OFFICIAL
BOY
SCOUT
HANDBOOK

By William 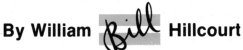 Hillcourt

**in association with the
BOY SCOUTS OF AMERICA**

Photo by Carson Buck

Ninth Edition • Eleventh Printing
300,000 February 1988
Total Copies of Ninth Edition—4,100,000
Total Printing Since 1910—32,560,000

William "Green Bar Bill" Hillcourt
Author, Naturalist, World Scouter

Dedicated to the American Scoutmaster who makes Scouting possible

IN APPRECIATION
This handbook, based on the experience of the
Boy Scouts of America in the United States
since its founding in 1910, is administered under the leadership of
Charles M. Pigott, *President*
Ben H. Love, *Chief Scout Executive*

NATIONAL BOY SCOUT HANDBOOK TASK FORCE

Alec Chesser and Bruno Hanson, *chairmen;* Thomas Allen; Donald H.
Flanders; Marvin A. Gershenfeld; Reuben Hitchcock; William E. Towell; and
James R. Neidhoefer

Featured artist: Norman Rockwell

National Staff Support Committee

Rebel L. Robertson, *chairman;* Bruce Ayars; George Bett; Fred Billett; Roy E. Bradshaw; J.
Jay Cassen; Michael Caterina; Loody S. Christofero; Judson Compton; Paul Dunn;
Richard D. Dutcher; J. Tracy Emerick; Walter A. Hasbrook; James A. Hess; William
Hillcourt; William H. Hofmann; James C. Langridge; Joseph L. Merton; John C. Page; and
Leroy Tatem

Editor: John C. Page
Copy editors: Richard L. Lehman and James W. DeLaney
Editorial assistants: Audrey F. Clough, Doris Cornelius, and Alice Fodor
Design and layout: Michael Feigenbaum, Michael Caterina, and Lloyd B. Nacion
Production: Robert Anderson, Gino Bartolucci, Philip Borri, Marti Briefer, James
Demules, Anne Ehlert, Barbara Guisto, Verna Glock, Helen Gold, Sophie Mozgai, Ellen
O'Meara, Theodore Tobias, Robert Varker, and Al Wheelhouse, Jr.
Artists: Joseph Csatari (frontispiece), Joseph Forte, Taylor Oughton, and Bernard Barton

Copyright 1979
BOY SCOUTS OF AMERICA
Irving, Texas
Library of Congress Catalog Card No. 78-72563
ISBN 0-8395-3227-X
No. 3227   Printed in U.S.A.   300M288

2

CONTENTS

Welcome
to the
Adventure
of Scouting

Welcome to the fun and adventure of Scouting. As a Boy Scout there are some wonderful experiences in store for you. You can go hiking and camping with your buddies in your patrol and troop. You can discover different plants and animals and learn how to take care of yourself in the out-of-doors. You can advance in rank and earn badges as you follow the trail to Eagle. You can experience democracy as you take part in choosing your leaders. You may find out what it feels like to be a leader, yourself.

I sincerely hope that many years from now this copy of *The Official Boy Scout Handbook* will serve as a dog-eared reminder of the great times you had when you were a Scout. I also hope you will appreciate all the important lessons you learned at troop meetings and at camp as you climbed Scouting's ladder. Most importantly, I hope the knowledge and skills you gained will help you in your life's work and as you take your place as an active citizen. Your participation will make our country even greater.

Good luck and good Scouting!

Ben H. Love
Chief Scout Executive

Norman
Rockwell

WHAT SCOUTING IS

Come and Get It
by Norman Rockwell, 1970

7

ALL OUT FOR SCOUTING!
by Joseph Csatari, 1976

To all Scouts, Scouting is a way of life. To most Scouts, Scouting is also their favorite sport. As a matter of fact, Scouting is a whole string of sports: camping and backpacking, hiking and orienteering, swimming and canoeing, and many more.

Your Life as a Scout

Today you are an American boy. Before long you will be an American man. It is important to America and to yourself that you become a citizen of fine character, physically strong, mentally awake, and morally straight.

Boy Scouting will help you become that kind of citizen. But also, Scouting will give you fellowship and fun.

Yes, it's fun to be a Boy Scout! It's fun to go hiking and camping with your best friends . . . to swim, to dive, to paddle a canoe, to wield an ax . . . to follow the footsteps of the pioneers who led the way through the wilderness . . . to stare into the glowing embers of a campfire and dream of the wonders of the life that is in store for you . . . .

It is fun also to learn to walk noiselessly through the woods . . . to stalk close to a grazing deer without being noticed . . . to bring a bird close to you by imitating its call. It is fun to find your way cross-country by map and compass . . . to make a meal when you are hungry . . . to take a safe swim when you are hot . . . to make yourself comfortable for the night in a tent or under the stars. In Scouting you become an outdoorsman.

But Scouting is far more than fun in the outdoors, hiking, and camping. Scouting is a way of life. Scouting is growing into responsible manhood, learning to be of service to others.

The *Scout Oath* and the *Scout Law* are your guides to citizenship. They tell you what is expected of a Scout. They point out your duties. The *Scout motto* is "Be Prepared"—prepared to take care of yourself and to help people in need. The *Scout slogan* is "Do a Good Turn Daily." Together, the motto and slogan spell out your ability and your willingness to serve.

Your life as a Scout will make you strong and self-reliant. You will learn Scoutcraft skills that will benefit you as you grow. In time, you will develop skills of leadership as well.

So pitch in! Swing into action! In your patrol and your troop you will have some of the best times of your life.

IT'S EASY TO BECOME A BOY SCOUT

So you want to get in on all the fun and excitement that Scouts have? There are three things you have to do to become a Boy Scout and enjoy the fellowship of a patrol and a troop.

First, you must be a boy 10½ years old and have completed the fifth grade or be 11 years of age or older but not have reached age 18. Second, you have to find a Scout troop near your home. Third, you have to know the rules of Scouting and the signs of a Scout.

YOUR AGE. If you have met the requirement of 10½ years old and fifth grade or 11 years, and not yet 18, fine! You can become a Boy Scout right away.

If you haven't met that requirement, you'll have to wait and let time turn the trick. But in the meantime, if you are in the second grade (or 8 years old), you can be a member of the younger branch of the Boy Scouts of America—Cub Scouting. Here you will have a wonderful time with other boys of your own age. Then, as you get close to 11 and are in a Cub Scout pack's Webelos den, you will learn all you need to know to become a Boy Scout.

FINDING A SCOUT TROOP. If you are a Cub Scout you will want to join the Scout troop that works with your Cub Scout pack. If not, ask the boys in your school. Some of them are probably Boy Scouts already. They will invite you to their next meeting. If you don't know where to join the Scouts, phone the Boy Scouts of America in your town. If it isn't listed in your phone book, write to: Boy Scouts of America, 1325 Walnut Hill Lane, P.O. Box 152079, Irving, TX 75015-2079. They'll tell you where to find a troop or how to become a Lone Scout.

It is easy for any boy to become a Boy Scout. But it is easier if you are a Webelos Scout. It is especially easy if you have earned the Arrow of Light Award.

When you are ready, pledge yourself to the Scout Oath in front of the troop. You are then a Boy Scout.

Your patrol leader in the patrol you join will help you master the Scout tests.

LEARNING ABOUT SCOUTING. What you now have to do is to satisfy your Scoutmaster that you:

- Understand and intend to live by the Scout Oath or Promise, the Scout Law, the Scout motto, and the Scout slogan.
- Know the Scout salute, sign, and handclasp and when to use them.
- Understand the significance of the Scout badge.
- Understand and agree to follow the Outdoor Code.

You will find the first three points on pages 27–49. You will find the Outdoor Code on pages 54–57.

When you have done these things, you can register as a Scout. You will then probably also want to subscribe to the Boy Scouts' monthly magazine, *Boys' Life*.

Fill out the membership application. Have your parent or guardian sign it. Give it and your registration fee to your Scoutmaster. When you have done this, you are a Scout and can wear the uniform and the Boy Scout badge. Your Scoutmaster will give you the temporary certificate of membership. You will get the regular certificate later.

NOTE: A graduating Webelos Scout who has earned the Webelos badge has thereby completed the joining requirements for Boy Scouting and may receive the Boy Scout badge upon joining the troop when approved by his Scoutmaster.

In a good patrol in a good Scout troop you will have
some of the best times of your whole life.

YOUR SCOUT PATROL

The Scout patrol is the finest boys' club in the world. The patrol is the unit that makes Scouting go. It is a group of boys, usually six to eight, who pal together because they like to do the same kinds of things.

A patrol is a team. All the members play the game of Scouting. All of you work toward the same goal. All of you have a wonderful time. In the patrol, you learn what fun it is to plan exciting things to do with some of your best friends ... to hike and camp together ... to sing and laugh together homeward bound from a strenuous hike or around a flickering campfire ... to work together to meet the tests that will carry all of you onward and upward in Scouting.

THE NAME OF THE PATROL. Every patrol has a name of its own. If you join an existing patrol, learn the history and tradition behind its name. If you are a new patrol, you'll want to spend a lot of time discussing a name. You'll want to decide on one that really fits your patrol.

NAME OF MY PATROL IS

_____

MY PATROL CALL IS

_____

Patrol Names and Calls

Alligator	Grunting hiss
Antelope	Shrill snort
Bear	Deep growl
Beaver	Clap hands sharply once
Bison	Lowing "Um-mooww"
Bobwhite	"Bob-bob-white"
Crow	"Caw-caw-waw"
Eagle	Shrill "Kreee"
Flaming Arrow	"Whsss"
Fox	Sharp bark
Frog	"Jug-o-rummm"
Hawk	High shrill whistle
Moose	"Oh-ah, oh-ah, oh-ahhh"
Owl	Loud "Coo"
Panther	"Keeook"
Pine Tree	Whistle imitating wind
Raccoon	Thin whine "Mm-mmm"
Rattlesnake	Rattle pebbles in can
Raven	"Kar-kaw"
Seal	Soft bark
Whippoorwill	"Whip-poor-will"
Wolf	Loud howl "Hoo-ooo"

For other names make up your own
patrol calls.

13

Most patrols pick the names of animals or birds. Those names have the real flavor of the outdoors. A Maine patrol may decide to become the Moose Patrol. A Rocky Mountain patrol may call itself the Eagles. But don't just call yourselves the "Eagle Patrol." There are thousands of them. Become the Soaring or the Screaming Eagles. Or how do names like Diving Seals, Roaming Buffaloes, or Speedy Beavers strike you? Naturally, you'll expect the Seals to be expert swimmers, the Buffaloes rugged hikers, the Beavers crack pioneers.

PATROL FLAG AND EMBLEM. Your patrol has a flag that displays the emblem or "totem" of your patrol. The best kind of patrol flag is one the patrol has designed and made itself. Many patrols put secret marks on their flags. But until you make your own, you can get one from your local Scouting distributor.

You wear the patrol medallion with your emblem on your right sleeve. It tells the world where you belong and what you stand for.

You'll probably want to paint or stencil your emblem on your camping gear. You'll also learn to draw it with a few quick lines. Add it to your signature when you sign your name as a Scout. The best patrol in the troop—you're part of it!

PATROL CALL. Every patrol has a call. If your patrol is named for an animal, you use its sound. For example, as a Hawk or a Fox or an Owl, you use the call of your namesake— the whistle of the hawk, the bark of the fox, the hoot of the owl. Even if the patrol is not named for an animal, you will still use an animal call. Indians used animal sounds for warnings. Students of bird life attract birds by imitating their calls.

The patrol call is meant to be used. When your patrol wins a contest you shout out your call and give your yell to let the troop know who you are. Hiking in deep woods, your patrol leader sounds the call for the patrol to gather. The members of the patrol will understand, but others will think that it is just one of the natural sounds of the woods.

14

Patrol flags come in many shapes and sizes. The best kind of flag is one the patrol made for itself.

YOUR PATROL LEADER. To have a good Scout patrol you have to have a good leader. To make sure that you have one, all the members of the patrol elect the Scout you respect the most as your patrol leader—one who has the energy and the will to work to make the patrol the finest possible.

The patrol leader is responsible for what happens in the patrol. He says to the rest of the gang, "Come on, let's go!" and starts off. He leads the patrol at troop meetings, on hiking and camping trips. He suggests Good Turns to be done. He thinks up ways for everyone in the patrol to make progress in Scouting, to do something, be somebody. He shares his leadership with all of you to give you a chance to learn what it means to be a leader.

To help him do his job, the patrol leader picks another Scout for assistant patrol leader. The assistant takes over when the patrol leader is absent.

There is a job for everyone in the patrol. For you, too, even if you have just joined. A Scout who writes well is the patrol scribe. He keeps the patrol diary. A Scout good at figures is the patrol treasurer. He handles the dues. If your patrol has camp gear of its own, you may need a quartermaster. And for special occasions your patrol leader may give out special duties. He may assign a hikemaster to find a new hike route, a grubmaster to come up with new patrol menus, a cheermaster to line up songs and stunts.

It is up to all of you in the patrol to give your patrol leader full cooperation through thick and thin. You've got to stick together for the good of the patrol. At times you may not want to go along with patrol plans. But Scouting is based on cheerful cooperation. Put aside your own comforts if it will benefit the patrol. "All for one—one for all." That's the idea.

PATROL DOINGS. An honest-to-goodness, live-wire patrol does plenty of things on its own. It always has a lot of interesting plans under way. You make plans for future patrol meetings, hikes, camps, Good Turns, stunts, making camp equipment, or for fixing up a patrol corner or den.

You are lucky if your patrol has a den it can call its own. A corner of a garage or basement that you can decorate will do.

PATROL MEETINGS. Your patrol meets often. At every troop meeting a part of the time is set aside for each patrol to meet by itself, in its own corner. Other patrol meetings are held regularly in the home of one of the Scouts in the patrol or in the patrol's own den.

You are lucky if you have a special place for a den. The corner of a garage or basement works as a clubhouse. You can decorate it and make furniture for it.

At patrol meetings the Scouts help one another with Scout advancement. It is at patrol meetings that all the great things you want to do as a patrol are decided.

PATROL HIKES AND CAMPS. Good patrols do lots of things outdoors. They take off regularly for a day of patrol hiking. These hikes are approved by your Scoutmaster in advance.

Good patrols go overnight camping by themselves. Your patrol can do it if you have a patrol leader your Scoutmaster can approve as an overnight camping leader. If your patrol leader does not yet have the necessary training, your patrol can still go camping on its own. One of the Scout fathers can go along. Or a troop leader may camp with you.

The goal of a patrol should be to be so well trained in camping that it can take off on its own overnights.

Hikes and camping trips are the high points in the patrol's life. It is around the campfires that patrol spirit reaches its peak. There each of you comes closer to the heart of Scouting.

All these patrol events are planned by the whole patrol. Your patrol leader is full of ideas. That's one of the reasons why he was chosen. He will suggest things to do. You will all be in on deciding. And you will all pitch in on whatever is decided on.

When the patrol has set a date and a time for a hike or a camp or for getting a job done, it is up to you to be there, on the dot, rain or shine. A "sunshine Scout" who only shows up when the sun is shining isn't of much value to a patrol or to himself. It's the "all-weather Scout" who makes a patrol hum and who gets the most fun out of Scouting.

18

BADGES AND INSIGNIA

The badges on your uniform will tell how far you have advanced in your Scout life.

IDENTIFICATION. The first badges you wear will indicate the patrol, troop, and council to which you belong.

Patrol medallion

Council shoulder insignia

Troop numeral

ADVANCEMENT. The dream of every Scout is to advance to Eagle. Along the way you have to earn skill awards, merit badges, badges of rank before your 18th birthday.

Skill award

Eagle badge

Merit badge

BADGES OF OFFICE. Some day, when you prove your ability, your friends may elect you as their patrol leader. Special ability earns these badges.

Patrol leader badge of office

Scribe badge of office

ACTIVITIES. For all the big events in which you will take part there will be special, colorful patches. They will remind you of all the good times you have had.

Order of the Arrow lodge insignia

Jamboree insignia

Camp insignia

In the patrol leaders' council, the patrol leaders, the senior patrol leader, and Scoutmaster plan the program of the troop.

YOUR SCOUT TROOP

The patrol does not stand alone. It is part of the troop. Most troops are made up of three or four patrols. Some may have even more.

Around your neck you wear the neckerchief in your troop's colors. On your left sleeve you wear the troop number. Every Scout is proud of his troop. Every Scout does his best so that the troop, in turn, will be proud of him. For years to come, you'll be a member of that good old troop. While living in it, you'll build memories that will last a lifetime—of troop songs around the fire on a cold winter's night, swims at camp, treasure hunt, father-and-son camps, parents' nights, courts of honor, Scouting Anniversary Week displays, troop Halloween parties, Thanksgiving Good Turns!

The way in which you make certain of that kind of memories is by getting behind the troop leaders. Back them up in their work to make your troop the very best.

YOUR TROOP LEADERS. Now, who are your troop leaders? First, there's your *Scoutmaster*. He spends hours planning the fun and adventure you will have in your troop. He takes training to learn exciting new things for you to do. He is present at every troop meeting and goes hiking and camping with the troop. He is the friend to whom you can always turn for advice. He coaches the patrol leaders. He gives his time and effort without pay. Why does he do all this? Because he believes in Scouting. Because he likes boys and wants to help them become real men.

Your *assistant Scoutmasters* help your Scoutmaster and take charge of the troop when needed. Like the Scoutmaster, the assistant Scoutmasters spend a great deal of time in planning and working on your behalf.

Then there's your *senior patrol leader*. He helps all the patrols with their program. He runs the troop meetings. *Junior assistant Scoutmasters* and, possibly, *leadership corps members* are responsible for things like games and contests. They are young men who have had plenty of Scout training.

Behind these leaders is the *troop committee*. This is a group of people who are responsible for the troop's welfare and who are ready to help it. Behind the troop committee, in turn, is the chartered organization—the church or synagogue, school, or service club that has accepted the Scouting program as one of its ways of helping youth.

THE PATROL LEADERS' COUNCIL. What the troop does is planned by the patrol leaders' council. This council is made up of the patrol leaders, the senior patrol leader, and the Scoutmaster. Other leaders may join the patrol leaders' council if their help is needed.

It is through this council that the boy leaders assume their jobs of running the troop. It is there that they get the training they need to lead their patrols effectively.

The patrol leaders' council meets each month to plan meetings, hikes, and camps of the troop as a whole. Before the council meeting your patrol leader talks over with your patrol what ideas you have for troop activities. He then takes them to the meeting and passes them on to the other leaders. Together, the members of the patrol leaders' council decide on what's to happen.

There's a lot of variety in the program of a good troop meeting. You'll learn something new at each of them.

TROOP MEETINGS. Most troops meet every week. Some meet twice a month and have patrol meetings between.

At troop meetings there are games—some for Scoutcraft training, some just for fun. There are contests among patrols, demonstrations and practice in Scoutcraft, and, of course, songs, stunts, and ceremonies.

Not all troop meetings are held at the regular place on the regular night. Occasionally, a troop may visit a fire station to start you off on earning the Firemanship merit badge. Another time it might be swim fun at a local pool. Or the troop might go to city hall to see your government in action. And one Saturday your troop might visit a factory, a power plant, a museum, or a zoo.

TROOP HIKES AND CAMPS. Every troop has a vigorous outdoor program. Once a month, year-round, the troop takes a hike or goes camping overnight. On these occasions each patrol tries to prove that it is the best patrol in the troop.

The biggest event in the Scouting year is summer camp when all patrols spend a week or longer camping together.

On these troop hikes, in troop overnight camps, and in troop summer camp, each Scout learns to take care of himself in the outdoors. As each member becomes skilled and self-reliant, the patrol becomes better and better.

It is by taking part in all the doings of your troop and your patrol that you learn to be a Scout.

Come to troop meetings promptly. Join the games and contests with all the energy and enthusiasm you have. Show up for a troop hike no matter what kind of weather. Aim to become one of the troop's best all-around outdoorsmen.

Remember that everything that happens in the patrol and in the troop happens because YOU and other boys like you are excited and proud of being Scouts. The success of your patrol and your troop depends on the efforts and Scout spirit that YOU and other boys like you put into it. The more you give of yourself to Scouting, the more Scouting will give to you.

When the troop goes camping each patrol has its own campsite and puts up its own camp.

YOUR DISTRICT AND COUNCIL

In Scouting, the area in which your troop is located is called a district. In a large city a district could be one or more neighborhoods. In the country it could take in several counties.

A number of districts make up a council. Your council has a staff of trained people who work full-time to make Scouting a success. The council has a service center. Here your Scoutmaster can get books, badges, and all kinds of help.

Training is an important council task. All councils make arrangements to train Scoutmasters and assistants as well as troop committees and others associated with Boy Socuting. There is a concern that all troops conduct a quality program. Training for youth leaders is a continuing cycle. As soon as recruited, the youth leader gets an introductory explanation of his job and its duties. From there, he goes through increased training for added responsibilities, such as the Junior Leader Orientation Workshop, Troop Junior Leader Training, Junior Leader Training Conference, and The National Junior Leader Instructor Camp.

DISTRICT AND COUNCIL DOINGS. There are many other troops besides your own in your district and council. Together they can do things that no single troop could do alone.

Many districts and councils have an annual camporee. This is a weekend event where all troops camp together. Each troop shows off its camping ability. And the patrols of different troops compete in Scoutcraft. Some councils also put on big shows. They may be called Scoutoramas, expos, circuses, or see'n'dos. Here troops put on Scout skills for the public to see.

The biggest and best council activity each year is summer camp held on the council's own camping property. In most cases this is where you will go for summer camp with your troop. Water activities are big in these council camps: swimming, boating, canoeing. You have hours instead of minutes to learn Scout skills. You have the equipment you need to do them. And have staff members who really know their stuff.

24

At a large council camporee thousands of
Scouts may camp together and hundreds of
patrols will show their camping skills.

25

I Will Do My Best
by Norman Rockwell, 1945

In the Scout Oath you will find a clear statement of what is expected of you as a Scout. When you take it you pledge yourself to live up to your duties to God and your country, to other people, and to yourself.

The Spirit of Scouting

It is easy to *become* a Scout. But it is not easy to *be* one. To be a good Scout you need guts and determination.

Scouting is a game. And like all games, it has rules you must follow to be a member of the team. The rules of Scouting are found in the Scout Oath or Promise, Scout Law, Scout motto, and Scout slogan. It is by following these rules that you become a true Scout.

SCOUT OATH OR PROMISE

On my honor I will do my best
To do my duty to God and my country
and to obey the Scout Law;
To help other people at all times;
To keep myself physically strong,
mentally awake, and morally straight.

THE MEANING OF THE SCOUT OATH OR PROMISE. When you pledge yourself to an oath or a promise you must know the meaning of it. So read carefully the paragraphs that follow. They will help you understand.

On my honor . . . The men who founded our country more than 200 years ago had great faith. They believed that every human being had the God-given rights of "life, liberty, and the pursuit of happiness." They fought to gain those rights for all of us. They pledged to each other their lives, their fortunes, and their "sacred honor." To them, their "sacred honor" was their loyalty to the high ideals they had set for themselves.

As a Scout and a good American, you must hold your honor sacred. When you pledge yourself to do something on your honor it means that you will do your utmost to live up to the high standards you set for yourself.

27

The founding fathers knew that signing the Declaration of Independence might cost them their lives. Benjamin Franklin remarked, "We must all hang together, or assuredly we shall all hang separately."

. . . I will do my best . . . Scouting does not expect you to become the perfect boy. It does expect you to strive toward the highest goals you can achieve. Not every boy has the ability to get high marks in school or to become a star athlete. But every boy has within him the power to do his best. That is what Scouting asks of you.

. . . To do my duty to God . . . Your parents and religious leaders teach you about God, and the ways in which you can serve. By following these teachings in your daily life, you do your duty to God as a Scout.

. . . and my country . . . As you look back into our country's history, you learn about men and women who toiled to make America great. Many of them gave their lives for it. They built it into what it is today. It is your duty to carry their work forward by working for our country's best interests. You can do this by obeying its laws. You can do this by working to solve some of its vast challenges.

. . . and to obey the Scout Law; . . . The 12 points of the Scout Law are not only rules for the game of Scouting, they are also rules that apply to your whole life. The Scout Law sets forth ideals for ways to act. In obeying the Scout Law you will find yourself growing into a gentleman and a respected citizen.

. . . To help other people at all times; . . . There are many people who need you. Your young shoulders can help them carry their burdens. A cheery smile and a helpful hand may be all that is necessary.

It will serve to make life easier for someone, old or young, who needs help. By helping whenever help is needed and by doing a Good Turn daily, you prove yourself a Scout. In that way you do your part to make this a happier world.

... To keep myself physically strong, ... You owe it to yourself to take care of your body. Protect it and develop it so that it will serve you well throughout your life. That does not mean building bulging muscles. It means building strength and endurance. Scouting will help you develop and keep a strong body.

... mentally awake ... You also owe it to yourself to develop your mind. Strive to increase your knowledge. Make the best possible use of your abilities. By being mentally awake you will live more completely in one day than a dull boy does in a month. With an alert attitude, you will get more out of life.

... and morally straight. And you owe it to yourself to aim to become a man of strong character. Be thoughtful of the rights of others. Be clean in speech and actions. Be faithful in your religious beliefs. Your life as a Scout will take you along the trail that leads to strong, self-reliant manhood.

There is only one oath out of the past that ranks with the Scout Oath. That was the Athenian Oath taken by the young man of Athens when he became 17.

THE OATH OF
THE YOUNG MAN OF ATHENS

"We will never bring disgrace on this our City, by an act of dishonesty or cowardice.

We will fight for the ideals and Sacred Things of the City both alone and with many.

We will revere and obey the City's laws, and will do our best to incite a like reverence and respect in those above us who are prone to annul them or set them at naught.

We will strive increasingly to quicken the public's sense of civic duty.

Thus in all these ways we will transmit this City, not only not less, but greater, and more beautiful than it was transmitted to us."

SCOUT LAW

The Scout Law is the foundation on which the whole Scouting movement is built. In the Scout Law is expressed the conduct which a Scout tries to live up to.

There have always been written and unwritten laws by which men have tried to live. When you are a Scout, the Scout Law becomes your code.

There is something about the Scout Law that makes it different from other laws. The laws of the nation, state, and city are mainly concerned with do's and don'ts. Not the Scout Law. The Scout Law is a statement of facts: "A Scout is trustworthy ... loyal ... helpful ... friendly ... courteous ... kind ... obedient ... cheerful ... thrifty ... brave ... clean ... reverent." By doing your best to live up to the Scout Law, you are a Scout. If you should *willfully* break the Scout Law, you fail as a Scout.

The ideals of the Scout Law are high—they are meant to be! It is only by striving toward high ideals and keeping faith with them that you can become the man you want to be.

THE MEANING OF THE POINTS OF THE SCOUT LAW. Each point of the Scout Law is expressed in a single word. Each of these words has a deep meaning. You should understand that meaning so well that you can explain it in your own words. What follows will help you to this understanding.

A Scout is TRUSTWORTHY. *A Scout tells the truth. He keeps his promises. Honesty is part of his code of conduct. People can depend on him.*

Your parents and teachers and friends know that as a Scout you tell the truth and keep your promises. When your mother or father asks you to do something, they know that you do it. When your troop has a meeting, your leaders know that you will be there. When you have said that you are going on a patrol hike or to camp, the other fellows know that you will be ready to go at the time agreed on.

SCOUT LAW

A SCOUT IS:

TRUSTWORTHY. A Scout tells the truth. He keeps his promises. Honesty is part of his code of conduct. People can depend on him.

LOYAL. A Scout is true to his family, Scout leaders, friends, school, and nation.

HELPFUL. A Scout is concerned about other people. He does things willingly for others without pay or reward.

FRIENDLY. A Scout is a friend to all. He is a brother to other Scouts. He seeks to understand others. He respects those with ideas and customs other than his own.

COURTEOUS. A Scout is polite to everyone regardless of age or position. He knows good manners make it easier for people to get along together.

KIND. A Scout understands there is strength in being gentle. He treats others as he wants to be treated. He does not hurt or kill harmless things without reason.

OBEDIENT. A Scout follows the rules of his family, school, and troop. He obeys the laws of his community and country. If he thinks these rules and laws are unfair, he tries to have them changed in an orderly manner rather than disobey them.

CHEERFUL. A Scout looks for the bright side of things. He cheerfully does tasks that come his way. He tries to make others happy.

THRIFTY. A Scout works to pay his way and to help others. He saves for unforeseen needs. He protects and conserves natural resources. He carefully uses time and property.

BRAVE. A Scout can face danger even if he is afraid. He has the courage to stand for what he thinks is right even if others laugh at or threaten him.

CLEAN. A Scout keeps his body and mind fit and clean. He goes around with those who believe in living by these same ideals. He helps keep his home and community clean.

REVERENT. A Scout is reverent toward God. He is faithful in his religious duties. He respects the beliefs of others.

To learn loyalty to your country, get to know how your government works.

A Scout can be trusted to act honestly in all business deals.

From time to time you may get yourself into trouble—all boys do. Your baseball may smash a window, your elbow may knock down a vase, your big feet may trample a flowerbed. By quickly admitting what you have done and making good the damage, the incident is forgotten.

It is a great thing to have people trust you. Your reputation for being trustworthy will be important to you in your future life. It will help you get a good job. It will help you get credit in stores, loans in banks. It will help you make the best kind of friends.

A Scout is LOYAL. *A Scout is true to his family, Scout leaders, friends, school, and nation.*

Loyalty starts within your family. You show this loyalty best by turning yourself into the kind of boy your parents would like you to be. Make them realize that you appreciate what they do for you. Speak about your home in such a way that people understand that you love it.

A chain is as strong as its weakest link. The success of your patrol and your troop depends on the loyalty of each boy in it—in the way you stick to your leaders and pitch in with the team, in the way you act as a Scout.

32

Hundreds of thousands of Americans have shown their loyalty to our country by fighting for it and dying for it. But there are many everyday ways of being loyal, too. Help in community projects. Show respect for our flag and our government. Obey our country's laws.

A Scout is HELPFUL. *A Scout is concerned about other people. He does things willingly for others without pay or reward.*

As a Scout you are concerned about other people. In pledging yourself to the Scout Oath you promised "to help other people at all times." The Scout motto tells you to "Be Prepared." The Scout slogan reminds you to "Do a Good Turn Daily." These three things hang together: you *promise* to help, you *can* help because you have learned how, and you *do* help.

A boy who knows first aid can help someone who is hurt. A boy who knows his town can help a stranger find his way. As a Scout you prepare yourself to be helpful, then look for ways to help.

Scouts may work for pay, but they don't take money for being helpful. If you do a Good Turn in the hope of receiving a tip, it isn't a Good Turn at all.

To be truly helpful you must know what to do.
Learn as many worthwhile skills as you can.

A Scout is FRIENDLY. *A Scout is a friend to all. He is a brother to other Scouts. He seeks to understand others. He respects those with ideas and customs other than his own.*

Friendship is like a mirror. When you greet a person with a smile on your face and a helping hand, you will receive a smile in return and help when you need it. The way to have a friend is to be one.

The moment you join a patrol and a troop, you enter a brotherhood that spans the world. The boys in it are of different countries and colors and creeds, but they are brother Scouts together. They live up to the same Scout Oath and Law that you are following.

Making a friend is fairly easy if you are friendly yourself. Keeping a friend is more difficult. You know that each person is an individual with ideas and ways of his own. To be a real friend you must accept the other person as he is, show interest in him, and respect his differences.

A Scout is COURTEOUS. *A Scout is polite to everyone regardless of age or position. He knows good manners make it easier for people to get along together.*

This is just another way of saying "A Scout is a gentleman." You will have many chances every day to show whether you are one or not.

First of all, be courteous in your own home. A "Please" and a "Thank-you" are easily said. Little helpful things are easily done. Yet they make your father and mother and the other members of the family feel that you really appreciate what they do for you.

Good manners always please and attract people. Open a door for a lady. Offer a seat in a bus to an elderly person. Rise from your chair when a guest enters the room. Help your mother be seated at the family table. Say "Pardon me" or "Sorry" when needed. They are manly things to do.

The courtesy you practice as a boy will make you a finer man as you grow up.

A Good Sign All Over the World
by Norman Rockwell, 1963

You will find the greatest expression of Scout friendship at a world jamboree. Scouts from Scotland may teach you a dance. Scouts from Indonesia and India may help. Other Scouts may join the fun.

It is always in fashion to be a gentleman and to act like one.

A Scout is kind to people. He is kind also to animals that cannot tell him their needs.

A Scout is KIND. *A Scout understands there is strength in being gentle. He treats others as he wants to be treated. He does not hurt or kill harmless things without reason.*

The knights of old were always ready to fight. They fought for their king, their religion, and their honor. But they could be the gentlest of the gentle in another duty they had. They protected the old and the weak, women, and children. They knew that there was a special strength in being gentle when gentleness was called for.

As a Scout, follow the example of the knights. Fight for your convictions. Be kind to those in need and those who cannot defend themselves.

Such kindness involves animals as well as human beings. If you have a dog or other animal pet of your own you are probably already kind to it. But you need to be kind also to the wild animals and birds you come upon when hiking and camping. The more you get to know wildlife, the more you will want to help it and protect it.

A Scout is OBEDIENT. *A Scout follows the rules of his family, school, and troop. He obeys the laws of his community and country. If he thinks these rules and laws are unfair, he tries to have them changed in an orderly manner rather than disobey them.*

Obedience begins in your home. If your parents have made rules for you to follow, follow them cheerfully. The rules they made show that they love you and care for you. Their rules will protect you. When you are older you can make your own decisions based on the experience you have gained.

There are others to whom you owe obedience. When a teacher tells you to do a thing, it is usually for your own good. When your employer gives you an order, it is for the good of the business. And when your Scout leader asks you to do a job, it is for the good of the patrol or the troop. That means it's good for you, too.

Being obedient also means obeying your country's laws. Here, obedience works for the good of everyone. Just imagine how much money would be available for education and other worthwhile purposes if people were so law-abiding that we could close our prisons. And think of the lives that could be saved on our highways each year if people obeyed the traffic laws.

A Scout obeys immediately when the attention signal is given. This signal is the Scout sign held up high.

37

Saving is one of the five things that make up thrift.

A Scout is cheerful even when the weather is foul.

A Scout is CHEERFUL. *A Scout looks for the bright side of things. He cheerfully does tasks that come his way. He tries to make others happy.*

There is an old saying: "Smile and the world smiles with you—weep and you weep alone."

There are people who always see the dark side of things. There are others who are cheerful always. They make life easier for themselves, and they help make others happy, too.

It is not the good times you have that will make you the man you want to be. It is only as you learn to overcome difficulties with a smile that you will grow to be a real man. In Scouting, you will have lots of fun on sunny days. But the memories that will live the longest in your heart will be of the times when you overcome obstacles cheerfully. It is when the patrol fights its way home from a hike against a storm. Then every step seems to be a mile. It is when a drenching downpour puts out your campfire. It is when your tent blows down in the middle of the night. These are the times when your cheerfulness is tested and your manliness grows.

A Scout is THRIFTY. *A Scout works to pay his way and to help others. He saves for unforeseen needs. He protects and conserves natural resources. He carefully uses time and property.*

Real thrift consists of five different things: earning, saving, spending wisely, sharing, and conserving.

It is a wonderful thing to be able to pay your own way. It is good to earn money for your own clothes, for your Scout uniform, and your camp equipment. And it is good to pay your troop dues out of your own pocket.

It is good also to be able to put money in the bank. But while you are young, it is more important for you to spend it on a good education that will give you a better future. Learn also to share whatever you earn with others.

Conservation is one of the most important ways in which you can show that you are thrifty. Protect and conserve our country's natural resources—its soil and water, its woods and fields, its wildlife. When you realize that waste is the worst enemy of thrift and act to stop it, you do your part to keep America beautiful.

A Scout is BRAVE. *A Scout can face danger even if he is afraid. He has the courage to stand for what he thinks is right even if others laugh at or threaten him.*

From the founding of the Scouting movement in America in 1910, more than 1,700 Scouts have earned the Honor Medal for Lifesaving. They saved a life at the risk of their own. Those boys had a grand chance to prove their bravery. They came

Bravery consists in knowing what to do, then doing it.

through with flying colors. Your chance may come. You, too, will win out, even if you are afraid, if you have prepared yourself to face danger and have learned what to do.

But lifesaving is not the only way you can prove your bravery. You can show it in your everyday life.

It takes bravery to do what is right when others call you a coward or a chicken for doing it. It often takes real courage to speak the truth and nothing but the truth. It takes backbone to admit a mistake and to apologize for it. It takes courage to defend a friend when he is under attack by others.

A Scout is CLEAN. *A Scout keeps his body and mind fit and clean. He goes around with those who believe in living by these same ideals. He helps keep his home and community clean.*

The simplest way to be clean is not to get dirty in the first place. That goes not just for your clothes and your body. It also goes for your thoughts and words and deeds.

You never need to be ashamed of the dirt that will wash off. If you play hard and work hard you can't help getting dirty. But when the game is over or the work done, that kind of dirt gives way to soap and water.

You never have to worry about dirt that washes off.

You show your reverence by the way you serve and worship God.

But there's another kind of dirt that won't come off by washing. It is the kind that enters your mind. An important part of your battle against that kind of dirt is selecting the right friends. Keep away from fellows who seem to get a kick out of swearing and telling dirty stories. Get in with a clean crowd where you will hear clean speech, and find clean sportsmanship, and get a clean outlook on life.

A Scout is REVERENT. *A Scout is reverent toward God. He is faithful in his religious duties. He respects the beliefs of others.*

Take a penny out of your pocket and look at it. What do you see on it? Just above Lincoln's head are 12 little letters: "In God we trust." They remind us of our faith. As a nation we trust in God. We try to live and work faithfully. You show that you are reverent to God by helping other people, and by following the religious teachings of your parents and religious leaders.

All your life you will be with people of different faiths and customs. The men who founded the United States of America gave us a heritage of religious freedom. It is our duty to respect others whose religion may differ from ours, even though we do not agree with them. The Scout benediction is "May the Great Master of all Scouts be with us till we meet again."

41

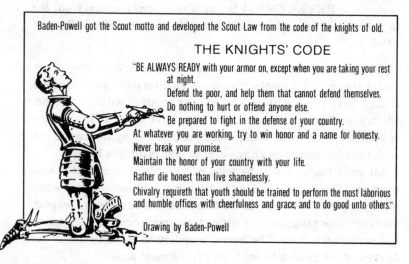

Scouts are often called into service when disasters strike. They are prepared to help.

SCOUT MOTTO

The Scout motto is BE PREPARED. The motto of the knights of old was "Be always ready." A Scout is a modern knight. He is a young man who keeps himself strong, who learns how to meet problems, who never lets himself be taken by surprise.

Someone once asked Baden-Powell, the founder of Scouting, "Be prepared for what?" "Why," said B-P, "for any old

Baden-Powell got the Scout motto and developed the Scout Law from the code of the knights of old.

THE KNIGHTS' CODE

"BE ALWAYS READY with your armor on, except when you are taking your rest at night.

Defend the poor, and help them that cannot defend themselves.

Do nothing to hurt or offend anyone else.

Be prepared to fight in the defense of your country.

At whatever you are working, try to win honor and a name for honesty.

Never break your promise.

Maintain the honor of your country with your life.

Rather die honest than live shamelessly.

Chivalry requireth that youth should be trained to perform the most laborious and humble offices with cheerfulness and grace; and to do good unto others."

Drawing by Baden-Powell

Scouts are prepared for any kind of emergency. For an ice rescue they know about throwing a line, sliding out a ladder or board, making a human chain.

thing." That's just the idea. The Scout motto means that you are always ready in mind and body to do your duty and to face danger, if necessary, to help others.

The more Scoutcraft you know, the better able you are to live up to the motto.

Someone has an accident. You are prepared to help because of your first aid training. A child falls into water. You are prepared to save the child because of the lifesaving practice you have had. A building is burning. You are prepared to do what needs to be done because you have practiced what to do.

With proper training, you will be prepared to meet any emergency because you are sure that you can handle the problem.

But Baden-Powell wasn't thinking just of being prepared for accidents. His idea was that every Scout should prepare himself to become a useful citizen and to give happiness to other people. He wanted every Scout to be prepared to work for all the good things that life has to offer and to face with a strong heart whatever may be ahead.

BE PREPARED *for life*—to live happy and to die happy, knowing that you have done your best. That's the big idea.

SCOUT SLOGAN

The Scout slogan is DO A GOOD TURN DAILY. This does not mean that you are to do *one* Good Turn during the day and then stop. It means looking for chances to help throughout each day, then helping quietly, without boasting. Doing them should be an automatic, normal part of your life.

Some Good Turns are big things—saving a human life at the risk of losing your own . . . rescue work in floods . . . service in hurricane-stricken areas . . . helping to fight a forest fire . . . working with your patrol on a conservation project.

But Good Turns more often are small things, thoughtful things. They might be helping a child cross the street . . . clearing trash off the highway . . . picking up broken glass from the street.

Remember always that a Good Turn is an extra act of kindness. It is not just something you do because it is good manners. To answer the question of a driver about reaching an address is not a Good Turn. That is common courtesy. But to draw a map for him that will show him how to get to where he wants to go—that's a Good Turn.

Children often need a Scout to do a Good Turn.

A Good Turn may require a certain skill. You need to know your town to be able to show the way.

MANY WAYS OF HELPING

Find a lost child.
Put out a grass fire.
Raise school flag daily.
Deliver church circulars.
Sort books in the library.
Wheel crippled person to church.
Pick up broken glass from the street.
Get child's kite down from a tree.
Put on a first aid demonstration.
Move furniture for an old person.
Make a scrapbook for a hospital.
Take part in a safety campaign.
Do errands for a sick person.
Clean trash off a vacant lot.
Help someone change a tire.
Help blind person on a bus.
Give first aid to someone.

Where a hurricane strikes, Good Turn chances are plentiful.

Many Scouts do special Good Turns for handicapped people.

Scout sign   Scout salute

When you make the Scout sign, your lower arm is at a right angle to your upper arm. In the Scout salute, the angle between them is 45 degrees.

SIGNS OF A SCOUT

When you become a Scout, you show in different ways that you belong to the world brotherhood of Scouting. You use the Scout sign, salute, and handclasp. And, of course, you wear the Scout badge and the Scout uniform.

SCOUT SIGN. The Scout sign marks you as a Scout anywhere in the world. You use it when you recite the Scout Oath and Law. When held high the Scout sign is an attention signal. If a leader running an event raises his hand in the Scout sign, all Scouts make the sign and come to silent attention.

To give the Scout sign, cover the nail of the little finger of your right hand with the thumb. Then raise your right hand, palm forward, with the three middle fingers upward. Hold your upper arm straight out to the side with your forearm straight up.

The three upstretched fingers stand for the three parts of the Scout Oath. The other two fingers represent the bond that ties all Scouts together.

SCOUT SALUTE. The Scout salute signifies respect and courtesy. You use it to salute the flag of the United States of America. You may also use it to salute a leader or another Scout in formal ceremonies or as a sign of courtesy.

To give the Scout salute, place the fingers of your right hand in position as for the Scout sign. Bring the hand smartly up to your head, palm sideways, until your forefinger touches the edge of your headgear. If you are bareheaded, touch your forehead above the right eye. When the salute is completed, snap your hand down quickly to your side.

SCOUT HANDCLASP. The Scout handclasp is a token of friendship. That is why it is made with the left hand. This is the hand nearest to the heart, the hand of friendship.

To give the Scout handclasp, extend your left hand with the thumb separated from the other four fingers. Grasp your friend's hand and clasp it firmly.

Scout handclasp

When you shake hands with a brother Scout, you do it with your left hand. That's the way it's done all over the world.

North point of the mariner's compass

Iris flower

Arrowhead

SCOUT BADGE

The complete Scout badge, which is also used on the First Class badge of rank, was adapted from the north point of the old mariner's compass. The design is often called a *trefoil*—a flower with three leaves. It is also known by its French name, *fleur-de-lis*—lily or iris flower. It goes so far back in history that it is uncertain whether it actually stands for a flower or an arrowhead.

With slight changes, the trefoil badge is used by Scouts around the world.

The *trefoil* means that a Scout can point the right way in life as truly as a compass can in the field.

The *three points,* like the fingers of the Scout sign, stand for the three parts of the Scout Oath.

The *two stars* symbolize truth and knowledge, and the outdoors in Scouting.

The *eagle with the shield* stands for freedom and readiness to defend that freedom.

The *scroll* with the Scout motto is turned up at the ends. It is a hint that a Scout smiles as he does his duty.

The *knot* at the bottom of the scroll is a reminder to "Do a Good Turn Daily."

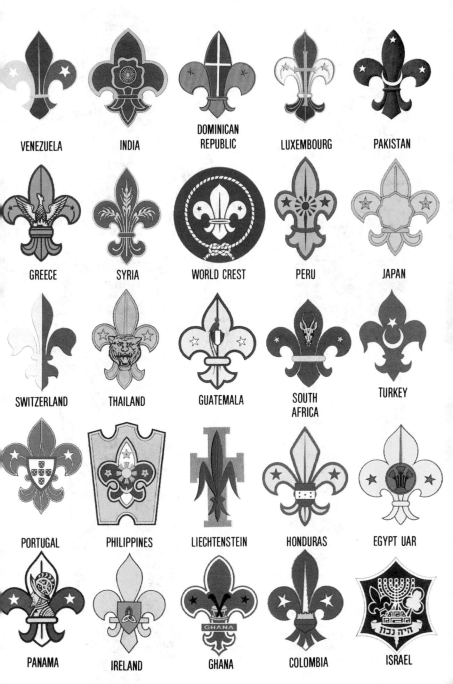

VENEZUELA

INDIA

DOMINICAN
REPUBLIC

LUXEMBOURG

PAKISTAN

GREECE

SYRIA

WORLD CREST

PERU

JAPAN

SWITZERLAND

THAILAND

GUATEMALA

SOUTH
AFRICA

TURKEY

PORTUGAL

PHILIPPINES

LIECHTENSTEIN

HONDURAS

EGYPT UAR

PANAMA

IRELAND

GHANA

COLOMBIA

ISRAEL

49

The uniform with shorts and short-sleeve shirt is just right for vigorous hiking and camping.

The Scout uniform with long-sleeve shirt and trousers is popular for year-round wear.

The troop chooses the headgear that its members will wear. There are four choices: beret, field cap, broad-brim hat, visored cap.

SCOUT UNIFORM

Your uniform is part of the thrill of being a Scout. Put on your uniform and you feel ready for hiking, camping, and other active Scout events.

There is real significance to that khaki uniform.

First of all, it shows that you belong. You are a member of the largest youth movement the free world has ever seen. It stands for the spirit of true democracy. It puts rich and poor on an equal basis in the spirit of brotherhood. It also helps build team spirit in your patrol and your troop.

The uniform is a steady reminder to yourself and to others that here is a boy who can be trusted to help when needed. Dressed as a Scout, you want to act as a Scout.

And finally, its color and design make the Scout uniform the ideal clothing of the outdoorsman.

THE PARTS OF THE UNIFORM. The Scout uniform consists of cap, beret or broad-brim hat, shirt, trousers or shorts, belt, socks or stockings, shoes or hike boots. Your troop decides what you will wear. For cold weather, the long-sleeve shirt and trousers are preferred. When the weather is hot, the favorite uniform is the short-sleeve shirt, shorts, and long stockings.

Throughout the world, the neckerchief is the mark of the uniform. Its color tells what troop you belong to.

HOW TO GET THE UNIFORM. The moment you get into the troop and have been registered as a Scout, you will want a uniform. Ask your Scoutmaster what store is the Scouting distributor. Take your registration card to the store. There you can buy your uniform, your community strip or council shoulder insignia, troop numeral, and patrol medallion.

WEARING THE SCOUT UNIFORM. Wear your uniform proudly. Wear the complete uniform correctly at all Scout events:
- Wear it at all patrol and troop meetings, hikes, camps, and rallies.
- Wear it when you appear before a board of review or a court of honor.
- Wear it when you take part in any Scout service project.
- Wear it during Scouting Anniversary Week in February.

CARE OF THE UNIFORM. As a Scout, you are careful of your clothes at all times — your uniform and your regular clothes. Fold your uniform carefully after use or hang it on hangers.

Keep your uniform clean and in good repair. Remove spots as soon as possible. If you like, have it dry-cleaned. Otherwise, wash in lukewarm water with a mild soap or detergent. Hang up to dry. Pull gently into shape. Iron while slightly damp.

Neckerchief

Neckerchief Slides

HOW TO WEAR A SCOUT NECKERCHIEF

Roll the long edge of the neckerchief to about 6 inches from the tip. Turn your collar under, if your troop wears the neckerchief over the collar. Otherwise place the neckerchief smoothly around your neck under your collar. Hold it in place with a slide. Tie the ends with a slipknot, if that is your troop's custom. Also, bolo ties are authorized and are worn under the open collar.

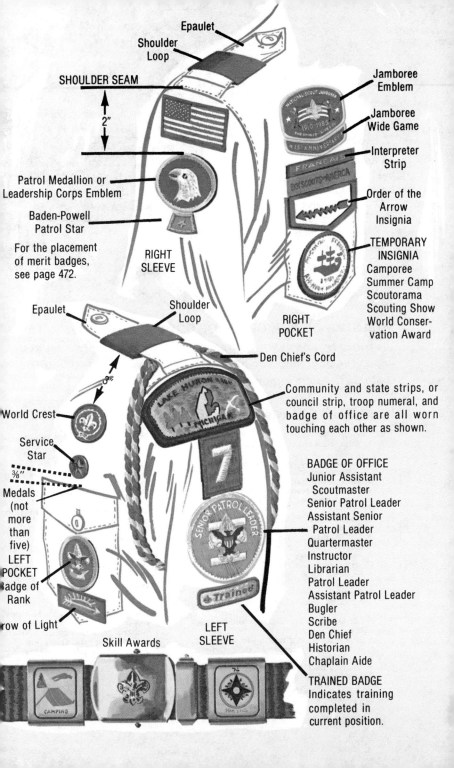

Epaulet

Shoulder Loop

SHOULDER SEAM

2″

Jamboree Emblem

Jamboree Wide Game

Interpreter Strip

Patrol Medallion or Leadership Corps Emblem

Baden-Powell Patrol Star

For the placement of merit badges, see page 472.

RIGHT SLEEVE

Order of the Arrow Insignia

TEMPORARY INSIGNIA
Camporee
Summer Camp
Scoutorama
Scouting Show
World Conservation Award

RIGHT POCKET

Epaulet

Shoulder Loop

Den Chief's Cord

World Crest

Community and state strips, or council strip, troop numeral, and badge of office are all worn touching each other as shown.

Service Star

⅜″

Medals (not more than five)

LEFT POCKET
Badge of Rank

Arrow of Light

Skill Awards

LEFT SLEEVE

BADGE OF OFFICE
Junior Assistant Scoutmaster
Senior Patrol Leader
Assistant Senior Patrol Leader
Quartermaster
Instructor
Librarian
Patrol Leader
Assistant Patrol Leader
Bugler
Scribe
Den Chief
Historian
Chaplain Aide

TRAINED BADGE
Indicates training completed in current position.

OUTDOOR CODE

As an American, I will do my
best to—
Be clean in my outdoor manners,
Be careful with fire,
Be considerate in the outdoors,
and
Be conservation-minded.

OUTDOOR CODE

MEANING OF THE OUTDOOR CODE. Whenever you and all
the other Scouts of your patrol hike or camp and wherever you
are in the outdoors, you are expected to live up to the Outdoor
Code. It has four important points:

THE SEVEN KEYS TO LOW-IMPACT CAMPING

1. Pretrip plans
   * Wear uniform or other dark colored gear.
   * Package food in burnable or pack-out containers.
   * Take trash bags.
   * Plan 12 or fewer in your party.
   * Select an area few people visit.
2. Travel
   * Stay on the trail.
   * Avoid cutting across switchbacks.
   * Let muddy trails dry.
   * Select hard ground for cross-country travel.
3. Campsites
   * Select a spot free from succulent plants.
   * Camp out of sight of trails, streams, and lakes.
   * Avoid tent ditching.
   * Limit stay in one place to four days.
4. Fires
   * Use a lightweight gas stove.
   * Use an old fire circle in heavily used areas.
   * Burn small wood gathered from the ground.
   * Make sure your fire is out.
   * In little-used areas, cover fire sc[...] with twigs.
5. Sanitation
   * Wash away from streams a[...] lakes.
   * Pour wash and dish water int[...] hole.
   * Dig latrines 200 feet or more fr[...] camp and water.
   * Cover wash-water holes a[...] latrines.
   * Pack out nonburnable trash.
6. Horses
   * Keep number to a minimum.
   * Tie to sturdy trees or rope.
   * Hobble or picket in dry areas.
   * Scatter manure.
7. Courtesy
   * Hikers step off trail when hors[...] pass.
   * Control pets if they are allowed
   * Do not pick wild flowers.
   * Avoid making loud noises. Lea[...] radios home.

54

As an American I Will Do My Best To—

BE CLEAN IN MY OUTDOOR MANNERS. *I will treat the outdoors as a heritage. I will try to improve it for myself and others. I will keep my trash and garbage out of America's waters, fields, woods, and roadways.*

The beauty of our land has been spoiled by tons of garbage, newspapers, tin cans, bottles, cardboard boxes. Our streams are being choked with trash.

The way to stop this plague is for you to join the war against litter. You do this by helping remove the trash that is destroying the place where you live. You do it also by never being a litterbug yourself.

BE CAREFUL WITH FIRE. *I will prevent wildfire. I will build my fire in a safe place and be sure it is out before I leave.*

As a Scout camper you will know exactly what to do to have a safe fire. You will know how to pick the proper spot for it. You will make certain that it cannot possibly spread. You will put it dead-out after use.

As a Scout, with eyes in your head, you may have to watch out for other people's fires. You will, of course, report any forest fire or grass fire. You will also be prepared to help local fire wardens or conservation agencies in cases of fire emergencies.

You are a guest. Wherever you hike or camp you are the guest of a landowner. All land is owned by either a private person or all citizens through their government. Act like a guest who wants to be invited back.

Put trash and garbage in a trash can if there is one near your camp. If not, bring it home with you. Never bury garbage. When hiking, put papers like candy wrappers in your pocket and then in a wastebasket at home.

Litter attracts litter. Clean up littered yards, vacant lots, streets, and campsites even if you didn't cause the litter. Clean places stay clean longer. Dirty ones quickly get dirtier.

BE CONSIDERATE IN THE OUTDOORS. *I will treat public and private property with respect. I will remember that use of the outdoors is a right that I can lose by abuse.*

When you visit the homes of other people you always behave. You want them to invite you back. Behave the same way in the outdoors.

When the first settlers came here, the whole vast country belonged to everybody. Today, every square inch belongs to somebody. It is private, state, or Federal land. No matter where you go, you are someone's guest. Act like one!

No guest would think of breaking his host's windows or carving up his host's furniture. Neither would a Scout damage things he comes upon when hiking nor would he destroy trees and shrubs where he is camping. No guest would keep a household awake by brawling far into the night. Neither would a Scout keep nearby campers from sleeping by shouting or yelling.

In a public park, heed the advice of "the man with the badge"—the park ranger, forest ranger, or game warden. Follow rules for the use of the picnic spot or camping area you are using. Clean up after you so that the place looks the way you would like to have found it yourself when you arrived.

Protect wildlife. You are the guests of the birds and animals, too. Help them. Don't hurt them. Then they'll be there for you to enjoy now and in the future.

Protect live trees against thoughtless vandalism. Their beauty is spoiled by meaningless initials.

BE CONSERVATION-MINDED. *I will learn how to practice good conservation of soil, waters, forests, minerals, grasslands, wildlife, and energy. I will urge others to do the same.*

There is a great need for conserving our country's natural resources. All you have to do is to look around you. Wherever you hike you may notice where the land is used properly and where it is not. You will learn from the good examples. And you may be able to help where poor methods have been used.

To do something about conservation, you must know how to go about it. One of the best ways is to earn the skill awards in Environment and Conservation. In each of these you carry out projects that will help your community.

In addition to working on skill awards, you will want to work with your patrol and troop on projects. Later you may be the one to set up projects for the other Scouts in the patrol and the troop.

In these ways you prove that you are truly conservation-minded.

Prevent erosion. Don't dig unless you must. If you do dig, save the sod, if any. Put it back in place before leaving.

Use deadwood for camp gadgets.

WHAT SCOUTS DO

Men of Tomorrow
by Norman Rockwell, 1948

To Camp! To Camp!

Camp! There's a word that's filled with adventure for every real boy! Camp stands for freedom, fun, and adventure!

Camp! Just breathe the word. Immediately you think of days full of excitement. You think of a tent under the open sky, of bacon sizzling in the pan. You imagine yourself sitting with your best friends at night around a blazing fire.

Camp is the high spot of your free and happy Scouting life. You'll learn more about Scouting in a few days in camp than you'll learn in months in the patrol den or the troop room.

Out in camp you'll have a glorious time. But you'll do more than that. You'll build up your health and your strength. You'll learn to be resourceful, self-reliant. You'll deepen your love of nature. You'll come to appreciate our country's natural resources. And in camp you'll learn to get along with others.

To get the greatest benefit from camping you need to be a good camper. It's the good campers who have the most fun in camp. To them, each camp is a success. It makes no difference whether the sun shines or the rain pours. There's work in making a camp successful. But then, everybody works. And there's real joy in it, too: When everyone does his share of the work, everyone has time for his share of the fun, too. You'll come home from each camp with a stronger patrol spirit. And you'll come home with more Scouting knowledge for yourself.

For every camping experience you have, you'll want more and still more. There'll be no holding you back. You'll want to become a year-round camper, an all-kinds-of-weather camper.

PREPARE FOR CAMP. You begin preparing for camp the day you join a patrol and a troop. The games you play at patrol and troop meetings will show you the knots you will use in camp. The contests you take part in will teach you how to handle an ax, to pack a pack, to pitch a tent. On patrol and troop hikes you will practice the safety tricks of the outdoors.

KINDS OF CAMPING. In Scouting you have a chance to do several kinds of camping. Make up your mind to get in on all of them.

Short-Term Camping. Runs over short weekends—Saturday-Sunday. Or long weekends—Friday-Sunday. Or over holidays. This kind is done on a campsite close to home: your troop's campsite, council camp, or a nearby state park.

Long-Term Camping. Takes in a week, 10 days, or longer. That's the kind of camping your troop does every summer. It is mostly done on the camp grounds of your local council.

Hike Camping: Backpacking. For this you travel to a starting point, then take off, pack on your back, on the trails of a state or national park or wilderness area.

High-Adventure Camping. Done far from home, perhaps even in a foreign country. It takes you to places where you may learn special ways of camping. You may also pick up such outdoor skills as fishing, canoeing, sailing, scuba diving, burro packing, horseback riding, rock climbing and several others.

PLANNING FOR CAMP. When the day has been set for a camp, you get together in your patrol to do the planning.

- **Personal Gear.** What'll I need? How will I take it?
- **Patrol Gear.** Tentage and cooking gear. Who'll carry what?
- **Menu and Food Lists.** What'll we eat? What'll it cost? Who'll do the buying? Who'll do the cooking?
- **Transportation.** Will we hike from home to camp? Or do we line up special transportation for getting there? Do we need a tour permit?
- **Campsite.** Where do we go? What permission do we need?
- **Firebuilding.** Must we have a permit?
- **Time.** Time of leaving. Time of return.
- **Permission.** Parents' permission for each boy going.
- **Plan of Activities.** What'll we do? What kind of equipment must we take for the activities we've decided on?

You'll have a busy patrol meeting doing all this kind of planning. It will be an exciting one and a happy one as well.

YOUR PERSONAL GEAR FOR CAMP

CLOTHING FOR CAMP. You'll certainly want to wear your Scout uniform. For hot weather, this will mean short-sleeve shirt, shorts, long stockings. For cool weather, you will wear long-sleeve shirt, trousers, socks. For cold weather, you will want to wear or bring a sweater or a jac-shirt. For rainy weather, you will be prepared with a poncho or a raincoat. For any kind of weather, you'll need rugged shoes.

Put into your pockets what you always carry. But add a Scout knife, matches wrapped in foil, a few sheets of toilet paper, and a couple of adhesive bandages.

STOWING CAMP GEAR. Lay out your personal camp gear the way it is listed on page 65, ready for packing.

A Scout pack is "a bag of bags." Things that belong together—eating utensils, toilet articles, repair items, extra clothing—go into their own bags. This makes it easy to pack your pack and to find things. The bags can be cloth or plastic.

Personal Camping Gear

You can check off your needs on the five fingers of one hand: sleeping, eating, being clean, being prepared, extras.

SLEEPING. You want to sleep well. To do this you must be warm. For your first overnight camps, one to three blankets will do. Eventually you will want a sleeping bag. Before you buy one, ask the advice of some camp-trained Scouts.

Buy the best sleeping bag you can afford. A bag filled with polyester fiberfill is good. Down is better. If the winters are severe, buy a winter-weight bag. Open it up for summer use.

You also want to be comfortable. Many campers use a shoulder-to-hip-length polyurethane pad. Others like an air mattress. You place it on top of a plastic ground sheet.

For nightwear bring pajamas.

EATING. You want to eat. Here you'll need an eating kit or separate knife, fork, spoon. Eating utensils as well: plate, cup, bowl, or a one-man cook kit that includes all three.

BEING CLEAN. Bring soap in a plastic container, washcloth, toothbrush and toothpaste, comb and metal mirror, hand towel. Perhaps a plastic washbasin.

If the camp is to last for several days, bring extra underwear, T-shirt, spare uniform parts, possibly moccasins or sneakers. You will then also take soap powder (in a small plastic bottle) for laundering.

BEING PREPARED. Put in your pack a flashlight and a small individual supply of toilet paper wrapped in plastic.

For a long-term camp, better also bring a repair kit. Put in it thread, buttons, safety pins, spare shoelaces.

When you are not wearing them, outer-clothing items go into your pack.

EXTRAS. You will want to take with you the Bible, Testament or prayer book of your faith. Probably also this handbook.

Finally, if you're like most campers you have a few favorite items you can't get along without. Bring them along.

PERSONAL CAMPING GEAR

☐ Pack

☐ Sleeping bag OR 2–3 blankets
☐ Foam pad OR air mattress
☐ Ground sheet, plastic

☐ Sweater OR jac-shirt
☐ Poncho OR raincoat and rain hat
☐ Pair rubbers, lightweight
☐ Pair sneakers OR pair moccasins

☐ Clothes bag(s) containing:
    ☐ Extra uniform parts   ☐ Extra socks
    ☐ Change of underwear
    ☐ Pajamas OR sweat suit
    ☐ Extra handkerchiefs   ☐ Swim trunks

☐ Eating kit containing:
    ☐ Knife   ☐ Fork   ☐ Spoon
    ☐ Plate   ☐ Cup   ☐ Bowl

☐ Toilet kit containing:
    ☐ Soap in box   ☐ Washcloth
    ☐ Toothbrush   ☐ Toothpaste
    ☐ Comb   ☐ Metal mirror
    ☐ Washbasin, plastic
    ☐ Hand towels
    ☐ Laundry materials

☐ Repair kit containing:
    ☐ Needles   ☐ Thread   ☐ Buttons
    ☐ Safety pins   ☐ Shoelaces

☐ Toilet paper, in plastic wrap
☐ Flashlight
☐ Scout knife
☐ Bible, Testament, OR Prayer Book
    according to your faith
☐ Personal first aid kit
☐ Coin (emergency phone call)

Extras you may want to take:
☐ Watch   ☐ Camera   ☐ Film
☐ Notebook   ☐ Pencil   ☐ Pen
☐ Drinking cup   ☐ Canteen
☐ Mosquito repellent   ☐ Nylon line
☐ Musical instrument   ☐ Songbook
☐ Purse or wallet with money
    and identification   ☐ Sunglasses
☐ *Boy Scout Handbook*   ☐ Air pillow

Make a check mark with a soft pencil in each
square as you lay out your equipment for camp.

Personal Camping Gear: PACKS

The kind of pack you'll want depends on the kind and the amount of camping you expect to do.

SOFT-BACK PACKS. For close-to-home camping, a soft-back pack is fine. Most of these packs have just one large compartment. Some have outside pockets for packing small items.

Yucca-Ranger Pack. This popular, all-around Scout pack is made of lightweight, water-repellent nylon. It has wide-web shoulder straps and outside pockets.

Scout Haversack. This smaller pack is made of canvas. Your bedding probably won't fit inside. So roll it into a long sausage, cover it with your plastic groundsheet, and strap or tie it to the brass rings on the outside, horseshoe style.

FRAME-BACK PACKS. In backpacking, a soft-back pack resting against your body may make you hot and sticky. To keep the pack away from your back you will then want to carry it attached to a pack frame. Such frames are usually made of aluminum tubing. Some, like the Horizon I and II, adjust to fit the height of the bearer. The Frontiersman frame has a bottom shelf for stowing a sleeping bag. The Yucca-Ranger pack can be mounted on these frames.

Cascade and Max Packs. These are large nylon packs with three and five outside pockets. The Cascade is sold only as a combo pack with frame. The Max pack, sold with or without frame, has two compartments and makes a fine combo with the Horizon frame.

PACKING THE PACK. In packing, put those items farthest down that you will use last after getting to camp. Place the softest bags in the part of the pack that will be touching your back. Keep rainwear at the top where you can get at it easily.

If your pack is of sufficient size, you may be able to get your bedding into it. If you have a pack frame, you may roll up your bedding in a plastic sheet and carry it beneath your pack.

When packed for an overnight camp, your pack should not be heavier than one-fourth of your own weight.

Scout haversack

Haversack, packed
(internal view)

Haversack
(horseshoe blankets)

Yucca-Ranger

Yucca-Ranger on
Frontiersman frame

Soft-back pack
with side pockets

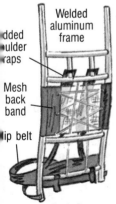

Welded
aluminum
frame

dded
·ulder
·raps

Mesh
back
band

·ip belt

Pack frame

Max pack
on Horizon I frame

Cascade
Backpacking Combo

PATROL CAMPING GEAR

When it comes to patrol camping gear, think EFFICIENCY: Think of what you want to get done as quickly as possible the moment you get to camp. You want the tents set up. You want the fireplace built, the fire lit, the cooking under way. The way to do this is to divide the patrol into two crews—a tenting crew and a cooking crew. Then split up the equipment to fit these two crews as listed on page 69.

TENTING CREW EQUIPMENT. A real camping troop will have enough tents to go around. They will probably be one of the models shown on page 71. Packed in with these tents should be the necessary poles, pegs, and guy lines for pitching them. The dining fly should come equipped the same way.

To make camp, the tenting crew needs woods tools: ax, saw, and camp spade. It also needs a few other items to keep the equipment in shape and the camp in good order.

COOKING CREW EQUIPMENT. Here, topping the list, we have pots and pans and all the tools needed for cooking. An old patrol will probably have a Trail Chef Kit of nesting pots and pans. If you don't have a kit, you can probably borrow what you need from the kitchens of a couple of patrol members. The same goes for the Chef's Kit of kitchen knives, forks, and spoons. Next in importance come plastic bags and containers for bringing the foodstuffs to camp.

In addition to the actual cooking, the cooking crew is responsible for fire building, water hauling, and cleanup. It will need fire starters, water containers, and cleanup materials.

GETTING THE EQUIPMENT TO CAMP. When the equipment is lined up, the fellow acting as patrol quartermaster distributes it. Each patrol member carries his share to camp.

When everything is packed, the patrol is ready to hike off. If the camp is beyond hiking distance, patrol fathers or troop leaders will have arranged for transportation.

PATROL CAMPING GEAR

TENTING CREW EQUIPMENT

- [ ] Two-man tents, with poles, pegs, and guy lines
- [ ] Dining fly, 10x10 ft. minimum, with poles, pegs, and guy lines
- [ ] Patrol flag on staff
- [ ] Small U.S. flag, with halyard
- [ ] Ax   [ ] Saw   [ ] Camp spade
- [ ] Repair kit containing
  - [ ] Mill file, 8-in., for ax sharpening
  - [ ] Sharpening stone   [ ] Thin wire
  - [ ] Twine or nylon line   [ ] Nails
- [ ] Sewing kit containing:
  - [ ] Thread   [ ] Needles   [ ] Safety pins
- [ ] First aid kit
- [ ] Toilet paper in plastic bag
- [ ] Electric lantern

COOKING CREW EQUIPMENT

- [ ] Cook kit (Trail Chef Kit) containing:
  - [ ] Pots (4)   [ ] Frying pans (2)
  - [ ] Serving plates (4)   [ ] Cups (4)
- [ ] Chef's kit containing:
  - [ ] Carving knife   [ ] Spoon, large
  - [ ] Fork, large   [ ] Ladle
  - [ ] Pancake turner or spatula
  - [ ] Potato peeler, "knee action"
  - [ ] Can opener   [ ] Hot pot tongs
- [ ] Water container, collapsible, plastic, 2½ gallons OR desert water bag
- [ ] Plastic washbasin for cooks
- [ ] Plastic food bags, various sizes
- [ ] Sugar container   [ ] Salt-pepper shaker
- [ ] Roll of aluminum foil
- [ ] Plastic sheets (2), 4x4 ft. minimum
- [ ] Matches in waterproof case
- [ ] Fire starters
- [ ] Cleanup materials:
  - [ ] Dish mop   [ ] Scouring pads
  - [ ] Paper towels in plastic bag
  - [ ] Liquid soap in plastic bottle
  - [ ] Sanitizing tablets for rinse
- [ ] Heavy-duty trash-can liner
- [ ] Ax   [ ] Saw   [ ] Camp spade

Patrol Camping Gear: TENTS

When you think of camping, you think of tents. But what kind? The kind depends on the kind of camping you'll be doing.

YEAR-ROUND TENTS. For patrol and troop overnight camps and for summer camp you'll want a two-man tent that is easy to put up. You want it roomy, with a ground surface of about 2.5 m² (30 sq. ft.) per camper. You want it high enough so that it won't cramp you, preferably about 2 m (6 ft.). But also, you want a tent made of sturdy and fire resistant material. It has to take the wear and tear of being handled by new Scouts as well as by skilled campers. The official Boy Scout tents fit all these points. They are made of a tough poly-cotton-blend fabric.

Voyageur. An A-shaped tent. It sets up with two poles. It has side haulers to give you extra room.

Grizzly. A family or patrol headquarters tent with no-stoop headroom. Screened doors and windows provide ventilation.

Explorer. If you want to make your own tent, the Explorer may be your choice. It is like a Voyageur with a short ridge. It can be set up without inside poles, using outside shear legs.

LONG-TERM TENTS. If you're going to the council summer camp, you may be in one of these canvas tents that's set up for the whole summer:

Wall. Looks like a small house, with walls and sloping roof. It sets up with two poles and a ridge pole.

Baker. Has an open front, with a large front flap that extends for shade and ventilation.

BACKPACK TENTS. When you have become an expert camper, you may want to take off with a buddy for a backpacking trip. For this you'll want a tent of lightweight material.

Adventurer. Made of rip-stop nylon. It sets up with two poles. This tent model comes in three sizes.

Free Spirit. This tent is set up with four poles for easy entry, and a ridge pole. It has an extra roof for ventilation.

NO TENT IS
FIREPROOF

Explorer

Wall

NO FLAMES IN
OR NEAR TENTS

Free Spirit

Grizzly

Adventurer

Voyageur

Baker

THREE STEPS TO TENT PITCHING

Before pitching an A-type tent, close the door flaps. Peg down four corners at right angles.

Assemble front and rear poles. Put pegs into the ground for front and rear guy lines. Put up tent poles. Attach lines to pegs. Use taut-line hitch.

Put pegs into the ground for side haulers. Attach hauler lines. Check all lines to make ridge taut and tent sides smooth.

TENT CARE. When you are ready to leave, strike the tents carefully. Follow the three steps above, but in the opposite order. Then spread out the tents on the ground.

Brush off dirt, grass, leaves, twigs. Then fold and roll up the tents. In the case of wall and voyageur tents, pull out the triangular door flaps and fold them over before folding the tent. Store the tents in a dry place. If the tents were rolled up wet, hang them out to dry before storing them.

Make yourself comfortable on flat ground by using clothing for padding.

YOUR CAMP BED

For the simplest type of camp bed, spread out your plastic ground sheet. If you have a foam pad or an air mattress, place it on the ground sheet. If you don't, fold up pieces of clothing and use them for padding. Lie down on the ground sheet in sleeping position. Place the padding under the small of your back, your head, and your middle thighs. Stand up and put blankets or sleeping bag over padding.

Remember the old camp rule: Have as much under you as over you. In that way you are not only warm against the cold night air, but also against the coolness of the ground.

If you use only one blanket on a summer's night, place one third of it on the bed and lie down on it. Bring the rest of the blanket over you so that the middle third is on top of you. Roll over slightly and tuck the last third under you. Lift legs and bring bottom of blanket under your feet.

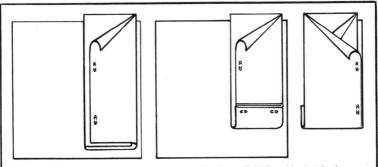

Blanket sleeping bag is made from two blankets. Fold first blanket in three layers. Pin down free edge with blanket pins. Place on half of second blanket. Bring bottom up and pin. Fold other half of second blanket over first blanket. Pin edges. Fold bottom under.

YOUR PATROL CAMPSITE

Your patrol and troop may already have a number of favorite campsites. Some of them may be in your local council camp. Others may be on the grounds of private owners. If you don't have a campsite yet, you'll have to find one for all the overnight camping you and your patrol will be doing.

- **The ground.** The ideal campsite is a fairly open, grass-covered spot. It should be gently sloping for rainwater to drain off easily, yet level enough for comfortable sleeping. If it is too steep, you will slide or roll out during the night.

- **Shelter.** Your site should have shelter against the prevailing winds. So choose a campsite with trees or shrubs to the west and north.

- **Wood.** It should have wood for fuel and for the camp improvements you want to make. Woodsman's tools should be stored properly and the wood preparation area protected.

- **Safety.** Your site should be safe. In the woods, do not pitch your tents under trees with dead branches. They may suddenly come crashing down. Do not pitch your tents in a gully. A rainstorm may turn the gully into a raging river. And do not camp under a cliff. A rockslide may occur.

- **Privacy.** It should be far enough away from people so that you have privacy, yet close enough to your hometown to be reached without spending too much time and money on traveling. For backpacking and summer camp you will, of course, go much farther afield.

- **Beauty.** And then, your site should be beautiful. This may not seem important to you. But it will add to your enjoyment without your realizing it.

When you have located what you consider a good campsite, get permission to camp there. Be sure to follow any rules the owner may set for its use.

The moment you arrive on your campsite you plant the patrol flag.

Camp Making

Well, there you are with the whole patrol on your favorite campsite. Now for putting up camp!

Not right away, though. Not if yours is a smart patrol.

Before you do anything else, all of you put your packs down in a straight row. Put them close together. Turn them all the same way. The duffel line is formed! It looks neat. It ought to. You're a top-notch patrol. Next, with your patrol leader in the lead, the whole patrol strolls over the campsite. You talk over how to set up camp most effectively. Then, with everyone knowing exactly what needs to be done, you all go to work.

ORGANIZED FOR CAMP MAKING. In a good patrol, the work of putting up camp is divided evenly among the members. Half of the gang may be a tenting crew responsible for pitching the tents, digging a latrine, laying the evening campfire. The other half may be the cooking crew. The Scouts get water and wood, build the fire, lay out foodstuffs and cooking gear, cook and serve.

It is a joy to see a well-organized patrol at work. The tents seem to jump up out of the ground. The fire crackles under the pots. Before you know it, the head of the tenting crew reports, "All done!" And the head cook yells, "Come and get it!"

Camp Health

CARE OF FOOD. Think of camp food in three groups:

- Food like fresh milk and fresh meat will spoil unless kept at a low temperature.
- Fresh vegetables, fresh fruit, butter, cured meats such as bacon, smoked ham, frankfurters need to be kept cool.
- Canned, dehydrated, and freeze-dried foods will keep at any temperature.

Place foods of the first two groups in some kind of refrigerator. If a brook runs by your campsite, use it. Put the foods into a covered pot and place this in the cool, running water. Weight down the pot with rocks. If the weather is warm, you may decide to take a plastic cooler to camp. If the weather is hot, don't take fresh milk and fresh meat. Use powdered milk and canned or freeze-dried meat.

DRINKING WATER. Use safe water only (page 181). Keep cooking and drinking water in a plastic water carrier. Or keep it in a covered pot, protected against dust, insects, and animals. In hot weather you can have cool water by using a desert water bag (page 97). Hang this where it is exposed to the breeze. Water seeps out through the canvas and keeps the contents cool by evaporation.

FIRE PROTECTION. It is advisable always to have water handy close to your tents. If you can't spare a pot for this purpose, a couple of large tin cans full of water will do.

GARBAGE. Know the rules for the place where you camp. Many camps have garbage cans with regular pickups.

If a brook runs through your camp, use it to keep your food cool. Place food in a covered pot. Weight it with rocks.

In other camps you may be permitted to get rid of garbage by burning. Use your cooking fire for this after you have finished cooking. Put several finger-thick sticks across your fireplace. Dump the garbage on them. After wet garbage has dried, add sticks to the fire to complete the burning.

Wash out empty cans and smash them flat. Wash out empty jars and bottles. Put them, with unburned trash, in a heavy-duty, plastic trash-can liner. Take everything out with you when you leave camp. Get rid of it in the nearest trash can or at home.

LATRINE. If there's no toilet near your campsite, you'll have to make a latrine. It should be located at least 30 m (100 ft.) away from tents and kitchen and from any stream or lake front. It should be screened from your campsite for privacy. The screening could be natural bush. Or it could be a piece of canvas tied up between nearby trees.

For an overnight camp make a simple straddle latrine. Dig it one camp-spade-width wide, six to eight spade-widths long, 30 cm (1 ft.) deep. If you dig the latrine in a grassy spot, save the turfs as described on page 88. Pile the dirt at one end of the latrine. Leave the spade stuck in the pile. Sprinkle a thin layer of dirt in the latrine after each use. Place toilet paper on a stick to keep it off the ground. Cover it with a plastic bag to keep it dry. Tell all campers where the latrine is as soon as it is made.

Dig a narrow trench for your latrine. Protect the turfs so that you can replace them later.

Make a trash "basket" by draping the top of a trash can liner over three upright stakes.

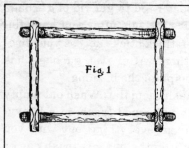
Fig. 1

ERNEST THOMPSON SETON's log cabin was in the *Official Handbook*, 1910. Your grandfather may have followed these plans using ax and saw. He began by placing four logs in a rectangle.

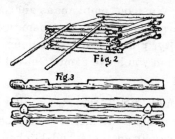
Fig. 2

Fig. 3

The upper part of the shorter logs were cut to an edge over each corner (1). The next logs were rolled in place on poles and V-notched to fit the edges of the logs below. Logs touched only in V-notches (2).

Fig. 4.

When the walls were almost high enough a piece was cut out of the next log for door and window (3). It was then turned over to lock in the logs below it. Wedges of wood were driven between the logs from top of door and window to the base log.

Then door and window were cut out (4). The cut went all the way into the base log. The door was made from two pieces of soft wood hewn to fit. The final logs were put on and two more across the top (5).

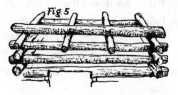
Fig. 5

Fig. 6

The ridge pole had to be as big as the other logs for it carried a lot of weight. Top end logs were beveled off (6). Many stout poles were laid side by side and pinned down with two long poles (7).

The poles were covered with a foot of hay or straw. Then clay was put over the roof. It packed the straw down into a tight waterproof layer.

Fig. 7

Building a cabin is hard work. Many more cabins were started than finished. Today you are not permitted to cut live trees. To build this small cabin would mean cutting down at least 20 straight-trunked trees.

WOODS TOOLS

Knife, ax, saw, and spade were the tools of the pioneers who settled on this land.

They used their knives in hunting and to whittle any number of household items. They needed their axes and saws to fell trees for log cabins and for fuel, and to clear the ground. They used their spades to turn the soil and make it ready for planting.

You don't have the same need for these tools today. But they come in handy for good camping. So learn to care for them and to use them the right way.

Your Knife

The official Scout knife is the most popular knife among outdoorsmen. It has a strong cutting blade and tools as well—can opener, cap lifter, screwdriver, leather punch or awl.

You can carry it in your pocket. Or you can hang it on your belt by the ring in its handle.

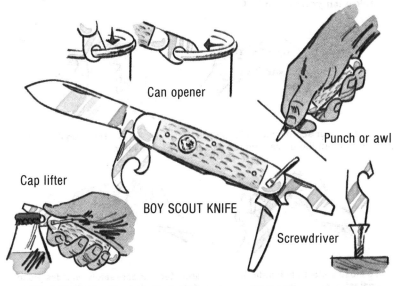

Can opener

Punch or awl

Cap lifter

BOY SCOUT KNIFE

Screwdriver

The official Boy Scout knife is the most versatile tool you can ask for.

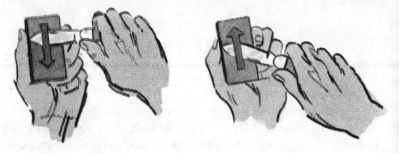

Sharpen your knife with a slicing motion, as if cutting into the stone.

SHARPENING YOUR KNIFE. Sharpen your knife on an oiled sharpening stone. Lay the blade edge on the stone. Raise the back of the blade slightly. Stroke the edge toward you and off the stone with a slicing motion, as if you were cutting into the stone. Turn the blade over and stroke it away from you the next time. Continue back and forth until the edge is sharp its full length. Wipe the blade.

USING YOUR KNIFE. For coarse cutting, grasp the handle with the whole hand and cut away from you to prevent injury.

For fine whittling, move the knife in short cuts, pushing the back with your thumb.

To open your Scout knife, hold it in your left hand. Put right thumbnail into nail slot. Pull out the blade until it snaps into open position.

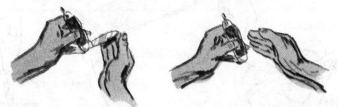

To close knife, hold handle with left hand. Keep fingers safely on sides. Push against back of blade with fingers of right hand. Let knife snap shut.

For whittling and fine cutting, move the knife in short cuts, pushing the back with your thumb.

For coarse cutting, as in trimming a branch, grasp the handle with the whole hand. Cut off twigs from thick end toward top.

CARE OF YOUR KNIFE. Your knife is a valuable tool. Take good care of it.

- Keep your knife clean, dry, and sharp at all times.
- Never use it on things that will dull or break it.
- Keep it off the ground. Moisture and dirt will ruin it.
- Keep it out of the fire. The heat draws the temper of the steel. The edge of the blade becomes soft and useless.
- Wipe the blade clean after using it. Then close it carefully.
- Treat the joints to an occasional drop of machine oil so that the blades will keep opening easily.

FUZZ STICKS

Fuzz sticks are the true woodsman's fire starters. And whittling fuzz sticks is an excellent test for proving your skill with a knife.

Use dry sticks, thumb–thick and a handspan long. Point one end. Hold the pointed end and fuzz the stick.

Cut shavings as long and thin as possible. But leave them on the stick to make it look like a Christmas tree.

When you are good at fuzz-stick making, you may want to take up real whittling. Then you will need a whittler's knife with special blades.

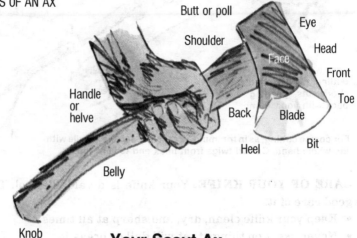

Butt or poll
Shoulder
Eye
Head
Face
Front
Toe
Handle or helve
Back
Blade
Bit
Heel
Belly
Knob

Your Scout Ax

If you are pitching camp on a spot that has been used for camping many times before, you'll have little chance to use your woods tools. But if you have permission to clear your own patrol campsite, you'll have plenty of use for ax and saw. You will need them also when you have to cut large pieces of wood into firewood. A good ax for these purposes is the official Scout pack ax. It has a 1¼-pound head set on a handle of hardwood or tubular steel.

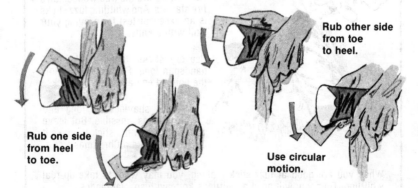

Rub other side from toe to heel.

Rub one side from heel to toe.

Use circular motion.

Hone the bit of your ax regularly with a dry sharpening stone. Use the stone also for removing the wire edge that forms when you file the ax.

SHARPENING YOUR AX. To keep your ax sharp, hone it regularly with a sharpening stone and touch up the edge when needed with a flat 20-cm (8-in.) mill file.

For **filing** to remove nicks lean the axhead against a log. Kneel on one knee. Place the file on the edge and push down hard. File the whole bit with long, even, straight strokes from toe to heel. Keep the file in very light contact with the blade on the return strokes. When you have brightened the entire length of the bit, turn the ax over and do the other side. Finish the job by honing the ax with a sharpening stone.

For **honing** hold the head of the ax in one hand in such a way that the handle points up and away from you. Rub the dry sharpening stone over the blade from heel to toe. Then turn the ax over with the handle now pointing down and hone the other side, from toe to heel. Keep it up until the bit is so keen that it no longer shows up as a bright line when you look at it.

CARE OF YOUR AX. Your ax deserves special care.

- Keep the edge, or bit, sharp—not just sharp enough for it to chew, but sharp enough to bite!
- Be sure the head is on tight. Some axes may need to have a screw tightened or a wooden wedge driven in harder.
- Never let your ax touch the ground. Driving it into the ground will nick it. Leaving it on the ground will rust it.
- Always have a chopping block under the wood you are chopping or splitting.
- When not in use, mask your ax. That is, cover the bit (blade). Stick it in a log or sheath it. On the trail, carry it in its sheath inside your pack.

For filing place the axhead against a log. To steady it you may want to firm the helve against the log with a couple of pegs.

Remember that a file is a one-way tool—it's designed to cut when it is pushed. Push the file downward with just enough pressure to bite into the steel. Return to the starting point and push. Handle the file carefully. Use a 3-inch-square piece of cardboard or leather as a guard on your file.

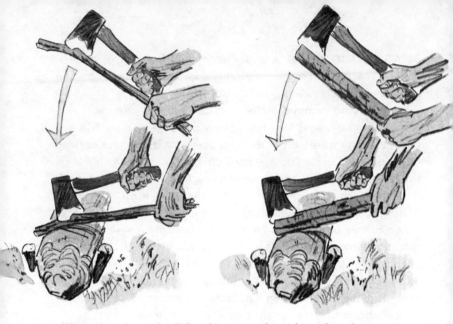

When chopping and splitting, keep ax and wood together—in contact.

CONTACT AXMANSHIP. For chopping and splitting you must have wood support under the stick. Otherwise the ax stroke will end up in the ground and not in the wood. A down tree or large chunk of wood will do.

For **chopping** a stick in two, hold the ax edge against the stick on a slant to the grain, not straight across. Raise stick and ax together with wrist motion and bring them down hard together on the chopping block. If the stick is not cut at this first stroke, raise stick and ax together in contact with one another and bring them down together. Repeat until cut.

If the stick is too thick to cut with this contact method, place the stick with the spot where you want to cut on the chopping block and cut it in two with a V-shaped notch. Make top of V as wide as the stick is thick.

For **splitting** a stick, hold one end of the stick in one hand. Rest the other end on the block. Place the ax blade on this end with a

If a stick is too thick to cut with a contact stroke, cut it in two with a V-shaped notch.

little of the blade overhanging it. Lift stick and ax together. Then bring down hard together on the chopping block. Just as you hit the block, twist the wood or the ax slightly to break the pieces apart.

If the wood for splitting is wrist-thick or thicker, first saw it into pieces about as long as your ax handle. Split the half pieces into quarters and the quarters into eighths.

AX SAFETY. Remember that not only wood but people can get chopped. So keep your buddies away when you use your ax.

Rest when you are tired. You have no control over your ax when you are tired. And an ax out of control is dangerous.

When you need to have your ax handy for use, stick it in a log. At other times sheathe it.

To pass an ax safely, hold the handle near the knob (end of the handle) with the head down. Pass with the bit (blade) facing out at right angles between you and the other person. Other person grips the handle just below your hand and says, "Thank you." That's your signal to release your grip.

Totin' Chip

1. Read and understand woods tools use and safety rules from the *Official Boy Scout Handbook.*
2. Demonstrate proper handling, care, and use of the Scout knife, ax, and saw.
3. Use knife, ax, and saw as tools, not playthings.
4. Respect all safety rules to protect others.
5. Respect property and not cut living trees.
6. I will subscribe to the "Outdoor Code."

I realize that my "Totin' Rights" can be taken from me if I fail in my responsibility.

Your Saw

For cutting wood, the right saw will do the job twice as fast as an ax. The ordinary saw is clumsy and does not work too well on the kind of wood you find in the forest. You need a saw that does not get stuck in the saw cut. For overnight camping, you may want to take a folding pack saw along. It is light and compact. Its blade folds into the wooden handle for packing. For a longer-lasting camp, you may prefer the traveling safety saw. This saw also folds to fit in your pack. When it is unfolded, the blade is held under tension with a screw device.

USING YOUR SAW. Your method depends on what's to be sawed. For general sawing, hold the wood firmly in place and use smooth and easy saw strokes. Pull the saw back and forth without downward pressure. Let the weight of the saw do the job for you.

Bucking—that is cutting wood into logs or small pieces—is easy with a saw. For thin wood, place one end of it over a log. Kneel down on one knee and put the opposite foot on the other

Sawhorse

Place the wood you are cutting so that the cut end falls free of the support.

When cutting saplings in clearing a campsite cut close to the ground.

Pack saw

Safety saw

The folding pack saw is just right for overnight camping. For a longer-lasting camp you may want the safety saw. This also folds up.

It is easy to touch up the teeth of a saw when they get dull. Use an ignition file. Stroke the file upward following the bevel of each tooth.

When pruning trees for a conservation project, prune close to the trunk.

part of the wood. Saw the end of the wood off so that it falls free of the log.

For larger wood, make a simple sawbuck by driving two stakes into the ground to form an **X** and lashing them together.

For a big sawing job, improvise a sawhorse by driving four stakes into the ground to form two Xs with their legs across a log. If necessary, lash each of the Xs.

When you have permission to clear a campsite of saplings and brush, saw them off just above ground level. If you saw them off higher, you'll trip over the stumps.

SHARPENING YOUR SAW. The folding and the safety saw both have fast-cutting blades. The blades come with the teeth filed and "set." This means that the points of the teeth are curved outward to each side. This makes the saw cut or "kerf" twice as wide as the thickness of the blade. Such a tooth setting prevents binding.

When the teeth grow dull, you can touch them up with an ignition file. Stroke the file upward following the bevel of each tooth. Finish one side of the saw. Then do the other.

The spade is an important conservation tool. You use it for removing turf from a grassy spot. You can then restore it.

Your Camp Spade

A spade is another tool for good camping. Not the large-size spade you use for gardening, but the small camp spade or shovel, with a blade only 10 cm (4 in.) wide. You need it to get your camp in shape, to conserve the land, and for cleanup.

Thoughtless campers often build their fires on a grass-covered spot or on top of rich forest soil. When such a fire has burned down, the organic matter in the soil is destroyed. It will take years for the land to recover.

USING YOUR SPADE. A thoughtful camper uses his camp spade to remove the topsoil or sod. The sod he removes in turfs the size of the spadeblade. He places the turfs out of the way, in a shady place so that they will not dry out. After the fire has been put out and the ashes have been "gardened" into the ground with the spade, the camper replaces the turfs. Thus he leaves no trace of the fire.

The spade has other uses around the fire. It is the perfect tool for picking up and moving glowing embers. This is important if you cook in aluminum foil, or use a bean hole, or roast and bake in Dutch ovens.

The spade is also a sanitary tool. A single dig with the spade will produce a "cat hole" for your own need. A short ditch will make a latrine for your patrol (page 77). A hole in the ground will take care of dishwater. Another hole may serve as an "icebox" to keep food from spoiling. In all cases the sod is preserved and replaced.

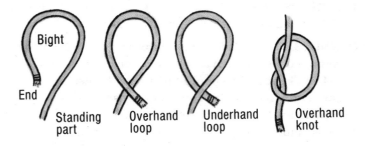

The parts of a rope are called end and standing part. All knots are made by combining bights, loops, or overhand knots in different ways.

ROPE AND KNOTS

You have probably already used a couple of knots around your home. For Scouting you need to know several more. You use knots in camp for setting up your tents and for improving your camp. You use them in pioneering, boating, and canoeing.

The trick is to know which knot to use for what and how to tie it right. So pick a knot that meets the tests of a good knot: It is easy to tie. It holds when tied correctly. It is easy to untie.

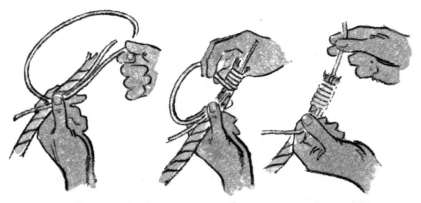

Whip the ends of a rope to keep them from raveling. Use a piece of twine at least 60 cm (2 ft.) long. Make it into a loop and place this at the end of the rope as shown. Wrap the twine tightly around the rope. When the whipping is as wide as the rope is thick, pull out the ends hard. Trim off the twine. Then whip other rope end.

MANY KINDS OF KNOTS. Old-time sailors know knots by the hundreds. A landlubber should know a dozen.

END KNOTS. These are tied in the end of a rope to prevent the end from being pulled through a hole or a block.

Overhand knot is the simplest of all end knots.

Figure-eight knot is also a part of the packer's knot.

Stevedore knot is the figure-eight with an extra loop.

Stopper knot has even more loops for added bulk.

KNOTS FOR JOINING. These are for tying together two rope ends of the same rope or of two different ropes.

Square knot is important in first aid (see also page 365).

Surgeon's knot holds better than the square knot.

Shoestring knot is a square knot tied with bights.

Fisherman's knot is used for tying fish lines together.

Sheet bend (page 93) joins ropes of different sizes.

Blood knot is used for tying nylon rope or filament.

Fisherman's "surgeon" knot is another nylon knot.

HITCHES. A knot is called a hitch when it is used to tie a rope to an object, such as a pole, a post, or a ring.

Half hitch is an overhand knot tied around an object.

Slippery half hitch is tied with a bight for easy untying.

Two half hitches will moor a boat (also on page 92).

Clove hitch is an important pioneering knot (page 95).

Timber hitch is another pioneering knot (page 92).

Taut-line hitch is used for tent pitching (page 95).

Lark's head is tied with the bight of a doubled rope.

KNOTS FOR LOOPS. These knots form permanent loops holding their size, or "running" loops varying in size.

Bowline is an important rescue knot (page 94).

Packer's knot is good for tying up newspapers for recycling.

Lariat knot is used by cowboys for making a lariat (lasso).

SHORTENING KNOTS. Instead of cutting a rope that is too long, these knots will shorten the rope without cutting.

Sheepshank will tighten a rope hung between two trees.

Trumpet knot is tied by intertwining three loops.

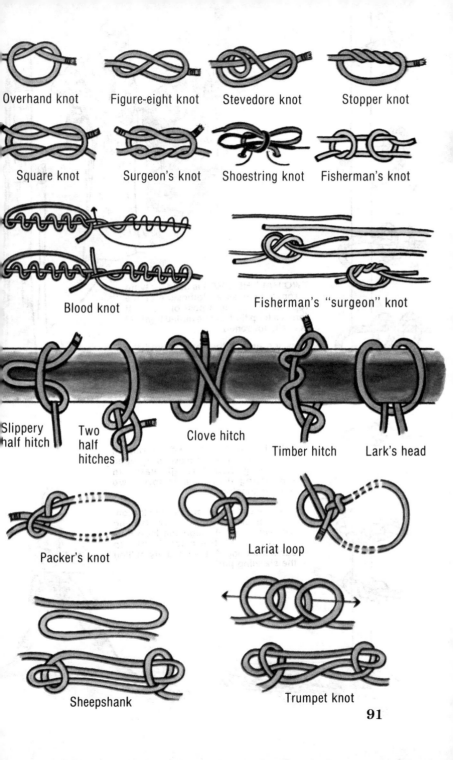

Overhand knot   Figure-eight knot   Stevedore knot   Stopper knot

Square knot   Surgeon's knot   Shoestring knot   Fisherman's knot

Blood knot   Fisherman's "surgeon" knot

Slippery half hitch   Two half hitches   Clove hitch   Timber hitch   Lark's head

Packer's knot   Lariat loop

Sheepshank   Trumpet knot

TWO HALF HITCHES is used for tying a rope—such as a clothesline or the rope of a boat—to a post or a ring. It forms a loop that can be pulled tight yet is easily loosened.

Pass the end of the rope around the post. Bring the rope end over and under its own standing part and through the loop thus formed. Do the same once more in front of this first half hitch.

TIMBER HITCH is used for raising logs, for dragging them over the ground or pulling them through water. In pioneering it is used to force two timbers together.

Pass the end of the rope around the log. Then under and over its own standing part twice and through the loop thus formed. Push the hitch firmly up against the log. Make it taut by pulling the standing part.

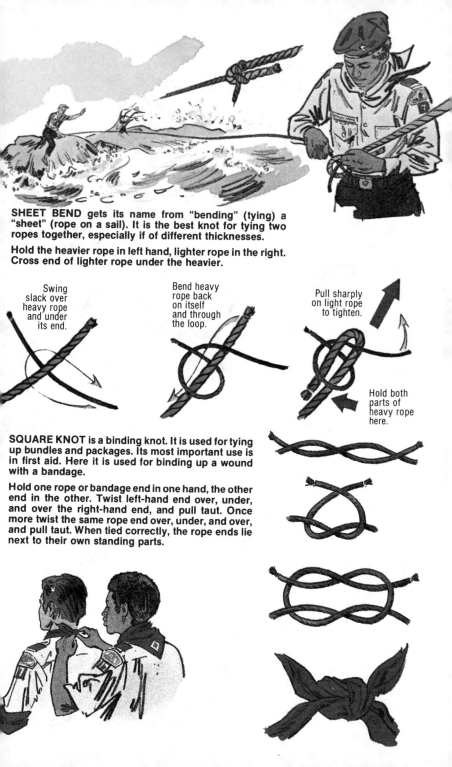

SHEET BEND gets its name from "bending" (tying) a "sheet" (rope on a sail). It is the best knot for tying two ropes together, especially if of different thicknesses.

Hold the heavier rope in left hand, lighter rope in the right. Cross end of lighter rope under the heavier.

Swing slack over heavy rope and under its end.

Bend heavy rope back on itself and through the loop.

Pull sharply on light rope to tighten.

Hold both parts of heavy rope here.

SQUARE KNOT is a binding knot. It is used for tying up bundles and packages. Its most important use is in first aid. Here it is used for binding up a wound with a bandage.

Hold one rope or bandage end in one hand, the other end in the other. Twist left-hand end over, under, and over the right-hand end, and pull taut. Once more twist the same rope end over, under, and over, and pull taut. When tied correctly, the rope ends lie next to their own standing parts.

BOWLINE forms a loop that will not close up. It is an important rescue knot for use in fires, mountain climbing, and water accidents.

Make an overhand loop in the standing part. Bring the rope end up through the loop, around the standing part and down through the loop. Tighten the bowline by holding on to the bend just formed and pulling hard in the standing part.

TAUT-LINE HITCH can be tied on a line that is taut. When used for tying a tent guy line, you can tighten or loosen the line by pushing the hitch up or down on the standing part.

Pass rope around the peg. Then bring the end under and over the standing part and twice through the loop formed. Again, bring the rope end under, over, and through the loop formed. Tighten the hitch around the standing part.

CLOVE HITCH (from cleave, to hold fast) is the most important knot for pioneering. It is used for starting and finishing most lashings.

Bring the rope end around the pole and in front of its own standing part. Bring the rope end once more around the pole. Finish by pushing the end under the rope itself. Then tighten as much as possible.

95

Comfort and Fun With Lashings

An overnight camp is quite simple. But if you are staying for a week or longer you'll want to make your camp comfortable.

Camp furniture and gadgets are fun to make. They show your inventiveness. They add the comforts of home. But don't go overboard and spend too much time making gadgets. Make just what you need. And remember to use only materials you are permitted to use.

LASHINGS. Most camp improvements call for tying sticks or poles together with lashings. Lashings can be made with binder twine, cord, or rope, depending on the thickness of the wood and the size of your project.

All lashings start with wrappings—that is, turns of the rope *around* the poles to hold them together. Some lashings also require frappings—that is, turns of the rope *between* the poles to tighten the wrappings.

When you know your lashings you can make many things for camp use: a clothes hanger, a towel rack, a raised fireplace, a dining table. You can pitch your tent with outside poles. You can put up a flagpole. And in troop and council camp where poles and ropes are available, you can even build a signal tower or a monkey bridge.

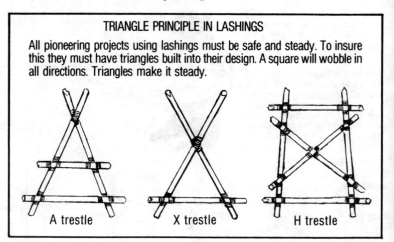

TRIANGLE PRINCIPLE IN LASHINGS

All pioneering projects using lashings must be safe and steady. To insure this they must have triangles built into their design. A square will wobble in all directions. Triangles make it steady.

A trestle   X trestle   H trestle

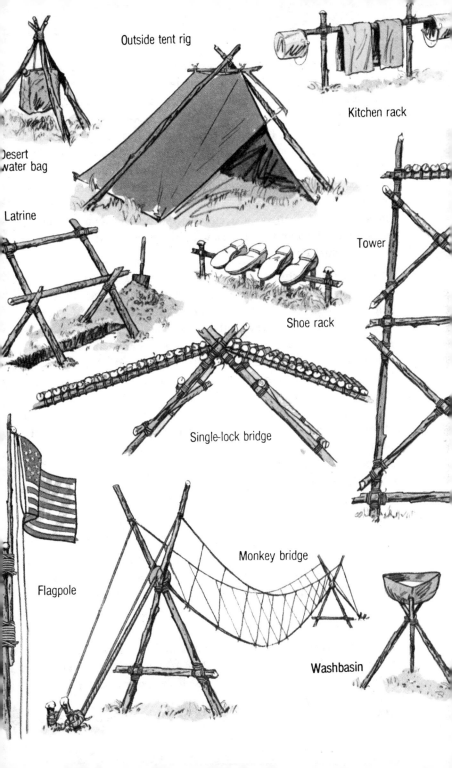

Outside tent rig

Kitchen rack

Desert
water bag

Latrine

Tower

Shoe rack

Single-lock bridge

Monkey bridge

Flagpole

Washbasin

Square Lashing. Place two poles on the ground, one cross-wise on top of the other. Tie a clove hitch around the bottom pole close to the crosspiece. Twist the free end of the rope around its own standing part. Now make three wrappings around both poles. Keep the rope taut. As you make the wrappings, lay the rope on the *outside* of the previous turn around the crosspiece, and on the *inside* of the previous turn around the bottom pole. Then make two frappings between the poles to tighten the wrappings. Tighten the frappings as much as possible. Finish off with a clove hitch around the end of the crosspiece. Remember: Start with clove. Wrap it thrice. Frap it twice. End with clove.

Diagonal Lashing. When you have to force two poles together to make them touch, use a diagonal lashing. This lashing is started with a timber hitch around the two poles where they cross. To make the timber hitch, pass the free end of the rope under and around the poles. Then carry the end around the rope's standing part and twist it around itself a few times before pulling the hitch taut. Now make three wrappings around both poles. For this, follow the lay of the timber hitch. Make the wrappings lie next to each other, not on top of each other. Continue with three more wrappings crosswise over the first three. Tighten the wrappings with two frappings between the poles. Finish with a clove hitch.

Shear Lashing. Place two poles next to each other. Lay a clove hitch around one of the poles. Then lash the poles together with seven or eight loosely laid wrappings. Make two frappings and finish with a clove hitch around the second pole.

Tripod Lashing. Place three poles alongside each other. Make a clove hitch around one of the poles. Then bring the rope over and under the poles five to seven times, figure-of-eight-wise. Finish with two loose frappings and a clove hitch around one pole.

Round Lashing. Place two poles side by side. Put a clove hitch around both poles. Make 8 or 10 wrappings around both poles. No frappings. Finish with a clove around both poles.

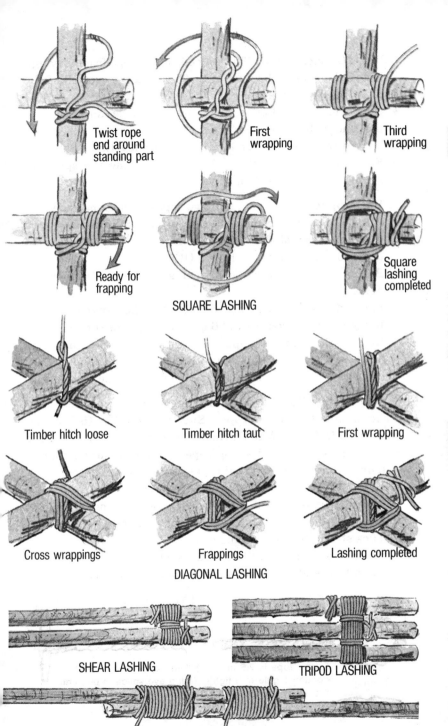

Twist rope end around standing part

First wrapping

Third wrapping

Ready for frapping

Square lashing completed

SQUARE LASHING

Timber hitch loose

Timber hitch taut

First wrapping

Cross wrappings

Frappings

Lashing completed

DIAGONAL LASHING

SHEAR LASHING

TRIPOD LASHING

ROUND LASHING

SPLICES. Back Splice. This splice keeps a rope from fraying.

- Unlay the rope end a few turns. Then make a crown knot by following drawings A, B, and C.
- Now bring the end of each strand over the strand next to it and under the strand next to that (D).
- Repeat this over-and-under movement a few times (E).
- Finish by trimming the ends and smoothing the splice by rolling it under your foot on the floor (F).

Short Splice. Use this to join two ropes of the same size.

- After unlaying the ends of each rope, push the two rope ends together, alternating the strands (A). Tie the strands down to prevent more unlaying (B).
- Bring strand 1 over the opposing strand and under the next.
- Bring strand 2 over strand 5 and under the next one.
- Bring strand 3 over strand 6 and under the next one.
- Remove tie and repeat operation with other rope end.
- Make two or more additional tucks with each strand.
- Cut off the ends of the strands. Smooth the splice.

Eye Splice. You use this to make a permanent loop and when making commando ropes. Such ropes, 2.5 m (8 ft.) long, were used in World War II. Each commando had his own rope around his waist. When a long rope was needed for climbing a cliff or scaling a wall, several ropes were locked together.

- Unlay the rope a few turns. Then bring strand 2 over strand c, under b, and out between strands a and b.
- Bring strand 1 over strand b and tuck it under strand a.
- Tuck strand 3 under strand c.
- Make two or more additional tucks with each strand.
- Cut off the ends of the strands. Smooth the splice.

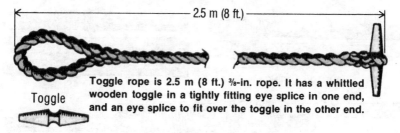

|← ──────────────── 2.5 m (8 ft.) ──────────────── →|

Toggle

Toggle rope is 2.5 m (8 ft.) ⅜-in. rope. It has a whittled wooden toggle in a tightly fitting eye splice in one end, and an eye splice to fit over the toggle in the other end.

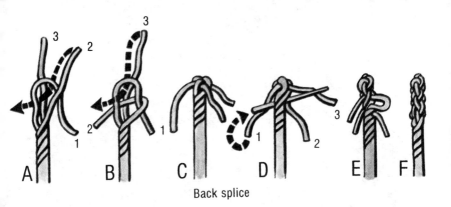

Back splice

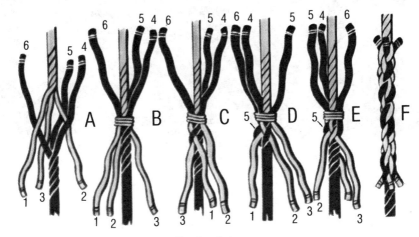

Short splice

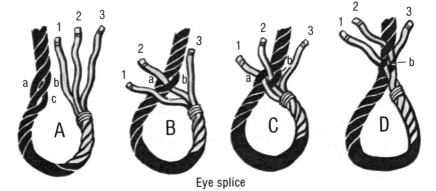

Eye splice

101

In a good patrol,
the whole patrol sits
down in style to eat its meals.

CAMP COOKERY

At home, you don't have to think too much about what's cooking. Usually someone has the food ready when mealtime comes around. But in camp you're on your own. There it's a matter of having the right amount of the right foodstuffs and necessary cooking gear on hand. There you have to know how to prepare kindling and firewood, how to build a simple fireplace and make the right kind of fire. There you have to know how to cook—not just for yourself but also for a buddy and, in patrol camp, for the whole patrol.

If you want to become a good camp cook, it'll pay you to become a good home cook first. Learn what it takes to cook a family meal. Help in the kitchen. Cook the kind of meals you like on the gas or electric range. Then use your knowledge in the wide-open spaces.

WHAT FOODS TO TAKE. In planning tasty meals for camp it is important to include the kind of foodstuffs you get at home. You need them for good health and for growth. For an overnight camp you don't have to worry too much. But for summer camp you should pick your foods from the four groups below to be sure you get what you need.

- **Meat, Poultry, Fish, Eggs.** You should have at least two helpings of meat (beef, veal, pork, lamb), poultry, or fish every day. Eggs may take the place of meat.

- **Milk and Milk Products.** At least 1 quart of milk daily to drink, with cereals, and in cooked foods. Cheese and ice cream can replace part of the milk.

- **Vegetables and Fruits.** Plan on at least four servings daily of things like these:
  Oranges, grapefruit, or tomatoes every day—served as is, as juice, or, in the case of tomatoes, also stewed.
  Dark-green and yellow-green vegetables at least every other day, some cooked, some raw: broccoli, spinach, collards, carrots, yellow squash, sweet potatoes.
  Potatoes, other vegetables, and fruits twice a day or as you like: potatoes, onions, celery, string beans, apples, pears, peaches, bananas, berries, melons, prunes.

- **Bread and Other Flour Products.** At least four helpings daily of enriched bread or whole-grain products: cereals, crackers, grits, macaroni or spaghetti, rice.

Accessories. In addition to the basic foods, certain other things are necessary in cooking: fats (butter, margarine, salad dressing), sweets (sugar, jam, jelly), and flavorings (salt, pepper, vinegar, mustard, cocoa).

For an overnight camp, most of your foodstuffs will be raw. Here you will bring fresh eggs, fresh meat, fresh vegetables, fresh fruits. For backpacking wilderness trips, it's a matter of traveling light. There you will make use of dried and dehydrated foods—egg and milk powder, instant potato, air-dried vegetables and fruits, freeze-dried meats.

When you have to plan three meals for a patrol overnight camp, you'll appreciate what it takes to feed your own family.

PLANNING YOUR MENUS. Let's say you're in charge of menus for a patrol overnight. How would you go about it?

Lining Up a Menu. Start by planning three meals that everyone in the patrol will like. You will want a complete dinner or supper, a solid breakfast, and an easy lunch. Study the recipes for routine camp dishes on pages 122-25. Also go through the fun dishes on pages 128-29. Then take your pick.

Food List. Once the menu is accepted, make a food list. List everything you'll need for each dish. Then check them off on the chart on the next page where the amounts are given in both the metric and the English systems. In the proper blank column, write down the amount of food for one boy. Use a soft pencil so that you can erase the numbers and use the column again in the future. Now multiply each amount by the number of those who will be going.

Price Out the List. Your next job is to check costs. Take the list to a grocery store or supermarket. Tell the owner or manager what you are doing—he may be willing to help you. But don't buy anything at this stage.

Cost for Each Person. When you have priced each item, add up the costs. Divide the result by the number of those going. This will give you the food cost per person.

Buying the Food. When all the Scouts who are planning to go have paid their shares, it's time to buy your supplies. Enlist a couple of patrol members to help you carry the groceries.

SIZE OF SERVINGS

	Metric	English	Breakfast	Dinner/Supper
Meat Group				
Steak	200-250 g	6-8 oz.		
Chops	125 g	4 oz.		
Stew	125 g	4 oz.		
Hamburger	125 g	4 oz.		
Frankfurter	125 g	4 oz.		
Chicken	350 g	12 oz.		
Ham, precooked	100 g	3 oz.		
Bacon	60 g	2 oz.		
Meat, canned	100 g	3 oz.		
Fish, fresh	200-250 g	6-8 oz.		
Fish, canned	100 g	3 oz.		
Eggs, fresh	2	2		
Eggs, dried	15 g	½ oz.		
Milk Group				
Milk, fresh	500 ml	1 pt.		
Milk, powdered	50-60 g	1½-2 oz.		
Cocoa, instant	1 packet	1 packet		
Cheese	60 g	2 oz.		
Ice cream	250 ml	½ pt.		
Vegetable-Fruit Group				
Orange	1	1		
Grapefruit	½	½		
Tomatoes	1	1		
Juice, canned	125 g	4 oz.		
Cabbage, raw	¼ head	¼ head		
Carrots, raw	1	1		
Vegetables, canned	125 g	4 oz.		
Vegetables, dehydrated	15 g	½ oz.		
Potatoes, raw	2-3 medium	2-3 medium		
Potatoes, instant	60 g	2 oz.		
Corn, raw	2 ears	2 ears		
Onions, raw	1 medium	1 medium		
Soup, canned	150 g	5 oz.		
Soup powder	¼ package	¼ package		
Fruit, fresh	1-2	1-2		
Fruit, canned	150-200 g	5-6 oz.		
Fruit, dried	60 g	2 oz.		
Bread-Cereal Group				
Bread	4 slices	4 slices		
Cookies	60 g	2 oz.		
Cakes	60 g	2 oz.		
Cereals—oatmeal	60 g	2 oz.		
Cereals—farina	50 g	1½ oz.		
Cereals—cold	20 g	3/4 oz.		
Pancake mix	100 g	3 oz.		
Rice, precooked	50 g	1½ oz.		
Spaghetti	100 g	3 oz.		
Macaroni	100 g	3 oz.		
Pudding powder	½ package	½ package		

OTHER ITEMS FOR COOKING: Salt, pepper, mustard, vinegar.   Catsup, relishes, salad dressing. Flour. Sugar. Butter, margarine, cooking fats. Jam, jelly, syrup, peanut butter.

105

For one-man cookery get the official one-man cook kit. It consists of frying pan, stewpot with lid, deep plate, and plastic cup. It comes in a cloth cover with a carry strap.

Eating kit consists of stainless-steel knife, fork, spoon. The pieces clip together to fit in a snap-shut plastic case.

For training in patrol cooking on overnight camps, you can make up a usable cooking kit from No. 10 tin cans. You can also make a charcoal burner to fit bottom of tin-can pot.

For patrol camping over a longer period, the Trail Chef kit comes in handy. It has two frying pans, three pots with lids, cocoa pot, four serving plates, and four plastic cups.

For a safe fire, clear the ground for a diameter of 3 m (10 ft.).

Safe Fire Building

Each year in our country around 10 million acres of woodlands and grasslands go up in smoke. Many of these fires are set by people who were careless with campfires. When YOU build a fire, you'll see to it that it's a SAFE fire.

Before building a fire anyplace, be sure you are permitted to do so. It is only in your local Scout camp that you are likely to be allowed to light fires without special permission. In public woods and parks you will need a permit. In some parks open fires are never allowed. Ask your Scoutmaster how to go about getting permission where required.

MAKE A SAFE FIRE SITE. A fire must always be under complete control. That means it must be built on a spot from which the fire cannot spread. So find a site away from tinder of any kind—including nearby trees, grasses, or mats of evergreen needles. Mossy soil should always be avoided—if once a peat fire gets started, it is extremely difficult to put it out.

Clean the fire site you have chosen down to bare soil, whether sand, gravel, clay, or rock. If the site is grassy, remove enough shovel-size turfs with your camp spade. Place the turfs right side up in a shady place. To be sure they will not dry out before you replace them, water them if necessary.

Next, clear the ground around the fire site for a diameter of 3 m (10 ft.). Remove anything that might catch fire from a flying spark. Clear away dry grass, dry leaves, twigs, pine needles. Place a pot of water close to the fire for emergencies. Now get your firewood ready and start your fire.

TINDER from bark of DEAD:
Cedar
Birch
Tulip
Basswood
Elm
Grapevine

TINDER from weed tops:
Goldenrod
Aster
Yarrow
Wild carrot
Milkweed
Cattail

PREPARE YOUR FIRE MATERIALS. Ernest Thompson Seton, first Chief Scout of the Boy Scouts of America, wrote a verse that tells you how to make a fire:

> *First a curl of birchbark as dry as it kin be.*
> *Then some twigs of softwood, dead, but on the tree.*
> *Last o' all some pine knots to make the kittle foam.*
> *An' thar's a fire to make you think*
> *you're sittin' right at home.*

The first line deals with *tinder*. The second is about *kindling*. The third is about *fuel*. You'll need all three.

Tinder. Tinder is the kind of stuff that flares up when you touch it with the flame of a burning match. As it burns it sets fire to the kindling.

In evergreen woods pick the tiny, dead twigs off the trunks of young trees. In broadleaf woods break off a dead branch and whittle it into thin shavings.

Some barks are excellent tinder. The outer bark of old grapevines and cedar comes off in long flakes. The bark of white and yellow birches peels off in thin "feathers." The outer bark of gray birch is especially good. But never take bark from a live tree, only from a dead limb or a rotting stump. The inner bark from a dead branch of tulip, basswood, and elm is also good.

In fields, last year's dry weed tops will do for tinder.

KINDLING
from DEAD
branches—
squaw wood:
Evergreens
Willow
Alder
Aspen
Cottonwood

FUEL from
DEAD trees:
Hickory
Oak
Beech
Birch
Maple
Ash
Mesquite

Kindling. Kindling catches the flame from the tinder. As it burns, it sets fire to the fuel wood.

In the woods in dry weather, you can use sticks you find on the ground. Even better are dead branches still on the trees. Such branches are known as "squaw wood," the kind that Indian women used to collect. Take branches that snap easily. If they bend they're too green. "If you can't snap it, scrap it!"

Fuel. For fuel, break dead branches into pieces about a foot long. Or cut them up with ax or saw. If the wood is wet, split it.

In woodless areas you may have to depend on charcoal.

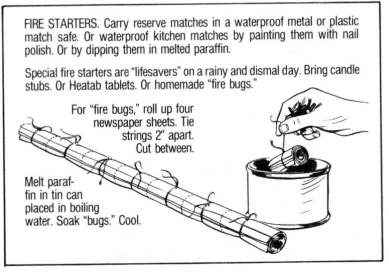

FIRE STARTERS. Carry reserve matches in a waterproof metal or plastic match safe. Or waterproof kitchen matches by painting them with nail polish. Or by dipping them in melted paraffin.

Special fire starters are "lifesavers" on a rainy and dismal day. Bring candle stubs. Or Heatab tablets. Or homemade "fire bugs."

For "fire bugs," roll up four newspaper sheets. Tie strings 2" apart. Cut between.

Melt paraffin in tin can placed in boiling water. Soak "bugs." Cool.

BUILDING THE FIRE. Now you are ready to lay and light your fire. Well, what kind shall it be? Almost any kind will give comfort on a cold day. But when it comes to cooking, campers have a slogan: "Flames for boiling. Coals for broiling."

Tepee Fire Lay. This fire lay will give you a quick fire for boiling in pots and frying in pans. Start it by placing a large handful of tinder on the ground in the middle of your fire site. Then lean a circle of kindling sticks around the tinder. The tips of the sticks should come together like the poles of an Indian tepee. Do a careful job. Otherwise the kindling sticks may flop over when the tinder has burned out.

To light the fire, crouch in front of the fire lay with your back to the wind. Strike a match. Cup your hands around it for protection. Let it burn into a real flame. Now touch the flame to the tinder close to the ground.

It caught! A few minutes later, the tinder has lit the kindling. Give the kindling a good start. Then feed the fire from the downwind side. Use thin pieces of fuel at first, then thicker pieces. Continue feeding until the fire is the size you want.

Lean-to Fire Lay. This is an improved version of the tepee fire lay. Start by pushing a green "lean-to stick" into the ground at a slant. Point its tip into the wind. This stick is to keep the kindling upright when the tinder has burned out. Place a handful of tinder under the stick. Lean kindling against it. Then place fuel against the kindling. Strike a match and light the tinder.

Fire-Stick Fire Lay. Use this fire lay to start a fire in a rock or hunter's fireplace. Lay a "fire stick" across the fireplace. Put a handful of tinder under the fire stick. Lean a number of kindling sticks against the fire stick. Build up the fire lay with thicker and thicker fuel. Then ignite the tinder.

Crisscross Fire Lay. This is just the thing when you want a bed of coals in a hurry for broiling or baking. Place two sticks on the ground parallel to each other. Put tinder between them. Then lay thin kindling sticks crosswise over the two supports, a little-finger -width apart. Continue with more crisscross layers. Increase the thickness from layer to layer.

FOUR KINDS OF FIRE LAYS

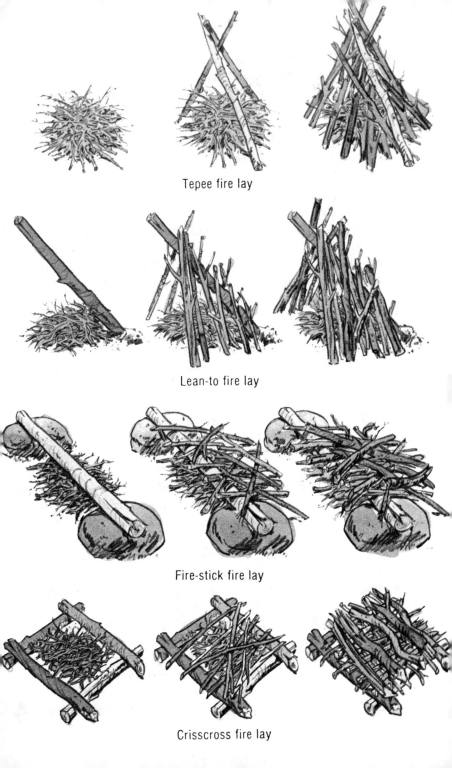

Tepee fire lay

Lean-to fire lay

Fire-stick fire lay

Crisscross fire lay

MANY KINDS OF FIRES. Pick what you like.

Three-Point Fireplace. This is the simplest fireplace for a single pot or pan. Just place three rocks of even size around your fire lay. Or push three metal tent pegs into the ground.

Rock Fireplace. Choose dry, flat rocks. Set them in two rows close enough together to support your pots. Don't use sandstone or wet rocks; they may explode when heated.

Hunter's Fireplace. If you have logs, use them for a "hunter's fire." Place two of them close enough together to support your utensils. Since the fire eats up the logs from the inside, you will have to replace them from time to time.

Trench Fireplace. In an open field, the trench fireplace is safer than an above-the-ground fireplace on a windy day. Mark off the trench with your camp spade, one spade width wide. Dig it enough spade widths long to make room for your utensils. Remove the sod in turfs and take proper care of them (page 88). Widen the windward end to catch a good draft.

Bean Hole. To cook bean-hole beans you need a hole in the ground large enough to hold a bean pot. Here, too, take care of the turfs. Light a fire in the hole. Use the fire to cook the beans until they are soft. Then use the coals to bake them.

Log-Cabin Fire. This is the ideal council fire for a whole camp of Scouts. It consists of a crisscross fire lay made from logs, with a smaller crisscross fire lay made from branches on top. You light this upper fire lay. As the campfire program progresses, the fire eats its way down through the pile.

Reflector Fire. This fire is built against a reflector of logs or rocks. It provides comfort on a winter's night. It is also good for baking or roasting in a reflector oven.

Star Fire. You start this Indian fire with a tepee fire lay. You then place four or five logs around it like spokes in a wheel. You keep the burning end slightly raised on a stick. As the logs burn, you push them farther into the fire.

Vigil Fire. Roll two logs close to a tepee fire. Raise them off the ground on a couple of sticks for draft. Place a third log on top, also supported on a couple of draft sticks. The fire will burn for a couple of hours without being touched.

112   **MANY KINDS OF FIRES**

Three-point fireplaces

Rock fireplace

nter's fireplace

Bean hole

Reflector fire

Trench fireplace

Star fire

Vigil fire

Log-cabin fire

Octagonal spindle is round at one end, tapered at the other.

Fireboard has gouged holes for spindle, V cuts for embers.

Best fire-by-friction woods are yucca, elm, red cedar, willow root, basswood, sycamore, cottonwood, poplar, soft maple, and white pine.

The real test is that you can go into the woods and make fire, using natural materials, a boot lace, knife, and ax.

Bow is stiff branch as long as your arm with a leather thong.

Hand block has smooth hole for top of spindle to spin freely.

Tinder is shredded cedar bark, inner elm bark, mouse nest.

Primitive Fire Making

Matches are OK for starting cooking fires. A campfire deserves better. Add to its romance by lighting it the way Indians and early settlers did it.

FIRE BY FRICTION. This was the Indian way of making fire. For this you need a fire-making set made up of spindle, fireboard, hand block, bow, and tinder.

To make fire by friction, put the tinder on the ground. Place the fireboard over the tinder. Kneel on one knee. Place the other foot on the fireboard. Twist bowstring once tightly around the spindle. Hold spindle upright with the hand block. Rest the hand holding the hand block against the knee.

Set the spindle spinning with long strokes of the bow. Increase the pressure. Keep going until heavy smoke rises. Knock the ember formed in the notch in the fireboard into the tinder. Blow it into flame with steady blows.

Fire has been made in 6.4 seconds. What's your aim?

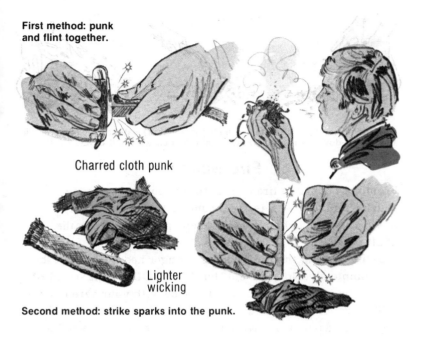

First method: punk and flint together.

Charred cloth punk

Lighter wicking

Second method: strike sparks into the punk.

FIRE BY FLINT-AND-STEEL. In colonial days people made fire by flint-and-steel. You can do the same. You will need a fire-making set consisting of a piece of flint, an old file, punk, and tinder.

The punk you will have to prepare in advance at home. It is the flammable material you need for catching the spark struck from the steel. You can use lighter wicking or charred cloth. To prepare the lighter wicking, light the end, then snuff it out. To char cloth, hang it from a stick. Light it. When aflame, drop it in a coffee can. Put on the lid to smolder the flame.

For tinder, your best bet is shredded dry cedar bark.

To make fire, hold flint and punk between fingers. With the steel, strike a glancing blow against the flint. Aim it in such a way that the sparks fly into the punk. Place the smoldering punk in the tinder and blow it into flame with long, soft blows.

Or place punk and tinder on the ground. Aim sparks into the punk. Lift up the smoldering punk and the tinder together and blow it into flame.

To extinguish a fire with water, sprinkle (do not pour) water on the embers. Stir the wetted-down ashes. Wet down smoldering sticks. Kill it COLD OUT!

Fire Safety

From the moment a fire is lit until it is put out, someone must watch it and see that it is under control. It is criminal to leave a fire unattended. To be extra safe, keep a pot of water near the fire at all times.

Extinguishing the Fire. When no longer needed, put out the fire completely. Not just "out" but "COLD OUT." What is left of it must be cool enough for you to touch with your bare hand.

With Water. Sprinkle (do not pour) water on the embers. Stir the wetted-down ashes with a stick and sprinkle again. Turn over smoldering half-burned sticks and wet them down on all sides. Wet the ground around the site. Give everything the COLD-OUT test.

Without Water. If water is scarce, work mineral soil into embers. That is, soil with nothing in it that will burn. Then stir and stir again until the last ember is out. Rub burned sticks against the ground until all sparks are out. Then give everything the COLD-OUT test.

Finally, "garden" the ashes into the ground. Replace carefully any turfs you have removed. Make the spot look as if no one had been there.

Ask your Scoutmaster about the "Firem'n Chit."

To extinguish a fire without water, work mineral soil into the embers. Stir and stir until the last ember or spark is gone. Kill it COLD OUT!

Getting Ready to Cook

The way you go about cooking in camp depends on the number of Scouts who will be eating. At times you may cook by yourself. At other times you and a buddy may cook together. The most interesting kind of cooking is when the whole patrol is to be served.

COOKING ALONE. For cooking alone you lay out your foodstuffs on a plastic sheet you brought along for the purpose. You then get out your cook kit. This may be a pot and a pan from your home kitchen. But much better is the official one-man cook kit (see page 106). You are ready to go!

COOKING BY BUDDIES. Here you have to decide between you who will do what. One of you will be the head cook. Or "bull chef," as they say in the Northwoods. The other will be the "flunky." The head cook lays out foodstuffs and gear on the plastic sheet. He then does the cooking and serving. The flunky is the fireman and water boy. For the next meal, the two of you change jobs. This way you both get training.

COOKING BY PATROL. For cooking in patrol camp, you make up a patrol roster (page 146). You take turns, in buddy teams, as wood-and-water boys, cooks, and cleanup crew. For this kind of cooking the official Trail Chef cook kit is the thing.

For quick pot and pan washing, smear soap powder paste or softened soap on the outside of pot before using. Soot then washes off in cold water.

Plan to have a substantial breakfast in camp. You have fasted during the night and you need a lot of energy for the day's exciting activities.

Breakfast in Camp

For breakfast in camp you want a big meal. There should be fruit, cereal, a main dish—such as eggs, bacon or ham, or pancakes—and a beverage.

On a cool day, have a hot cereal and cocoa.

On a hot morning, use cold cereal and milk.

FRUIT. Fresh Fruit. Year-round you can get and serve 1 or 2 oranges, bananas, or apples or ½ grapefruit. In season you can get melons and berries. In the fall look for wild berries.

Canned Fruit. Figure on 150 to 180 g (5 to 6 oz.) canned fruit, grapefruit segments, peach halves, pineapple slices, whole apricots or plums. Or you can have juice: ½ cup orange, grapefruit, or tomato juice.

Stewed Fruit. You'll want 4 to 6 prunes or dried apricots, 3 to 4 dried peach halves, or ¼ cup dried apples; sugar to taste. Cover with water, bring to a boil, then simmer—that is, keep just below the boiling point—for 15 to 30 minutes. When done, add 2 to 4 teaspoons sugar. You can shorten the time by soaking the fruit overnight.

CEREALS. Cold Cereals. Use 1 individual box of a kind you like. Serve with milk and sugar.

Hot Oatmeal. Bring 1 cup water to a vigorous boil. Sprinkle into it ½ cup quick-cooking rolled oats while stirring. Add a pinch of salt. Cook at a slow boil for 5 minutes, stirring frequently to the bottom of the pot.

Instant Hot Oatmeal. Bring ¾ cup water to a boil. Drop ½ cup instant oatmeal into a bowl. Pour the boiling water into the oats and stir until mixed. Sprinkle with salt and stir.

Hot Farina. Stir ¼ cup farina or similar cereal into ¾ cup of boiling water. Add a pinch of salt. Cook gently for 5 minutes, stirring frequently.

EGGS TO YOUR TASTE. Eggs, Fried.

Heat a teaspoon of butter or margarine or bacon fat in the pan. Break 2 eggs into the pan. Fry over slow heat until the white becomes firm.

Eggs, Scrambled. Beat 2 eggs in a bowl with a fork. Add a pinch of salt and 2 tablespoons of water. Heat butter or margarine in the pan over a slow fire. Pour in the beaten eggs and cook gently until set, scraping occasionally from the bottom of the pan with a fork. Serve plain or mixed with cubes of ham, crumbled fried bacon, or frankfurter chunks.

Eggs, Boiled. Bring water to a boil. Put 2 eggs in with a spoon, one at a time. Boil 3 to 5 minutes for soft-boiled, 10 to 15 minutes for hard-boiled. Put the boiled eggs in cold water for a moment. This makes the shells peel easily.

BACON AND HAM.

Bacon-and-eggs and ham-and-eggs are popular breakfast combinations.

Bacon, Fried. Put 3 or 4 slices bacon in a cold pan and cook over slow fire, turning the slices when half done. Do not overcook—the bacon will crisp as it cools. As the fat collects, pour it off into a container and save it. Bacon fat is excellent for all kinds of frying.

Ham, Fried. Heat a small amount of butter or margarine in the pan. Put in a slice of precooked ham, about 100 g (3 oz.). Fry the ham over a slow fire until it has become slightly browned. Turn and fry the other side.

PANCAKES AND FLAPJACKS.

Bake these in a large frying pan or on a griddle. Pancakes are about the size of the palm of

119

your hand. Flapjacks are supposed to fill the whole bottom of the pan. They use the same kind of batter. They are turned by being flipped with a knife or a pancake turner—or in the air if you have the courage and the skill.

Pancakes. Make a batter of ½ cup pancake flour according to the instructions on the box. (If you have no prepared flour, make your own by mixing ½ cup ordinary flour, ½ teaspoon baking powder, 1 pinch of salt, ½ teaspoon sugar. Add 1 egg and ¼ to ½ cup milk.) Heat your pan and grease it with a little butter or margarine or bacon fat. Pour in batter for enough cakes to fill the bottom of the pan. Fry over a slow fire. As soon as bubbles burst in the center of the cakes and the edges begin to brown, turn the pancakes and fry the other side. Serve with butter, jam, syrup.

French Toast. Beat lightly 1 egg, ¼ teaspoon salt, 1 cup milk. Dip (don't soak!) both sides of up to 8 slices of bread. Fry in greased pan or on griddle. Serve with butter and syrup.

SOMETHING TO DRINK. Milk. You will certainly want at least 2 cups of milk. If you can get fresh, pasteurized milk at camp, fine. Otherwise use dry powdered milk: Add ½ cup to 2 cups water and stir.

Cocoa. Use 1 or 2 packages instant cocoa. Bring 1 or 2 cups water to a boil. Add 1 package of cocoa per cup and stir. For a richer cocoa, add 1 or 2 tablespoons dry milk.

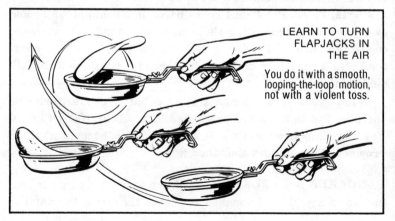

LEARN TO TURN FLAPJACKS IN THE AIR

You do it with a smooth, looping-the-loop motion, not with a violent toss.

Lunch is the simplest meal of the day in camp. On a hot summer's day you will want a cold meal. On a cold winter's day you would have a hot meal.

Lunch in Camp

Lunch comes during the hottest hours of the day. So you probably don't want to do much cooking. Nevertheless, you're starved—so what to do? A couple of sandwiches, a cold drink, a few cookies will fill you up at high noon. If you want to have your main meal in the middle of the day use the dinner recipes that follow.

SANDWICHES. For one serving: 4 to 6 slices enriched white or dark bread, butter or margarine, fillings. For fillings, use hard-boiled eggs, cold cuts, cheese, sardines, tuna or salmon, sliced tomatoes, peanut butter, jelly, jam, or whatever else you wish. A couple of lettuce leaves and a dab of salad dressing add to taste and looks.

HOT DISHES. If you are in a picnic mood, light a fire and fry a hamburger or grill a hot dog. Or make a toasted cheese sandwich by simply frying a regular cheese sandwich on both sides in a little butter or margarine. Or try one of the aluminum foil tricks on pages 126-27.

Hot Soup. This is perfect for a cold or rainy day. For one serving: ½ can condensed soup or 1 package of instant soup. Dilute condensed soup with an equal amount of water. Heat. Follow instructions on package for instant soup.

Supper or dinner should be the most enjoyable meal in camp. Plan a meal that everyone in the patrol will like. Take time to prepare it well.

Dinner or Supper in Camp

The evening meal is generally the main meal in camp. It will consist of a meat, poultry, or fish dish with a choice of vegetables, bread or biscuits, dessert, and beverage.

MEAT COOKING. There are many methods of cooking meat. Broiling is the fastest, stewing the slowest. Keep that in mind when you plan your menu.

Meat, Broiled. To broil meat over an open fire, use a wire broiler or make a rustic broiler from a green forked branch. Place a piece of meat of about 250 g (8 oz.) in the broiler and hold it 10 cm (4 in.) above a bed of glowing coals. Broil until the meat is done to suit your taste. A 2.5 cm (1 in.) thick steak needs about 8 to 10 minutes on each side to be medium done.

Meat, Pan-Broiled. Use 125 g (4 oz.) ground beef or steak, lamb, or pork chops. Heat a small amount of grease in the pan—just enough to keep meat from sticking. Drop in patties of ground meat or steak or chops. Cook over a slow fire, turning occasionally. Pour off the fat as it collects. Ground meat (hamburger) takes only a couple of minutes on each side; steak 6 to 8 minutes; lamb chops 8 to 10 minutes; pork chops 12 to 15 minutes. Pork should always be well done.

Meat, Stewed. Cut 125 g (4 oz.) beef, lamb, or veal into 2 cm (¾ inch) cubes. Rub flour and salt into them and fry them in the pot in a little fat until brown. Add enough water to cover them. Bring the water to a boil, then move the pot to a spot over the fire where the meat can simmer for about 1 hour or until tender. About 30 minutes before meat is done, season with a pinch of salt and add peeled and cut-up vegetables: 1 onion, 1 carrot, 1 potato. Continue simmering until done.

Chicken, Fried. Cut ½ frying chicken into two or three pieces and roll them in flour. Fry in 2 tablespoons butter or margarine, turning every now and then, until all pieces are a golden brown. Add 2 tablespoons water, put on a lid, and steam over low fire for about 20 minutes until done.

FISH. Figure on 250 g (8 oz.) fresh fish. Clean the fish first. Remove scales by scraping with a blunt knife from tail toward head. Cut the spine just behind the gills. Tear the head off with a slow forward motion—the entrails will come out with it. Slit open the belly and clean the inside. Cut off fins and tail.

Fish, Fried. Cut the spine of a small fish in several places to prevent it from curling up in the pan. Cut larger fish in pieces, or fillet them by removing backbone and skin. Wipe the fish dry with a cloth. Roll it in flour. Fry in a small amount of butter or fat until golden brown.

Fish, Poached. Drop fish into salted, boiling water. Simmer gently until the fish can be picked easily from the bones.

HAND THERMOMETER. Hold palm at place where food will go: over coals for broiling, in front of reflector oven for baking. Count "One-and-one," "Two-and-two," and so on, for seconds you can stand to hold your hand. Move your hand to find the temperature you want.

	Hand removed at count	Heat	Temperature
	6 to 8	Slow	120°C-175°C 250°F-350°F
	4 to 5	Moderate	175°C-200°C 350°F-400°F
	2 to 3	Hot	200°C-230°C 400°F-450°F
	1 or less	Very hot	230°C-260°C 450°F-500°F

VEGETABLES. Potatoes, Boiled. Peel and quarter 2 to 4 medium-size potatoes. Drop them into enough water to cover them. Add ½ teaspoon salt. Boil gently for about 20 minutes. Test with a fork—if it goes in easily, the potatoes are done. Pour out water. Place pot near fire to let moisture steam off.

Potatoes, Home-Fried. Boil 2 or 3 medium-size potatoes. Let them cool. Cut the cold potatoes into slices and fry in hot fat until brown. Fry sliced onion with the potatoes if you like.

Potatoes, Mashed. Boil 2 or 3 medium-size potatoes. When done, mash with the bottom of a cup from your cook kit. Add a knife-tip scoop of butter, a pinch of salt, and 1 or 2 tablespoons of milk. Beat the mixture with a fork.

Potatoes, Instant Mashed. Prepare from ½ cup instant potato flakes. Follow the directions on the box.

Vegetables, Boiled. Take your choice: ¼ small head of cabbage, 1 or 2 medium carrots, 2 ears of corn, ½ cup cut string beans or shelled peas. Clean the vegetables. Cut them up if too big. Cook in as little water as necessary. Cook at a soft boil, without a lid on the pot. Fresh cabbage cooks in about 7 to 12 minutes, carrots in 25 minutes, corn on the cob in 6 to 10 minutes, string beans in 30 minutes, peas in 10 to 15 minutes. Or use ½ cup canned vegetables. Just heat them.

SPAGHETTI, MACARONI, RICE could be your choice instead of potatoes or for adding variety to your meals.

Spaghetti. Bring 4 cups water to a boil in a large pot. Push into the water 100 g (3 to 4 oz.) spaghetti. Add ¼ teaspoon salt. Boil hard 5 to 9 minutes or until tender. Do not overcook; spaghetti should be slightly chewy. Drain. Serve with the spaghetti sauce you like best.

Macaroni. Drop 100 g (3 to 4 oz.) macaroni in 4 cups boiling water. Cook as for spaghetti 10 to 15 minutes. Serve with butter or spaghetti sauce.

Rice, Precooked. Bring ½ cup water to a boil. Add dash of salt and ½ teaspoon butter. Stir in ½ cup precooked rice. Cover. Remove from heat. Let stand 5 minutes, then fluff up the rice with a fork.

BREADSTUFFS. Biscuits. Follow the directions on the package for mixing dough out of ½ cup ready-mixed biscuit flour. Divide the dough into three or four parts and pat into biscuits about 1 cm (½ inch) thick. Place the biscuits on the greased pan of a reflector oven and bake in front of a steady fire for about 15 minutes. Test by pushing a straw into one of the biscuits—if the straw comes out clean, the biscuits are done.

Bannock. Make a stiff dough of ½ cup biscuit flour. Flatten to a thumb-thick cake to fit your pan. Fry 7-8 minutes over slow coals to brown bottom. Then tilt pan before a fire to finish top. Bake top 7 minutes or longer. Test with a straw.

DESSERTS. Fruit. Use the same as for breakfast (page 118). Remember that watermelon is in season during summer camp! So are berries.

Pudding. Follow directions on the box for making pudding from ½ package of instant pudding powder.

Cake, Cookies. 1 piece cake or 4 cookies should be enough.

Magic Lemon Pudding. Mix ¼ can sweetened condensed milk with the juice of ¼ lemon. You'll be surprised at what happens. To vary, crush some cookies and add them.

Shortcake. Mix dough as for biscuits, but add 2 teaspoons sugar. Make into two biscuits and bake in a reflector oven. Serve with crushed, sweetened berries.

Place the reflector oven, with biscuits or pies, before a reflector fire (see page 123). Use hand thermometer count of 2. Also for bannock.

Time the placing of the food so that everything will be ready together.

Cooking With Aluminum Foil

"Perfect camp meal—no pots or pans to carry, no utensils to clean afterward." How does that sound to you? Great! But impossible? Not at all—if you go in for aluminum foil cookery. You simply wrap your foodstuffs in a piece of heavy-duty foil in such a way that the steam cannot escape. Place the package on hot coals and turn it a couple of times during the cooking. When cooked, the foil is your plate.

The fire is important in foil cookery. You need a shallow bed of glowing coals that will last for the time required for cooking. Quickest way to get this is to make a crisscross fire lay and let it burn down to embers (pages 110-11).

Hamburger a la Foil. Make 125 g (4 oz.) hamburger into a thick cake. Peel 1 potato and cut it into strips. Peel and slice 1 onion. Scrape 1 medium carrot and cut it into sticks. Place the ingredients on a piece of foil. Sprinkle with salt. Close the foil into a package. Place the package on the coals and cook for 15 minutes.

Foil Stew. Cut 125 g (4 oz.) beef or lamb into 2 cm (¾ in.) cubes. Place on foil with 1 peeled and cubed potato, 1 peeled and quartered onion, 1 scraped and sliced carrot. Sprinkle with salt. Wrap up. Cook on coals 20 minutes.

Caveman Steak and Lyonnaise Potatoes. Place on foil 1 potato and 1 onion, peeled and sliced. Dab with butter and sprinkle with salt. Wrap up. Cook on coals for 15 minutes. Place a

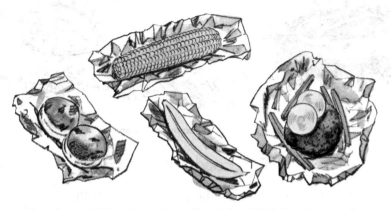

When done, open up the packages. Spread out the foil and use as plates.

250 g (8 oz.) steak on foil directly on the coals. Cook 2.5 cm (1 inch) steak 3 to 5 minutes on each side for rare, 8 minutes for medium, 10 for well done.

Chicken and Corn Roast. Smear 2 ears of corn, 1 chicken drumstick, and 1 thigh with butter. Sprinkle with salt and wrap in separate foil packages. Cook chicken on coals 20 minutes, corn 10.

Baked Fish. Wrap 1 or 2 slices of bacon around the fish. Wrap in foil and bake on coals 15 to 20 minutes.

Biscuits. Make biscuits according to usual recipe. Wrap in greased foil. Wrap loosely to permit raising. Bake 6 to 10 minutes. Turn halfway through the baking.

Baked Fruit for Dessert. Wrap apple or banana in foil. Bake apple about 30 minutes, banana 10. Try baking a whole fresh pineapple in foil some day. That's eating!

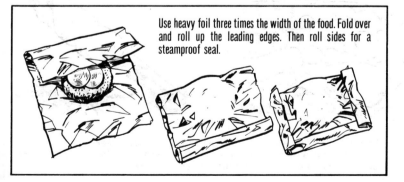

Use heavy foil three times the width of the food. Fold over and roll up the leading edges. Then roll sides for a steamproof seal.

Broil your steak directly on the coals or in a broiler over the coals.

Fun Food in Camp

Anyone can cook with pots and pans. Cooking without them is something quite different. Try it. You'll have fun doing it.

COOKING IN COALS. Roast Potatoes. Bury washed potatoes in a bed of coals. Bake until well done, about 40 minutes. Keep the fire going on top of the coals. Test for doneness by pushing a pointed stick into them. When it goes in easily, the potatoes are done.

Damper or Ash Bread. Pat stiff biscuit dough into a flat bread, 2.5 cm (1 in.) thick. Cover top and bottom with large leaves. Push coals and ashes aside. Lay dough on the hot ground. Cover with ashes and coals. Bake 10 minutes. Test with a straw. Push straw into bread. When it comes out clean bread is done.

COOKING ON COALS. Caveman Steak. Flatten the bed of coals with a stick. Place a 2.5 cm (1 in.) steak on top of the coals. Broil 3 to 5 minutes. Turn. Broil the other side.

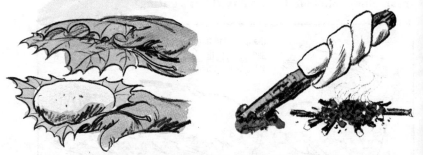

Use stiff biscuit dough for damper (left) and twist (right). Make dough by flour-bag trick: With a stick, stir a hollow in flour in plastic bag. Pour in ¼ cup water. Stir until you have a blob of dough on end of stick.

Kabob, shish-kebab, shashlick—suit yourself—is a favorite fun dish.

Roast Corn. Open the husks. Remove the silk. Close up the husks again. Dip the ears in water. Then place them on the coals. Roast 8 minutes. Turn a few times during roasting.

COOKING OVER COALS. Broiled Steak. Make a tennis-racket broiler from forked branch. Anchor the steak with short sticks. Place over a bed of glowing coals. Broil to desired doneness.

Kabob. Broil cubes of meat on a skewer, alone or with vegetables. Combine to suit yourself 3 cm (1¼ in.) cubes of beef, lamb, ham; chunks of tomato, onion, green pepper, zucchini, pineapple. Place meat and vegetables alternately on pencil-thin skewer of green wood. Broil over coals 10 to 15 minutes.

Twist. Roll stiff biscuit dough into a long sausage. Twist this around a stick as thick as an ax handle. Lean the stick over a bed of coals. Turn occasionally. Bake until done.

**JUNIOR LEADER TRAINING
CONFERENCE FEAST**

This is the traditional feast for Scouts and guests that winds up the boy leader training!

For each person, 1 Cornish game hen, 2 ears of corn, 1 Idaho potato, fresh salad plate, rolls, beverage, melon for dessert.

Impale hens on spits—up to four to a spit. Roast over charcoal 30 minutes or until done. Bake foil-wrapped potatoes 30 minutes, foil-wrapped corn 10 minutes.

129

You can make a small charcoal stove from a No. 10 tin can, and a larger one from a 5-gallon oil can.

Cooking on Charcoal Fires

In many public parks open wood fires are prohibited. And in many camping areas firewood is so scarce that you have to pack in your own fuel. You can solve these problems by using charcoal or, better, charcoal briquets. You can buy them in convenient packages.

CHARCOAL STOVES. Unlike a wood fire, a charcoal fire requires some kind of stove. What kind? There are dozens on the market. But why buy one when you can make your own?

For cooking a meal in a single pot or a small pan you can turn a No. 10 tin can into a charcoal stove. Cut off the top completely. Make holes for draft along the bottom with a juice-can opener. Make similar holes along the top edge, from the inside out. Cut off with tin shears the sharp tips of the tongues that result. To save charcoal, make a perforated grate from a can top. Rest it on a couple of wires pushed through the stove one-third or half-way down.

For broiling, barbecuing, and frying, you can make a larger, trough-shaped stove by cutting open a 5-gallon oil can.

CHARCOAL TIPS. A charcoal fire is quite different from a wood fire. Using wood you have a hot fire to start with, a slower fire later. Using charcoal you have a slow fire in the beginning, a hot fire later.

- Guess how much charcoal you will need for the whole cooking job. Ignite that much from the start.
- For sure, safe start, use twigs and wood shavings. Never use flammable fluids to start a charcoal fire. They burn off

130

Many commercial charcoal stoves fold up for easy carrying. Most of them have a charcoal pan that can be set high or low. They have a grill for placing utensils and broiling meat.

When ready to broil, start the charcoal fire as suggested below. Then spread out the coals. For boiling, confine the charcoal under the pot in a heat localizer—a sheet-metal collar.

fast, lighting only a little of the charcoal. Pouring on more is then very dangerous.

- Figure on about 20 minutes from starting the charcoal fire to having the heat you need. You can speed up the process by fanning the fire with a pot lid.
- For frying and broiling, spread out the charcoal. A single layer is usually sufficient.
- For boiling, confine the charcoal within a heat localizer ring—a sheet metal collar that keeps the heat directly under the pot. Or place the pot directly on the coals.
- If the fire gets too hot, dampen it by sprinkling a few drops of water on the glowing charcoal. Or use a squeeze bottle.
- Reclaim unburned charcoal. As soon as you have finished cooking and heating water for the cleanup, dump the glowing charcoal briquets into a pot of water to extinguish them. Drain them immediately and spread them out to dry. Retained heat, plus the heat of a summer's day, will dry them in no time for use for your next meal.

QUICK START FOR CHARCOAL

Make a charcoal fire starter from a large fruit juice can. Cut out the top and bottom. Place the can on the perforated charcoal pan. Half fill it with twigs. Then add the number of briquets you will use. Start the fire from below the pan. When all charcoal is glowing, remove can with a pair of pliers.

You need plenty of hot water for
a sanitary dishwashing job.

CLEANUP

CLEANUP AFTER COOKING. Get this job out of the way as
soon as you have eaten.

- **Garbage.** Some camps have trash cans for trash and garbage
  disposal. If not, all trash and garbage should be compacted into
  a plastic bag and carried home or to the nearest trash can.
- **Jars and Cans.** Wash out empty jars. Burn out empty tin cans
  and flatten them. Put jars and flattened cans in a tote-litter bag.
  Get rid of them at home or in the nearest trash can.
- **Extinguish Fire.** Put out the fire with water (see page 116). Cover
  the fire site with the material you scraped from it to make it safe.
  Or replace the turfs if you have dug up sod.
- **Firewood.** Stack unused firewood, ready for the next time.

DISHWASHING. The smart cook puts two pots of water over the fire the moment the cooking is done—one for washing, the other for rinsing. The water will be hot by the time you have eaten.

- **Wipe.** Rough-clean your utensils first. Wipe them out with paper towels or leaves. Burn the soiled towels or leaves on the remains of the cooking fire.
- **Wash.** Put soap powder or liquid soap into the dishwater. Use a dishmop to clean plates, cups, silverware. Clean pots and pans separately.
- **Rinse.** Dunk the washed utensils in the hot rinse water. You may have to hold the plates with hot-pot tongs. Be sure the rinse water is nearly boiling. This will heat the utensils so that they will dry by themselves. You will then not need a dishtowel. To be even more certain that the hot water will sterilize the dishes, you may want to add a chemical sanitizing powder to it. You can get this from your local Scouting distributor.
- **Air-Dry.** Spread out the rinsed utensils on a plastic sheet to air-dry. Store them when dry.

CLEANUP AFTER CAMPING. The really good camper aims to leave his campsite looking in such a way that no one can see that he has been there. To do this, check each of these points:

- Did I fill in all ditches and holes I made? Did I replace what turfs I dug up?
- Did I make certain that all fires were cold out? Did I restore all fire sites to their original looks?
- Did I get rid of all garbage? Did I pack out all empty cans and jars, aluminum foil, and other unburnable trash? Did I follow the slogan "If you can pack it in, you can pack it out."
- Did I make sure that I packed all the pieces of equipment I brought to camp so that I forgot nothing?
- Did I leave behind the only two things that a Scout camper always leaves behind on breaking camp:

    A campsite in better shape than he found it.

    His thanks to those who make the camp possible.

EDIBLE WILD PLANTS

In addition to the foodstuffs you bring from home you may be able to use foodstuffs that nature provides. It is a lot of fun to try to live off the land, to make a meal of the fish you catch and the edible plants you find.

For your first experiments with edible plants, eat them raw or cook them in your regular cook kit. Later, cook some of them the survival way, without utensils.

Now, what exactly does that word "edible" mean? Any plant might be considered edible. But you want more than edibility in what you eat. So when looking for edible plants consider these five points:

- The plant must be EATABLE. You should be able to chew it easily, either in its raw state or after you have made it tender by cooking.
- It must be WHOLESOME. All the plants on these pages are good for you. **But there are many plants that are not wholesome. And a few are poisonous. So before picking plants on your own, learn which ones to pick from someone who knows about edible plants. Learn them well enough to identify them positively even when they are not in flower.** Don't pick plants along roadsides. They may be contaminated by motor oil or leaded gas.
- It must be DIGESTIBLE. You can make a beautiful-looking dish out of grass. But it wouldn't do you any good. A cow or a horse can digest the cellulose in grass. You can't.
- It must be NUTRITIVE. The plants on these pages are full of nourishment. Some of them are richer in vitamins and minerals than some of the vegetables you eat at home.
- It must be PALATABLE. It must be agreeable to your taste. If you don't like it you won't eat it.

GREENS. Woods and fields are full of edible wild plants. Some are eaten raw and cold, others cooked and hot.

Salads. Salad greens can be nibbled raw. Or you can serve them as a regular salad—one kind only or several kinds

Chickweed

Common milkweed

Sheep sorrel

Dandelion

Watercress

Purslane

Black mustard

Lamb's-quarters

Chicory

Stinging nettle

mixed together. Wash them thoroughly and drain them before serving. A salad dressing will enhance the taste.

Of all wild salad greens, *watercress* is the king. Young spring leaves of *dandelion, chicory,* and *lamb's-quarters* come next. Sprigs of young *purslane* and *chickweed* follow. The sprouts on the tips of *cattail* rootstocks can be eaten raw from fall to early spring.

Leaves of *sheep sorrel* add a tangy taste to your salad.

Cooked Greens. Some greens are bitter all the time. Others become bitter as spring turns to summer. They become palatable by cooking.

In the spring, cut the shoots of *common milkweed* when they are just a few inches high. Boil them in enough water to cover. When almost done, pour off the water, pour on fresh water. Boil until tender. Serve like asparagus.

The same method of boiling in two changes of water is used for the tender tops of *lamb's-quarters* and *stinging nettle,* stems and leaves of *purslane,* leaves of *black mustard, chicory,* and *dandelion.* If you can't find enough of one of these plants, just mix several kinds together.

For a special treat, boil the young green flower spikes of *cattail* about 5 minutes, serve with butter, and eat like corn on the cob.

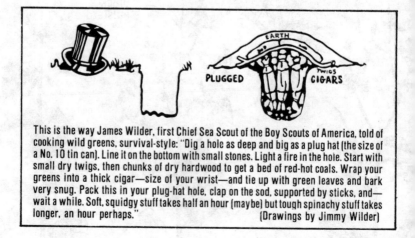

This is the way James Wilder, first Chief Sea Scout of the Boy Scouts of America, told of cooking wild greens, survival-style: "Dig a hole as deep and big as a plug hat (the size of a No. 10 tin can). Line it on the bottom with small stones. Light a fire in the hole. Start with small dry twigs, then chunks of dry hardwood to get a bed of red-hot coals. Wrap your greens into a thick cigar—size of your wrist—and tie up with green leaves and bark very snug. Pack this in your plug-hat hole, clap on the sod, supported by sticks, and—wait a while. Soft, squidgy stuff takes half an hour (maybe) but tough spinachy stuff takes longer, an hour perhaps." (Drawings by Jimmy Wilder)

WILD ROOTS AND TUBERS

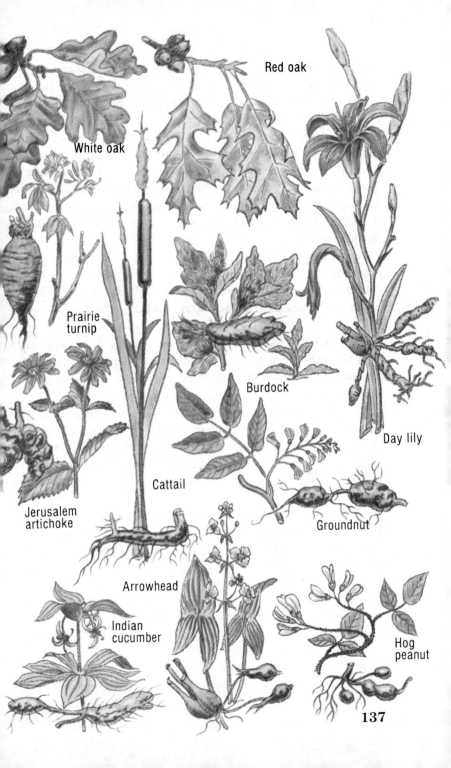

White oak

Red oak

Prairie turnip

Day lily

Jerusalem artichoke

Cattail

Burdock

Groundnut

Arrowhead

Indian cucumber

Hog peanut

137

BREADSTUFFS. Many Indian tribes depended on acorns, the fruit of the *oaks*, for their breadstuff. They ground up the raw or dried kernels into flour. Then their trouble started. Acorns are bitter because of the tannin they contain. So the flour had to go through a leaching process before it could be used. Some tribes put the coarsely ground meal into a basket and placed this in a running stream. Others leached out the tannin by soaking the flour, first in boiling water, then in several sets of cold water. You may want to try it sometime. If you do, mix the acorn flour half and half with regular flour for a better-tasting bread.

A much tastier bread can be made from a half-and-half mix of *cattail* pollen and flour. The pollen forms on the flower spikes of the cattail in early summer. It can be collected in great quantities by shaking the spikes into a plastic bag.

ROOTS AND TUBERS. You can get plenty of nourishment from the roots or tubers of *arrowhead, cattail, prairie turnip, groundnut, hog peanut, Jerusalem artichoke, day lily,* and the first-year roots of common *burdock,* dug in the fall.

In a pinch these roots and tubers can be peeled and eaten raw, but they are better boiled or roasted in the coals of your fire. For roasting, first wrap the roots in several layers of large leaves that have been dipped in water. The wet leaves will first steam the roots; then, as the leaves dry, the roots will be roasted.

The crisp roots of *Indian cucumber* can be munched "as is." They have a pleasant cucumbery flavor. But only dig a few where they are plentiful for a taste. In other places they should be protected.

BEVERAGES. The red fruit clusters of *staghorn sumac* make a refreshing "pink lemonade." Steep them in enough cold water to cover. Pour off the liquid and strain it through a cloth. Sweeten to taste.

You can make a pleasant-tasting hot tea by pouring boiling water over the leaves of *spearmint, peppermint, wild ber-*

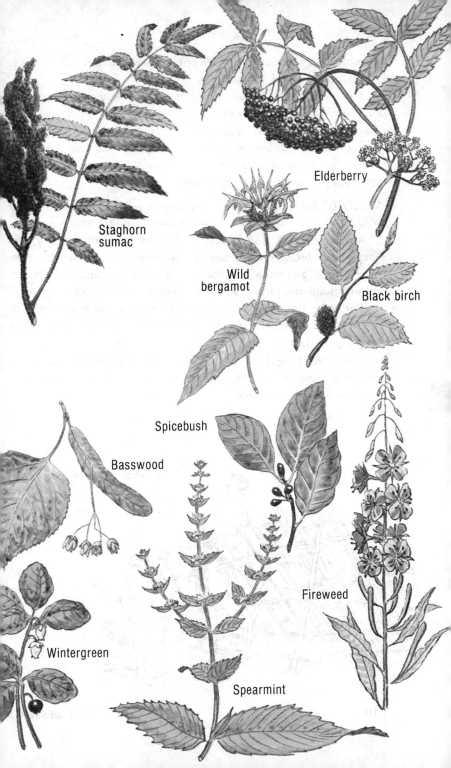

Staghorn sumac

Elderberry

Wild bergamot

Black birch

Spicebush

Basswood

Fireweed

Wintergreen

Spearmint

gamot, over the flowers of *elderberry* and *basswood*, and over the twigs of *spicebush*.

You can also make tea on the dried leaves of *wild strawberry*, *black birch*, *wintergreen*, and *fireweed*.

The roots of *dandelion* and *chicory* can be used as coffee "stretchers" or substitutes. Dry them first, then chop them up. Roast the chips on a pan to a dark brown. Then grind them between stones or in a coffee grinder.

WILD DESSERTS. When they are in season, you can't beat wild berries, fruits, and nuts for a flavorsome dessert.

Among berries and fruits, you'll like *wild strawberry*, *red raspberry*, *blackcap*, *dewberry*, *huckleberry*, *blueberry*, *cranberry*, *wild grape*. All of them, cooked with sugar, make excellent jams and jellies. Find the recipe in a cookbook.

The ripe *mayapple* fruit appeals to some. So does the fruit of the *prickly pear*. *Pawpaw* and *persimmon* are good when fully ripe in late fall or early winter.

And don't forget the nuts of *black walnut*, *butternut*, *pecan*, *hickory*, *hazel*, *chestnut*, and *piñon*. They make a perfect ending to a wilderness meal.

In survival camp, you'll be eating edible wild plants. Here you'll also use fibers of wild plants for lashing your shelter and making fish lines.

Chestnut

Piñon pine

k walnut

Pecan

Beach plum

Hazelnut

Hickory

Persimmon

Wild grape

Mulberry

Pawpaw

Red raspberry

Blackberry

Prickly pear

Blueberry

Strawberry

Cranberry

Mayapple

A camporee is a perfect dress rehearsal for your troop's summer camp.

YOUR SUMMER CAMP ADVENTURE

Summer camp is the biggest event in the whole Scouting year. There's something to look forward to! You *learn* camping on year-round overnights. You *practice* it in summer camp.

Active patrols and troops aim for at least 10 nights of camping during the year in addition to summer camp. The success of those short camps depends on each Scout having a job to do—and doing it. There's work to it—but then, everybody works. And there's real joy to it, too. Because when every member does his share of the work, everyone has time for his share of the fun.

The better you get at camping, the better you'll want your whole patrol to be. The more eagerly you'll help the new boys who join the patrol. You want your whole outfit to have a reputation for being the "campingest" patrol in the troop.

How can you be sure that yours is a good camping patrol?

You'll have a fair idea about it when you camp with the troop. But the best way to find out is in a district or council camporee where you match yourself against other patrols.

Here you can refine your patrol's camp organization and test your menus.

CAMPOREE CAMPING. In its simplest form a camporee is a demonstration of the outdoor skills of two or more patrols, or two or more troops camping together. It is usually a Friday-Sunday event full of fun and fellowship and exciting contests.

Camporee camping boils down to honest-to-goodness patrol camping. It uses a rating plan that'll show how well your patrol camps. The rating plan you'll be using may be developed by your local council or by your troop leaders. It rates everything that happens during the camporee.

It rates your equipment and how it is packed. It checks to learn if your patrol is organized for efficient camp making. It rates your camp for layout and looks and livableness. It seeks the answers to a lot of questions: Does each Scout have a definite duty? Does he carry it out? Is the patrol in all events? Is the Scout Law truly the law of the patrol's camp?

If your patrol is up to scratch on all these points you'll know that it is good. But even more important: If all the patrols of the troop measure up you are in for a marvelous troop camp this summer. Why? Because a *camporee is the perfect dress rehearsal for summer camp.*

You learn all the outdoor skills of Scouting on the year-round hikes and camping trips of your troop and patrol. You use all of them and become better at them in summer camp. Here you also have the chance to pick up such special skills as rowing and canoeing, fishing and pioneering, archery and marksmanship, and many others.

A Day in Summer Camp

The moment troop summer camp is announced in the spring, you'll be raring to go. You'll pitch in with your patrol to plan and work toward this wonderful event.

Troop camping is the Scout way of summer camping. It means that all the fellows in your troop camp together with your own Scoutmaster and assistant Scoutmasters. Each patrol lives as an individual unit within the troop area. Each patrol has its own tents and its own kitchen and is under the active leadership of its own patrol leader.

You wonder what troop summer camp will be like?

Well, to find out, imagine yourself out there in camp.

MORNING IN SUMMER CAMP. You awaken to an exciting new day with your best friends. You look out through the open tent door and see a smiling sun in a blue sky. You jump out of bed, grab soap and towel, and join the others for the morning wash. A few moments later you are back in your tent. You straighten up things, bring blankets out for airing, get dressed.

The patrol cooks of the day sound off: "Come and get it!" Not a moment too soon! You're positively starving!

After breakfast there's work to be done. Your camp must be made spick-and-span in a hurry. It is. Just in time, too. The troop leaders are coming around the bend for the morning checkup. Your patrol gets the honor flag of the day. You knew it would.

You and the whole troop gather around the flagpole. Old Glory goes aloft. Your eyes follow the flag—red, white, blue, against a clear summer sky!

After the ceremony, you're ready for the day's activities.

First there is work to be done. Your patrol has decided that your campsite needs a few improvements and additions. There's a clothesline to be put up. There's a raised fireplace to be built to make life easier for the cooks. With all of you working together, the jobs are out of the way in no time at all.

What's next? Perhaps this is the day you have planned to go adventuring. What'll it be? An exploration hike along that ancient overgrown trail? A nature hike, looking for animals and birds, rocks and minerals? An orienteering race, cross country with map and compass?

Hurry now! There's the call for swim! What a glorious feeling to jump into the lake and strike out for the diving raft with your buddy. Up on the raft and back into the water. Up again. In again. Not a care in the world.

"All out!" And, a moment later, "Lunch, everybody!" The patrol cooks are doing themselves proud! Every scrap of food disappears.

AFTERNOON IN SUMMER CAMP. Afternoon in camp has a way of rocketing by. So many things to do. More Scoutcraft. Perhaps archery or marksmanship. And then, of course, another swim. And maybe not just a swim. Maybe an exciting watersports event with patrol contests in swimming and lifesaving, rowing, and canoeing.

Time to get supper ready. You check the duty roster. It's your turn, with your buddy, to build the fire and haul in the water while another buddy team goes about the cooking.

Supper is probably the eating highlight of the day. It is also an opportunity for good fellowship.

After the cleanup, the whole troop gets together for an hour of action and fun. It may be a vigorous game of capture the flag. Or it may be a game of volleyball or soccer.

In camp you put up a roster of the buddy teams responsible for fuel and water, cooking, and cleanup.

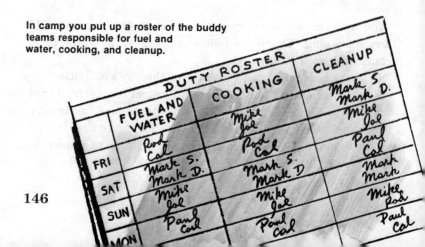

DUTY ROSTER

	FUEL AND WATER	COOKING	CLEANUP
		Mike Jal	Mark S. Mark D.
FRI	Rod Cal	Rod Cal	Mike Jal
SAT	Mark S. Mark D.	Mark S. Mark D	Paul Cal
SUN	Mike Jol	Mike Jal	Mark Mark
MON	Paul Carl	Paul Cal	Mike Rod
			Paul Cal

When you go summer camping jamboree-style your patrol chest becomes your food box and kitchen worktable. You eat your meals at your patrol table.

Extra PATROL CAMPING GEAR for LONG-TERM CAMP

FOR COOKING

- ☐ Patrol food chest
- ☐ Food canisters (plastic) with lids, various capacities—16 to 32 oz.
- ☐ Galvanized mop buckets for dishwashing (2), 14 qt.
- ☐ Rubber scraper
- ☐ Dishmop
- ☐ Scouring pads, nonrusting

FOR DINING

- ☐ Patrol table with benches
- ☐ Dining fly, 12 by 16 ft.
- ☐ Pole, pegs, and guy lines for fly

OPTIONAL ITEMS

- ☐ Charcoal stoves ☐ Charcoal briquets
- ☐ Reflector oven
- ☐ Griddle ☐ Dutch oven ☐ Pitcher
- ☐ Mixing jar, plastic, 1 qt., with short piece of chain to break up lumps
- ☐ Extra canteens for dry camping
- ☐ Plastic bags, various sizes
- ☐ Metal tent pegs
- ☐ Electric lantern
- ☐ Table cover, plastic or vinyl
- ☐ Personal appearance kit containing:
  - ☐ Shoe polish ☐ Polish brush
  - ☐ Polish rag ☐ Cleaning fluid

EVENING IN SUMMER CAMP. Darkness is falling. The campfire is about to start.

CAMPFIRE! There's nothing in the world that can compare with sitting with your best friends in a close circle, under the spell of the fire, watching the flickering flames, having a wonderful time together.

As the flames soar upward, the campfire leader opens a program that's a mixture of fun and seriousness.

Scouts with special abilities do their stuff. Each patrol puts on a skit. There may be a couple of campfire games.

And lots of songs. When the fire burns low, your songs turn into the soft, melodious kind. You end with *Taps*.

> *Day is done, Gone the sun*
> *From the lake, from the hills, from the sky.*
> *All is well. Safely rest. God is nigh.*

You walk back to your tent, silently. You crawl into your sleeping bag. A moment later you're fast asleep.

Happy dreams! Tomorrow is another day. It will be full of excitement and surprises. That's what every day is in the camp of a real troop of real patrols of real Scouts.

Memories of campfires will last long after the embers have faded.

Swimming is one of the most joyful sports in the world. If you don't know how, you'll learn in summer camp. If you know how, you can become an expert.

GO SWIMMING

"Come on in—the water's fine!" Next to "Come and get it!" that's about the most popular yell in summer camp.

Your whole troop is going swimming. Everything is ready at the waterfront for everyone to have an enjoyable swim.

Before you came to camp you had your doctor give you a medical examination. The first day in camp your swimming ability was tested. Now you are buddied up with a pal about as good at swimming as you are.

You and your friend check in at the buddy board with all the other Scouts of your troop. And there goes the whistle!

You dive or splash in. The race out to the raft is on. Up on the raft. Off the diving board. Up again, in again.

Suddenly a whistle pierces the air. There's a yell of "Buddy up!" The lifeguard counts to 10. You and your buddy quickly grasp hands. So do all the other buddy teams. The guard checks to see if all buddies are together. You'd better be! To break the buddy rule is one of the most serious offenses in camp.

Another blast of the whistle. "All right!" And the fun begins again until the call of "All out!" sounds.

Step 1. Adult supervision

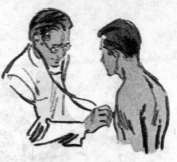

Step 2. Physical fitness

Step 5. Lookout

Step 6. Ability groups

SWIMMING SAFETY. The Safe Swim Defense used in Scout camps means safe swimming to all Scouts. It has eight steps:

- **Step 1.** An adult is in charge during a swim. He or she must be trained in water safety or use helpers who are.
- **Step 2.** Each swimmer must provide a current and complete health history from his parent, guardian, or medical doctor.
- **Step 3.** The swimming place is cleared of hazards. Areas are marked: no more than 1 m (3½ ft.) deep for nonswimmers, deeper for beginners, over the head for swimmers.
- **Step 4.** Strong swimmers take turns as lifeguards. Two stand on shore with a lifeline, ready to help.

Step 3. Safe area

Step 4. Lifeguards

Step 7. Buddy system

Step 8. Discipline

- **Step 5.** A lookout stands where he can see and hear all areas. He directs any help needed.
- **Step 6.** Scouts swim in ability groups in areas matching their ability. A nonswimmer is just learning. A beginner can jump into the water and swim 15 m (50 ft.). A swimmer can swim 100 m (300 ft.) and float.
- **Step 7.** Everybody swims with a buddy with the same swimming ability. Buddies check in together. They stay near one another during the swim. They check out together.
- **Step 8.** There is good discipline in the swimming area. Everyone understands and follows the water-safety rules.

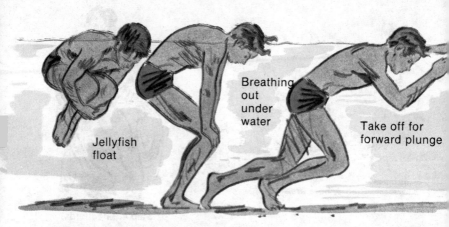

Jellyfish
float

Breathing
out
under
water

Take off for
forward plunge

LEARN TO SWIM. The first step in learning to swim is to get to know that the water will hold you up. So, with a good swimmer standing by, you wade into water waist-deep. You take a deep breath. You bend down. You fold your hands over your shins and drop your chin on your chest. You won't sink. You'll bob up and float like a jellyfish.

Next comes your breathing. For swimming you breathe in through your mouth and out through the nose. Try it in waist-deep water. Take a breath through your mouth. Put your head under water. Breathe out slowly through your nose. Repeat.

Now for a glide on top of the water. Take a deep breath. Push off with your feet and plunge forward with your arms stretched way ahead. Don't kick. Just glide.

SWIMMING THE CRAWL. Leg Kick. Practice the leg kick by resting your hands on the bottom with your legs straight back. Move your legs up and down. Keep them straight but not stiff. Move your legs from your hips, not your knees. Then take a glide with the leg kick added.

Arm Stroke. Practice the arm stroke while standing in waist-deep water. Bend forward so that the top of your body is in a swimming position. Stretch your right arm straight ahead. Swing the arm straight down to the hip. Then raise the elbow and stretch the arm forward again. Do the same with your left arm. Then with both arms alternately.

Legs and Arms Together. When you now combine leg kick and arm stroke, you're swimming the American crawl.

152

Forward plunge

Legs only

Arms only

Arms and
legs

AMERICAN CRAWL. The fastest stroke of all is the American crawl. It is the stroke usually used in swimming a freestyle race. Short distances can be covered very rapidly. But the stroke is tiring for untrained swimmers over long distances.

ELEMENTARY BACKSTROKE. This stroke will enable you to swim on your back for great distances without becoming tired. The end of each stroke

OTHER SWIMMING STROKES.

After you have learned to swim, using the American crawl, make up your mind to become a good swimmer. This means lots of practice. It also means taking up a number of other swimming strokes. They will lead you toward earning the Swimming merit badge.

SIDESTROKE. The driving force in the sidestroke is the scissors kick you perform with your legs. You spread your legs, then snap them together as if

permits a long glide. It is one of the easiest strokes to learn and do. And it is the best all-around stroke when you swim on your back.

Learn the elementary backstroke first. It is probably the most relaxing of all swimming strokes. Then continue with such strokes as sidestroke, breaststroke, trudgen, back crawl. These strokes are all described, with lots of illustrations, in the *Swimming* merit badge pamphlet.

you were closing a pair of scissors. At the same time, you thrust one arm forward and sweep the other arm downward with hands cupped.

REACH. If you have a stick handy, use it to reach victim.

REACH. If you have a handhold, sit down and stretch out a leg. This may get you within reach.

WATER RESCUES. It is good to know that you are safe when swimming. Every Scout should be a swimmer. And every Scout should be able to assist someone else in danger in the water.

This year, in the United States, more than 7,000 persons will drown while swimming or playing in the water. You may get the chance to prevent some of these drownings by learning and being ready to use basic lifesaving skills.

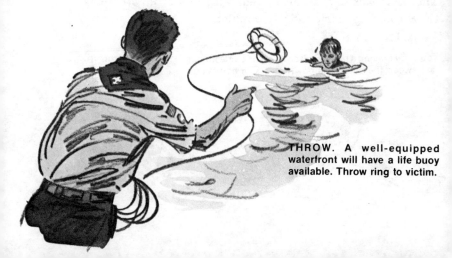

THROW. A well-equipped waterfront will have a life buoy available. Throw ring to victim.

An important point in attempting a water rescue is this: NEVER do it by swimming if you can do it a safe way, without risk to your own life. The safer ways are reaching, throwing, or going with support.

- **Reach.** Most water accidents happen close to shore or dock. You may be able to reach the victim with a helping hand, a pole, or a branch.
- **Throw.** A properly equipped waterfront will have a ring buoy prominently displayed, ready for immediate use. Use it. If no buoy is available, a coil of rope may do.
- **Go with support.** Too far to reach with a rope? Then get into a boat or canoe or onto a surfboard and go to the victim's assistance.

If Everything Else Fails. Under extreme circumstances, you may have to swim out to help a drowning person. *NEVER attempt a swimming rescue unless you are an excellent swimmer.* You do not want to add yourself to the drowning statistics.

If there is no other way to assist someone who is drowning, quickly strip down to undershorts while keeping the victim in sight the whole time. Take your shirt between your teeth at the back of the collar and swim rapidly toward the victim. When near, but still beyond arm's reach, grasp the shirt in one hand and flip the other end of it into the victim's hands. When he grabs it, tow him to safety. See illustration, page 39.

GO WITH SUPPORT. The best support is a rowboat. Row out quickly. When you are close, turn the boat and approach the victim stern first. Have him grab stern. Tow him.

Swimming Fun

The better you and your friends get at swimming, the more fun you'll have and the more stunts you can attempt. Such stunts are all safe for good swimmers under proper supervision. They should not, of course, be tried by beginners.

Floating. Arch your back and head way back. Take a deep breath and hold it. Hold your arms out and back to balance the weight of your legs. Whenever you breathe, blow out the air quickly and suck in another breath through your mouth.

Undressing. When you have mastered floating, try undressing in the water: Jump in with all your clothes on. Strip down to your underwear.

Looping the Loop. Use a combination of any strokes.

Underwater Orienteering. Test your compass skills. Dive in with a waterproof compass. Come up facing a given direction.

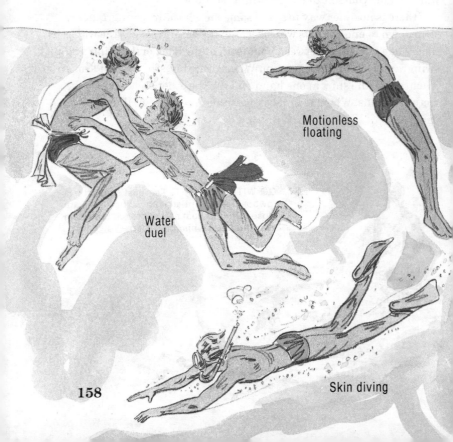

Motionless floating

Water duel

Skin diving

Skin Diving. For further fun you should now be ready to take up skin diving with flippers, mask, and snorkel.

BUDDY FUN. Water Duel. Challenge a buddy to a water duel. Put a Scout belt over your trunks. Slip a colored rag under the belt. The idea is to get your buddy's rag, keeping your own.

Tired Swimmer. Play tired swimmer with your buddy. Bring your buddy to shore with a *chin tow* (see illustration below). OR use *cross-chest tow:* Place one arm across his shoulder, over his chest. Swim with your free arm and a scissor-like kick with your legs. OR use a *back rest-push:* Have your buddy rest on his back with his hands on your shoulders and transport him with breaststroke. OR try *hair pull:* Grasp your buddy's hair with one hand. Swim sidestroke with the other. Then have your buddy try the same carries with you.

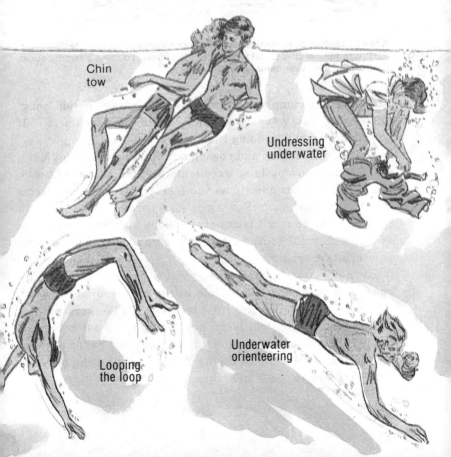

Chin tow

Undressing under water

Looping the loop

Underwater orienteering

Getting into boat

Feathering

Rowing straight course

When you enter a boat, step into the middle of it. For good rowing, "feather" your oars: turn the oar blades flat when out of the water. To row a straight course, keep a landmark over center of stern.

ROWING. In camp you'll probably be singing the old song, "Row, row, row your boat gently down the stream . . ." If you're lucky you'll be doing it, too.

Getting into a boat and rowing out into the lake is not just a fun activity. Rowing is an excellent sport for physical fitness. You will know this quickly as you feel the strain in your arms and in your abdomen. Rowing is an emergency skill as well. Knowing how to row a boat may give you a chance to rescue a swimmer in trouble. And if you like to go fishing, a rowboat is your craft for trolling.

Even if you are a nonswimmer you will have a chance to go rowing in summer camp. While in the boat you will always, like everyone else, wear a life preserver (PFD—personal flotation device). You will learn how to enter a boat correctly. You will learn to never stand up in a boat and never to overload a boat. You will pick up the proper way of using the oars and learn how to row a straight course.

160

Portaging

White-water canoeing

On a wilderness trip you will portage your canoe from river to river.

White-water canoeing will be your greatest thrill!

CANOEING. The canoe was handed down to us from the Indian. You can see him paddling along, without a sound, down the river, in his birchbark canoe.

The canoe used in camps today is made of wood, aluminum, fiberglass, or plastic. In summer camp you may have a chance to learn how to care for such a canoe, how to carry it, how to paddle it in smooth and fast water. But first you must be a good swimmer. Even the best of canoeists sooner or later will upset or be swamped. That's why knowing how to swim is important. That's also why even the most expert canoeist wears a life preserver.

When you have become a good canoeist, the day may arrive when you'll set out with a few fellow Scouts on a wilderness trip. Then you'll paddle over quiet lakes ... swoop down into white water ... portage your canoe around rapids ... land at night to make camp ... start out again the next morning for more exciting adventure.

In Indian-style camping you help keep alive the traditions of the earliest Americans. You learn to play Indian games and take part in Indian dances.

PRIMITIVE CAMPING

When you have mastered regular camping in patrol and troop you are ready for the primitive kind. To start with, you may turn a weekend or a couple of days in summer camp into primitive days. Later you may want to spend a week at it.

INDIAN-STYLE CAMPING. To prepare for Indian camping, study the *Indian Lore* merit badge pamphlet.

Your local council's camp equipment may include a couple of tepees. If you can arrange to borrow one, fine. If not, build wigwams by covering frameworks of branches with tarps.

Clothing is a simple matter. Loincloth and moccasins are your daylong wear. Use red or blue outing flannel for the loincloth. The cloth should be as long as you are tall, one-third your waist-measure wide. Make moccasins from a kit.

There's a lot to do in Indian camp. Go in for Indian hand wrestling and leg wrestling. Train in basic Indian dance steps and learn some of the special dances: buffalo dance, hoop dance, eagle dance. Light your cooking fires by friction. Roast or broil your food. Or cook it in the embers.

Wind up your days in Indian camp at campfires that feature Indian songs, dances, and ceremonies.

SURVIVAL CAMPING. For this you use as little equipment as possible: "bear skins" (blankets), Scout knives, axes.

You build a lean-to shelter by lashing branches together with plant fibers (page 140). You use plant fibers also for tying primitive fish hooks and fish spears.

For food, you use wild greens and roots, fruits and nuts as part of your diet (pages 134-41). And you cook whatever fish you catch over a fire started by a fire-by-friction set made on the spot.

PIONEER CAMPING. In pioneer camping your patrol becomes a wagon team of pioneers on the backwoods trail.

For sleeping quarters you put up covered-wagon-type shelters. For activities you go in for all kinds of pioneering.

You bake or roast your food in Dutch ovens. You barbecue your meat over a fire made by flint and steel.

And at your campfires you sing the songs of pioneer days.

COLD-WEATHER CAMPING. Winter camping in the snow is a special kind of primitive camping. Your main considerations are keeping warm and dry, sleeping warm and dry.

Keeping warm means vigorous activities, grub with extra heat-producing fats and sugars, and the right kind of clothing. Your clothes should not absorb water—wool is good, but some new synthetics absorb even less water. Whatever the material, your clothes should fit loosely with a windproof jacket over them. Your feet need special warmth. So, on with a pair of heavy socks over your regular socks. Then into beeswaxed boots or snow pacs, ski cap, and mittens.

Sleeping warm means proper tenting and bedding. If for any reason you don't have proper equipment, do not go cold-weather camping. A backpack tent with sealed seams, waterproof floor, and rain fly is recommended. So is a sleeping bag. Use a fiberfill or goose down bag with at least 2½ pounds of down. Keep the down bag absolutely dry. Place a foam pad over the tent floor and put your sleeping bag on top of the pad. In an emergency you can wear part or all of your clothes inside your sleeping bag.

Note: Don't depend on a fire. Winter storms are unforgiving, if you are not prepared. So, get the guidance of an experienced cold-weather camper.

Backpacking the trails of Philmont Scout Ranch or another wilderness area with some good Scout friends is an experience you will never forget.

BACKPACKING

After you have hiked with your patrol and your troop and have mastered the skills of camping, the day will come when you will want the thrill of hitting the trail with your pack on your back. From being just a camper you become a backpacker.

HOW MANY? HOW FEW? For backpacking, the whole troop may not be able to go—maybe not even the whole patrol. Anyway, for a wilderness expedition, a group should consist of no more than 8 to 10 persons including at least one adult leader. If more are going the group should be broken up into smaller crews, each crew organized to hike and camp on its own.

The best number for a backpacking crew is four. Four can easily pack the gear you need. And a crew that size is prepared for the worst: if an accident happens, one stays behind with the victim and two go for help.

164

Gear for Backpacking

FOOTWEAR. For hiking on smooth trails, the footwear you have used for regular patrol hikes (page 177) will do. For rough-trail and cross-country hiking you need something sturdier. Special hiking boots are expensive. Many backpackers get along with common work boots.

When buying the boots, have on your feet the socks you will be wearing—cotton socks inside, athletic socks on the outside. Break in the boots well before you take off. If your feet feel sore after wearing them, soak the boots in warm tap water. Then get into them with socks on and walk them dry.

CLOTHING. Wear what you usually wear for hiking. And be prepared with clothing for rain and cold (page 63 and 177). Carry extra clothing in your pack for change along the trail.

Put in your pockets what you usually carry for a hike. But add a Scout knife and matches wrapped in foil.

PACK. The pack you have been using for camp will probably be OK (page 66). If you want to step up to a new pack, think of where you will be hiking. Pick a frame-back pack if you'll be following smooth trails. Pick a soft-back pack for rough trails, rocky terrain, cross-country and mountain traveling, skiing.

Your pack should have wide shoulder straps with foam pads, and a padded hip belt. The hip belt reduces the strain on your shoulders by bringing the weight over your hips and legs.

CAMPING GEAR. Whether you backpack into a state park for a long weekend or spend the summer backpacking the length of the Appalachian or Pacific Crest Trail, you'll need the same gear. The difference is in the weight of food and fuel.

Use the gear you have collected during your Scouting days. But decide on what to leave out for backpacking. To do this, unpack after a trip. Place all your gear in three piles:
- Pile No. 1: things you used several times.
- Pile No. 2: things you used once or twice.
- Pile No. 3: things you didn't use at all.

Now, if you have the courage of your convictions, push piles 2 and 3 out of the way. Check what is left with the lists on page 167. You can get along without the items crossed out in red.

Personal Gear. *Sleeping.* One-third of your expedition will be spent in a sleeping bag. Be sure it is a good one (see page 64). Bring a pad for comfort, but no ground sheet: your tent should have a waterproof floor.

Eating. Most backpacking meals are cold. There may be occasional hot beverages and one-pot meals for supper. All the gear you need for eating is a bowl, a cup, and a spoon.

Crew Gear for Four. *Tentage and Tools.* You will need light-weight two-man tents, with rain fly, sewn-in floor, and screening, with the necessary poles, pegs, and guy lines. No dining fly. And definitely no ax, saw, or spade!

Cooking. Two pots will do: the smallest pot and the cocoa pot from the Trail Chef Cook Kit or their equivalent from home. Or bring two No. 10 tin-can pots with bails (page 106). A large spoon for stirring, a ladle for serving, and as many plastic bags and containers as you need for packing your food.

Cleanup. Each backpacker cleans his own dishes, so you don't need materials for sanitizing them. Just a soap pad for scouring the pots.

But these items should definitely be added:

Map of the area—preferably a topographic map.

Compass. One of the orienteering compasses, Silva model.

Stove. Where open fires are prohibited you'll need a stove. Stay away from gasoline and kerosine stoves: they require that you carry liquid fuel—a dangerous fire hazard. A butane stove, using a disposable cartridge, is safe. Or use a simple charcoal stove (page 130). You can carry enough charcoal briquets inside a stove to cook a half dozen meals. For places where open fires are permitted, bring a few extra aluminum tent pegs and set up your pots on three-point fireplaces (page 113). Fire starters (page 109) are "lifesavers" on a rainy day. IMPORTANT: When packed, your backpacking pack should weigh no more than one-fifth of what you weigh, stripped.

BACKPACKING GEAR

Overnight camp gear can be used for backpacking, but much of it can be left behind. The items crossed out in red are not needed for backpacking.

PERSONAL CAMPING GEAR

- [ ] Pack
- [ ] Sleeping bag ~~OR 2-3 blankets~~
- [ ] Foam pad ~~OR air mattress~~
- [ ] ~~Ground sheet, plastic~~
- [ ] Sweater OR jac-shirt
- [ ] Poncho OR raincoat and rain hat
- [ ] ~~Pair rubbers, lightweight~~
- [ ] Pair sneakers OR pair moccasins

- [ ] Clothes bag(s) containing:
  - [ ] Extra uniform parts [ ] Extra socks
  - [ ] Change of underwear
  - [ ] Pajamas OR sweat suit
  - [ ] Extra handkerchiefs [ ] Swim trunks

- [ ] ~~Eating kit containing:~~
  - [ ] ~~Knife~~ [ ] ~~Fork~~ [ ] Spoon
  - [ ] ~~Plate~~ [ ] Cup [ ] Bowl

- [ ] Toilet kit containing:
  - [ ] Soap in box [ ] Washcloth
  - [ ] Toothbrush [ ] Toothpaste
  - [ ] Comb [ ] Metal mirror
  - [ ] ~~Washbasin, plastic~~ emergency signal
  - [ ] Hand towels [ ] ~~Bath towel~~
  - [ ] ~~Laundry materials~~

- [ ] ~~Repair kit containing:~~
  - [ ] ~~Needles~~ [ ] ~~Thread~~ [ ] ~~Buttons~~
  - [ ] ~~Safety pins~~ [ ] Shoelaces

- [ ] Toilet paper, in plastic wrap
- [ ] Flashlight
- [ ] Scout knife
- [ ] Bible, Testament, OR Prayer Book according to your faith

Extras you may want to take
- [ ] Watch [ ] Camera [ ] Film
- [ ] Notebook [ ] Pencil [ ] Pen
- [ ] Drinking cup [ ] Canteen
- [ ] Mosquito dope [ ] Nylon line
- [ ] Musical instrument [ ] Songbook
- [ ] Purse or wallet with money and identification
- [ ] *Boy Scout Handbook* [ ] Air pillow

~~PATROL CAMPING GEAR~~
CREW CAMPING GEAR
~~TENTING CREW EQUIPMENT~~

- [ ] Two-man tents, with poles, pegs, and guy lines
- [ ] ~~Dining fly, 10x10 ft. minimum, with poles, pegs, and guy lines~~
- [ ] ~~Patrol flag on staff~~
- [ ] ~~Small U.S. flag, with halyard~~
- [ ] ~~Ax~~ [ ] ~~Saw~~ [ ] ~~Camp spade~~
- [ ] ~~Repair kit containing:~~
  - [ ] ~~Mill file, 8-in. for ax sharpening~~
  - [ ] ~~Sharpening stone~~ [ ] ~~Thin wire~~
  - [ ] ~~Twine or nylon line~~ [ ] ~~Nails~~
- [ ] Sewing kit containing:
  - [ ] Thread [ ] Needles [ ] Safety pins
- [ ] First aid kit [ ] Map [ ] Compass
- [ ] Toilet paper in plastic bag
- [ ] ~~Electric lantern~~

~~COOKING CREW EQUIPMENT~~
- [ ] ~~Cook kit (Trail Chef Kit) containing:~~
  - [ ] ~~Pots (2)~~ [ ] ~~Frying pans (2)~~
  - [ ] ~~Serving plates (4)~~ [ ] ~~Cups (4)~~
- [ ] ~~Chef's kit containing:~~
  - [ ] ~~Carving knife~~ [ ] Spoon, large
  - [ ] ~~Fork, large~~ [ ] Ladle
  - [ ] ~~Pancake turner or spatula~~
  - [ ] ~~Potato peeler, "knee action"~~
  - [ ] ~~Can opener~~ [ ] ~~Hot pot tongs~~
- [ ] Water container, collapsible, plastic, 2½ gallons
- [ ] ~~Plastic washbasin for cooks~~
- [ ] Plastic food bags, various sizes
- [ ] Sugar container [ ] Salt-pepper shaker
- [ ] ~~Roll of aluminum foil~~
- [ ] Plastic sheets (2), 4x4 ft. minimum
- [ ] Matches in waterproof case
- [ ] Fire starters [ ] Stove
- [ ] ~~Cleanup materials:~~
  - [ ] ~~Dish mop~~ [ ] Scouring pads
  - [ ] ~~Paper towels in plastic bag~~
  - [ ] Liquid soap in plastic bottle
  - [ ] ~~Sanitizing tablets for rinse~~
- [ ] Heavy-duty trash-can liner
- [ ] ~~Ax~~ [ ] ~~Saw~~ [ ] ~~Camp spade~~

FOODSTUFFS. Foods for backpacking must be lightweight. They must also keep well without refrigeration. That means dried, dehydrated, or freeze-dried foods. You will find most of what you want in a supermarket. Break open the packages and repack what you need in plastic bags for easy carrying.

Breakfast. Orange drink (powder); hot drink (instant); cereal, cold or hot (instant); milk (powder).

Lunch. Lemonade or fruit punch (powders); cheese, salami; melba toast, crisp rye bread; dried fruit; cookies.

Trail Snack. Sweet "gorp" mix of raisins, nuts, candy-coated chocolate; dry "gorp" of diced hard salami, diced hard cheese, nuts, goldfish crackers; hard candy.

Supper. Cold or hot drink; soup (instant); one-pot meal; macaroni and cheese, spaghetti and sauce; pudding (instant).

Sporting-goods stores sell lightweight meals made up in four-man portions. They are good but expensive.

On the Trail

Take off in the morning with a free spirit and a good conscience: the place where you camped shows no trace of you.

HIKING. Hike a steady, constant pace. And hike in single file. A trail is supposed to be narrow. Keep it that way.

In planning for the day's journey you may have settled on a destination 16 km (10 mi.) ahead. That would be an average backpacker's idea of a day's hiking. Some do less. Others do much more. If you only cover 13 km (8 mi.), so what? Don't be arbitrary about reaching your planned destination unless for a definite reason. You may find a campsite you like before you hit it. Or you may go on to something better.

RESTING. The rests you take along the trail should not be just for resting your body. They should be for refreshing your soul as well. Stop to look at the magnificent vista wherever the trail opens up. To admire the beauty of the flowers of a mountain meadow. To listen to the bird chorus. To feel the wind blowing through your hair.

In Camp

Stop in midafternoon to make camp. Or continue into the night if a full moon gives you enough light to put up tents.

Pitch the tents where they will do the least damage to the delicate vegetation. There can be no ditching even if rain is likely. So pick the spot accordingly.

COOKING. Set up your stove or build your fire if you are permitted to do so. Cook and serve your backpacking supper.

Scour individual cup, bowl, and spoon with sand or dirt. Rinse them in plain, cold water. Then let them air-dry.

Heat water in the pots to clean them. Scour with a soap pad if necessary. Rinse in cold water.

Many animals are scavengers. So get rid of food scraps and garbage immediately after cooking. Put all food in a plastic bag and swing it on a rope from an overhanging branch.

PERSONAL HYGIENE. It is all right on a wilderness trip to take a dip. But don't use a stream or lake for a soap bath. Carry water a distance away from the shore to bathe and do your laundry. Do not use detergent. Use plain soap. Soap is biodegradable—it disappears in the ground without damage to soil and plant life.

For elimination, scoop out and use a "cat hole" (page 182).

Don't take chances on drinking water. Even the purest-looking water in a mountain stream may be contaminated by the waste of some careless backpacker upstream. So disinfect your drinking water with water purification tablets (page 181). To make it more palatable, add some fruit-drink powder.

Whether you use a soft-back or a frame-back pack, pack the heaviest items high and close to your back. This places most of the weight on hip belt.

Good   Poor

Breakthrough for Freedom
by Norman Rockwell, 1967

At world jamborees you will meet brother Scouts from all over the world. In this picture, Norman Rockwell painted representatives from each of the five continents plus the Middle East.

HIGH-ADVENTURE OPPORTUNITIES

As you grow older in Scouting you will discover that many special adventures open up to you. Some of them are available to you if you are 13 by January 1 before your trip. Ask your Scoutmaster.

JAMBOREES. Tops among all high-adventure opportunities is a national or a world jamboree. World jamborees are held every 4 years. So if you are a Scout or Scouter in 1987, 1991, 1995 you may want to try for a place on the BSA contingent. National jamborees are held between world jamborees. Try your luck in 1989.

PHILMONT. You can find high adventure at the Philmont Scout Ranch and Explorer Base. This base consists of 137,493 acres of the old West. It is near Cimarron, N. Mex. Here you can fish, pan for gold, do burro packing, and climb 2-mile-high Old Baldy. Your council may have a trip scheduled for Philmont next summer. Or a group of old-timers in your troop may be going. If not, get in on a Philmont crew organized by the base itself.

MAINE NATIONAL HIGH ADVENTURE AREA. Here you have 6 million acres of privately owned woodlands, public waterways, and parks. Located in the untraveled and truly remarkable scenery of northern Maine, there are two high-adventure program bases: Matagamon Base is located near Baxter State Park on Grand Lake Matagamon. Seboomook Base is on Seboomook Lake at Pittston Farm. You can go canoeing, backpacking, backwoods camping, and fishing. You can try canoe sailing, float boating, bushwhacking, and other things you have never done before. Okpik, a winter camping weekend training experience, and Beyond the Roadhead outdoor leadership school, for 16- to 20-year-old youth, are conducted here.

NORTHERN TIER HIGH ADVENTURE. This is the jumping-off place for high adventure in the world's greatest canoe country. Here you will be canoeing, fishing, camping in northern Minnesota and the Quetico Provincial Park of Canada. These are rugged trips for experienced canoeists traveling the historic fur trade route where the French-Canadian voyageurs paddled their birchbark bateaux.

FLORIDA NATIONAL HIGH ADVENTURE SEA BASE. Through this gateway you have your choice of year-round aquatic activities. You can canoe where the Seminole Indians roamed. You can cruise the Gulf of Mexico on a 38 m (136 ft.) square-rigged brig. You can explore the coral reefs of the Florida Keys and the Bahamas on smaller vessels. And you can scuba dive in the crystal-clear waters.

OTHER HIGH ADVENTURE OPPORTUNITIES. Many local councils across the United States have developed excellent high-adventure programs in addition to the national programs. These are locally owned bases identified as nationally accredited local council high-adventure bases" and listed in *Horizons Unlimited.*

Let's Go Hiking

Why hike? Because you are an American boy! Because there's roaming in your blood. Because hiking gives you an outlet for your roving spirit.

There's adventure to hiking. There's a thrill to following the trails of the early settlers who built our country. There's excitement to exploring what's left of its wilderness. There's spirit to getting to know our land—its valleys and hills, its forests and plains, its rivers and lakes.

There's health in hiking, too. Hiking is one of the best exercises known. It strengthens your lungs and heart. It hardens your muscles and straightens your back. It makes your blood run tingling through your veins.

And there's fun to hiking. Not the laughing kind of fun but the joy of feeling free as a bird, fit and self-reliant. No roar of traffic. No blare from radios. No jabber from TV sets. All around you the sounds and sights of nature.

EVERY SEASON IS HIKING SEASON. The whole year is for hiking. Every season should find you on the open road.

Every good patrol and every good troop has a strong outdoor program. It gets you out under open sky at least once a month. If you take part in all these outdoor events, someday you will be a real hiker. But not until you have hiked through the soft breezes of spring, the heat of summer, the showers of autumn, the bitter winds of winter.

That kind of hiking is not for softies. It is only for those who have the guts to face whatever hardships come their way. You won't always have easy going on your hikes. There'll be fights with brambles and thorns. There'll be tough climbing over rocky trails. You won't always have fair weather. There'll be sudden thundershowers, driving rain. But you'll learn to take the hardships with good humor. They are part of the fun of hiking. And as you overcome them they will help you build yourself into the kind of man you want to be.

PLANNING YOUR HIKES. To get the most enjoyment and profit from a hike, you need to do some planning. So whether it is a patrol hike or a buddy hike, here are things to consider:

- What do we want to do or learn or accomplish?
- What permission do we need?
- What's our destination? How will we get there?
- What will we do on the way? And when we get there?
- What uniform will we wear? What other clothing?
- What equipment do we need? What food do we take?
- When will we take off?
- When will we be back home?

A Scout hike is not just a walk. It is a walk with a purpose. You may want to train in Scoutcraft. You may want to study nature or go exploring. Or you may simply want to hike for the sake of hiking—to roam the woods, to toughen your body.

Your hike may be a morning, an afternoon, or an all-day event. Your destination may be a hilltop, a lake, a beach.

Jot the details down. They're your hike plan. They will also help you make your hike report when it is all over.

Make a copy of your hike plan and leave it with your family at home. The family should know when to expect you home. They should also know where you will be in case they have to reach you in an emergency.

Most Scout hikes are from town or city out into the country. But country boys may get a special kick, occasionally, of a hike into town or city.

YOUR HIKING OUTFIT

For a successful hiking experience, you need suitable footgear and clothing, adequate equipment and eats.

FOOTGEAR FOR HIKING. For hiking, your most important gear are feet that are strong and well cared for. Keep them in shape through walking, running, jumping. Wash them often.

Your hiking shoes should be old friends, well broken in. They should have soft uppers and strong soles. They should have ample room in them for your toes to spread and to wiggle. They should hug the arch and heel snugly for support and to prevent friction. Official Boy Scout shoes meet these tests.

For most trail hiking, low shoes are all right. But in rough country ankle-high shoes or hike boots are better.

Scout socks and stockings are especially good for hiking. They are made of cotton or wool and stretch-nylon. Be sure there are no holes in them. Be sure also that they have no darns that will rub your skin. Some hikers like to wear a pair of thin nylon socks inside their stockings.

CLOTHES FOR THE SEASON. Whatever the season, your Scout uniform is your best clothing for hiking. It was designed for tough outdoor use. It is sturdy and comfortable.

For hot-weather hiking on open roads and across fields, short-sleeve shirt and shorts are perfect.

For cool weather and for cross-country hiking through brush and brambles, wear long-sleeve shirt and long pants. For cold weather, wear layers of clothing. The airspaces between them insulate you against the cold. Besides, several layers let you shed one or more if you get hot while you hike. For a winter hike you may need long underwear, heavy sweater, windproof jacket, mittens.

What about headgear? Scout field cap or beret makes you look sharp. For better protection for your head against sun and rain, the broad-brim Scout hat is your answer. In cold weather, wear a Scout cap with earflaps or a knit cap.

Most of the equipment you need for hiking will go into your pockets. If you are not certain of finding safe water, bring a canteenful from home.

HIKE EQUIPMENT. For every hike there are things you'll want to have in your pockets: notebook, pencil, a couple of adhesive bandages, book matches wrapped in foil, knife, handkerchief, toilet paper, phone money. If you are not certain of safe water along the way, you may bring a canteenful from home.

For general hiking and exploring, you'll need map and compass. If you plan to cook you'll bring a pot for a patrol meal or one-man cook kits for cooking by buddies. You'll then also need tools for eating. For a pioneering hike, you'll bring rope. For a photographic hike you'll take camera and film.

Whatever the hike, someone should carry a first aid kit. Then you will be prepared in case of injuries.

HIKE FOOD. Fix your hike food at home before you take off. One or two sandwiches, an apple, and a candy bar make a good lunch. Put it in a plastic sandwich bag.

"Birdseed" is a hike snack. This is a mix of dry, sugar-coated cereal, raisins, candy-coated chocolates, and peanuts or cashew nuts. Enjoy a handful when you are hungry.

For a patrol hike put all equipment and food in a single pack and take turns carrying it. For a buddy hike or a hike by yourself use a small hike bag swung over one shoulder.

ON THE HIKE

With everything planned and your equipment on hand you start off with your patrol. Everyone is in high spirits. We'll soon find out what kind of hikers you are.

If you know your business you'll start slowly, and slowly get into your stride. Not dawdling along, which tires you out. But walking with a free and easy stride.

HOW TO WALK. Learn to walk the way the Indian walked. Come down lightly on your heel, with your toes pointed straight ahead, and push off with your toes. Swing your arms easily. Keep your chin up. Glide along with a smooth, natural movement of your whole body.

When you hike with a pack, keep the weight of it high on your back. Lean forward with only a slight stoop.

YOUR HIKING SPEED. On a patrol hike you are out to enjoy the trail and the fresh air and to learn Scouting. You are not out to break speed records. So fit your speed to the purpose of the hike and the distance to be covered. If you are looking for animals or birds, the distance may be short and the time long. But if you are out exploring you may want to cover ground. For such hiking 5 km (3 mi.) an hour may be your speed.

A good test of your hiking speed is the talking test. When you move so fast that all talking stops, you're not hiking. You are just swallowing miles. Slow down to a speed that suits everyone. Swing along with a song, if you like.

For the best rest, lie down on the ground with the legs raised.

RESTING ON THE WAY. Stop for a rest every half hour or so. Make it short—3 to 5 minutes. If you rest longer, your leg muscles stiffen. You'll have trouble limbering up again.

To really rest, lie down on the ground. Place your legs up against a stump or a rock. That makes the blood run from them. When the minutes are up, get back in your stride.

While hiking, be your age. Stay away from candy and soft drinks. They only make you thirsty. So does continual sipping from your canteen. If you feel thirsty put a small, clean pebble in your mouth. It should be large enough so you won't swallow it by accident. You will be surprised at what this does to keep you from feeling thirsty.

SAFETY CROSS-COUNTRY. Scout hiking is done cross-country or along bypaths. Those bypaths may not be paths at all. They may be the bank of a river, the shore of a lake, the ridge of a hill. They may even be compass directions that'll take you straight through the underbrush.

When you travel cross-country like this, the big rule is "Watch your step!" It may be fun to jump from rock to rock and to hurdle a fallen tree. But a rock may be slippery and a log rotten. Then what? A sprained ankle is no fun on a hike.

So put your feet down on solid ground. Don't place your foot on a loose rock. It may throw you. Don't step on a log. Step over it. And watch out when you use trees or shrubs for handholds in scaling a slope. The tree must be sound and the shrub firmly rooted.

SAFETY ON ROADS. A Scout hike is meant to take you through woods and over fields. But you may often have to follow a main route for a while before you reach a place where a trail leads off to adventure.

Roads are built for cars—not for hikers. When you use them for hiking, you must look after yourself.

To be safe walking along a road, keep as far over to the left as possible. In this way you can see an oncoming car and can get off the road. If there is a shoulder along the road, use it.

For night hiking, carry a flashlight. Also, tie a white handkerchief flat around your lower right leg. Even better, wear reflective tape

When hiking at night, make yourself visible to drivers of oncoming cars.

around your leg and on the back of your shirt. It will bob up and down as you walk. Drivers will see it before they see you.

These safety rules hold true whether you hike alone or with the patrol. In the patrol you should move single file far over to the left or completely off the roadway. The patrol leader walks a few steps ahead of the first Scout. The assistant patrol leader walks a few steps behind the last.

SAFE WATER FOR DRINKING. When it comes to drinking on a hike: Drink safe water only.

The water you carry in a canteen from home is safe. But you can't be sure of the water from a spring or a stream. Even crystal clear brook water may contain dangerous germs. Some states mark pure roadside springs with signs that say "Safe Drinking Water."

If you are not certain of your water, make it safe for drinking by killing the germs in it. This can be done most easily with water purification tablets. You can buy them at your local Scout shop or in a camp equipment store. Follow directions on the container.

If you must boil the water, don't let it merely come to a boil and then take it off, but let it boil fully for 10 minutes as germs are tough customers. Let it cool before drinking.

181

Let no one say—and say it to your shame

FOLLOW THE RULES. In all your hiking, live up to the Outdoor Code. That is expected of all Scouts at all times.

- Obey all "Keep Off," "Private," and "No Trespassing" signs. Cross private property only with the owner's permission. Leave gates the way you found them. And remember that fences are put up to keep somebody out or something in—not for climbing.
- Never cross a planted field before it is harvested or a meadow before it is mowed. To do this is to damage a farmer's crop. Woodlands are crops, too. You want to conserve them, not mar or destroy them. Domestic animals are someone's property. Cows give more milk when left in peace. Horses are in the field to rest and to feed. Do not molest them.
- Walking on railroad tracks and trestles is against the law. It is also extremely dangerous. Stay off!
- Hitchhiking is out! It isn't hiking at all, and it may be unlawful in your state.
- If you need to go to the "bathroom," find a spot off to the side. Scoop a "cat hole" in the ground with the back of a heel. After using, push the dirt back in.

that all was beauty here until you came.

- If you stop someplace to cook, be sure you have permission to light a fire. In many places, a written fire permit is required. After eating, clean up the grounds. Take your gargage and trash out with you in a plastic trash bag.

SCOUT'S PACE. There'll be times when you'll want to move faster than your usual hiking speed. When an old wolf wants to hurry, it lopes. A Scout uses Scout's pace.

Scout's pace is a mixture of jogging and walking. Jog about 25 paces (double-steps) at an easy dogtrot, then walk 25 paces. Then repeat.

Scout's pace serves two useful purposes. One is to cover ground without being tired. The other use is to measure distance. With a bit of practice you can develop a steady rate of 1 miles in 12 minutes or 2 kilometers in 15 minutes, not varying 15 seconds either way. To learn this timing method measure a half mile with a car's odometer. Scout's-pace the distance forward and back until your timing is right.

Then, when you are good at Scout's pace, use it often. If you like to run, work out your own faster timing rate.

FIND YOUR WAY

Many of the hikes you will take with your patrol and troop will be to nearby, familiar places. But from time to time you will want to take off for places where you have never been before. To do this you'll need map and compass.

Your Hike Map

A map is simply a picture of a piece of land as it looks from the air. If you flew over the area you would see roads and rivers, fields and forests, villages and towns. On a map the most important of these details are shown by symbols.

You already know several kinds of maps. You have studied the maps in your schoolroom of the whole United States and of the world. You know the road maps that are used by auto drivers. But none of these maps is of any use for hiking.

The kind of map you need for hiking is the kind produced by the U.S. Geological Survey. It is called a topographic map—from the Greek *topos* (place), and *graphein* (to write).

Topographic maps come in many different scales. A good scale for a hike is the scale of 1 in. to 24,000 in. It appears on the map as 1:24000. A distance of 1 in. on this kind of map means a distance of 2,000 ft. in the field (1 mm means 24 m).

HOW TO GET A MAP. To get a topographic map, first send a postcard to Branch of Distribution, U.S. Geological Survey, 1200 South Eads Street, Arlington, Va. 22202. Ask for a map index of your state and an order form.

The index is a map of the state divided into sections called "quadrangles." Find out which quadrangle covers your hiking area. Then order the map by giving the name of the quadrangle and sending a money order or check for payment. Send your order for a map of an area east of the Mississippi River to the Branch of Distribution in Arlington, Va. Send your order for a map of an area west of the Mississippi to Branch of Distribution, U.S. Geological Survey, Federal Center, Denver, Colo. 80225.

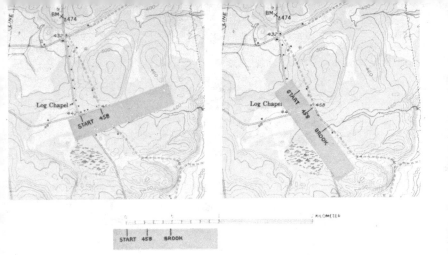

To measure distances on a map, use a paper strip as described in text.

WHAT THE MAP TELLS. A good map tells five things:
- **Description.** Any map gives you the name of the area. A topographic map also tells you where on earth it is found.
- **Details.** Landscape features are shown on the map by easily understood signs. They are called map signatures.
- **Directions.** The top of the map is usually north. That makes the bottom south, the left side west, the right side east.
- **Distances.** The scales in the bottom margin of your map give you the means for measuring distances on the map.
- **Designations.** Lakes, rivers, towns, and other features are designated by their names in various type styles.

USING A MAP. Before you set out, spread out the map and look at it. Plan to start from a point you know, such as a road crossing. Next, decide on your destination—a hilltop, for instance. Finally, lay a route on the map to get you there.

How long will the hike be? Measure the distance this way: Place a paper strip on the map with one edge along the first lap of your route. Put a mark at the edge for your starting point and another for the end of the lap. Mark off the other laps the same way. Then lay the paper strip against the distance ruler on your map. Check the distance between the marks against the scale.

Open pit, mine	⚒
Index contour	～～
Intermediate contour	～
Fill	⊥⊥⊥⊥⊥⊥⊥⊥⊥
Cut	
Power line	‥‥‥•‥‥‥•
Telephone line, etc.	– – – –
Railroad	+–+–+–
Hard surface roads	
Improved road	
Unimproved road	=======
Trail	– – – – –
Bridge	
Footbridge	– –✕– ✕– –
Perennial streams	
Water well · Spring	○ ⌒
Lake	
Marsh (swamp)	
Buildings (dwelling)	▪ ▪ ▮ ▨
School · Church · Cemetery	⌂ ╪ ⊤
Buildings (barn, etc.)	▫ ▭ ▨
Sand area	
Woods	
Orchard	
Scrub	

Map Symbols

To learn the map symbols, study the map and symbols on these pages first. Then spread out a topographic map and try to find all the map symbols it contains.

BLACK. Everything printed in black is the work of man: roads, railroads, bridges, buildings, boundaries, names.

Black lines are roads. A good road is shown by two solid lines, a poor one by two broken lines. A path is a single broken line. Hard surface roads may be indicated by red ink between two black lines.

Black rectangles are buildings. If topped by a flag it's a schoolhouse.

BLUE. Anything blue is water. A blue line is a brook. A blue band is a river. A blue blotch is a lake.

GREEN. Woodland areas are printed in green. So are orchards and scrub lands. Also marshes and swamps, but with broken blue lines and grass tufts to show that they are wetlands.

BROWN. Hills and valleys are shown by brown lines. These lines are called contour lines. Every point along one of these lines is the same number of feet above sea level. Contour lines tell you the ups and downs of the countryside. Where the lines are far apart the ground is gently sloping. Where the lines are close together the hill is steep.

Follow one of the heavier brown lines on your map and you will come upon a number—100, for instance. It is an index contour. Everything on that line lies 100 feet above sea level. If the sea should rise 100 feet, this line would become the new shoreline. If it should rise 20 feet more, the next thin line would be the shoreline. And so on, for every 20 feet of rise. (See illustrations on page 188.)

On certain maps, the difference in height or interval between contour lines is only 10 feet. Check in the bottom margin to find this "contour interval."

187

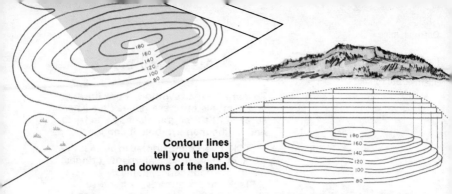

Contour lines
tell you the ups
and downs of the land.

You are at your starting point, ready to go! But in what direction? You will know as soon as you have oriented your map. To orient a map means to line up all directions on it with the same directions in the field.

Orienting a Map by Inspection. Locate in the field some features that are shown on your map—a crossroad, a building, a bridge. Inspect your map and find the map symbols for the features on it. Then turn the map until the symbols fit the actual features in the field. You have now oriented your map "by inspection." North of the map—the top of it—has been turned toward true north. All directions are correct. You are ready to follow the route you laid.

Every time you finish a lap, orient the map for the next lap. Continue until you reach your destination.

To get back home, you simply follow the laps of your route in the opposite direction.

Map is oriented when the map symbols fit the features in the field.

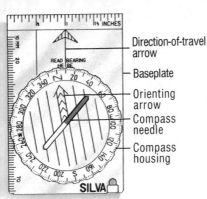

Direction-of-travel arrow

Baseplate

Orienting arrow

Compass needle

Compass housing

Each official Boy Scout compass, Silva system, is more than a compass. The box that houses the compass needle is attached to a baseplate that acts as a direction pointer, a tool for taking compass bearings, and a ruler for measuring map distances. The two most popular Silva models are the Polaris and Explorer III.

Your Compass

But maybe you don't want to follow roads or trails. Maybe you want to hike right smack through the countryside. For that kind of traveling you need a compass.

HOW A COMPASS WORKS. The important part of a compass is a magnetized needle. This is balanced on a pinpoint, free to swing around. When left to itself the needle eventually comes to rest; it then always points in one certain direction. The reason for this is that there is a force in the earth that pulls at the needle. The whole earth is like a tremendous magnet, with one pole in the north, the other in the south.

The earth's magnetism makes one end of the compass needle point toward magnetic north. This end is clearly marked as the north end. It may be painted red or black. Or shaped like an arrowhead. Or stamped with the initial N.

THE COMPASS POINTS. When you know from the compass needle where north is, you can find the eight main points of the compass:

Face north. South is then right behind you. West is on your left. East is on your right. Halfway between north and east is northeast. Halfway between east and south is southeast. Halfway between south and west is southwest. Halfway between north and west is northwest.

Or, starting from north and going clockwise: north, northeast, east, southeast, south, southwest, west, northwest, and back to north.

This way of reciting the compass points is called "boxing the compass."

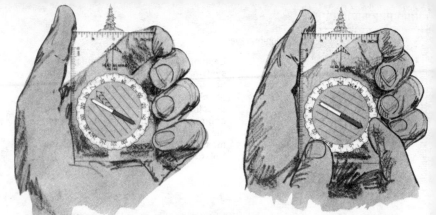

It is easy to read a compass bearing when you use a Silva compass.

READING A COMPASS BEARING.

Let's say that you want to read a compass bearing in the field. That is, you want to find the direction to a certain point expressed in degrees.

Face the landmark to which you want to know the bearing. Hold the compass level in front of you, at waist height or a little higher. Point the direction-of-travel arrow on the base plate straight ahead of you toward the landmark.

Now twist the compass housing until the compass needle lies over the orienting arrow. This arrow is on the inside bottom of the housing. Make sure that the north part of the needle points to the letter N (north) on top of the housing. Read the number on the rim of the compass housing at the spot where the direction-of-travel line touches the housing. There you have the bearing expressed in compass degrees.

To orient a map by compass, first set compass bearing at N (360°). Place compass on map with one edge alongside the magnetic north line in the margin. Turn compass and map together until the needle lies over orienting arrow with north part pointing to N. Map is oriented.

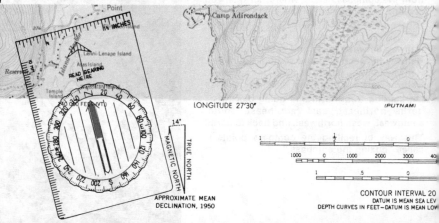

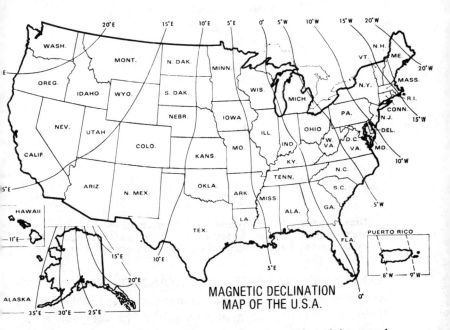

MAGNETIC DECLINATION
MAP OF THE U.S.A.

Find where you live on this map. Then check out the number of degrees of declination E (east) or W (west). Remember the number you arrive at.

TWO NORTHS. When you use map and compass together, remember that there are two norths. Your map is based on *true north*. All lines on it from bottom to top point to the geographic North Pole. The north end of your compass shows *magnetic north*. It points to the magnetic North Pole located on Canada's Bathurst Island in the Arctic Ocean 1,600 km (1,000 mi.) south of the real North Pole.

The difference between the lines of your map and the pointing of the compass needle is called "declination." Because of the difference, each time you set your compass from the map you must reset it to fit the declination. You do not have to do this on a line that runs from the east coast of Florida to the magnetic North Pole. But you have to *add* the degrees shown on the declination angle on your map if you are *east* of this line. You have to *subtract* the degrees shown on your map if you are *west* of this line.

To make things much simpler, make your map speak "compass language" as described on the next page.

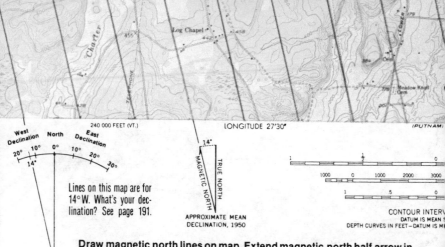

Lines on this map are for 14° W. What's your declination? See page 191.

240 000 FEET (VT.)

West Declination
20° 10° 0°
14°
North
East Declination
10° 20°
30°

LONGITUDE 27'30"

(PUTNAM)

14°

MAGNETIC NORTH

TRUE NORTH

APPROXIMATE MEAN
DECLINATION, 1950

Center

1   1   0
1000   0   1000   2000   3000
1   5   0

CONTOUR INTERV
DATUM IS MEAN S
DEPTH CURVES IN FEET—DATUM IS M

Draw magnetic north lines on map. Extend magnetic north half arrow in map margin. Or mark off the declination number you found on page 191 on diagram to the left. Run line from center to mark and over map.

MAKE YOUR MAP SPEAK "COMPASS LANGUAGE." To overcome the difference between map directions and compass directions, make your map agree with the compass at all times. Do this by drawing magnetic north-south lines on it:

Locate the magnetic north half arrow in the bottom margin of your map. Extend this half arrow line up through the map. Then draw several other lines parallel with this line, a ruler's width apart, as shown on the map at the top of this page.

USING MAP AND COMPASS TOGETHER. With magnetic north-south lines on your map, use map and compass together by following the three steps on the next page.

Practice this method a number of times, setting the compass to the directions on the map. Soon you will be ready for a cross-country journey.

Lay out a route on your topographic map. Connect five or six clearly shown landmarks: road crossings, buildings, bridges, and the like. Set the compass for the direction from your starting point to the first landmark and get going. When you reach that first landmark, reset the compass for the next leg of the route toward the next landmark. Continue in this manner until you have covered the entire route and have reached your final destination.

USING MAP AND COMPASS TOGETHER

IMPORTANT: As you set out to learn these three steps, make use of your compass. If you do not have a compass yet, use the practice compass as described on page 575.

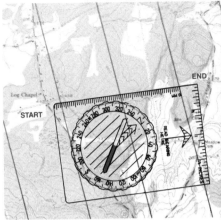

Step 1. ON THE MAP, LINE UP THE EDGE OF COMPASS WITH YOUR ROUTE. Place the Polaris compass on map so that the edge of its baseplate touches your starting point and your destination, with the baseplate's direction-of-travel arrow pointing in the direction you want to go. Look at the map.

Step 2. ON THE COMPASS, SET THE HOUSING TO THE DIRECTION OF YOUR ROUTE. Hold baseplate firmly on the map. Paying no attention to the needle, turn the compass housing until the north arrow on the bottom of it is parallel with a north-south magnetic line drawn on your map, north to the top.

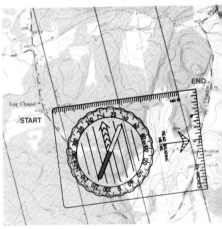

Step 3. IN THE FIELD, FOLLOW DIRECTION SET ON THE COMPASS. Hold compass in front of you with direction-of-travel arrow pointing straight ahead. Turn yourself until north part of compass needle covers north arrow on bottom of compass housing. The direction-of-travel arrow now points at your destination. Pick a landmark in that direction and walk to it, then another landmark.

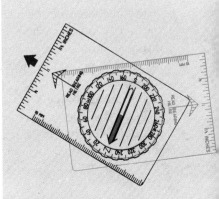

Your First Orienteering Trip at Home

Before you set out on an orienteering trip in the field, take the trip first at home on the map on the next page.

Let's say that you want to start at the crossroads marked 442 just to the south of the Log Chapel. A short expedition might then take in the road-T marked 179 north of Meadow Knoll Cemetery, the farmhouse at road bend 149, the crossroads at 432 north of the Log Chapel, and back to 442.

SETTING YOUR COMPASS. Your first job is to set your orienteering compass for the first lap of the journey.

If you have an orienteering compass this is where it gets a workout. If you don't, you can get along with the training compass you made from the parts on page 575.

So set the compass for the first direction as described on page 193. What is the setting? Check the degree number where the housing touches the direction-of-travel line.

Next lap: from road-T to the farmhouse at road bend marked 149. How many degrees? Next set the compass from the farmhouse to the crossroads marked 432 slightly off north from Log Chapel. Finally from crossroads 432 back to 442.

FOLLOWING THE ROUTE. The route is laid. But would you actually follow these straight lines in the field? Not if you are a real orienteer. You would use all the knowledge you have to pick the easiest and fastest route. You would use all your cunning. That's why orienteering is called "cunning running."

Look at the map again. Instead of following a beeline, you take the short road east to the point marked 458. You then go southeast until you hit the brook. You follow the brook down into the valley, then continue cross-country to point 179. From there you follow the road north to the farmhouse. Here you take the dirt road west to point 432, then the main road south past the Log Chapel to the crossroads at 442.

With this for a starter, you are ready for orienteering in the field. So get an *Orienteering* merit badge pamphlet and set out on the thrilling sport of orienteering.

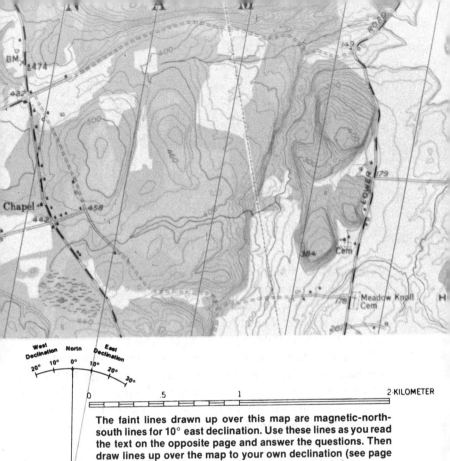

The faint lines drawn up over this map are magnetic-north-south lines for 10° east declination. Use these lines as you read the text on the opposite page and answer the questions. Then draw lines up over the map to your own declination (see page 192), and answer the same questions and those below.

1. Where is the highest point on the map? How high is it?

2. What is the air distance from the Log Chapel to the Meadow Knoll Cemetery?

3. Does the brook starting south of the Log Chapel run slow or fast?

4. How long will it take you to hike from the farmhouse at 149 to crossroads 432 if you walk 5 km an hour?

5. On what kind of road will you be hiking?

6. Compare the two hills in the middle of the map with the two hills toward the right of the map. Which are higher?

7. Where will you cross water hiking from the farmhouse at 149 to the Meadow Knoll Cemetery?

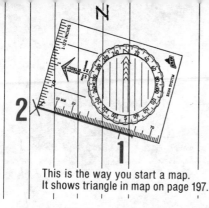
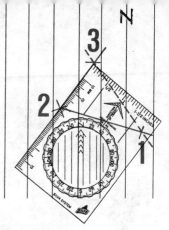

This is the way you start a map.
It shows triangle in map on page 197.

MAPPING

Mapping is as simple as 1, 2, 3. All you need is a Silva compass, a ruled paper pad, and a sharp pencil.

Let's say you want to make a map of your camp area to the west. You start at a road fork. Mark it with a dot on one of the rules at the right of your paper. That's point 1.

Point 2 is the tree where the road turns right. Set your compass for the first bearing as described on page 190. Don't bother to note the degrees—that chore is eliminated when you use a Silva compass. Place the compass on the paper with the edge of the baseplate touching point 1. Move the compass to line up the lines on the bottom of the housing with the rules on the paper. Draw a line along the edge of the baseplate. Next pace the distance to point 2. Mark off the distance on the line. Use the millimeter scale for your paces: 1 mm = 1 pace.

Point 3 is the next road turn. Set your compass for the bearing. Transfer bearing to paper as just described. Pace distance. Mark point 3 that many millimeters from point 2.

(You may want to check your accuracy: At point 3 take the bearing to point 1. Is it within a few degrees of a dotted line on your map connecting 3 and 1? Measure the distance on your map in millimeters between 3 and 1. Then pace the distance from 3 to 1. The number of paces should be close to the number of millimeters.)

Now continue your mapping from point 3 until you have covered your area. Finish map by drawing in details.

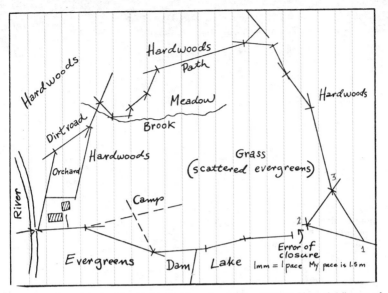

This is how a completed survey of a closed area would look. Note the "error of closure." Not even a top mapmaker will come out on the dot.

Finished map sketch should contain magnetic north half arrow, scale, name of area, details of landscape features, name of mapmaker, and date.

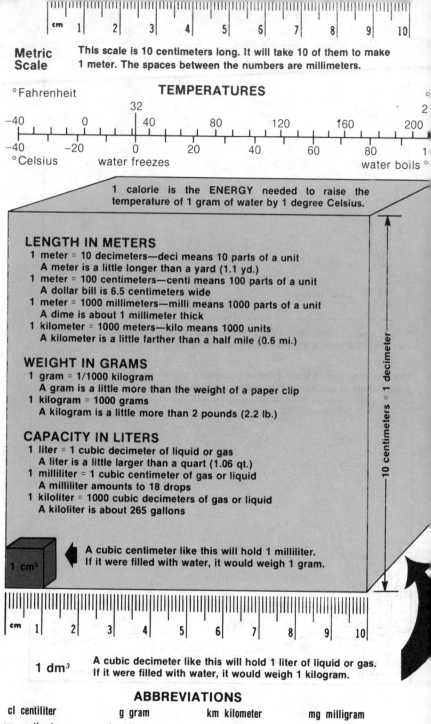

Metric Scale

This scale is 10 centimeters long. It will take 10 of them to make 1 meter. The spaces between the numbers are millimeters.

cm 1 2 3 4 5 6 7 8 9 10

TEMPERATURES

°Fahrenheit

−40   0   32 40   80   120   160   200

°Celsius   −40   −20   0   20   40   60   80

water freezes   water boils

1 calorie is the ENERGY needed to raise the temperature of 1 gram of water by 1 degree Celsius.

LENGTH IN METERS
1 meter = 10 decimeters—deci means 10 parts of a unit
   A meter is a little longer than a yard (1.1 yd.)
1 meter = 100 centimeters—centi means 100 parts of a unit
   A dollar bill is 6.5 centimeters wide
1 meter = 1000 millimeters—milli means 1000 parts of a unit
   A dime is about 1 millimeter thick
1 kilometer = 1000 meters—kilo means 1000 units
   A kilometer is a little farther than a half mile (0.6 mi.)

WEIGHT IN GRAMS
1 gram = 1/1000 kilogram
   A gram is a little more than the weight of a paper clip
1 kilogram = 1000 grams
   A kilogram is a little more than 2 pounds (2.2 lb.)

CAPACITY IN LITERS
1 liter = 1 cubic decimeter of liquid or gas
   A liter is a little larger than a quart (1.06 qt.)
1 milliliter = 1 cubic centimeter of gas or liquid
   A milliliter amounts to 18 drops
1 kiloliter = 1000 cubic decimeters of gas or liquid
   A kiloliter is about 265 gallons

10 centimeters = 1 decimeter

1 cm³

A cubic centimeter like this will hold 1 milliliter. If it were filled with water, it would weigh 1 gram.

cm 1 2 3 4 5 6 7 8 9 10

1 dm³   A cubic decimeter like this will hold 1 liter of liquid or gas. If it were filled with water, it would weigh 1 kilogram.

ABBREVIATIONS

cl centiliter   g gram   km kilometer   mg milligram
cm centimeter   kg kilogram   l liter   ml milliliter
dm decimeter   kl kiloliter   m meter   mm millimeter

MEASURING IN METRICS

Do you know what the five countries Brunei, North and South Yemen, Burma, and the United States have in common? They are the only countries today that do not use the metric system.

A few years from now—certainly by the time you reach manhood—the main system of our country for measuring will be the metric. It is the most logical system ever invented. And it is the easiest to work with because it is a decimal system.

Whenever you multiply or divide by 10, or 100, or 1,000, etc., you simply shift the decimal point.

PERSONAL MEASUREMENTS. On hikes and while camping you often have to measure a distance, a height, or a width. You can do this easily by using the ruler you always carry with you: yourself. The most important personal measurements you will use are shown below. Take these measurements—in metrics—and write them in the proper spaces. Then remember them and make use of them.

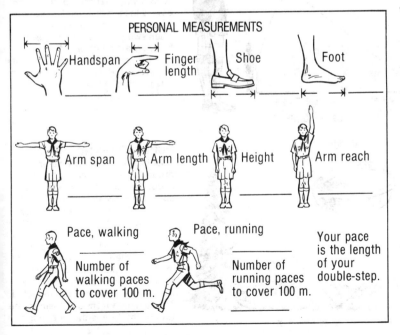

PERSONAL MEASUREMENTS

Handspan — Finger length — Shoe — Foot

Arm span — Arm length — Height — Arm reach

Pace, walking

Number of walking paces to cover 100 m.

Pace, running

Number of running paces to cover 100 m.

Your pace is the length of your double-step.

METRICS AT A GLANCE

MEASURING HEIGHTS

Pencil method

PENCIL METHOD. Place a buddy whose height you know against the tree, or make a mark for your own height on the trunk. Step back. Hold a stick or pencil up before you in your outstretched hand. With one eye closed, measure off on the stick with your thumbnail the height of your buddy. Then move the stick up to see how many times this measurement goes into the height of the tree. Multiply the height of your buddy with the number found. This gives you the height of the tree.

Tree-felling method

TREE FELLING METHOD. Hold a stick upright in your outstretched hand. Move backward away from the flagpole (or tree) you want to measure. Sight to the flagpole in such a way that the tip of the stick covers the top of the pole. The place where your thumb is, is its foot. Then swing the stick 90 degrees to a horizontal position. Notice the point where the tip of the stick hits the ground. Pace the distance from this point to the foot of the flagpole to get its height.

Muddy water method

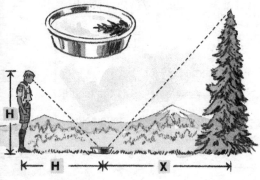

MUDDY WATER METHOD. Place a washbasin with muddy water on the ground between you and the tree, at a point which you estimate to be approximately as far away from the tree as the tree is high. Step back from the basin a distance equal to that from your eyes to the ground. You should now see the top of the tree reflected in the water. If not, move basin (keeping yourself at the same distance from the washbasin) until you see the tree top reflected. The distance from the basin to the foot of the tree is the tree height.

MEASURING WIDTHS

NAPOLEON METHOD. Stand on one shore. Bow your head, chin against chest. Hold your hand to your forehead, palm down. Move hand down until the front edge of it seems to touch the opposite shore. Now make half right turn, "transferring" the distance to your shore. The distance to the point which the edge of your hand seems to touch is the width of the river. Pace it. Napoleon would have used the brim of his hat instead of his hand. So would you if you had on a broad-brim Scout hat.

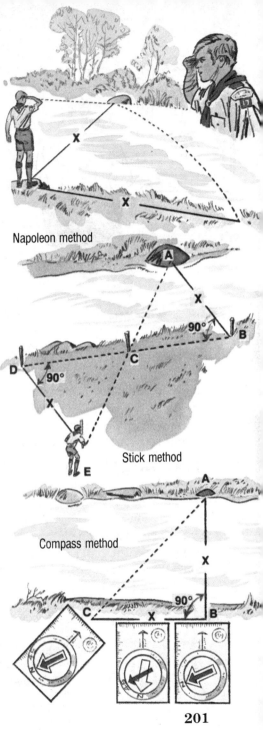

Napoleon method

STICK METHOD. Notice a rock on the other side of the river (A). Place a stick on this side opposite the rock (B). Walk along the shore at right angles to AB. Take any number of paces (say 50). Place another stick here (C). Continue walking along the shore in the same line for as many paces as before (in this case 50). Place another stick here (D). At this point walk at right angles to DB. When you sight stick C and mark A in a straight line, stop (E). DE is distance across river.

Stick method

COMPASS METHOD. Stand on one side of a river (B). Notice a rock exactly opposite to you on the other side of the river (A). Point the travel-direction arrow of your compass at the rock. Turn the dial until the compass needle lies over the orienting arrow, north point pointing N. Read the degrees (in this case 120). Add 45° (making it 165). Walk along the river, pointing the travel arrow toward A. When the compass is oriented, stop (C). Distance CB is the width of the river.

Compass method

201

In a large city there will be many special features to investigate: maybe an art gallery, a zoological garden, a natural history museum.

TOWN AND CITY HIKING

Most Scout hikes take you out into the open country, away from populated areas. But on occasion you will want to take a town or city hike. It will be entirely different. But it can be just as interesting when you plan it that way.

TOWN HIKE. If you live in a small town you may think you know all about it. But do you? You may know its streets like the back of your hand without really knowing the town. Ask yourself some questions about it. Then set out to find the answers along these lines:

Which is the oldest house in town? Who is the oldest person? Where does he or she live? Which is the oldest grave marker in the cemetery? Who was buried under it? When? Where is the largest tree? From what location will I have the finest view of my town?

CITY HIKE. If you live in a large city, imagine yourself an investigator trying to find places where you have never been before. If you are an out-of-towner, play tourist. Get a map of the city and plan an itinerary in advance of what you want to see. There may be a famous museum you should visit. Or an art gallery, a city park, a zoo, a historic site.

A Scout Is Courteous. In city traffic, stay on the sidewalk. Walk in single file or by twos. Follow the traffic flow of other walkers. Jaywalking—that is, careless walking or crossing in the middle of the block—is illegal in most cities. Cross only at intersections. Watch traffic signals. Consider other people when you walk: talk softly.

Follow Your Route. Unless you have a guide, stick to the route you laid in advance. Fold the map to the area where you are. Locate your exact position. Orient your map by inspection: hold it so that the street on the map and the real street lead straight ahead. Every time you turn a street corner, turn your map so you are looking down the new street. If you get lost, ask a policeman.

Toilets. There are public restrooms in bus, railroad, and subway stations. You will find them in libraries and in government buildings. Sometimes there are pay toilets. You will need "emergency coins" to use one.

With a map of the city on hand and street signs to guide you, you can easily find your way. Cross at intersections only. Obey traffic signs.

203

You'll have plenty of excitement hiking with your patrol and troop.

ADVENTURE HIKES AND GAMES

Most good Scout troops have an outdoor experience every month. Sometimes it'll be a hike, sometimes a camp. From time to time your patrol may take off on its own. Some of these troop and patrol hikes will be built around a "big idea" in some Scoutcraft skill. Others will be for testing your ingenuity or endurance. Still others will be in the form of games—games with a purpose—to make you a better Scout, strong in body and alert of mind.

Let's take a look at some typical troop and patrol hikes:

TREASURE HUNT. At a troop meeting, the senior patrol leader announces: "Next week's hike is a treasure hunt!"

This is the way it works: Your patrol leader gets a sealed envelope. On it is a small sketch map with an X and these words: "Proceed to X. Then open envelope." X is easily located. The envelope is opened. There's a message inside: "Go to the tallest oak you can see from here. Follow the directions of its largest branch 90 m." You do and find an overturned stone. Under it is the next clue: "235° to tree with unnatural fruit." The tree is a hickory with pine cones tied to its branches. At its foot starts a trail of Indian trail signs. They lead to another tree.

No clue there! Someone looks up. High overhead, a tag is

Snow time is the best time for learning the skill of tracking.

tied to a branch. The patrol's best climber goes up for it. The tag says, "Look 157°." He does. He points: "There's a red neckerchief in a tree over there." Off at a gallop! A clue is pinned to the neckerchief: "150 m, 95°." Here is the last clue: "Dig under the dead chestnut." You locate the tree, dig under it and find—well, maybe not a chest of gold doubloons but certainly at least a bag of peanuts for the lucky treasure hunters.

LOST-CHILD HIKE. The whole troop is alerted. Your patrol rushes to the mobilization point. When all the patrols are gathered, a troop leader announces: "A child is lost. A search has been going on all night. The only area not scoured is a stretch of woodland. It is indicated on a map sketch which each patrol will receive. Our help has been requested. Are you ready to give it?"

Of course you are. Your patrol leader tells you what is expected of you. And you are on your way, with orders to meet at a certain spot at a certain time whether you have found the child or not.

In this particular case, the "child" is a life-size doll, made up of pillows and child's clothing. But some other time it may be a real child.

ORIENTEERING. When you have learned the use of map and compass you can experience the thrill of orienteering.

Beeline Hike. Your first try at orienteering could be a beeline hike for the whole patrol. Get out your topographic map and decide on a starting point and a destination about 5 km (3 mi.) apart. Draw a line from starting point to destination and set the bearing on your compass. Take off and follow the bearing right smack through the countryside, overcoming all obstacles on the way. Each Scout in the patrol takes his turn leading the rest of you.

Orienteering Race. When you are really good at map and compass, challenge another patrol to an orienteering race. Get someone who knows orienteering and is familiar with the countryside to lay out a course with five or six control points. Then divide the patrols into buddy teams. Each team has an orienteering compass and a map with the control points marked. Teams are sent off 5 minutes apart.

You and your buddy take off. You set the compass for the first control point and get going. When the point is reached, you reset the compass for the next point. You continue this way until you have covered the whole course.

Now find out which team has made the best time with all control points passed. You may not come in the winner the first time you try. But someday you will.

MANY KINDS OF HIKES. With a bit of imagination you can think up any number of ideas for patrol hikes. Here are some suggestions to start you off:

206

Exploration Hike. Take off for territory that's brand-new to all the Scouts in the patrol. There may be a mountain, a cave, a lake to be explored. Or, in studying your map you may see where a small river starts in the hills south of your camp. Set out to discover the source.

Tracking Hike. Tracking hikes are especially exciting when snow makes it easy to follow the tracks. Here you have the straight track of a fox, here the erratic prints of a rabbit. At this point a couple of deer got scared and took off in long jumps. There are stories to read in the snow.

SOAR Hike. SOAR stands for Save Our American Resources. Hike to a nearby picnic spot, a lakeshore, or a brook. Bring cleanup tools and plastic bags. Clean up the area to Scout standards.

10-Mile Hike. Get your patrol established as a 10-mile club by taking at least three 10-mile hikes. Then take the next step and go metric. Turn your hikes into 20-km hikes and your patrol into a 20-km club.

Night Hike. Some night in camp don't turn in after campfire. Instead, turn out for a night hike along familiar trails around camp. Absolutely no talking. The darkness and silence will give you a very special experience.

Night Orienteering. This is the toughest kind of orienteering. You have to find your way in the dark, with map, compass, and flashlight your only tools.

207

The climax of a "Lost-Child Hike" comes when the "child" is found.

DIRECTIONS WITHOUT A COMPASS

DIRECTIONS BY STARS. North Star Method. Find the North Star (page 317). Then push the longer of two sticks upright into the ground. Place the shorter stick where, when you sight over the tips of both sticks, you hit the North Star. A line between the sticks is a true north-south line.

DIRECTIONS BY THE SUN. Shadowless Shadow-Stick Method. Push a short straight stick into the ground so it makes no shadow. Wait until it casts a shadow 15 cm (6 in.) long or longer. The shadow will be pointing east from the stick. A line across the shadow line will be north and south.

    Equal-Length-Shadow Method. Push a straight stick, 1 m (3 ft.) long, upright into the ground. In the morning, place a small peg at the tip of the shadow. Tie a string around the pole with a bowline. Using this string, with the distance from the shadow-stick to the peg as radius, draw an arc of a circle. In the afternoon, place another peg where the tip of the shadow hits the arc. A line between the pegs is a west-east line, with west at the morning peg. A line across it is north-south.

DIRECTIONS BY THE MOON. Shadowless Shadow-Stick Method, used with the sun, works just as well with the moon if this is bright enough to cast a shadow.

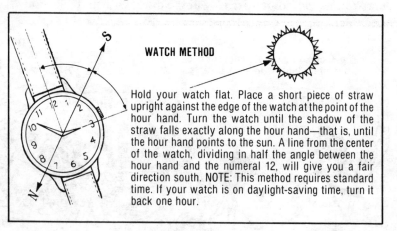

WATCH METHOD

Hold your watch flat. Place a short piece of straw upright against the edge of the watch at the point of the hour hand. Turn the watch until the shadow of the straw falls exactly along the hour hand—that is, until the hour hand points to the sun. A line from the center of the watch, dividing in half the angle between the hour hand and the numeral 12, will give you a fair direction south. NOTE: This method requires standard time. If your watch is on daylight-saving time, turn it back one hour.

THREE WAYS TO FIND NORTH

North by North Star

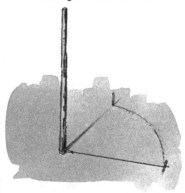

Shadowless shadow-stick method by sun. Also by moon if this is bright enough to cast a shadow.

Equal-length-shadow method

Line up three landmarks ahead of you for a straight course.

LOST!

Someone once asked Daniel Boone, "Were you ever lost?" Dan thought it over for a while, then replied, "No, I was never lost. But once I was a mite bewildered for 5 days." Dan was right. No person is really lost if he knows how to find his way.

HOW NOT TO GET LOST. The main rule for not getting lost is to know at all times where you are.

When you hike with your patrol or your troop, be alert. Note the directions of the roads, of streams you cross, of lakeshores you follow. And note and remember outstanding features of the landscape, natural or man-made: hills, cliffs, large trees, TV towers. Jot down the details in your notebook or make a sketch map of the hike territory.

When you expect to travel in an area where you have never been before, always take along a map and a compass.

LOST BY YOURSELF. If you are on a hike by yourself and get lost, the main thing is to be calm. Take it easy. Sit down on a rock or under a tree. Then reason your way out.

In your mind, trace your course back to the point where you definitely knew where you were. "Where did I go wrong?" Recall other hikes you have taken through the same territory, and try to remember the features. "How do the roads run? Am I north or south, east or west of camp?"

After having threshed everything out unhurriedly, decide on the most sensible direction to take. Then set out.

210

If you have a compass, it will be easy for you to hold your course. If you have no compass, follow a beeline. Line up two landmarks in the direction you want to go—trees, rocks, or whatnot. From the first one, line up a third landmark ahead of the second one. Then proceed. Continue in this way, always keeping two landmarks in a straight line in front of you. Eventually you will find some familiar spot or see a trail or a stream that will bring you back to camp.

STRAYED FROM THE PATROL. But if you ever become separated from your friends on a wilderness expedition, the thing to do is to let *them* find *you*, rather than for *you* to attempt to find *them*.

As soon as your absence is noted, someone will start looking for you. So stay put and have faith that someone will find you. Prayer will help. Make yourself as comfortable as possible and wait.

To assist the searchers, try to let them know where you are. The universal distress call is some kind of signal repeated three times, at frequent intervals. Three shouts, for instance. Or three blasts with a whistle. Or three columns of smoke. To make such a smoke signal, clear the ground for a safe distance. Build three small fires 2 m (6 ft.) apart and make them smoke by throwing grass or green leaves on them. This signal will soon be spotted, possibly from a fire tower or some other lookout, maybe from a search plane. When the searchers have heard you or have spotted you, they will answer you by an OK signal of two shouts, or two whistle blasts, or two gunshots.

If you doubt that you will be found before nightfall, collect firewood to last through the night. Find a windbreak: a rock, down log, or cliff. Build a fire for warmth and sit between the fire and the windbreak. If you need to leave your base for food or water, mark the trail with broken branches so you can find your way back.

But whatever you do, stay put. You will be found.

WHERE SCOUTS ROAM

So Much Concern
by Norman Rockwell, 1975

213

If you have the patience and the skill you can bring home a photographic record of the adventures you have in your pursuit of nature.

Nature Around You

The more hikes and camping trips you take, the more you will come to appreciate nature around you. The more also you will come to realize that "nature" is not just one thing. "Nature" is a multitude of things with tremendous variety.

The nature of a forest is vastly different from the nature of a desert, or a meadow, or a seashore. The nature you find at the top of a mountain is different from what you find at the foot. Each of these nature areas is its own kind of environment: a home for particular plants and animals that live together and depend for their survival on each other and on the conditions that surround them. Each environment is a complicated system, an ecosystem—from the Greek word *oikos*, meaning a home. The study of environments, of the relationship between living things and their surroundings, is called ecology—the study of the home.

It will help you understand what goes on in an environment of nature if you think of it as being not too different from the man-made environment in which you live.

In your home environment boys and girls, men and women live together. Your house shelters you. Nearby stores have the kind of food you need. Public utilities provide you with light, heat, and water. Your street or backyard or garden gives you space to move about.

It is much the same in an environment of nature.

Plants grow where they grow because they have found living conditions suitable. They have found the soil and water, light and temperature to their liking.

Animals live where they live first of all because all animals depend on plants for their food. Some animals, such as deer, squirrels, and seed-eating birds live on plant life directly. Other animals, such as foxes, shrews, hawks, and owls, live on plant life indirectly: the small animals they feed on are plant eaters. But in addition to food, animals need plants for other reasons. Trees and shrubs, weeds and tall grasses give them shelter against the heat and the sun and inclement weather. They provide them with concealment for resting and sleeping and raising the young. They also furnish escape cover for a quick getaway when an enemy is about.

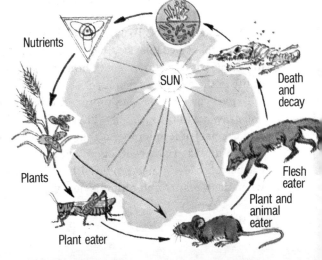

FOOD CHAIN. Plants get energy from the sun. Animals get energy from food. The mouse eats a root and gets energy from it. The fox gets energy from eating the mouse. Body waste from both gets into the soil as food for plants, called nutrients. When animals die they also return to the soil.

Nutrients

SUN

Death and decay

Plants

Flesh eater

Plant and animal eater

Plant eater

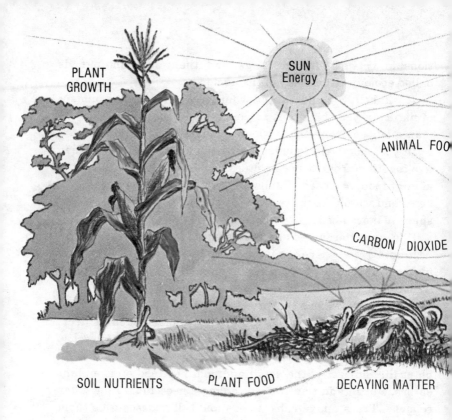

PLANT
GROWTH

SUN
Energy

ANIMAL FOO

CARBON DIOXIDE

SOIL NUTRIENTS   PLANT FOOD   DECAYING MATTER

Sunlight is the source of all energy. This energy works with the green
chlorophyll in plants to make sugars from water and carbon dioxide.

TWO LIFE CYCLES

LIFE-GIVING SUN. To understand how living things live you need
to know about a couple of cycles. A cycle is a process which continues
in a circle with no start or end. The most important cycle for all kinds
of life is the oxygen-carbon cycle.

To live, you and all other living creatures must breathe. To do this,
you draw air into your lungs. The lungs absorb oxygen from the air
and use part of it in a process that can be compared to burning. The
carbon dioxide that results goes out into the air when you exhale.
Carbon dioxide is also produced by burning all kinds of fuel and
when dead plants and animals decay.

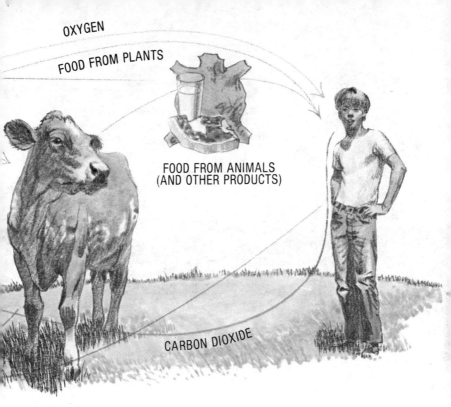

OXYGEN

FOOD FROM PLANTS

FOOD FROM ANIMALS
(AND OTHER PRODUCTS)

CARBON DIOXIDE

Plants take carbon dioxide from the air and give off oxygen. Man and other animals use oxygen and give off carbon dioxide. The cycle goes on.

Plants need this carbon dioxide to grow. By a miraculous process they combine the carbon in it with water to produce simple sugars. In doing this, they give off oxygen as a by-product. This process is known as photosynthesis—making things with the aid of light. In this process the plants make use of the energy of sunlight and of a green coloring matter in their cells called chlorophyll. The plants further combine the sugars with nitrogen and minerals to form many other foods: starches and oils, protein and vitamins.

All food eaten by you and other animals can be traced to the oxygen-carbon cycle. Bread and cereals, vegetables and fruits come directly out of the cycle. Milk, eggs, and meat are produced by animals that live on plants.

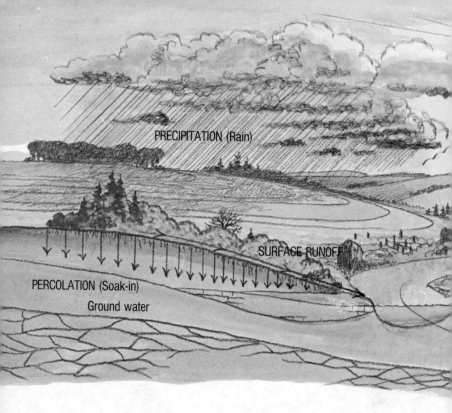

PRECIPITATION (Rain)

SURFACE RUNOFF

PERCOLATION (Soak-in)

Ground water

Plant and animal life depend on water. Man can live for weeks without food. He lasts only for a short time without water. So do plants.

LIFE-SUSTAINING WATER. All living things must have fresh water for life and growth. Here again everything depends on the sun. The sun evaporates the water out of the salt water that covers two-thirds of the earth's surface and out of lakes and rivers. It then distributes the water back on earth. To understand the cycle in which water moves, you need to know a few technical words:

Evaporation is the process by which water is changed into vapor. It is speeded up by wind and high temperature. When cooled in the upper air, the vapor forms clouds.

Transpiration is the loss of water from plants to the air in the form of vapor. The water entered the plants from the water supply in the soil.

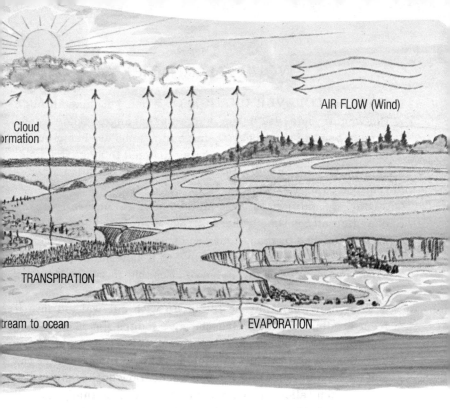

The sun evaporates water from oceans and lakes. Winds created by the sun carry the vapors inland. When cooled the vapors turn into rain or snow.

Precipitation is the way in which water falls from the clouds. This can be as rain, hail, sleet, or snow. It happens when the clouds cool so much that the air can no longer hold the water.

Surface runoff takes place where the droplets fall faster than the soil can soak them up. The excess water runs downhill to streams, rivers, and, finally, to lakes and oceans.

Percolation is what happens to the droplets that don't run off the land. This water soaks into the soil and is used by plants. It also moves deeper into the ground to become part of the ground-water supply. When all space in the ground is filled, the water flows along cracks to come up as springs or rivers, to return to the lakes or oceans from which it came.

YOUR ENVIRONMENT

NATURE FOREVER CHANGING. When you hike through the countryside you'll see numerous changes being made around you. New roads are being built. Dams are being put up to create lakes. Marshes are being drained to make dry land. Whenever man changes the environment, plant life and wildlife soon change as well.

But in addition to man-made changes, nature goes on changing all the time by herself. When you look at any piece of land untouched by man, it may seem as if nothing is happening to it. But you are actually looking at a slow slow-motion picture. The changes may not be noticeable in ten years or a hundred, but changes are taking place just the same.

A shallow lake may be filling up with silt washed into it from eroding hillsides. Grasses and sedges get a chance to move out from the old shoreline. In decaying they build up the soil. Rushes and cattails take hold. They, in turn, prepare the soil for field grasses and various weeds. Low bushes may get a start—then taller bushes and small trees. Eventually the soil may be suitable for larger trees. These, in the end, may grow into a stand of magnificent trees in what is called a climax forest. Provided, of course, that the climate is right and that nature has had her own way with the spot. For man, in 1 day, can undo what has taken nature hundreds or even thousands of years to create.

Keep these changes in mind as you take imaginary hikes into the environments on the pages that follow.

A lake, over hundreds or even thousands of years, may fill up and turn into climax forest.

Succession of plant life as a lake turns into forest. From left: Lake with submerged plants; grasses and sedges; rushes and cattails; weeds; shrubs; small trees; large trees.

BROADLEAF WOODLANDS. For real Scouting enjoyment, we "take to the woods." In the East, those woods are made up mostly of broadleaf hardwood trees. They thrive because the soil, the rainfall, and the moderate year-round temperatures suit them. In the Northeast the winters are more severe. There evergreen trees mix with the hardwoods. In the humid South, sandy soils, fires, and cattle grazing may keep down the hardwoods. There pines take over.

You'll have plenty of excitement hiking through a broadleaf forest any time of the year.

In the spring, flowers of many colors cover the forest floor. Dogwood trees put on their white display. Redbuds open their pink flowers. Spicebushes turn yellow. Within a couple of weeks you walk through the forest under a green roof.

In the summer the forest teems with wildlife. From afar comes the steady hammering of a woodpecker. You hear the scolding of a blue jay, the cawing of a crow. A deer breaks through the underbrush. A gray squirrel jumps from branch to branch overhead.

It is along the forest edge that you'll see most of the forest's birdlife. Red-eyed vireos and redstarts, tanagers and grosbeaks, veeries and wood thrushes and warblers play hide-and-seek in the tangle of wild grape and bittersweet.

With the coming of fall, the leaves of the broadleaf trees lose their green color. Birches and sassafras turn bright yellow. Sugar maples flame in yellow or orange, or in scarlet like the scarlet oak. Tupelo and dogwood turn red. Beech and hickories take on all shades of brown. Then the leaves fall. And the trees stretch their naked branches toward the sky.

Main Broadleaf Areas of the U.S.A.

MAMMALS		
1	Gray squirrel	10 Common screech owl
2	White-tailed deer	11 Cooper's hawk
3	Raccoon	12 Scarlet tanager
4	Long-tailed weasel	13 Black-capped chickadee
5	Eastern chipmunk	14 Hairy woodpecker
6	White-footed mouse	15 Wood thrush
7	Shrew	16 Ruffed grouse
		17 Ovenbird

BIRDS
8 Red-eyed vireo
9 Blue jay

REPTILES
18 King snake
19 Box turtle

REPTILES
(continued)
20 Ringneck snake

AMPHIBIANS
21 Wood frog
22 Red eft

TREES AND SHRUBS
23 Sassafras
24 Gray birch
25 White ash

26 Dogwood
27 White pine
28 White oak
29 Spicebush
30 American beech
31 Viburnum
32 Shagbark hickory
33 Sugar maple
34 Rhododendron

PLANTS
35 Ferns

EVERGREEN WOODLANDS. Dense woodlands stretch along the border to Canada. In the East they poke an arm southward along the Appalachians. In the West they push an even broader arm down over the Rockies, still another deep into California. They cover half of Alaska. These woodlands are made up of trees with needle-shaped leaves: pine and spruce, fir and hemlock.

In the North these trees live through long, cold winters with lots of snow. In the Northwest they grow in weather that is cool and damp. But we have pines in the Southeast as well. There they thrive in the warm, humid climate. All these trees are green throughout the year. They shed some of their needles from time to time. But there are millions more to shed.

You stop beside a tall pine. Under it you notice a number of small, oval clumps. They are pellets spit out by an owl. You look up. The owl is sitting high in the tree. In another pine nearby a red squirrel is tearing a cone apart. In another a porcupine is sleeping.

Ahead of you the woods open up into a glade. Here you find a different kind of plant life. The trees may be birches or aspens. The ground cover will be ferns and low shrubs, blueberries and huckleberries. Here you will come upon most of the birdlife: kinglets and thrushes, juncos and finches, jays and chickadees.

The deeper you get into the northern and western woods, the better your chance to see our country's largest animals. High up in Maine you may surprise a black bear or a moose. In the West a mule deer or a black-tailed deer may force its way through the thicket. You may even see an elk.

Main Evergreen Woodland Areas of the U.S.A.

MAMMALS
1 Abert squirrel
2 Elk
3 Mule deer
4 Bobcat
5 Red squirrel
6 Fisher
7 Porcupine
8 Black bear
 (brown phase)

BIRDS
9 Northern goshawk
10 Golden eagle
11 Great horned owl
12 Steller's jay
13 Western tanager
14 Clark's nutcracker
15 Oregon junco

TREES
16 Lodgepole pine
17 Ponderosa pine
18 Douglas-fir
19 Quaking aspen
20 Englemann spruce
21 White fir

FIELDS AND PRAIRIES. In most parts of the country, you won't be many miles out of town before you see farms, fields, or prairie.

In the East, these open spaces were once great forests. If farming stopped, they would turn back into woodland. On the Great Plains, the areas were prairie. If they were no longer farmed, they would again become prairie. In parts of the Southwest, irrigation has turned desert into fields. If the water should stop flowing, desert would again take over. But there is no chance that these lands will ever return to what they were. America needs her farms to feed her ever-growing population.

The main plants of fields and prairies are wild or cultivated grasses. The animals are those that live in high grass or low shrubbery.

As you walk along a wheatfield or cornfield, you may see a meadow mouse scurry in among the stalks and disappear. Its worst enemy, a black racer snake, slithers in after it. A woodchuck scampers across your path. A chipmunk disappears in a stone pile. A cottontail runs off.

You follow the hedgerow between two fields. Lots of birdlife there: Different kinds of sparrows flit in and out. Towhees rustle up the dry leaves. Suddenly a pheasant takes flight.

If your hike is in the East, you may spot a red fox. On the Great Plains, coyotes may tune up for an evening concert. In the West, ground squirrels or prairie dogs may look at you from their holes.

You may even spy a pronghorn antelope in the distance. It takes off as it catches your scent.

Main Prairie Areas of the U.S.A.

FIELDS		11	Meadowlark
		12	Lark sparrow
MAMMALS			
1	Red fox	REPTILES AND AMPHIBIANS	
2	Cottontail	13	Leopard frog
3	Striped skunk	14	Garter snake
4	Meadow vole		
		TREES AND SHRUBS	
BIRDS		15	Cottonwood
5	Red-tailed hawk	16	Walnut
6	Barn swallow	17	Pin cherry
7	Ring-necked pheasant	18	Sumac
8	Common bobwhite	19	Apple
9	American crow	20	Multiflora rose
10	Eastern bluebird	21	Blackberry

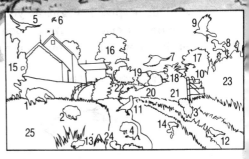

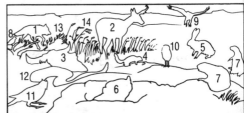

PLANTS
22 Wheat
23 Corn
24 Lichen
25 Pasture (grasses)

PRAIRIES

MAMMALS
1 Coyote
2 Pronghorn antelope
3 Bison skull
4 13-lined ground squirrel
5 Jackrabbit

6 Badger
7 Prairie dog

BIRDS
8 Lark bunting
9 Prairie falcon
10 Burrowing owl
11 Horned lark

REPTILES
12 Prairie rattlesnake

PLANTS
13 Sagebrush
14 Grama-grass

WETLANDS. Our main wetlands are marshes and swamps. Well, what's the difference? A marsh is a wet lowland overgrown with cattails, sedges, and many kinds of grasses. A swamp is wetland with shrubs and trees, such as cypress or tamarack. It is water that makes an area a marsh or swamp. The amount of water, soil, and climate decide what plants will grow there. The plants, in turn, decide the wildlife you'll see.

The marsh you explore today was probably once a lake or pond. The swamp may also have been a lake. Or it may have been woodland that got overflowed with water. Marsh and swamp are both in-between stages in the changing of nature. They may turn into dry fields someday. The natural process is slow. It is often speeded up by drainage.

Are you ready to go "bog trotting"? You may get your feet wet hiking along the edge of marsh or swamp. But you'll have lots of fun. In a northern or western marsh, you are almost certain to see ducks. Here are the nesting grounds of mallards, pintails, black ducks, teals, and others. In a swamp in the South, you'll come upon herons and egrets and other wading birds.

All around you birds are calling or singing. You hear the twitter of swallows, the warble of warblers, the quack of ducks, the gurgle of red-winged blackbirds. Maybe even the "pump" of the bittern, the "clack" of the rail.

As you walk along the water's edge, you'll hear the plop of frogs jumping in. The sleek brown body of a mink vanishes without a splash. Right at your feet you may come upon the remains of crayfish. A raccoon feasted there last night. And out in the water you may spot a swimming muskrat.

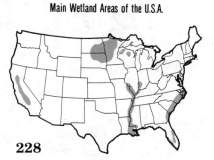

Main Wetland Areas of the U.S.A.

MAMMALS
1 Muskrat
2 Mink

BIRDS
3 Mallard
4 Northern harrier
5 Great blue heron
6 Red-winged blackbird
7 Black-crowned
   night heron
8 American coot
9 Bank swallow
10 Sora
11 American bittern
12 Pied-billed grebe
13 Common pintail
14 Green heron
15 King rail

REPTILES
16 Water snake
17 Cottonmouth
18 Snapping turtle
19 Painted turtle

228

AMPHIBIANS
20 Leopard frog
21 Bullfrog
22 Spring peeper

INSECTS
23 Damselfly
24 Dragonfly

TREES AND SHRUBS
25 Red maple
26 Poison sumac

27 Pussy willow
28 Black willow

PLANTS
29 Cattails
30 Arrowhead
31 Reeds
32 Spatterdock
33 Sedges
34 Rushes
35 Wild rice
36 Wild celery
37 Sundew
38 Pitcher plant

STREAMS AND LAKES. Our lakes and streams are like the veins and arteries in your body. They carry life-giving water through our land. Where water flows, plant life and wildlife abound.

If you hike along a gently flowing river, you may come upon a colony of beavers. Or you may catch sight of a muskrat or a mink. The reeds, sedges, and cattails that grow along the riverbank form a wet jungle. It is alive with birds.

Where the river runs into a lake, you have your best chance to study our diving ducks. Here you may see canvasbacks, redheads, scaups. An osprey soars overhead. A kingfisher takes a power dive into the water—and comes up with a fish in its bill. Look carefully along the water's edge. The ground may be crisscrossed by tracks of deer, raccoon, and opossum.

The large lakes of our northern states were formed during the ice age more than 2 million years ago. They will probably remain lakes until another ice age comes along. Shallow lakes may become marshes and fields. But other lakes are being formed. Numerous farm ponds are added each year. And the damming of rivers for electric power or flood control has created hundreds of new lakes.

A lake may seem peaceful and quiet. Not so. It is full of surging life. Water insects flit over the water. And your eyes may catch the flash of a fish below the surface. What kind will it be? It all depends. In a weedy lake, it may be a sunfish or a perch, a pickerel or a crappie. In a clear lake it may be a bass or a pike or a muskellunge. In a muddy pond or a slow-moving river it may be a catfish or a sucker. But if you want to see a trout you must look for it in a fast-moving stream.

Main Streams and Lakes of the U.S.A.

MAMMALS
1 Beaver
2 Raccoon

BIRDS
3 Tree swallow
4 Osprey
5 Belted kingfisher
6 Canada goose
7 Common loon

REPTILES
8 Ribbon snake
9 Painted turtle

AMPHIBIANS
10 Spotted newt
11 Bullfrog

FISH
12 Trout
13 Pickerel

FISH
(continued)

14 Crappie
15 Black bullhead
16 Yellow perch
17 Pumpkinseed
18 Largemouth bass

INSECTS
19 Mayfly
20 Dragonfly

TREES AND SHRUBS
21 Cottonwood
22 Alder
23 Tamarack

PLANTS
24 Pickerelweed
25 Pond lillies
26 Hornwort

SEASHORE. If you live near an ocean or a gulf, a hike may take you to the shore. There is plenty to see. That goes whether you walk along the rockbound coast of Maine or California, along the beaches of the east coast, or the flats of the Gulf.

The plant life is decided by the soil—or the lack of it—and by temperature and tide, wind and salty spray. Along a rocky coast you may walk through groves of storm-gnarled pines. Along sandy shores you may reach the water's edge through dunes held in place by beach grass.

Where the coast is rocky look for a tidal pool. This is a hole where some of the water was trapped when the tide went out. Count the number of periwinkles and other small snails. Search for tiny crabs, starfish, mussels, barnacles.

On a sandy beach watch for the tracks and holes of fiddler crabs or ghost crabs. Pick up shells of mussels, chitons, and whelks. Along a cool-water shore you may come upon the quaking masses of stranded jellyfish. Where the water is warm you may find the bloated balloons of Portuguese men-of-war. Sandpipers sweep down in flocks of a dozen or more. They run along the water's edge, thrust their bills into the sand, come up with tasty food bits. Terns skim over the water on long, pointed wings. Gulls settle down on the waves for a few moments of rest.

You may have the idea that the plant life of the sea is not important. You'll be wrong. Besides seaweed, the ocean is full of tiny plants. These plants—algae—are the main food of small water creatures and of tiny fish that are the food of larger fish which, in turn, are eaten by still larger ones.

Main Seashore Areas of the U.S.A.

MAMMALS
1 Porpoise
2 Deer mouse

BIRDS
3 Herring gull
4 Bald eagle
5 Common tern
6 Sandpiper

FISH
7 Skate egg case
8 Common mackerel

9 Bluefish
10 Porgy
11 Sand shark
12 Flounder

SEA CREATURES
13 Horseshoe crab
14 Left-handed whelk
15 Razor clam
16 Common starfish
17 Sand shrimp
18 Ghost crab
19 Scallop shell

SEA CREATURES
(continued)
20 Moon shell
21 Sand dollar
22 Fiddler crab
23 Hermit crab
24 Portuguese
   man-of-war
25 Soft-shell clam
26 Mole crab
27 Sea anemone
28 Limpets
29 Common mussels

30 Sea urchin
31 Oyster drill
32 Oyster
33 Rock barnacle
34 Blue crab
35 Periwinkle

PLANTS
36 Rockweed
37 Kelp
38 Sea lettuce
39 Blue-green algae

DESERTS. To most people, a desert is a desolate place with little beauty. They just haven't taken the time to look. Or they have picked the wrong season. Come into the deserts of Arizona or New Mexico or California in April or May when rain sweeps across the parched land. Then the desert blooms. Cactus and yucca open up their blossoms. The ground is covered with flowers so tiny that you must lie on your belly to see them.

There you have proof that water is the only thing needed to turn a desert into a garden spot. The soil of most of our deserts is rich in plant food. Where the soil can be watered, the desert becomes orchard or farm land. Citrus trees flourish toward the south. Fields of grain spread toward the north.

In the middle of the day a desert seems without life. Most animals and birds hide from the heat. A roadrunner may scurry over the sand. And you may see and pick up a horned toad—not a toad at all but a lizard. But don't pick up a Gila monster if you find one. It is our only poisonous lizard.

In the cool of the evening the desert comes alive. Desert mice, pack rats, kangaroo rats, and ground squirrels leave their burrows. They hustle about for plant and insect food. Diamond rattlers and sidewinders go hunting. The tiny elf owl flies out from its nest in a hollow cactus. Jackrabbits, spotted skunks, foxes, and coyotes go on the prowl.

By daybreak most of the animals seek shelter. But that is the time to see the desert's birdlife. Warblers and orioles sing from their perches. Woodpeckers hammer for insects. Flycatchers snap insects from the air. Thrashers peck for them in the sand.

Main Desert Areas of the U.S.A.

MAMMALS
1 Peccary
2 Spotted skunk
3 Kit fox
4 Yuma antelope squirrel
5 Black-tailed jackrabbit
6 Kangaroo rat

BIRDS
7 Gila woodpecker
8 Red-tailed hawk
9 Turkey vulture
10 White-winged dove
11 Elf owl
12 Road-runner
13 Gambel's quail
14 Cactus wren

REPTILES
15 Diamondback rattlesnake
16 Desert tortoise
17 Collared lizard
18 Gila monster

234

REPTILES
(continued)
19 Sidewinder
20 Zebra-tailed lizard
21 Garter snake
22 Horned toad

DESERT CREATURES
23 Centipede
24 Tarantula
25 Scorpion

TREES AND PLANTS
26 Saguaro cactus
27 Palo verde
28 Cholla cactus
29 Yucca
30 Barrel cactus
31 Ocotillo
32 Creosote bush
33 Mesquite
34 Staghorn cholla cactus
35 Prickly pear cactus
36 Beaver tail cactus

GARDENS AND PARKS. The first task of the early settlers arriving in the British colonies in North America was to create homes for themselves and their families. They cleared the woods for farming. They cut down trees to build their cabins. And as soon as they were well established they planted a garden to make their surroundings look like the homes they had left in the "old country." They created their own man-made environment of growing things. And as more and more settlers arrived and moved together in villages and towns, they set aside some of their acres as parks for the enjoyment and recreation of all.

The same tradition is with us today. Wherever people build houses for their families, they surround them with growing things: lawns, flowers, flowering shrubs, trees. Some of these plants are native American, transplanted from the wild. Others are imports from all over the world.

It is in spring and early summer that gardens and parks are most beautiful. The grass is luscious. The leaves of the broadleaf trees and the shoots of the evergreens are juicy-green. The flowering shrubs are in full bloom. The bracts of the dogwood flowers shine white against the green background. The brightly colored flower clusters of the lilac give off their sweet scent.

Where there are trees and sheltering underbrush you will find squirrels and chipmunks and rabbits. Birds will be busy feeding their young: woodpeckers and flickers with insect larvae from the bark of the trees, robins with earthworms from the lawn. A birdbath will bring in other birds. A small lily pond will attract frogs and toads.

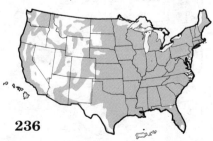

Populated Areas of the U.S.A.

MAMMALS
1 Chipmunk
2 Cottontail rabbit
3 Raccoon
4 Gray squirrel

BIRDS
5 Blue jay
6 Common flicker
7 Mourning dove
8 American robin
9 Downy woodpecker

REPTILE
10 Box turtle

AMPHIBIANS
11 Bullfrog
12 American toad

ANNELID
13 Earthworm

236

INSECTS
14 Dragonfly
15 Monarch butterfly

TREES AND SHRUBS
16 Scotch pine
17 Cedar
18 Hemlock
19 Blue spruce
20 Dogwood

21 Gray birch
22 Lilac
23 Sycamore
24 White oak
25 Blueberry
26 Blackberry

PLANTS
27 Cattail
28 Pond lily

CITY. A city is a man-made environment of stone and brick, steel and cement, aluminum and glass. Big buildings tower against the sky. Asphalt covers the ground. But even so, plants and animals have a way of moving in whenever they have a chance.

Wherever a building is razed, weeds soon take over the vacant lot: dandelions and ragweed, plantain and bindweed, and a dozen kinds of mosses. In dying, they form mulch that gives weed trees a chance to get started: ailanthus and locust first, then other trees that get along on poor soil.

Birdlife begins to flourish. House sparrows and domestic pigeons gone wild come to pick up seeds. Other birds try their luck, feeding on what is in the ground or on top of it: robins and starlings, house finches and blue jays. Chimney swifts pick insects from the air during the day. Nighthawks do it at night.

This kind of wildlife is of no harm to human beings. But when humans are careless, trouble starts. When garbage and trash are dumped in a vacant lot, unsavory creatures move in. In the beginning they may be insect pests: houseflies and cockroaches. But soon after, four-footed creatures appear. The first to come is the old-world house mouse. This is soon followed by the detested Norway rat. This rodent arrived in America as a stowaway on sailing ships many years ago. It now thrives throughout the country where it can find conditions filthy enough to suit it. It is a carrier of various diseases. A filthy vacant lot is not only an eyesore; it is a danger. That is why many Scout troops take on the task of cleaning up trashy vacant lots as Good Turns to their communities.

Main Big-City Areas of the U.S.A.

MAMMALS		
1	Gray squirrel	
2	House mouse	
3	Norway rat	

BIRDS		
4	House finch	
5	Chimney swift	
6	House sparrow	
7	Herring gull	
8	Common nighthawk	
9	European starling	
10	Blue jay	
11	American robin	
12	Pigeon	

INSECTS		
13	Clothes moth	
14	Mosquito	
15	Housefly	
16	Cockroach	
17	Ant	
18	Silverfish	

ARACHNID
19 Spider

CHILOPOD
20 Centipede

CRUSTACEAN
21 Pillbug

TREES
22 Ailanthus
23 Silver maple

24 Locust
25 Sycamore
26 Mulberry
27 Cedar

PLANTS
28 Ragweed
29 Moss
30 Privet
31 Grass
32 Dandelion
33 Plantain
34 Bindweed

You'll be astonished at the amount of animal and plant life you can find in a plot only 1 meter square. Use a magnifying glass to identify the species.

MINI-ENVIRONMENTS

The environments in which you have roamed as a Scout have been as vast as your eyes could measure. But there are small environments that are also worth your study.

PLOT OF GROUND. One of these mini-environments is in the ground right under your feet. Measure off a square plot with sides 1 meter long: 1 square meter of ground. (Or make it a plot 2 feet by 5 feet: 10 sq. ft.) Pick a plot with plenty of plants.

Now get down flat on your belly and check on what's there. Start with the plants. List the kinds you see. Then the living creatures: ants and other insects and whatever else you can find. Use a magnifying glass if you have one.

Then carefully remove the sod from an area two spade-widths square. Dig up the dirt and check it out for more living things. Put back the dirt and sod when you are through.

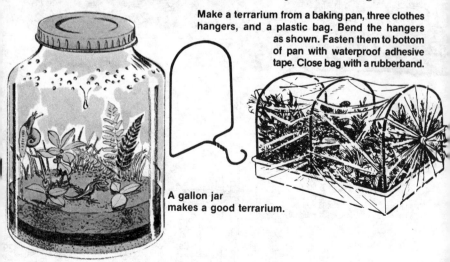

Make a terrarium from a baking pan, three clothes hangers, and a plastic bag. Bend the hangers as shown. Fasten them to bottom of pan with waterproof adhesive tape. Close bag with a rubberband.

A gallon jar makes a good terrarium.

TERRARIUM. You can continue your study of a mini-environment right in your own home, in a terrarium. The definition of a terrarium is "a fully enclosed container for the indoor cultivation of plants." By enclosing the plants, the moisture in the container stays the same. You need do no regular watering.

For a simple terrarium, use a gallon jar. Spread in it, in layers, 1 cup coarse gravel, 1 cup finely crushed charcoal, 3 cups topsoil. Insert some small rooted plants or sow some grass seed. Add ¼ cup water. Put in such animals as salamanders, land snails, crickets. Screw the lid on tight. Place the terrarium in a window but out of direct sunlight. Open as needed to feed the animals.

AQUARIUM. An aquarium, as the word tells you (*aqua* is Latin for water), is a watery mini-environment. For this you need a fishtank or bowl with a layer of clean sand on the bottom. Fill the tank with pond water. Anchor a couple of local aquatic plants in the sand. Then introduce a few water snails and a couple of minnows or other small fish.

If you can't get pond water, use tap water and let it stand a few days to lose its chlorine. And if you can't collect your own plants and fish, get them from a pet shop. Here you can also buy aquarium fish food. The main point in feeding is: Don't overfeed. Feed once a day and only enough to last the day.

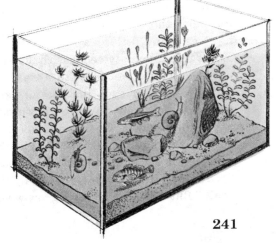

Most aquarists buy exotic fish for their aquaria. You will have more fun if you stick to native fish you have caught yourself. Shiners, minnows, darters, killifish, sunfish, sticklebacks, daces do well. Include a few snails. Snails are scavengers—they will keep your aquarium clean.

Study this picture carefully. Notice all signs and marks left by animals.

GET TO KNOW WILDLIFE

When hiking with your patrol, you breathe the fresh air, smell the good earth. Ahead stretches a whole day of adventure.

Now what kind of time will you have? It depends on how well you use your senses. It depends on how observant you are.

Some fellows get very little out of life. They have eyes for seeing. But they notice nothing. They have ears for hearing. But what they hear goes in one ear and out the other. They have as many little gray brain cells as you have. But their minds remain empty because they have no curiosity, no power of concentration, no ability to store what they learn.

Not you! Your eyes and ears are keen. Your mind is full of questions you want to have answered. You want to know all about the world in which you live. And you are not satisfied with finding out about the "What is it?" You want to know the "Why is it?" as well. Not just "What animal is that?" But also "Why does it live where it lives?" Not just "What tree is that?" But also "Why does it grow where it grows?"

Make a list of all the evidence you have found. Then turn to pages 246-47.

PRACTICE DOES IT. On a patrol hike there's nothing like a nature game to help you become observant.

Far and Near. Your patrol leader reads a list of 20 things worth looking and listening for, with a number of points for each, such as:

Barn swallow	2 points	Oriole's nest	10 points
Deer track	5 points	Squirrel	5 points
Garter snake	10 points	and so on	

The first Scout to observe one of these things reports to the patrol leader and scores the number of points decided on. The Scout with the largest score at the end of the hike wins.

Nature Hunt. Each Scout receives from the patrol leader a piece of paper listing some items he is to find, such as:

Cracked nut	Antler of deer	Owl pellet
Feather, 5 cm	Rabbit droppings	Groundhog hairs
Gnawed cone	Shed snakeskin	Moth cocoon

The Scout who finds most items within 1 hour wins.

SIGNS AND MARKS. In trying to know wildlife, it is not just a matter of seeing the animal. It is also a matter of discovering evidence of its presence: signs and marks it left behind.

Look for such evidence wherever you are. It ranges the whole way from a nest in a treetop and a branch gnawed by a beaver to the skin shed by a snake and a pinecone belabored by a squirrel.

OBSERVE AND REMEMBER. In all your outdoor pursuits, train yourself to observe and remember. Get into the habit of scanning the environment in which you find yourself. Sweep your eyes over it from left to right, from right to left, zigzag-style, from the tops of the trees to the ground at your feet. Observe details and try to remember them.

And get as much practice as possible in the skills of observing and remembering through games in your patrol, particularly variations of Kim's Game. Here is a sample:

Nature Kim's Game. Your patrol leader spreads out 20 animal signs and marks and covers them with a neckerchief. He uncovers them and gives you 1 minute to observe what is there. He covers the items again and gives you 2 minutes to write down the items you remember.

How good are you?

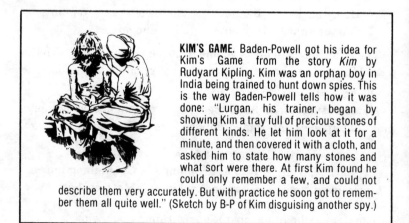

KIM'S GAME. Baden-Powell got his idea for Kim's Game from the story *Kim* by Rudyard Kipling. Kim was an orphan boy in India being trained to hunt down spies. This is the way Baden-Powell tells how it was done: "Lurgan, his trainer, began by showing Kim a tray full of precious stones of different kinds. He let him look at it for a minute, and then covered it with a cloth, and asked him to state how many stones and what sort were there. At first Kim found he could only remember a few, and could not describe them very accurately. But with practice he soon got to remember them all quite well." (Sketch by B-P of Kim disguising another spy.)

Nuts gnawed by squirrels

Feathers

Porcupine quills

Shed snake-skin

Pinecones eaten by squirrel, mouse, grosbeak

Chrysalis

Hazelnut chewed by mouse

Insect skin

Rabbit · Gray fox · Red fox · Deer
Droppings/Scat

Cocoon

Stick gnawed by rabbit

Branch gnawed by beaver

Dropped antler gnawed by mice

Abandoned birds' nests

Deer skull (antlers shed)

Study this picture. Check it against your list of things on pages 242-43.

Environment Kim's Game. Turn back to pages 242-43. Study the picture carefully for 2 minutes. Let your eyes go over it the way you let your teeth go over a corncob. Then put the book away. Write down every sign or mark you remember that showed animal life. Now compare your list with the picture above. How many things did you catch? NOTE: You can do the same with each of the environments on pages 222-39.

Signs-and-Marks Kim's Game. Open up to page 245. Follow the same procedure as for the Environment Kim's Game you just played. But spend only 1 minute looking. What's your score? Twelve would be good, 16 excellent, 20 incredible.

Make a mix of plaster of Paris. Turn a cardboard strip into a collar by notching the ends together. Place it around the track and pour in the mix. Let it harden. Remove it and brush off the dirt.

Now add to the list of marks and signs the names of the animals making them.

GETTING CLOSE TO WILDLIFE. On a hike you'll get a kick out of seeing a deer leap across your path or a raccoon scurry into the thicket. But wouldn't it be far more fun if you could get so close to the animal that you could see what it is doing, how it lives? Of course it would.

To do that you have to be quite an outdoorsman. You have to be familiar with trailing, tracking, and stalking skills.

Trailing is the ability to follow the beaten path made by an animal as it moves back and forth between shelter and feeding ground. It is also the ability to follow the trail marks made by one outdoorsman for another to show where he is going.

Tracking means to follow the marks—tracks and signs—of an animal as it roams through woods and across fields. It takes keen observation to see such marks and to follow them until you see the animal or hit upon its hiding place.

Stalking is one of the most American of all Scoutcraft skills. The early Indians and pioneers were expert stalkers. When you are good at stalking you can sneak up close enough to an animal to watch what it is doing without scaring it away.

247

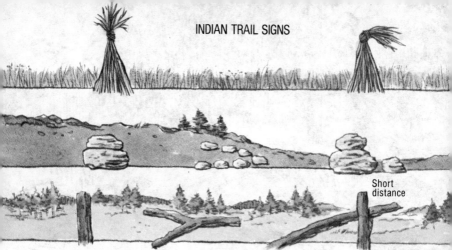

"This is the way."   "Turn right."

Trailing

There will be occasions on hikes and camping trips where part of the patrol is sent ahead to investigate a certain area or to find a good campsite. That's when you need to know how to make and read trail signs.

SCOUT TRAIL SIGNS. Scout trail signs are scratched in the ground with the point of a stick. Or you can shape them from pebbles or twigs. A small arrow means "This is the trail." An X is a warning placed where trails may cross, "This isn't the trail—don't go this way." A square with a number in it and with an arrow means "I've hidden a message in this direction, as many paces away as the number says." A circle with a dot in the middle tells you "This is the end of a trail," or "I have gone home."

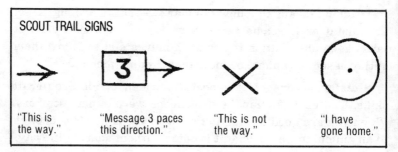

SCOUT TRAIL SIGNS

"This is the way."   "Message 3 paces this direction."   "This is not the way."   "I have gone home."

248

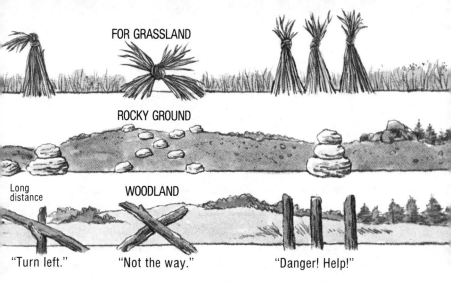

FOR GRASSLAND

ROCKY GROUND

Long distance | **WOODLAND**

"Turn left." | "Not the way." | "Danger! Help!"

When you follow a trail of trail signs, use your eyes and take it easy. Be sure that each sign is actually a sign and not one you are just imagining. If you think you have missed a sign, go back to the spot where you wiped out or undid the last one and start off again. Wiping out or undoing a sign is very important. Unless you do it you may confuse other patrols or even yourself the next time you hike through the same place.

INDIAN TRAIL SIGNS. When you have used the Scout trail signs for a while, you will probably want to learn to use Indian trail signs. The Indians made their signs by placing small stones in certain ways, by knotting grass into small tufts, or by pushing sticks into the ground. Study the illustrations on these pages and pick the trail signs that suit your patrol.

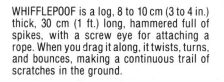

WHIFFLEPOOF is a log, 8 to 10 cm (3 to 4 in.) thick, 30 cm (1 ft.) long, hammered full of spikes, with a screw eye for attaching a rope. When you drag it along, it twists, turns, and bounces, making a continuous trail of scratches in the ground.

249

Tracking

If you happen to live in snow country, you will find tracks all around you in the wintertime. You can follow them easily. At other times of the year and in other parts of the country, you'll find lots of tracks at the edges of rivers and lakes.

FOLLOW A TRACK. To follow a track successfully, there are a few simple rules you should know:

- **Study a Single Track.** Before you set out to follow a track, fix the details of a single track in your mind. Measure the track. Make a simple sketch of it if you like. Then you can be sure that you are always following the right one, even when other tracks may be mixed in with it.
- **Track Into the Eye of the Sun.** If possible, track against the sun. Small details then show up much better by the shadows they cast. The tracks look deeper and sharper.
- **Look at the Track as a Whole.** As you follow the track, look up and ahead. Through grass a track looks like a streak because the bent grass reflects the light differently than the rest. On hard ground the track may show up by displaced pebbles, cracked twigs, turned-over leaves.
- **Imagine Yourself in the Place of the Animal.** If you lose the track at any time, say to yourself, "Where would I go from here if I were the animal?" Look in that direction. Then act according to your imagination.
- **Mark the Last Imprint.** If you have come to a dead end, mark the last imprint with a stick or with your handkerchief and cast around the marker—that is, walk around it in an ever-widening spiral until you find the track again.
- **Notice Important Landmarks as You Proceed.** Don't get lost when following tracks. Be alert to your surroundings. Notice and remember landmarks you pass that will guide you back to your starting point.

Careful now! Those last tracks look as if they are freshly made. The animal you are tracking may be just ahead of you. Stop, look, and listen! There it is! Now stalk up close to it!

Fore Fore

Fore

Fore Fore

Hind

Hind Hind

WOODCHUCK

MUSKRAT

OPOSSUM

Hind

Hind

Hind

RCUPINE BADGER SHEEP

MOUSE
(Meadow)

DEER

Fore Fore

Fore Fore

Fore

Fore

Hind

OTTONTAIL
ABBIT

Hind

OTTER

Hind

SQUIRREL

Hind

SKUNK

Hind

RACCOON

Fore Fore

Fore

Fore

Fore Fore

Hind Hind

DOG FOX

Hind

MINK

Hind

CAT

Hind

RAT

Hind

DEER MOUSE

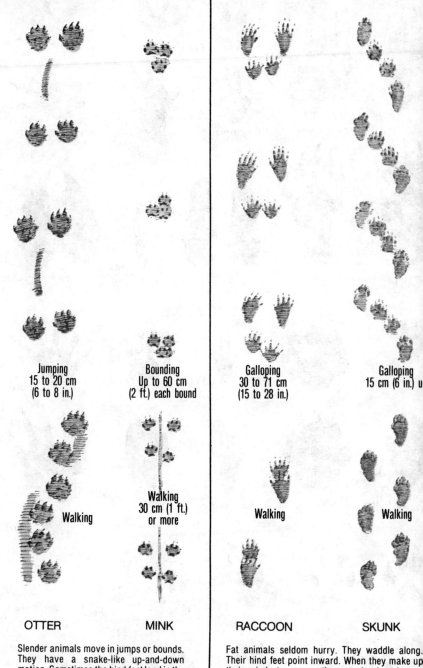

Jumping
15 to 20 cm
(6 to 8 in.)

Bounding
Up to 60 cm
(2 ft.) each bound

Galloping
30 to 71 cm
(15 to 28 in.)

Galloping
15 cm (6 in.) u

Walking

Walking
30 cm (1 ft.)
or more

Walking

Walking

OTTER

MINK

RACCOON

SKUNK

Slender animals move in jumps or bounds.
They have a snake-like up-and-down
motion. Sometimes the hind feet land in the
prints of the forefeet. In walking, they fall
behind. In running, they land in front.

Fat animals seldom hurry. They waddle along.
Their hind feet point inward. When they make up
their minds to scurry, they run in short jumps.
Forefeet and hind feet show in paired tracks. Close
prints make them easier to track.

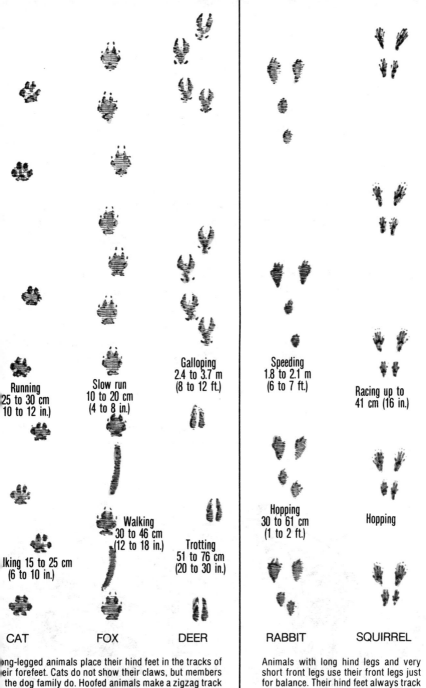

Galloping
2.4 to 3.7 m
(8 to 12 ft.)

Speeding
1.8 to 2.1 m
(6 to 7 ft.)

Running
25 to 30 cm
10 to 12 in.)

Slow run
10 to 20 cm
(4 to 8 in.)

Racing up to
41 cm (16 in.)

Walking
30 to 46 cm
(12 to 18 in.)

Hopping
30 to 61 cm
(1 to 2 ft.)

Hopping

lking 15 to 25 cm
(6 to 10 in.)

Trotting
51 to 76 cm
(20 to 30 in.)

CAT   FOX   DEER   RABBIT   SQUIRREL

ng-legged animals place their hind feet in the tracks of
eir forefeet. Cats do not show their claws, but members
the dog family do. Hoofed animals make a zigzag track
mething like the track of a fox or dog. Fox walking in
ow shows marks of its tail dragging.

Animals with long hind legs and very
short front legs use their front legs just
for balance. Their hind feet always track
ahead of their forefeet. Tracks will be
much closer in deep snow.

Stalking

There is adventure to stalking. It is also a wonderful physical-fitness conditioner. It takes plenty of muscle control to walk silently and to keep your body in perfect balance at all times. And it takes strength to move forward in the unaccustomed positions that stalking calls for. You will be using muscles you don't realize you have.

STALKING HINTS. Some animals have sharp eyesight—others are nearsighted: They see movement but not details. Most of them depend on their keen senses of smell and hearing for protection.

- **Stalk Against the Wind.** If an animal gets your scent or hears you, good-bye! Therefore, approach it carefully with the wind in your face. If you have discovered it from the wind side, make a half circle around it before you continue. To find the wind direction on a still day, wet a finger in your mouth and hold it up. The side toward the wind will feel cooler.
- **Move Slowly and Carefully.** A quick jerky motion is easily detected. Move silently as well. Watch where you place your feet—the cracking of a dry twig may sound like a pistol shot. Move ahead swiftly when wind rustles the leaves.

254

- **Have Your Body Under Complete Control.** If the animal detects you, "freeze" on the spot—that is, become absolutely motionless. If you keep perfectly still, the animal may look directly at you without noticing you. Did you ever see a cat "freeze" in front of a mousehole? That's the idea.
- **Choose the Right Background.** In Scout uniform you blend naturally into underbrush and grass. But against the sky you show up sharply. So keep low when crossing a ridge.
- **Make Good Use of Anything That Will Hide You.** Hide behind trees, stumps, bushes, rocks, and in large clumps of grass. Do not look out from the side of a tree. Get down low next to the trunk. Do not look over a rock. Look around it with your head close to the ground.
- **Use the Right Positions.** The way you hold yourself depends on how close you are to your quarry and the cover you have to hide behind. Far from your quarry, among trees and high shrubs, use an upright position. In low bushes, crouch and move ahead with knees bent and your body leaning from the hips. Closer to your prey, get into a cat creep—creep on hands and knees with back flat, and buttocks low. In low grass, worm along in a belly crawl—flat on the ground, push yourself forward by drawing up one leg, digging it in, straightening it out.

255

The closer you get to an animal in stalking,
the closer you must hug the ground.

Trailcraft Fun

The trailcraft of trailing, tracking, and stalking is not something you can learn by reading about it. You need practice—lots of it. And the best practice you can get is right in your own patrol. Here you can play games until you can trail and track your patrol pals with ease and stalk up to them without being heard or seen.

TRAILING GAMES. For these games you can use materials you find in the field. Or you can use equipment brought from home.

Hare and Hounds. One Scout is the "hare." He is sent ahead to lay a trail by Indian trail signs. Give the "hare" 10 minutes to get going. Then set out in pursuit to trail him down before he reaches his goal 1.5 km (or 1 mi.) away.

Hunting the Whifflepoof. One Scout is the "whiffler." He takes off, dragging along his pet animal, known as a "whifflepoof" (page 249). The patrol follows 5 minutes after. The whiffler must be trailed down before he reaches his goal.

TRACKING GAMES. Only expert trackers can track the actual footprints of a person through woods and across fields. To give the Scouts in the patrol a chance, you may have to make the track with tracking irons, or place marks and signs along the way.

Track the Tracker. Get someone to make a set of tracking irons for the patrol. One Scout puts on the tracking irons and

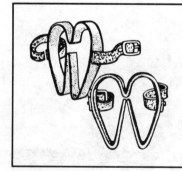

In the 1910 *Official Handbook,* Ernest Thompson Seton showed how "iron hoofmarks," screwed onto the sole of boots could be used to imitate deer tracks. Baden-Powell improved on the idea by suggesting "tracking irons" made of hoop iron and attached to the shoes with leather straps. They became a popular Boy Scout Supply Service item.

takes off, trying to make the kind of trail a deer might make through the woods. The rest of the patrol follows him 5 minutes later. At his destination the deer takes up the position as the "deer" of the Deer Stalking game.

Wounded Spy. The "spy" has a 1-minute start. He drops a few drops of "blood" (corn sprayed with red paint) every few steps. He must cross the "border" (a brook or road) 1.5 km (or 1 mi.) away before the "FBI men" (the rest of you) catch him.

STALKING GAMES. You don't need much space for these. They can be played where you stop for lunch on a hike or in a backyard.

Sleeping Pirate. A blindfolded "pirate" sits on a log with his "treasure" (an empty matchbox) at his feet. The others form a circle around him about 30 m (100 ft.) away. The idea is to stalk up to the pirate, take the box, and return without being heard. If the pirate hears you, he claps his hands and points. If he points at you, you're out. The successful stalker becomes the next pirate.

Deer Stalking. The "deer" stands in a forest or a field. The others walk away from him 60 m (200 ft.) in different directions. Here they fall down flat. On a whistle signal, they stalk toward the deer. They use whatever cover is available. When the deer sees a Scout he points and yells to him to stand. The Scout who comes closest without being seen is the next deer.

Wary Wolf. One Scout is the "wary wolf." The others stand in a line 60 m (200 ft.) from him. Whenever the wolf turns his back, they stalk toward him. Whenever he turns quickly, everyone "freezes." Any Scout making the slightest move goes back to the starting line to begin again. First Scout to touch the "wolf" wins. He is the next wolf.

In stalking, practice hiding behind trees and rocks. To look out from behind a tree, get down low next to the trunk. To look from behind a rock, keep head close to the ground.

OUR AMERICAN MAMMALS

You may be a pretty smart outdoorsman. But did you ever stalk up close enough to watch one of the furry, four-legged, warm-blooded creatures we call mammals? Brother, that's a trick that takes patience and skill.

The best first step for learning to stalk mammals is to find out what kinds are found where you live. Read about them. Check up on their habits. Then, when you're hiking, you'll know where and when to look for them.

SOME EASY ONES. Start stalking some of the easy ones.

Sometime on a hike when you pass a stone pile or an old log, you may catch a glimpse of a couple of chipmunks—long, slender brown bodies with black and buff stripes. Stand perfectly still. As soon as the chipmunks get used to you, they'll go about filling their cheek pouches with food.

Do you have oaks or hickories around camp? Then you'll find gray squirrels around, too. Among hemlocks and pines the red squirrel, or chickaree, is most common. "Freeze" and kiss the back of your hand with a squeaky smack. A curious squirrel may come up so close that you can almost touch it.

In an open field what looks like a stone may suddenly move. The "stone" is a woodchuck. It scampers off and pours itself into its hole. Move close and flatten yourself to the ground. Some minutes go by. A head peers up cautiously. Then the whole, chunky body comes out.

While hiking, you can't help scaring up a rabbit from time to time, especially at dusk. It jumps up as if it wants to run in all directions at once. Because of this confusion, you often see dead rabbits on highways, killed by automobiles.

The same fate overtakes many a skunk. Not because it is scared, but because it can't be bothered moving out of the way.

SOME HARDER ONES. A red flash among the bushes gives you your greatest stalking challenge: Mr. Fox is on the warpath! With some luck you may come upon a fox's "earth," the burrow under a tree or a rock where it lives. You have some

INSECT AND PLANT EATERS ▶

Mole

Shrew

Meadow
mouse

White-footed
field mouse

Flying squirrel

Squirrel

Chipmunk

Woodchuck

Beaver

Opossum

Rabbit

Porcupine

Muskrat

watchful waiting before you! Eventually papa comes along, a rabbit in his teeth. The pups come rushing out, yapping for food.

Someday a couple of deer may bound before you, tails bobbing like flags in the breeze. Freeze instantly. The deer stop and look around. A moment later they graze peacefully, and you can stalk nearer.

On an evening hike along a lake or river you may see a nose parting the surface of the water like the wake of a canoe. It's a muskrat. You follow it with your eyes toward a round-topped hut of rushes stuck together with mud.

If luck is with you, you may have the rare chance to find an "otter slide." Here you will see the funniest sight of the animal world. The otters run to the top of the bank, then "toboggan" down on their bellies into the water.

Along the brook you discover tracks that look like small hands, clearly showing five fingers. Station yourself nearby and wait while dusk falls. A chunky creature, with a black mask across its eyes and a bushy, ringed tail, arrives and begins to fish for frogs and crayfish. A raccoon is having supper.

If there's a beaver dam near your camp you can spend an exciting evening there. Around the large, dome-shaped lodge all is quiet. But soon a single guard appears and swims back and forth. If you disturb it, it warns the rest with a loud whack of its broad tail on the water. If it feels the coast is clear, the other beavers come out to feed on bark, or to cut down trees.

PROWLERS OF THE NIGHT. A moonlight hike is interesting in itself. It is doubly so when you combine it with stalking, stopping regularly to listen to the sounds around you.

There may be a rustle in the leaves next to the path. Turn on your flashlight. There's a gray animal about the size of a cat, but looking like a large rat, with a long, naked tail: an opossum. Up and after it! As you head it off, it goes limp and turns over. Dead from a heart attack? No, sir! It is "playing 'possum." If you leave it on the ground and stand still next to it, it soon "revives" and scampers off.

Mink

kunk

Weasel

Raccoon

Otter

Badger

Spotted skunk

Something is moving overhead. You look up. Flying squirrels are playing among the trees. They run up one, then take off and land far away and farther down on another. They aren't actually flying. A wide fold of skin between their fore and hind feet acts as a parachute.

THROUGH THE WILDWOODS. So far, most of the animals we have talked about are found in all sections of our country. But in certain parts of it are mammals you won't see anywhere else.

In remote, wooded parts of our country you may come upon the fresh, flat-footed tracks of black bear. Generally the black bear is harmless. But a mother with cubs may become dangerous anytime. So keep your distance! If you are close enough to see them, you are too close. In fact, if you find bear tracks, go immediately in the opposite direction.

Up in the north woods lives a queer animal. It may come right into your camp, snooping for food. It takes its time because it has little fear. It is well protected with a whole armory of stiff quills. You guessed it. It's the porcupine.

Also in really wild woodland you may come upon an animal that looks like an overgrown housecat. Its short tail, tufted ears, and spotted coat tell you it is a bobcat or bay lynx.

In pioneer days the gray wolf could be found almost everywhere. Today it is almost extinct in the United States. So you aren't likely to see any. And look as you may, you'll probably never see a cougar or mountain lion in the wild. Not only because it is scarce, but because it knows how to hide.

Far up in the north in the big woods, near the Canadian border, moose still roam. You may see them at dusk on the shore or swimming as you paddle your canoe over a quiet lake. You may attract their attention if you can imitate their grunt using a birch bark "trumpet."

MAMMALS OF PLAINS AND DESERTS. If you happen to live on our Great Plains, you'll know the jackrabbit. It is related to the cottontail, but has larger ears, longer hind legs. It looks funny when it runs. After a few long jumps, it leaps

LARGE MEAT EATERS

Mountain lion

Lynx

Bobcat

Grizzly

Black bear

Gray fox

Red fox

Coyote

Wolf

straight up in the air, then speeds off again with more flat jumps.

The jackrabbit has plenty of reason to be scared. A coyote (pronounced ki'-ote) may be on its trail. You'll know you're in coyote country; you will hear them barking in the night.

The West gives you the opportunity to study burrowing mammals. Here you will find whole "towns" of burrowers with hundreds, or thousands, of inhabitants.

Prairie dogs live that way. When you approach a "town" you see sentinels sitting up on their hind legs, guarding the feeding "dogs." When they notice you, they give off a piercing whistle of alarm. Immediately there is a scuffle for the holes. Now "freeze." Soon the prairie dogs come out again.

IN THE WILDS OF THE ROCKIES. In the Rocky Mountains you may come upon the wapiti, or American elk. Next to the moose it is our largest member of the deer family. You will be thrilled when you see a wapiti bull with its widely branching antlers. The antlers are dropped every year and grow out again in about 4 months.

The pronghorn or American antelope roams the plains in the Rocky Mountains region. It is our speediest animal. When it dashes along in the sun, a racehorse can barely keep pace with it. You'll have no trouble recognizing it when you see its white rump patch flashing.

The mule deer is a native of the foothills of the Rockies. You will know it by its large ears, the two Y-shaped forks in each horn, and the black-tipped, white tail. The Columbian black-tailed deer lives in the forest along the Pacific coast. Its tail is black on the upper surface.

As you climb up and up in the mountains you may see the Rocky Mountain sheep or bighorn. Or you may catch sight of the Rocky Mountain goat. It can scale mountain walls where hardly a ledge can be seen. When posed against the snow, the mountain goat is almost invisible in its shaggy white coat. But against a dark mountainside it stands out clearly.

HOOFED MAMMALS

Mule deer

White-tailed deer

Black-tailed deer

Elk

Moose

Caribou

Bighorn

Pronghorn

Mountain goat

WINGED FRIENDS

Some summer morning while camping with your patrol you wake up before the rest. You are just about ready to turn over for another snooze when you catch the notes of a bird song. You can't identify the singer. Just as you think it must be a warbler, it breaks into a robin's "cheerily." Then it interrupts itself with a loud "meow." It's a catbird entertaining you.

From the distance comes the buzzing "chip-chip-chip" of a chipping sparrow and the unsure warble of a bluebird. Suddenly you hear a gay, rollicking song. The tiny singer, a wren, sits perched on a branch before your tent. You listen for a while. The bird songs are getting you. You slip out of your blankets, get into your clothes.

You step out of your tent. It's early. The sun is just coming up, and there is still dew on the grass. You look around. The lake is calling you. You set out on the trail.

As you reach the lakeshore, you see a few birds running around on thin legs, looking for food. Their spotted breasts give them away as spotted sandpipers.

Bank swallows skim over the water catching insects in

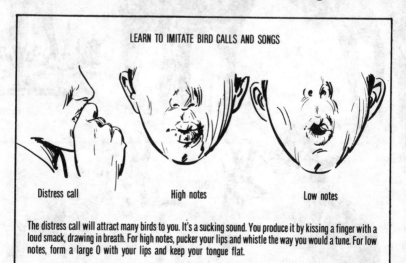

LEARN TO IMITATE BIRD CALLS AND SONGS

Distress call   High notes   Low notes

The distress call will attract many birds to you. It's a sucking sound. You produce it by kissing a finger with a loud smack, drawing in breath. For high notes, pucker your lips and whistle the way you would a tune. For low notes, form a large O with your lips and keep your tongue flat.

Bobolink

Yellow-headed
blackbird

Belted kingfisher

Black
tern

Killdeer

Spotted
sandpiper

Sora

Common
snipe

Wood
duck

Blue-winged
teal

Least
bittern

Mallard

American
bittern

Black-crowned
night heron

Pied-billed
grebe

Common
loon

American
coot

their graceful flight. From the other side of the lake comes a familiar "quack-quack." You can just make out the green, white, and maroon of the male mallard and the brown of its mate.

Something has disturbed the birds swimming near the shore. Some of them, gray with blackish heads and white bills, take off after pattering their lobed feet on the surface of the water. Those are the coots or mud hens. The others, larger, black-and-white-checkered, dive under and come up farther out. They are loons, renowned as expert divers.

As you sit down quietly at the water's edge, a yellow warbler settles in the willows to sing you its song of "sweet, sweet, sweet."

A belted kingfisher in its bluish-gray coat takes off from the branch above you. It plunges headfirst in a high dive and comes up with a small fish wiggling in its bill.

The sun is mounting in the sky. Time has flown. You rush back to camp. You find the patrol cooks of the day busily at work and the rest of the patrol popping out of their tents.

As you tell about your expedition, the chances are that someone will say, "Let's all go tomorrow." So it's a bird hike for the whole patrol.

YOUR PATROL'S BIRD HIKE. The best time for a bird hike is early morning, soon after sunrise, before the sun gets too hot. Dress warmly, for mornings are often cool.

Bring along notebook and pencil, and if you have them, field glasses.

Each Scout must know how to move quietly and softly, without jerky motions, and keep his eyes and ears wide open. When you see a bird, "freeze" on the spot and watch it carefully. Bring your field glasses up to your eyes with a long, slow motion.

As far as possible, stalk with the sun at your back. The sun will then shine full on the birds in front of you and you will see the finest shadings of their colors. When the sun is in your face you see birds only as dark silhouettes.

Brown-headed cowbird

Common grackle

Red-winged blackbird

Rose-breasted grosbeak

Downy woodpecker

Red-headed woodpecker

Wood thrush

Brown thrasher

Fox sparrow

American robin

Orchard oriole

Rufous-sided towhee (or chewink)

Baltimore oriole

Scarlet tanager

Northern cardinal

American goldfinch

Yellow warbler

Common yellowthroat

Prairie warbler

Eastern bluebird

Blue jay

Indigo bunting

RECOGNIZING THE BIRDS. You will have a much better time on your bird hike if you recognize the birds and know them by name. Six S's will help you in the identification:

Size. It is easy to see how important it is to notice size. A bird may be as tiny as a humming bird and as large as a great blue heron. A ruler won't help you. So estimate the size as compared to a bird you know: About as big as a house sparrow. Slightly smaller than a robin. Almost as large as a crow.

Shape. Some birds are long and slim. Others are short and plump. Some have long legs, others short. The tail may be long or short, pointed or squared or forked. The bill may be thin or thick or broad. The head may be rounded or crested.

Shadings. The general color may tell you what it is. Black may be a crow. Blue could be an indigo bunting. Red might be a scarlet tanager. But many birds can be told apart only by the distinct shadings of their field marks. A gray bird smaller than a robin may be one of several; a black cap identifies it as a catbird, a white band across the tip of its tail as a kingbird.

Song. Very often the first you will know of a bird's presence is its song or call. The cowbird squeaks like a rusty hinge. The chickadee sings its name. You may wonder about a dull-colored, sparrow-size bird. An insect-like buzz will tell you it's a grasshopper sparrow. Quick chirps mean it's a chipping sparrow, and a melodious tune a song sparrow.

Sweep. Sweep stands for whatever movement a bird makes. How does it fly? Does it swoop and skim like a swallow? Does it soar like an eagle or bound up and down like a woodpecker? Does it walk like a starling or hop like a sparrow?

Surroundings. Some birds prefer open fields. Others like woods, still others marshland and lakes. Small birds haunting the shores of lakes or oceans are almost certainly sandpipers, snipes, plovers. Small brownish birds in the fields are members of the sparrow tribe.

Sometimes just one of the S's will tell you the story. But most often you have to add several together to identify your bird. Jot down notes and look it up in a good bird guidebook.

270   **BIRDS BY SIZES AND SHAPES**

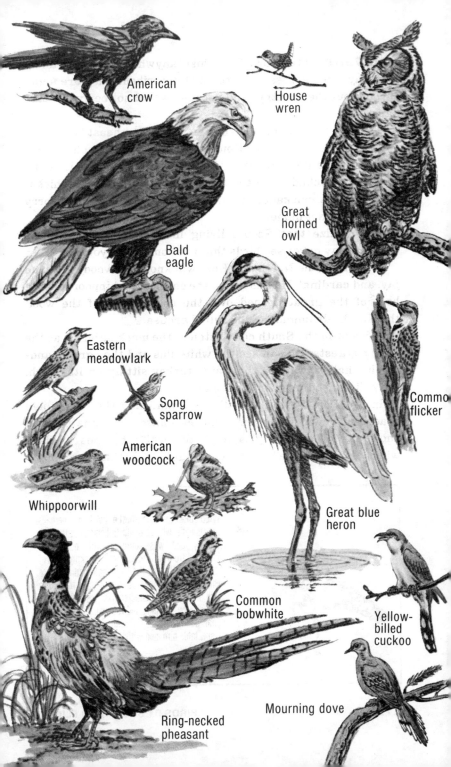

American crow

House wren

Great horned owl

Bald eagle

Eastern meadowlark

Song sparrow

Common flicker

American woodcock

Whippoorwill

Great blue heron

Common bobwhite

Yellow-billed cuckoo

Mourning dove

Ring-necked pheasant

OUR VAST AMERICA. On a hike anywhere in our country you may come across the birds just described. They are found throughout the country. And yet they would not be exactly the same.

The tiny black-capped bird seen in the Northeast is a black-capped chickadee. In the Southeast it's a Carolina chickadee. On the Plains it's a long-tailed chickadee. In the Rockies it's a mountain chickadee. In the Southwest it's a Mexican chickadee. Enjoy a chickadee when you see one. Let others worry about the exact name.

But realize that Scouts living in another section of the country may never see birds that are common to you.

A Scout of the North and East will know the woodcock, blue jay, and cardinal. He has heard the call of the whippoorwill, the hoot of the great horned owl, the organ song of the wood thrush, the drumming of the ruffed grouse.

A Scout in the South can "listen to the mockingbird," as the song suggests. He can see the white ibis and the egret standing in shallow waters, the water turkey sitting on its perch, the pelican gliding over the ocean.

In the Far West, the California quail and the long-tailed roadrunner will lead you a merry chase. The phainopepla shows its crest. Magpies flash the white patches of their wings. And the sage hen struts through its mating ceremony.

WILD TURKEY—our largest native bird—perhaps got its name when brought to England in the 16th century and was confused with guineafowl imported from Turkey. Benjamin Franklin wrote of it in 1784. "I wish the bald eagle had not been chosen as the representative of our country, he is a bird of bad moral character; like those among men who live by sharping and robbing, he is generally poor, and often lousy. The turkey is a much more respectable bird, and withal a true original native of America."

Osprey

Northern harrier

Cooper's hawk

Peregrine falcon

Turkey vulture

Red-tailed hawk

Swallow-tailed kite

Common nighthawk

Common tern

Chimney swift

Barn swallow

Herring gull

REPTILE FACTS

Reptiles are cold-blooded animals. Their temperature is the same as their surroundings. They all have lungs and breathe air, even those that spend most of their time in the water. Most of them are beneficial to man. The main diet of the smaller ones is snails, worms, insects, and their grubs. The larger ones go after rats, mice, and other rodents. Even the poisonous snakes rid fields and woods of rats and mice.

OUR POISONOUS SNAKES. Get to know the poisonous snakes first. We have four kinds in the United States. It is quite easy to tell them apart.

What makes them dangerous is the fact that they have glands in their heads that produce a strong poison. They can shoot this poison into the flesh of a victim through fangs that act like hypodermic needles.

Rattlesnakes are found in the lower 48 states. They vary in size from babies of about 20 cm (8 in.) to adults up to 2.5 m (around 8 ft.). You can't mistake them for other snakes. The tail is provided with a rattle: a horny, jointed structure. The buzz of this rattle is a warning signal—one it is best to heed!

The copperhead hangs out in rocky, wooded haunts in the eastern half of the country. It may grow to be 1.2 m (4 ft.) long. You can tell it by its copperish-brown color with hour-glass-shaped cross bands of a darker shade.

The cottonmouth or water moccasin lives in streams and marshes of the South. This chunky, muddy-brown snake may reach a length of 1.5 m (5 ft.). When angry, it raises its head and opens its mouth. The inside of the mouth is cotton-white.

The coral, or harlequin, snake is the fourth of our poisonous snakes. It ranges from Florida to North Carolina, the lower Mississippi valley, and Texas. It is a small, slender, and brilliantly colored snake. Bands of bright yellow separate broader black and coral-red bands. It spends most of the day underground. It comes out at night to find food. For that reason it is seldom seen.

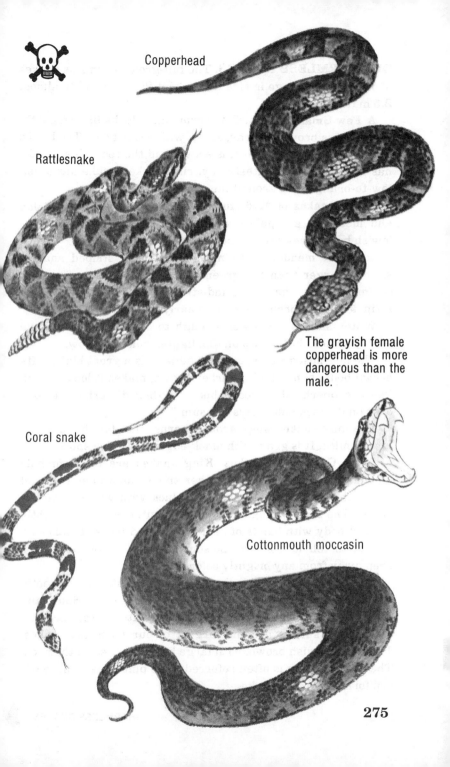

Copperhead

Rattlesnake

The grayish female copperhead is more dangerous than the male.

Coral snake

Cottonmouth moccasin

OUR HARMLESS SNAKES. The full-grown harmless snakes of our country range in size from about 20 cm (8 in.) to almost 2.5 m (around 8 ft.).

A Few Small Snakes. The worm snake looks like an earthworm but is brownish-gray, scaly, with a tiny head. The brown snake, as you can imagine, is brown and the red-bellied snake has a red belly. The steel-gray, ring-necked snake has a yellow-to-orange ring around the neck.

Some Snakes of Medium Size. The green snakes of fields and meadows are pale green above, with a whitish or yellowish belly. They grow to be 60 cm (2 ft.) long.

In moist meadows you may see several striped snakes, slightly larger than the green. The garter snake—our most common snake—has three indistinct stripes on its body. The stripes on the ribbon snake are clearly defined.

Water snakes swim well enough to catch fish. They have stocky bodies, dull-brown on top, lighter-colored below.

The hog-nosed snake, or "puff adder," is a great bluffer. Its brown body, banded with darker brown, makes it look enough like a copperhead to scare hikers. When disturbed, it rolls over on its back and "plays 'possum."

The milk snake hangs around barns—not for the milk but for the mice. It is gray, with black-edged brownish spots.

Some Good-Size Snakes. King snakes are the cannibals among our snakes. They eat other snakes as well as rats and mice. The common king snake is black with white or yellow bands. The scarlet king snake of the Southeast has a brightly colored body with bands of red, yellow, and black. It takes an expert to tell it from the poisonous coral snake. So, better keep away from any brightly colored snake.

The black racer or blacksnake of the East has a smooth, black upper surface. The brownish coachwhip of the South and the striped whipsnakes of the West are related to the racers.

The bull snakes are the largest of our harmless snakes. They are grayish brown, with large black patches on the back. The eastern form is often referred to as pine snake, the western form as gopher snake.

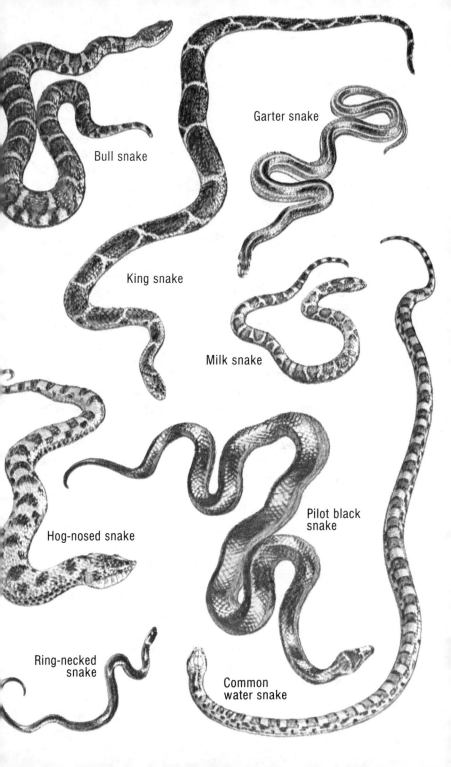

Bull snake

Garter snake

King snake

Milk snake

Hog-nosed snake

Pilot black snake

Ring-necked snake

Common water snake

LIZARDS. You may have heard of the horned toad of our American deserts. It is plenty horned, but it isn't a toad! It is a lizard and should really be called horned lizard.

Lizards may almost be considered snakes with legs. You can tell a lizard by its movable eyelids. No snake has those.

A couple of our lizards live in the northern part of the country. They are the grayish-brown, rough-scaled fence lizard and the striped, smooth-scaled skinks.

Most lizards live in dry, hot desert lands. Here you will find the desert lizards, collared lizards, and swifts, all with long, slender tails. You can't confuse them with the fat, sluggish Gila (pronounced "heela") monster. It is covered with black and pink warts. They look like "beadwork." The Gila monster is our only poisonous lizard.

Lizards make interesting pets. You can install them in a terrarium and feed them mealworms, earthworms, and flies.

TORTOISES, TERRAPINS, TURTLES. Turtles may be considered in three groups: Those that live on dry land as tortoises; those of ponds, streams, and marshes as terrapins; those designed for life in the water with flippers for legs, as turtles.

Our largest tortoise is the gopher tortoise of the Southwest. It may weigh up to 7 kg (about 15 lb.). The one you see more often in northern woods and fields is the box tortoise or box turtle. When you disturb it, it pulls in its head, legs, and tail and closes up its shell.

The famous dish "Maryland terrapin" is made from the diamondback terrapin. It lives in the brackish waters of the Atlantic and Gulf coasts. Almost as good for stew or for soup is the snapping turtle. It is a ferocious creature found in lakes and ponds. Here, too, you may look for the much smaller painted and spotted turtles. Their shells are smooth. The shell of the wood turtle is rough.

The wood turtle may well go into a stew pot, too, but don't use the musk turtle or stinkpot. It gives off a musky smell that is enough to discourage any hungry soul.

278   OTHER REPTILES

Wood turtle

Snapping turtle

nted turtle

Spotted turtle

Box turtle

Diamondback
terrapin

Musk turtle

Swift

Gopher tortoise

Horned toad

Collared lizard

Gila monster

A FEW AMPHIBIANS

Some summer evening when you are out hiking, pay special attention to the sounds of the night. There is a humming chorus all around you. Crickets chirp. Katydids sing. From the lake comes a steady "banjo" tune. Suddenly a booming call breaks through all the other sounds. "Jug-o-rum" it goes. The bullfrog, our best-known amphibian, is croaking his serenade.

Amphibians are creatures that spend part of their life in water, part of it on land. Most of them lay their eggs in water. Frogs and toads start life in the water as tailed tadpoles.

FROGS AND TOADS. Adult frogs and toads are tailless. Frogs have moist bodies with smooth skin. Toads have dry warted skin.

The drab-green bullfrog is our largest frog. The leopard frog is our most common. It is green, with brown rounded spots with light borders. The pickerel frog looks like the leopard but has yellow or orange hind legs. The green frog is the banjo player of the lake. The reddish-brown wood frog is common in damp woods. In the West you will find the brightly colored red-legged and yellow-legged frogs.

The common tree frog has sticky pads on his toes. It can hang onto branches and leaves. So can the spring peepers that fill the early spring days with their high-pitched singing.

Of the fat, sluggish toads the best known are the American toad and the Fowler's toad. They are both squatty and warty.

SALAMANDERS. Salamanders do not lose their tails when they grow up. And, unlike the scaled lizards, they have a smooth, naked skin.

The most common salamander is the newt. When it lives in the water it is olive-green. When it lives on the land it turns bright orange-red. The spotted salamander is black with two rows of yellow spots. The tiger salamander has yellow spots.

Most salamanders are very small, but the mud puppy of the East and Midwest gets to be 30 cm (12 in.) long. The ugly hellbender of the East and South is twice as big.

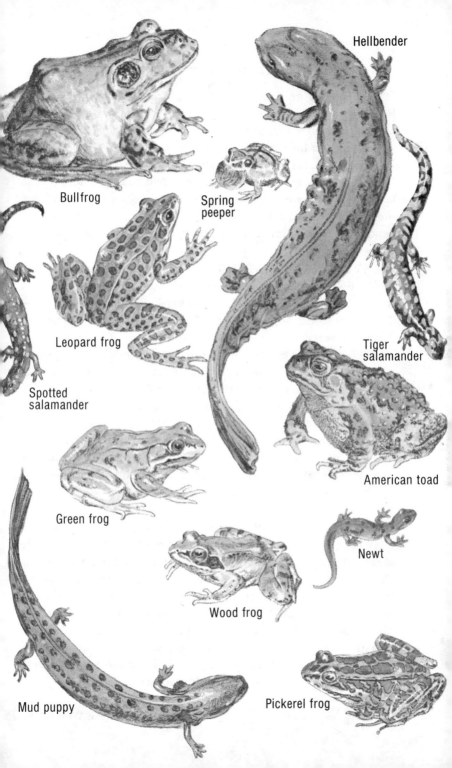

Bullfrog

Spring peeper

Hellbender

Leopard frog

Spotted salamander

Tiger salamander

American toad

Green frog

Newt

Wood frog

Mud puppy

Pickerel frog

LET'S GO FISHING

Do you like to go fishing? Do you like to sit at the edge of a lake with your homemade fishing rod? Do you get a kick out of seeing your cork signal that some sunfish or sucker has taken your dangling angleworm?

Or are you the ambitious type? Do you prefer to wade in a mountain stream? Do you get a thrill from casting a fly on the surface of the swirling water? Have you known the breathless moment when a dark shadow rises to your lure, grabs it and sends your reel spinning?

MANY KINDS OF FISHING. Still fishing is the simplest kind of fishing. For this you use a pole twice as long as you are tall, length of line, a float (cork), a sinker, and a couple of hooks. The angleworm will be your favorite bait. But a minnow, a grasshopper, a cricket, or a hellgrammite will do as well.

Once you have caught the fishing fever you'll probably want to get into more advanced fishing. Then you will need special rods, special lines and reels, hooks and lures. You will also need plenty of advice on picking the right tackle and using it correctly. That goes whether you take up spinning or bait casting, spin-casting or fly-fishing. Some of this advice you can get from the *Fishing* merit badge pamphlet. You can get even more advice from an old-timer who really knows his fishing.

IDENTIFYING YOUR FRESHWATER CATCH. It will be easy for you to recognize members of the trout family by their streamlined shape. Their markings tell what kind they are. The sides of the brook trout have red spots, often surrounded by rings of blue. The brown trout is also red-spotted, but has black spots as well. The fully grown rainbow trout has a sparkling rainbow stripe along its sides.

The green, blue, red, and common sunfish or pumpkinseed may weigh up to 0.5 kg (about 1 lb.). They are splendid panfish. So are their relatives, the bluegill and the crappie.

Muskellunge

Pickerel

Northern pike

Largemouth bass

Catfish

Walleyed pike

Rock bass

Brook trout

Yellow perch

Crappie

Bluegill
sunfish

The smallmouth and largemouth bass also belong to the sunfish family. They have greenish bodies and look almost alike. You tell them apart by the length of the lower jaw. The rock bass, another sunfish, is easy—it has red eyes.

The yellow perch of weedy lakes has green bands over a yellow body. The large, glassy eyes of the pikeperch has given it the nickname of walleye or walleyed pike. It is not a pike at all but a true perch.

The pikes are the wolves of the freshwater. It is hard to tell them apart. Among them, the muskellunge is grayish with darker blotches. The northern pike is greenish with yellow spots. The pickerel is greenish with a chainlike design.

You will know the bullhead catfish by its catlike whiskers and its lack of scales. And you can't mistake the sucker. It has a sucking mouth that opens downward.

IDENTIFYING SALTWATER FISH. It is not too difficult to identify freshwater fish. There are just a few hundred species in our rivers and lakes. It is different with saltwater fish. There are more than 4,000 different species in the waters around our country. Most of them are found far out at sea. But some of them can be caught close to shore, from piers or docks, or from a drifting boat. Some can be taken in the surf.

The striped bass—dark-striped up and down its silvery body—is a fisherman's joy. So is the channel bass or red bass which is not a bass at all. It belongs to the croaker family. So does the weakfish, which is not weak at all. It got its name from its tender mouth, easily torn by a hook.

The tiger-like stripes on its silvery body identify the mackerel. The dark bands around the body tell you that a fish is a sheepshead. Color distinguishes bluefish and blackfish.

These are only a few of our saltwater species. Books can be written—and have been—about the majestic salmon and the lowly eel, the vicious barracuda and the bright-colored dolphin. And many tales can be told of the giants of the two oceans that wash our shores: tuna and marlin, sailfish and swordfish, tarpon, and a hundred different sharks.

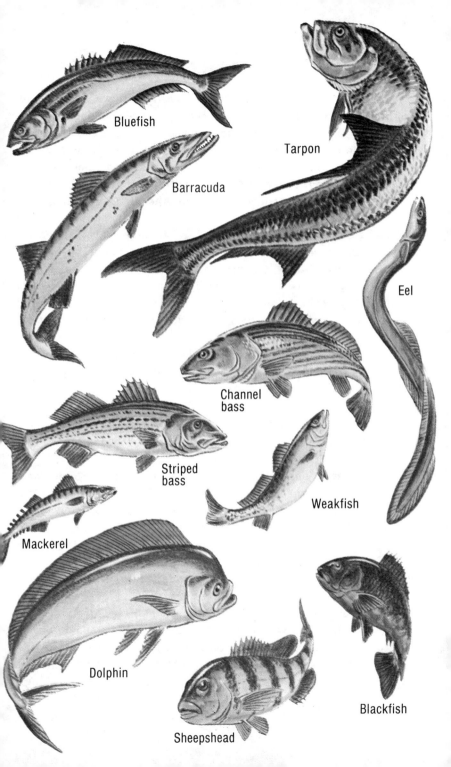

Bluefish

Tarpon

Barracuda

Eel

Channel
bass

Striped
bass

Weakfish

Mackerel

Dolphin

Blackfish

Sheepshead

THE SIX-LEGGERS

Squat down anywhere outdoors and look down and around. Soon you will see small, six-legged creatures moving about.

Six legs and three sections to their bodies are the way you tell the half-million kinds of insects on this earth. Spiders are sometimes mistaken for insects. But look at them closely. Notice their eight legs and bodies with two parts, and you can rule them out of the insect kingdom. And what a kingdom!

INSECTS RULE THE WORLD. Rattlesnakes are dangerous. Yet, more people are killed each year through the bites of some mosquitoes. Rodents destroy the farmers' fields. But they are not as bad as grasshoppers. Fire wastes acres of forests and thousands of houses. But that is nothing compared with the damage done by bark beetles, gypsy moths, termites.

Man spends millions of dollars every year to keep down the billions of dollars' worth of damage done by insects. The situation is not all bad, though. The help we get from many insects outweighs the harm the others do.

BUTTERFLIES AND MOTHS. Butterflies and moths are the most beautiful insects. They all have four broad wings that are covered with tiny scales.

How can you tell butterflies and moths apart? This way: Butterflies fly around in the daytime. Moths fly at night. Most butterflies at rest hold their wings straight up. Most moths keep theirs out flat or curled around their bodies. Butterflies have antennae or feelers on their head shaped like tiny clubs. Moths have thread-shaped or featherlike antennae.

Of the butterflies, the swallowtails will give you the greatest thrill. They have bright colors and "tailed" wings. But there are others worth following in their flight: The fritillaries have silver-spotted undersides and black-streaked orange tops. The purplish-black mourning cloaks are decorated with wide borders of yellow and rows of blue dots. The admirals are red-banded. The anglewings have "question mark" markings.

Cabbage butterfly

Common sulphur

Question mark

Viceroy

Tiger swallowtail

Red admiral

Monarch

Regal fritillary

Mourning cloak

Gypsy moth

Luna moth

White-lined sphinx

Io moth

Promethea moth

Cecropia moth

Even the white cabbage butterflies, and the bright yellow common sulphurs are worth knowing.

The monarch or milkweed butterflies are amazing for the way they travel. In the fall they migrate in large numbers, flying from Canada almost to the Gulf of Mexico. Birds do not like the taste of monarchs. This has benefited another butterfly, the viceroy, which looks much like the monarch.

ANTS, BEES, AND WASPS. If you are looking for wisdom rather than beauty, follow King Solomon's advice: "Go to the ant, thou sluggard; consider her ways, and be wise."

The ants have close relatives, the bees and the wasps. Some of them live together in large communities. They do many of the same things that man does.

Take carpentry, for example: The carpenter ants drill and cut holes in old wood. They build homes with many rooms. Dairying: Ants use aphids, tiny sucking insects, for cows. When stroked on the back, aphids make a sweet liquid which ants feed to their larvae. Gardening: Some ants prepare soil and raise a small fungus, like mushrooms. Sugarmaking: Did man ever produce sweeter sugar than the honeybee? Masonry: Mud daubers build nests of clay for their eggs and larvae. Papermaking: The hornet knew how to make paper from wood pulp long before man caught on to the trick.

BEETLES. Beetles, like bees and wasps, have four wings, but one pair only is used for flying. The other pair consists of two hard shells. They protect the body and the other wings when the insect is not flying.

Beetles are of many sizes. The giant stag beetle with its branching "horns" is 5 cm (2 in.) long. The tiny snout beetle is only 6 mm (¼ in.) long. But size has little to do with the damage, or good, that beetles do. The tiny ones are among the worst. Here we find the cotton boll weevil, the Colorado potato beetle, the cucumber beetles, and many others.

But beetles are some of our best helpers. The round lady beetle eats harmful insects in great masses. The burying beetle rids fields of dead things.

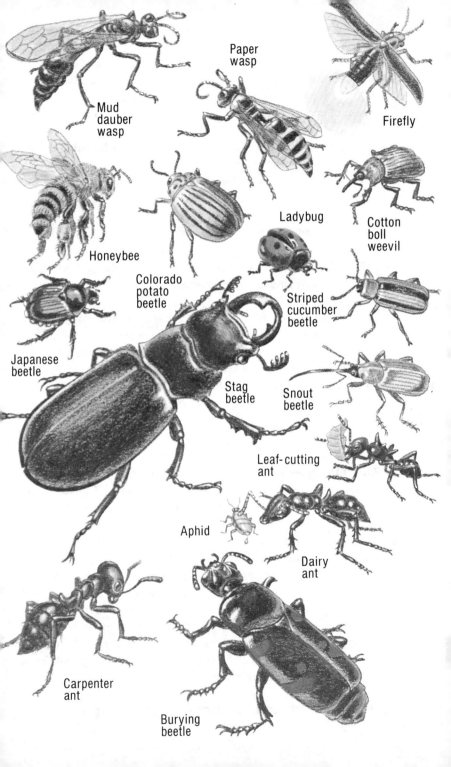

Mud dauber wasp

Paper wasp

Firefly

Honeybee

Colorado potato beetle

Ladybug

Cotton boll weevil

Japanese beetle

Striped cucumber beetle

Stag beetle

Snout beetle

Leaf-cutting ant

Aphid

Dairy ant

Carpenter ant

Burying beetle

Among beetles, don't overlook the amazing fireflies or lightning bugs. You have seen them on warm summer evenings. They are neither flies nor bugs. They have solved the problem of producing cold light. So far we can't copy them.

FLIES AND MOSQUITOES. The two-winged insects, the fly and mosquito, are the most dangerous to man.

Flies spread typhoid fever. Mosquitoes spread malaria and yellow fever. We can stop these diseases by controlling the carriers. We do this in their breeding grounds: flies in filth and garbage, mosquitoes in stagnant water.

GRASSHOPPERS AND THEIR RELATIVES. Do you like music? You will find most of the insect musicians among the grasshoppers, crickets, and katydids.

The grasshoppers fiddle along on warm summer days. They use their wing covers for violins, their hind legs for bows.

The katydid does its fiddling at night. It is a long-horned grasshopper that lives in trees. It makes music by rubbing its outer wings together. Only the males debate whether "Katy did" or "Katy didn't." Katy herself can't fiddle.

Of all the insect musicians the cicadas are the most powerful. They buzz from morning to night during the hot months.

BUGS. Many people call all insects "bugs." But true bugs form a definite group. Bugs have four wings. Two of these wings generally have a front part that is hard and the back part that is clear and thin. Besides, all true bugs have mouth parts made for sucking—unfortunately! Just ask someone who has had experience with bed bugs.

The aphids and the scale insects that suck sap out of plants and trees are true bugs. So are the stinkbugs you come across when you go berry picking. The chinch bugs eat corn and grain. Spittle bugs hide in their frothy spittle on weed stalks. The water striders, boatmen, and back swimmers of lakes and streams are bugs. So are the tiny tree hoppers that appear in an endless number of varieties.

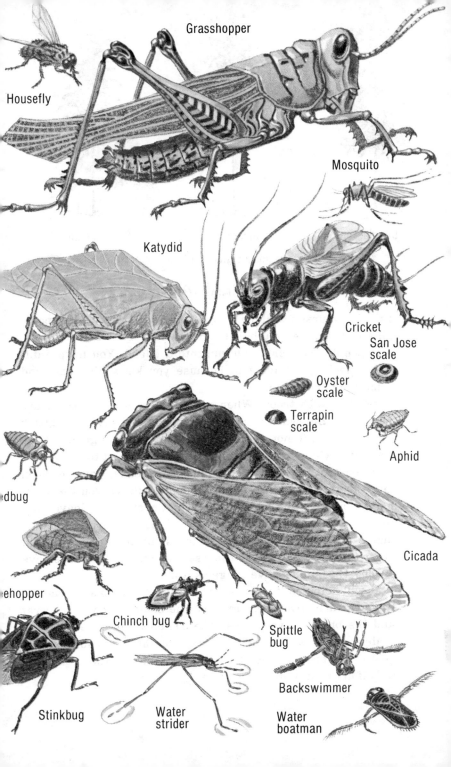

Housefly

Grasshopper

Mosquito

Katydid

Cricket

San Jose scale

Oyster scale

Terrapin scale

Aphid

dbug

ehopper

Cicada

Chinch bug

Spittle bug

Backswimmer

Stinkbug

Water strider

Water boatman

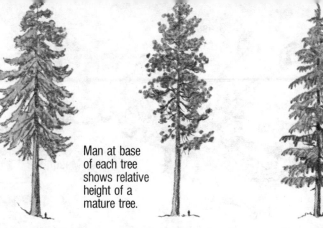

Man at base
of each tree
shows relative
height of a
mature tree.

Douglas fir   Ponderosa pine   Western hemlock

Our largest trees are the evergreens inland from the Pacific slope.

OUR AMERICAN TREES

Imagine yourself walking down Main Street. There are people all about you, yet you hardly notice them. They are all—well, just people. Suddenly you run into a friend. You have a different feeling toward him because you know his name and something about him.

So it is with trees. When you don't know them, trees are just trees. But when you can recognize, let's say, a shagbark hickory, you will notice shagbarks whenever you go on a hike. The same will be true with all other trees you get to know.

Some trees, like spruces, pines, and elms, you will soon learn to know by their shape. The bark will tell you the sycamores, birches, and beeches. You can't mistake the leaves of a tulip, sassafras, or holly. And you will have no trouble recognizing dogwood, magnolia, and locust by their flowers. Still other trees you can tell by their seeds or fruits. The oaks have acorns, the maples have winged keys.

It will help you if you remember that the trees are generally grouped in two large groups: the conifers (cone bearers) and the broad-leaved trees. The conifers have needlelike or scalelike leaves that usually stay on the trees for several years. The broad-leaved trees have flat leaves that generally fall off in the autumn.

292

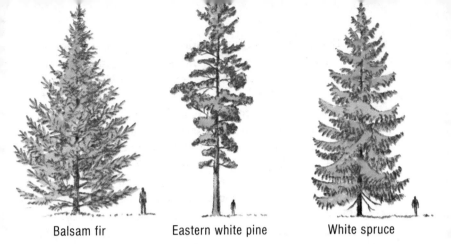

| Balsam fir | Eastern white pine | White spruce |

Most evergreen trees have the Christmas-tree look of an inverted cone.

GET TO KNOW YOUR LOCAL TREES. Now, to know the trees, you'll need a certain amount of memory, but an even greater amount of common sense.

We have more than 600 native trees in the United States. Some trees like it hot, others cool. Some like to have their roots wet, others dry. Your common sense will tell you they won't all be in your neighborhood, not even in your state.

So find out which trees are native to your section of the country. Get someone in the troop who knows his trees to show you the more important local ones. Learn to recognize a couple of dozen trees. If you do, you'll know most of the trees that you are apt to come across in your locality.

SOME IMPORTANT CONIFERS. The conifers are often referred to as "evergreens." They do not lose their needles—or scalelike leaves—when the weather turns cold.

The Pines. It is easy to recognize the pines. The mature trees have straight trunks, free of branches partway up. Higher up whorls of branches form open crowns.

To distinguish among the different pines, look at the needlelike leaves. They grow in small clusters, with five, three, or two needles to a cluster.

In the Northeast, the white pine is the only pine with five needles to a cluster. Pitch pine has three, jack and red pine two. In the Southeast, the longleaf and loblolly pines have three needles to a cluster, slash and shortleaf pines only two.

In the mountains of the West, you will find the most majestic of our pines. Here tower sugar pines, sometimes to a height of more than 60 m (200 ft.). This pine and the western pine have five needles to the cluster. Ponderosa, Jeffrey, and knobcone pines have three. Lodgepole pine has two.

Spruces and Firs. These are the common "Christmas trees." Spruce needles are four-sided. They sit singly all around the branch. Fir needles are flat. They seem to be arranged in two rows on the sides of the branch.

In the North and Northeast, spruces are the blue-green, soft-needled Engelmann and the silvery-blue, stiff-needled blue spruce. The Sitka spruce is our tallest American spruce.

The balsam fir of the East and the white fir of the West are stately, fragrant trees. The flat needles are dark green on top. The underside shows two white lines.

Tamarack or Larch. The soft needles, growing in tufts on old growth, fall off in winter. The cones are small.

Hemlocks. Eastern and western hemlocks are large trees. They have small cones and small, flat, round-tipped leaves.

The West has a giant tree related to the hemlocks. It is a botanical puzzle. It is called Douglas spruce, Douglas fir, red fir, Oregon pine. Yet it is neither spruce, fir, nor pine.

The Sequoias. In California you will find the largest and oldest trees of the world: the redwood and the big tree or giant sequoia. Some of the redwoods tower to a height of 105 m (350 ft.). Big trees reach a diameter of 7.5 m (about 25 ft.). Some of these trees are more than 4,000 years old!

Cedars, Junipers, and Cypresses. The leaves of the cedars are tiny, bright-green scales. They are arranged like small shingles on flattened twigs. An eastern cedar, the arborvitae, is much used in parks. Western red cedar is a lumber tree.

Red cedars are actually junipers. They have two kinds of leaves. Some are scaly and flat, others are awl-like and prickly. Their cones are berrylike and blue.

The bald cypress of the South gets "bald" in the winter. It drops its needles each year. Cypresses grow in low swamplands where they send up cone-shaped stumps called "knees."

Douglas fir

Red spruce

Giant
Sequoia

Rocky
Mountain
juniper

Pacific
yew

Eastern
red cedar

Bald
cypress

Eastern
white pine

Redwood

Tamarack

Eastern
hemlock

Balsam fir

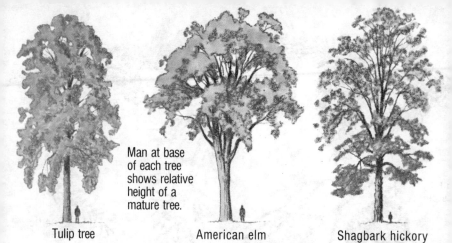

Man at base of each tree shows relative height of a mature tree.

Tulip tree   American elm   Shagbark hickory

Deciduous trees flourish in the temperate climate of the Northeast.

SOME BROAD-LEAVED TREES. Another term for these trees is deciduous—from *decidere*, to fall off. They lose their leaves in winter.

Willows and Poplars. The proper name of the "pussy willow" is glaucous willow. In the spring its straight branches bear furry, silvery catkins. The sandbar willow is one of the first plants to grow on new sand bars formed by shifting river banks.

The trembling of its leaves make the poplar, or aspen, easy to recognize from afar. It is caused by the wind shaking the long flat leaf stems. While the aspens are small trees with smooth bark, the cottonwood is large, with rough, furrowed bark.

Nut Trees. The walnuts and the hickories look pretty much alike. Their light foilage gives a feathery effect to the broad crowns. The walnuts have many (11 to 23) leaflets to each leaf. The hickories have fewer (3 to 9). The fleshy husk remains on the walnuts. The husk of the hickories opens up in four sections.

After the husk has rotted off, it is easy to crack butternuts, but very hard to crack the nuts of black walnuts.

The nuts of shagbark hickory and its relative, the pecan, are good eating. Mockernut, bitternut, and pignut have small and bitter kernels.

296

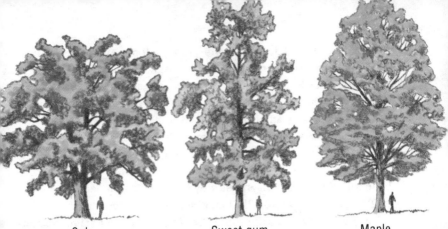

Oak   Sweet gum   Maple

Many broadleaf trees change from green to vivid colors in the fall.

The Birch Family. This family includes birches, hornbeams, and alders.

The Indians used the bark of the paper birch to build canoes. They called it "canoe birch." The outside layers of its bark peel off in papery "curls." So does the bark of yellow birch. The gray and the black birches have closely fitted bark.

The wood of the smooth-barked American hornbeam is so tough that the tree is often called ironwood.

Alders grow in moist ground throughout the country. They have broad leaves, stalked buds, and small, conelike fruits.

Beech and Chestnut. You can tell a beech tree by its smooth, pale gray bark. Its leaves have a strong mid-vein and parallel side veins. Its burlike fruit contains two triangular nuts.

The chestnut used to be an important eastern forest tree. But the chestnut blight killed off a great number of the trees. The chestnuts have burs with brown, edible nuts.

The Oaks. The wood of our native oaks has played a large part in American life. The ship *Old Ironsides* was built from oak. Hand-hewn oak beams were used in the houses of the colonists.

There are three groups of oaks:

WHITE OAKS have leaves with rounded lobes. Their sweet-kernel acorns mature in 1 year.

297

BLACK OAKS have bristle-pointed lobes on their leaves. Their acorns are bitter and take 2 years to mature.

LIVE OAKS keep their leaves for several years. If it weren't for their acorns, you wouldn't know that they are oaks. Their leaves have smooth edges without lobes.

Elms and Hackberry. The American and slippery elms have leaves that are egg-shaped, lopsided, and saw-toothed along the edges. Many of the magnificent old elms of the East have been killed by a fungus spread by the Dutch elm beetle.

The hackberry looks like an elm but has berrylike fruits.

Magnolias and Tulips. The best known of our native magnolias is the cucumber tree. Its fruit is a cone-shaped mass of many small "pods."

The trunks of tulip trees rise high in straight columns without a single side branch for a great distance. The grayish bark is deeply furrowed. In the spring it has tulip-shaped, greenish-yellow flowers.

Custard and Tea. The common pawpaw is a member of the custard apple family. The fruit looks like a short, chubby banana.

Tea made from the root bark of the sassafras tree is an old household remedy for colds. On the same tree you'll find some leaves that are oval and others that are shaped like mittens. Still others remind you of the trefoil of the Scout badge.

SMOKE PRINTS

Smear butter or petroleum jelly on a piece of cardboard. Smoke it up over a candle flame. Place leaf, vein side down, on the smoked cardboard. Place newspaper sheet over it. Rub to have veins pick up soot. Transfer smoked leaf to white paper. Cover with newspaper and rub.

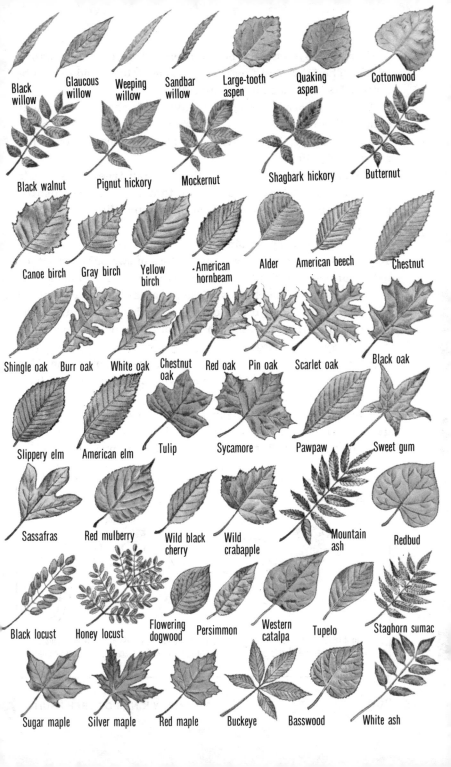

Black willow
Glaucous willow
Weeping willow
Sandbar willow
Large-tooth aspen
Quaking aspen
Cottonwood

Black walnut
Pignut hickory
Mockernut
Shagbark hickory
Butternut

Canoe birch
Gray birch
Yellow birch
American hornbeam
Alder
American beech
Chestnut

Shingle oak
Burr oak
White oak
Chestnut oak
Red oak
Pin oak
Scarlet oak
Black oak

Slippery elm
American elm
Tulip
Sycamore
Pawpaw
Sweet gum

Sassafras
Red mulberry
Wild black cherry
Wild crabapple
Mountain ash
Redbud

Black locust
Honey locust
Flowering dogwood
Persimmon
Western catalpa
Tupelo
Staghorn sumac

Sugar maple
Silver maple
Red maple
Buckeye
Basswood
White ash

Gum and Sycamore. The sweet gum tree has star-shaped leaves. The juice that flows from it dries into a good gum substitute. Its fruits look like spiny balls.

The sycamore has similar balls, but they are without spines. Even from afar you will know a sycamore by its bark. The trunk looks like a patchwork of large blotches of white, green, and yellow.

Plums and Cherries. If you find a small tree in the woods with shiny oval leaves and fruits that look like reddish or purple plums, you have found the wild plum. We have a dozen wild varieties.

Wild bird cherry or pin cherry are small trees with tiny, shiny, red cherries, singly or in clusters of two or three. Other wild cherries have fruits arranged in bunches like grapes.

The Maples. The leaves of the maples are arranged in pairs, opposite each other on the branch. Their main veins come out like fingers from the base of the leaf. The fruits are winged keys.

Buckeyes. The fruit gave the buckeyes their name. The large, shiny brown seed looks somewhat like the eye of a deer. The leaves have 5 to 7 leaflets.

The Ashes. Our American ashes have feathery crowns of dark green leaves. The leaves come in pairs, opposite to each other on the twigs. Each leaf is made up of many leaflets.

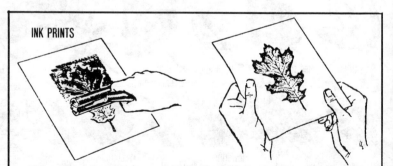

INK PRINTS

With a rubber roller, roll out a small dab of printer's ink on a glass plate. Ink underside of leaf. Place leaf, inked side down, on white paper. Cover with a piece of newspaper and run roller over it.

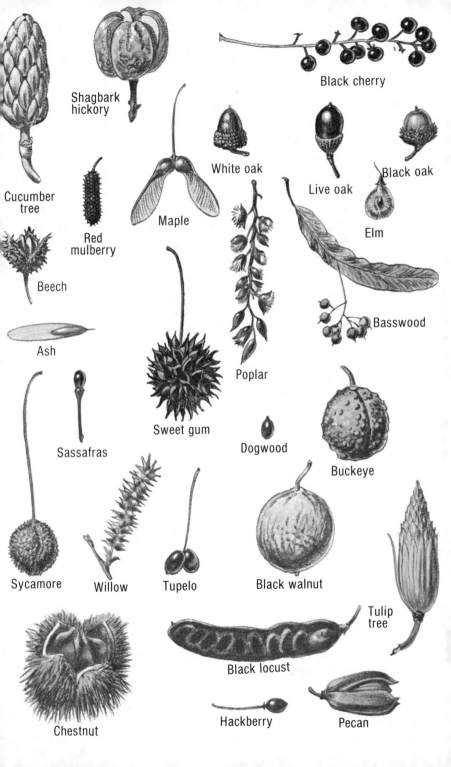

Shagbark hickory

Black cherry

Cucumber tree

White oak

Live oak

Black oak

Maple

Elm

Red mulberry

Beech

Basswood

Ash

Poplar

Sassafras

Sweet gum

Dogwood

Buckeye

Sycamore

Willow

Tupelo

Black walnut

Tulip tree

Chestnut

Black locust

Hackberry

Pecan

FLOWERS OF THE YEAR

One of the best things about a spring hike is seeing the first flowers of the year. You'll find them poking their heads through the dead leaves.

Jack-in-the-pulpit stands proudly erect with its three-part leaves. It hides tiny flowers under a striped hood. Hepatica bobs its pale lilac flowers, bloodroot opens its white crown. If you are lucky, you may come upon a moccasin flower swinging its pink "moccasin" high on a downy stem. Or you may see a wake-robin unfolding its three-leaved maroon flower.

You might wish to pass the ill-smelling skunk cabbage. Don't! Instead, stoop down. See how the leaves unfold from bright green cones. Study the colors of the leaf that surrounds the small flowers on the clublike stalk.

Then continue your hike. Keep your eyes open for rue anemone, spring beauty, trout lily, dutchman's breeches, wild columbine.

SPRING MARCHES NORTH. Now, what you see on your spring hike depends on where you live.

On a hike in Georgia, for instance, in early March, you will see the spring flowers that people around New York will not see until late in April. That's 6 or 7 weeks later. Along our ocean coasts, spring marches northward at the rate of about 20 km (13 mi.) a day. In the middle of our country spring moves faster once it gets started.

WHERE TO GO. In the early spring you will find most of the flowers in woods and marshes. But soon the trees are in full leaf. They form an almost solid ceiling that shades the underbrush. Then the time for finding flowers in the woods has passed. There will be only a few there: Boneset and baneberry reach high to get as much light as possible. Jewelweed shows its bright orange flowers along a forest brook.

At that time of the year the open fields come into their own. The early flowers of the fields are the dandelion, clover, and

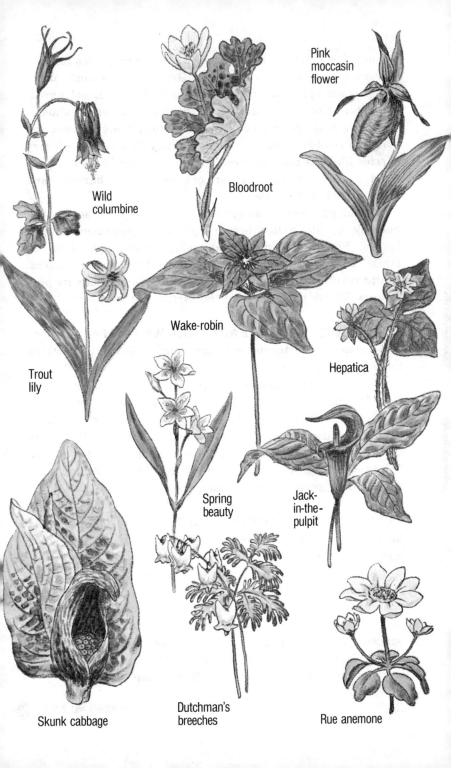

Wild columbine

Bloodroot

Pink moccasin flower

Trout lily

Wake-robin

Hepatica

Spring beauty

Jack-in-the-pulpit

Skunk cabbage

Dutchman's breeches

Rue anemone

cinquefoil, all close to the ground. As the grass grows tall, the flowers must reach up above it. Queen Anne's lace, oxeye daisy, black-eyed Susan, yarrow, butterfly weed, goldenrod, and aster raise their heads above the grass on slender stalks.

As you hike along a country lane, many flowers greet you from the roadside. Mullein sends up its yellow spikes, chicory carries high its blue flowers. There are many kinds of hawkweed, some clear yellow, others orange. Thistle, burdock, and tansy grow in thick masses.

Should you paddle along the lakeshore, you'll see cattail pushing up its yellow-brown spikes among sword-shaped leaves. Bittersweet nightshade winds itself high along its stalks. Pickerelweed displays its dense, blue flower clusters. White turtlehead opens its mouth. Milkweed spreads its pink flowers. Yellow pond lilies dot the surface of the water.

NORTH AND SOUTH, EAST AND WEST. Most of these flowers are found throughout our country, but some sections have flowers of their own.

It is in the Northeast where you may find the fringed gentian, Virginia cowslip, day lily, Oswego tea, and showy aster. On the west coast grow the golden-yellow California poppy, shooting stars, blue and scarlet wonder, the snow flower. In the dry parts of the Southwest you will come upon cactus in bright colors. In the South there are coral plant, orange milkwort, purple gerardia, and meadow beauty.

TELLING THE FLOWERS APART. With so many flowers about, it seems almost impossible to tell them apart, to get to know their names.

Naturalists interested in flowers—botanists—have tackled this problem. They have noticed that some flowering plants seemed to be related. They had the same type of flower and seed, the same kind of stalk, the same leaves. So, related flowers were grouped in families. The families were given names, and the descriptions of them were arranged in keys. In such a key you can follow the details of a flower step by step.

Tansy

Yarrow

New England aster

Black-eyed Susan

Bittersweet nightshade

Boneset

White baneberry

Turtlehead

Butterfly weed

Hawkweed

Pickerelweed

Red clover

Early goldenrod

Common mullein

Thistle

Yellow pond lily

LEARN THE IMPORTANT FAMILIES. To get to know a plant family, begin with a flower you know well.

Let's say you pick the wild rose. Look at it from below. First you see five small, green leaves. They are the sepals. Together these form the calyx. Above them come the five pink petals that make up the corolla. In the center of the flower is a large number of pollen-bearing pins. These are the stamens. They form a ring around a cluster of green, threadlike pistils.

Five sepals, five petals, many stamens, many pistils—together they spell "rose family." Some of the members may vary from this rule. Most of them follow the pattern closely. Wild strawberry, meadowsweet, raspberry, cinquefoil, agrimony, and such trees as apple, pear, plum, cherry belong to the rose family.

It is a good idea to begin your study early in the spring. You will find that most spring flowers belong to just two families: lily and crowfoot. In summer, pink, mustard, rose, pea, evening primrose, parsley, figwort, and mint families take over. Late summer and fall are ruled by the composite (daisy) family with its asters, goldenrods, and thistles.

Get to know the main features of these families. Add to them the members of the grass family. If you do, you will be able to find your way among almost two-thirds of the flowers of our country.

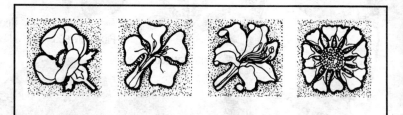

PLANT FAMILIES. Each plant family has its own characteristics. In a flower belonging to the rose family, the parts are divisible by 5, in the mustard family by 4, in the lily family by 3. What looks like a single flower of the composite (daisy) family may actually be hundreds of flowers, some of them tube-shaped, some of them tongue-shaped.

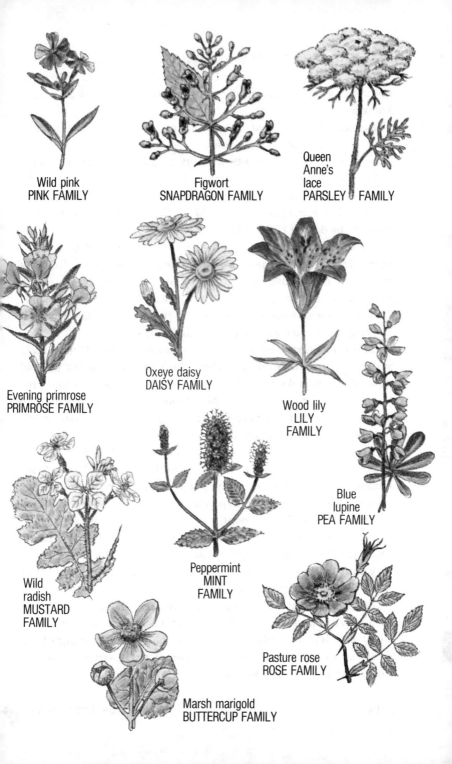

Wild pink
PINK FAMILY

Figwort
SNAPDRAGON FAMILY

Queen
Anne's
lace
PARSLEY FAMILY

Evening primrose
PRIMROSE FAMILY

Oxeye daisy
DAISY FAMILY

Wood lily
LILY
FAMILY

Blue
lupine
PEA FAMILY

Wild
radish
MUSTARD
FAMILY

Peppermint
MINT
FAMILY

Pasture rose
ROSE FAMILY

Marsh marigold
BUTTERCUP FAMILY

NOT ALL PLANTS ARE FLOWERS. The flowers, of course, are all plants, but not all plants are flowers. You will come upon many flowerless plants on your hikes. It is just as well to know a bit about them.

Plants are arranged into two large groups: those that produce seeds and those that don't.

Low on the list of plants without seeds are the algae. Some of them are tiny—the blue green scum on a quiet lake. Others grow to great sizes—the green, brown, and red algae or seaweeds of our coasts. One of them, the big brown kelp, may grow to be 45 m (150 ft.) long.

To see the bacteria you need a microscope. But in spite of their tiny size they have a great effect on our lives. Some of them are harmless. Some are useful. Others cause infection and diseases. Strep throat is an infection caused by germs. The diseases of cholera, pneumonia, tuberculosis, and the venereal diseases are all caused by bacteria.

The fungi are seedless plants of wide variety: Green mold grows on bread. Mildew makes black spots on tents packed down while still damp. Blights and rust kill chestnuts and pine trees. Yeast raises bread. Mushrooms grow in woods and fields. Some of the mushrooms make good eating. Others are poisonous. It takes an expert to tell them apart.

The lichens appear as grayish scale patches on trees, rocks, and soil. These patches are not individual plants. Each lichen is two plants, alga and fungus. They grow together in an amazing partnership, depending upon each other for life.

Liverworts—flat, ribbonlike, green plants—and mosses of many shapes are among the seedless plants. So are the horsetails, the ferns, and the club mosses. Some of the ferns are so tiny that you hardly see them in the rock cracks in which they grow. Others grow to tree size.

But of all plants, the seed producers are the most important to us. Without them there would be no human life on earth. They nourish us, clothe us, give us shelter. They range from grasses and trees to the vegetables of our gardens, and the flowers in the florists' shops.

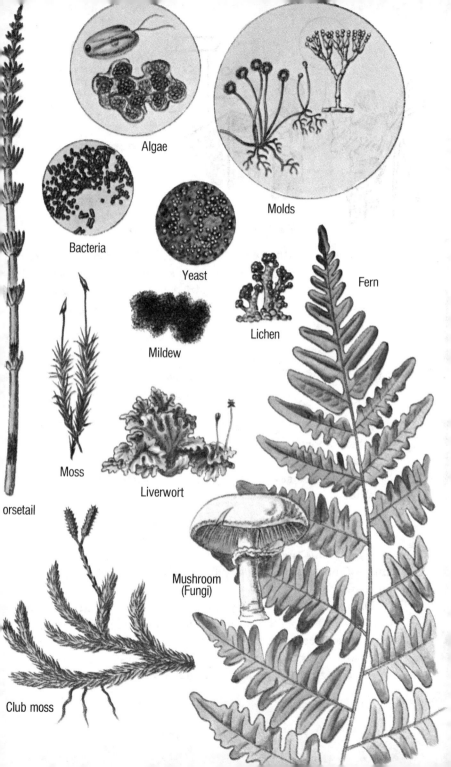

Algae

Molds

Bacteria

Yeast

Fern

Lichen

Mildew

Moss

Liverwort

orsetail

Mushroom
(Fungi)

Club moss

WIND AND WEATHER

"Some are weatherwise, some are otherwise," Benjamin Franklin once said. In his day, it was very important for farmers and sailors to be "weatherwise." They had to figure out the weather for themselves. They did it by whatever knowledge they had picked up about weather signs.

That's where we are lucky today. We can get our daily weather reports and predictions by radio or TV. They are based on photographs from satellites and on the observations of thousands of people throughout the country—meteorologists, persons who specialize in weather.

When in camp you won't have much chance to listen to weather reports. And yet, if you intend to go on a hike or take a canoe trip, you'll want to be sure that the good weather will hold. There are several things that will help you forecast the weather.

TELLING WEATHER BY THE WIND. In the continental United States, the wind blowing from the west is the prevailing wind. This means that the weather that people have 800 km (500 mi.) west of you today is the weather you will have tomorrow.

This west wind almost always brings clear, bright weather (except in California and west Florida where it carries moisture inland from the sea). East of the Rockies, the east wind generally brings rain. The north wind brings a clear cold. The south wind brings heat and often quick showers.

310

When the wind blows from the northeast you can expect rain in the summer, snow in the winter. The northwest wind brings cooler weather in the summer, cold waves in winter. The wind from the southwest is warm—in the summer often scorching. The wind from southeast is the wettest of them all.

TELLING WEATHER BY WEATHER SIGNS. Watch the weather carefully and mind some of the old weather sayings.

Fair-Weather Signs. You will then learn that *fair weather* is ahead when you see some of these signs:

- "Red sky at night, sailors' delight." The dust particles in the dry air of tomorrow's weather produce a red glow.
- "Swallows flying way up high mean there's no rain in the sky." Swallows catch and eat insects on the wing. At high air pressure that comes with fair weather, insects are carried up high by air currents.
- "If smoke goes high no rain comes by." Smoke of your fire goes straight up. With high air pressure smoke rises.
- "When the dew is on the grass rain will never come to pass." Dew forms when air moisture condenses on cooled-off vegetation. This happens during nights of dry air and clear skies.

Poor-Weather Signs. On the other hand, there's *poor weather* in store when you notice these signs:

- "Red sky in morning, sailors take warning." Dry, dust-laden air is leaving toward the east. Moist air is coming in from the west.
- "Swallows flying near the ground mean a storm will come around." At low air pressure, insects fly close to the ground on heavy, moist wings. Swallows follow.
- "If smoke hangs low, watch out for a blow." Low air pressure prevents smoke from rising.
- "When grass is dry at morning light, look for rain before the night." On a cloudy night, grass does not cool off enough for dew to form.
- "Mackerel scales and mares' tails make lofty ships carry low sails." "Scales" and "tails" are cloud formations that warn of changing weather.

CIRRUS or "*FEATHER*" clouds are usually with a clear day. Highest of formations. From about 5 to 6 miles. Calm sea

CIRRO STRATUS "*TANGLED WEB*" A high thin whitish cloud Altitude about 5½ miles. Produces halos. Calm sea

CIRRO CUMULUS or "*MACKEREL*" clouds. Small flakes arranged in groups or lines Height about 4 miles. Calm sea.

ALTO CUMULUS or "*SHEEP*" Rather large white masses or groups often spread into lines. Height varies from 3 to 4 miles.

ALTO STRATUS A thick grey "*CURTAIN*" like cloud. Shows a bright patch where sun or moon hides. Height about 3 miles. Squally weather

"Cloud Types Tell the Weather," from the

STRATO CUMULUS
"TWIST" shaped clouds of dark color. Not very thick showing blue sky in spots. Does not bring rain. Height about 1 mile

NIMBUS *"UMBRELLA"*
"OVER ALL" Rain clouds. Thick and dark. Small ragged pieces floating at low level are known as *"SCUD"* Holes may be seen

CUMULUS *"WOOL PACK"*
Huge masses of varying height. Bright opposite the sun. On same side as sun is dark with bright edges

CUMULO-NIMBUS -*"THUNDER"* or *"SHOWER"*. Like Cumulus but has *"False Cirrus"* at top and *"Nimbus"* underneath. These clouds come very low

STRATUS —*"SPREAD SHEET"*
Horizontal sheet of lifted Fog. Torn apart is known as *"Fracto Stratus"*

WEATHER RECORD

DATE _____

	a.m.	p.m.
Temperature		
Relative humidity		
Wind direction		
Wind velocity		
Rainfall		
Sunshine		
Clouds		

Your Weather Record

Know your climate and you'll better understand your own environment. Weather records will help you learn. Use information from local newspapers, radio, or TV, if available. If not, set up a simple weather station. Take readings twice a day for those weather features listed on the chart. At the end of the month use the information to interpret your weather.

WEATHER AS A HOBBY. If you want to make weather one of your hobbies, get in touch with people interested in meteorology. Your science teacher may suggest names to you. Get a *Weather* merit badge pamphlet and meet the requirements.

WIND-SCALE NUMBERS
(Simplified Beaufort Scale)

When you see this:		Wind speed is:	
		KM/H	MPH
0 Calm. Smoke goes straight up. *No wind.*		0-1.6	0-1
1 Direction of wind shown by smoke drift, but not by wind vane. *Slight wind.*		1.6-5	1-3
2 Wind felt on face. Leaves rustle. Wind vane moves. *Light breeze.*		6-11	4-7
3 Leaves and small twigs move steadily. Small flag held straight out. *Gentle breeze.*		13-19	8-12
4 Dust and loose paper raised. Small branches move. *Moderate wind.*		21-29	13-18
5 Small trees sway. Waves form on lakes. *Fresh wind.*		30-38	19-24
6 Large branches move. Wires whistle. Umbrellas are hard to use. *Strong wind.*		40-50	25-31
7 Whole trees in motion. Hard to walk against wind. *High wind.*		52-60	32-38
8 Twigs break from trees. Very hard to walk against the wind. *Gale.*		62-72	39-46
9 Small damage to buildings. *Strong gale.*		74-87	47-54
10 Much damage to buildings. Trees uprooted. *Whole gale.*		88-101	55-63
11 Widespread damage from wind. *Violent storm.*		102-116	64-72
12 Violence and destruction from wind. *Hurricane.*		117+	73+

KM/H—kilometers per hour   MPH—miles per hour

Weather Instruments

RAIN GAUGE. Use a No. 10 can or a coffee can. Whatever you use must have top, sides, and bottom the same diameter. Measure rainfall daily with a ruler. Empty the can after each measurement.

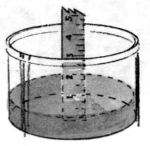

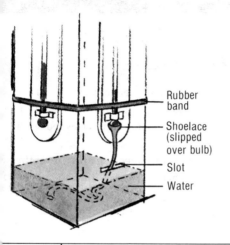

Rubber band

Shoelace (slipped over bulb)

Slot

Water

HUMIDITY. Use a milk carton and two thermometers. Measure humidity by noting the difference between the wet-bulb and dry-bulb thermometers. Use the chart below to find the percent of relative humidity.

Difference between wet-bulb and dry-bulb readings		TABLE OF RELATIVE HUMIDITY—MEASURING MOISTURE							
		Temperature of air, dry-bulb thermometer in Celsius (°C) and Fahrenheit (°F)							
°C	°F	-1°/30°	5°/40°	10°/50°	15°/60°	21°/70°	26°/80°	32°/90°	37°/100°
.5	1	90%	92%	93%	94%	95%	96%	96%	97%
1.1	2	79%	84%	87%	89%	90%	92%	92%	93%
1.6	3	68%	76%	80%	84%	86%	87%	88%	90%
2.2	4	58%	68%	74%	78%	81%	83%	85%	86%
3.3	6	38%	52%	61%	68%	72%	75%	78%	80%
4.4	8	18%	37%	49%	58%	64%	68%	71%	74%
5.5	10		22%	37%	48%	55%	61%	65%	68%
6.6	12		8%	26%	39%	48%	54%	59%	62%
7.7	14			16%	30%	40%	47%	53%	57%
8.8	16			5%	21%	33%	41%	47%	51%
9.9	18				13%	26%	35%	41%	47%
11.0	20				5%	19%	29%	36%	42%
12.1	22					12%	23%	32%	37%
13.2	24					6%	18%	26%	33%

HEAVENS ABOVE

The campfire is over. You and the other members of your patrol are on your way back to your tents. The trees form a dark wall all around you. But above you the sky is clear. It is crowded with thousands of sparkling stars.

Or you have just finished a winter patrol meeting and are on the way home. Half a moon hangs overhead. Around it stretches the wide expanse of the skies.

Either time is perfect for beginning your star study.

"CON"—TOGETHER. "STELLA"—STARS. For thousands of years people have grouped the stars together into pictures—constellations. The custom probably goes back to times when men spent the nights under the stars, watching their sheep. The shepherds of old Greece and Rome thought they could see pictures of heroes, kings and queens, men, maidens, and monsters in the stars. They named the figures to suit their imagination. We still use the same names.

Today the constellations help us find our way by ship across the ocean. They guide a plane flying, a rocket racing through space. One of them will help you find north on a night hike.

Find the North Star. Draw a line from it to the ground. A landmark here will be true north of you.

This is how the "pointers" help you find the North Star in the starry sky.

STARS TO THE NORTH. For an easy way to learn the constellations, you need a good starting point. You can't ask for a better one than the Big Dipper. So set out to locate it in the sky. There it is: Four stars make up its bowl, three its handle. Three, did we say? Not so fast. Look at the second star in the handle. If you have good eyesight you'll see that it is really two stars. The Indians used the two to test the sight of their children. They called the larger star the horse, the other on its back the rider.

Now let the "pointers" of the Big Dipper—those two stars farthest from the handle—guide you to the polestar of North Star. The distance is about five times the distance between the two stars. True north on earth lies at the horizon directly under the North Star.

If you look close you notice that the North Star is at the end on the handle of a smaller dipper: The Little Dipper. Between the two dippers dangles the Dragon—a long line of faint stars.

Now find the Big Dipper on page 319. Continue from the pointers through the polestar to a W formed of five stars. This is Cassiopeia, the queen. King Cepheus is nearby.

N

On a summer's night begin your travels of the sky by first locating the stars that swing around the North Star: the dippers and the W of Cassiopeia.

Trace a line between the Big Dipper and the W. Then draw another line across this line, crossing it at the North Star. In one direction along this line you'll see a bright star with a tilted box of four smaller stars near it. This bright star is Vega, in the constellation the Lyre. Now look the other way from the North Star. See the bright star with three faint ones near it? It is Capella in the Charioteer, a rather vague five-sided constellation.

The seven constellations you have located so far are in the sky the year round. But at times Vega dips under the northern horizon when Capella is high in the sky. At other times, it's Capella that dips under. This dipping is not caused by the stars. It is caused by the movement of the earth.

Back again to the Big Dipper. This time follow the pointers away from the North Star. Keep going till you locate the sickle-shaped Lion. Its brightest star is Regulus. Between the Lion and Capella are the Twins, Castor and Pollux. Between Capella and the W is the Perseus constellation. Between the W and Vega five stars form a wide cross—the Swan or Northern Cross.

Now, turn the book upside down.

Back to the Big Dipper once more. Follow the curved line of the handle until you reach Arcturus. It is the brightest in a group of stars that looks like a big kite. This is Boötes, the Herdsman. Next to the Herdsman you'll find a half circle of faint stars. This is Corona, our Northern Crown. As you continue, you'll see Hercules. It is shaped like a lopsided H. And so you find yourself back at Vega.

Now look south. Right in front of you hovers Scorpius. Its tail swings toward the horizon. Its head points toward Spica, the bright star of the Y-shaped Virgin. In the other direction from the Scorpion flies the Eagle. It looks like a bird with spread wings.

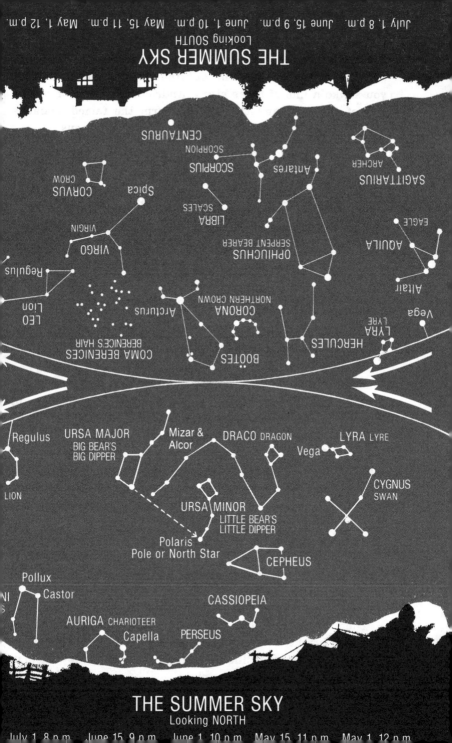

WINTER STARS. On a winter's night, start from the Big Dipper. Follow the pointers through the polestar and the W, till you strike a line of three stars: Andromeda. The star at one end of the line, and three more, form the famed Pegasus square. The other end of Andromeda points to Perseus.

Now, turn the book upside down.

The finest group of stars in the winter sky is Orion to the south. Two bright stars make up his shoulders. Three small ones form his head and two more his legs. Three stars are his belt. Three more his sword.

Draw a line upward through Orion's belt. First you come to the red star Aldebaran, the "eye" in the V-shaped head of the Bull. Continuing further you find the Pleiades or Seven Sisters. If you have good eyesight, you can count six. In a telescope you'll see more than 200.

Back to Orion again. This time follow the line through his belt in the opposite direction till you hit Sirius. Next to our own sun, it is the brightest star in the sky.

THE PLANETS. Our sun has a family. The earth belongs to this family. So do other bodies that swing through the sky.

The old observers of the stars noticed five stars that did not behave like the others. They didn't twinkle—they glowed with a steady light. They didn't follow the other stars—they moved among them. The observers called them by the Greek name *planetes*, or "wanderers." Today we know nine planets, including the earth.

The five seen by the ancients—Mercury, Venus, Mars, Jupiter, Saturn—are still visible with naked eyes. Mercury is a weak dot that can sometimes be seen soon after sunset. The others look like bright stars. To find out which of them are in the sky on a certain night, check them out in an almanac.

Then watch for them in the evening just after sunset, before the stars brighten. Then you can easily locate the visible planets because of their brilliance. And you can then follow them in their courses throughout the night.

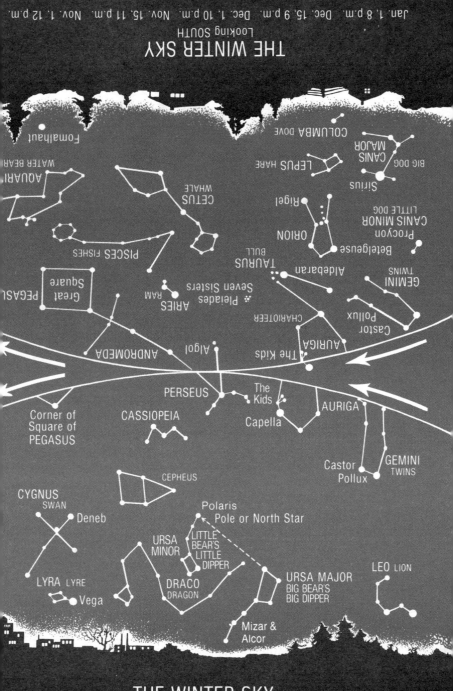

Jan. 1, 8 p.m. Dec. 15, 9 p.m. Dec. 1, 10 p.m. Nov. 15, 11 p.m. Nov. 1, 12 p.m.

THE WINTER SKY
Looking SOUTH

Fomalhaut

AQUARI WATER BEAR

CETUS WHALE

PISCES FISHES

PEGASUS

Great
Square

ARIES
RAM

Pleiades
Seven Sisters

TAURUS
BULL

Aldebaran

CHARIOTEER

AURIGA
The Kids

ANDROMEDA

Algol

COLUMBA DOVE

CANIS
MAJOR

LEPUS HARE

Big DOG

Sirius

Rigel

ORION

CANIS MINOR
LITTLE DOG

Procyon

Betelgeuse

GEMINI
TWINS

Castor
Pollux

PERSEUS

The
Kids

CASSIOPEIA

Corner of
Square of
PEGASUS

The Kids

Capella

AURIGA

Castor
Pollux

GEMINI
TWINS

CEPHEUS

CYGNUS
SWAN

Deneb

Polaris
Pole or North Star

URSA
MINOR

LITTLE
BEAR'S
LITTLE
DIPPER

LYRA LYRE

Vega

DRACO
DRAGON

URSA MAJOR
BIG BEAR'S
BIG DIPPER

LEO LION

Mizar &
Alcor

THE WINTER SKY
Looking NORTH
Jan. 1, 8 p.m.   Dec. 15, 9 p.m.   Dec. 1, 10 p.m.   Nov. 15, 11 p.m.   Nov. 1, 12 p.m.

This will be a better world when all people work together for pure water, litter-free land, clean air, fertile soil, wildlife and energy conservation.

Protect Your World

The early settlers found America a land full of natural resources of tremendous value. Virgin forests covered a large part of our country. The soil was fertile. Woods and prairies teemed with wildlife. Clear streams and lakes abounded in fish. The air sweeping across the land was clean. Minerals of all kinds lay hidden in the ground. The resources were so vast that it seemed as if they could never be used up.

So forests were cut and prairies broken and turned into farmland. Water from rivers and lakes was used for factories and mills. Wildlife was shot for food or was driven away. Minerals were wastefully tapped. And as each natural resource diminished, all the others suffered.

Within a short time, the results became obvious. Where previously forest or grass-covered soil held the water, the exposed land shed heavy rains, causing destructive floods. Fertile topsoil was washed away—or blew away in dust storms. Rivers were filled with silt from eroding farms and wastes from factories. The air was polluted by smoke and poisonous gases. Minerals and oil showed signs of giving out.

The voices raised in warning went unheeded for a long time. But other voices were being heard. Today every intelligent person realizes the importance of conservation.

The way a farmer tills his soil in Kansas, or an engineer builds a dam in Tennessee, or a hunter kills a predator in Maine used to be the private concern of each of them. Not any more. The way they go about it may influence all of us by the processes they set in motion. A flood in Missouri, a drought in Texas, a dust storm in Oklahoma used to be local matters. Not any more. They may be symptoms of poor use of the soil that may ultimately affect us all.

WHAT IS CONSERVATION? To the world at large, conservation traditionally has meant "the wise use of natural resources for the greatest good of the most people for the longest time." Now we include the improvement or renewal of these resources.

To each individual, the word "conservation" has its own meaning. To some, conservation is an enormous dam for producing electricity. To others, it is a compost heap in the garden for making humus to enrich the soil. To some it is planting a thousand trees. To others it is refraining from throwing a burning cigarette out of a car window. It is obeying game laws and willow-planting a stream bank. On a farm it is contour plowing a field. In the city it is trash removal and salvaging newspaper and setting down the thermostat dial.

By making conservation a part of your everyday thinking and acting, and by working with others in using proper conservation practices, you are helping make a richer and better country. You are helping protect the world.

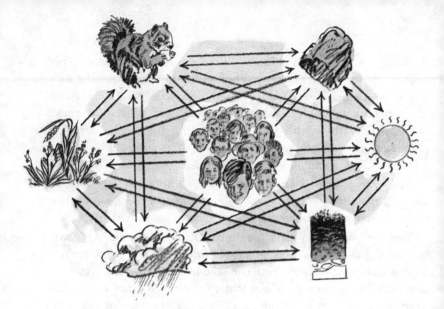

Soil, air, water, plants, animals, rocks, and sun are in a web of nature. This web makes up the fabric of life on earth as we know it.

WHAT YOU CAN DO. From the day it was founded, the Boy Scouts of America has been one of the strongest fighters in the conservation battle. You will want to be in there fighting, too! Three things are required of you in this fight:

- That you recognize the need for conservation.
- That you learn about the sources of our conservation problems.
- That you do something to help solve the problems.

To recognize the need, all you have to do is look around you—or smell around you. In the city you will see the litter in the street, the trash awaiting collecting, the sooted-up buildings. And you will smell the stench of exhaust gases in the air. In the country you will see the murky or muddy rivers, the scum on some of the lakes, the eroded trails underfoot.

Some of your world is that way today. But don't accept those parts of it! Decide to do something to better them. You will find lots of suggestions on the pages that follow. They cover our country's six main conservation concerns.

Pure Water

There's as much water on earth today as there ever was or ever will be. The circulation of it in the water cycle is never-ending. The glass of water you drink today might have flowed down the Danube River last month. Or it could have been some of the Atlantic that carried Columbus to America.

It seems as if there is an abundance of water on earth. There is. But it is mostly salty seawater of no use for drinking, nor for the thousands of other needs we have for water. Only 3 percent of the world's water is fresh water, and a large percentage of that water is now so polluted that the cost of purifying it is almost prohibitive.

The causes of water pollution are many: Silt from soil is the biggest water polluter. Agricultural chemicals washed into streams from poorly managed farms and other watershed areas are another. Highway and building construction creating erosion and further silting adds to the problem. Sewage from individual homes and community disposal plants dumped into rivers and streams. Wastes from industrial and chemical plants poured into lakes and waterways. Oil spills from tankers and barges. Trash and litter thrown into lakes and streams.

The pollution of water has many devastating effects. In countless lakes, fish life has been partly or completely destroyed. Lakes and rivers of recreational areas have been made unfit for swimming and boating and other water sports.

Many lakes are dying from being overnourished with runoffs from farms, city sewage, and industrial wastes. These feed algae. The dying and rotting algae rob the oxygen the fish need.

Some industries have had to close down for lack of the pure water they needed for manufacturing. Cities have difficulties providing for the ever-growing need for water for homes, factories, and recreation.

The prevention and correction of water pollution involve local laws and enforcement of these laws. You can help in small ways by refraining from polluting water and by saving as much water as possible.

WHAT YOU CAN DO ABOUT WATER. Some of the things you can do deal with water pollution. Others will save water.

- Get your patrol interested in cleaning up a section of a stream or part of a lake. Protect your feet with sneakers, your legs with old trousers, your hands with work gloves.
- For dishwashing and laundering in camp, use soap, not detergent. Soap breaks down in nature and disappears.
- Do not wash with soap in a stream or lake. Carry water inland 30 m (100 ft.) or more and wash there. Do your toothbrushing right in camp, not in stream or lake.
- At home, turn faucets off tightly. One drop a second wastes 25 l (6½ gal.) in 24 hours.
- Keep a plastic bottle of water in the refrigerator so that you do not have to let the tap run to get cool water.
- Cut a half-gallon plastic bottle in two. Place the lower part in the bottom of the toilet tank. In a family of four, the water you save will amount to 500 l (135 gal.) or more a month.
- Shower with the plug in the bathtub. Compare the amount of water with the amount you use for a bath. Which method uses less water?
- Shower the water-saving way: Wet yourself. Turn off the water. Lather up. Then rinse, first in warm water, then in cooler water.
- When you brush your teeth, turn the water on and off as you need it. Do not let it run unnecessarily.
- If you have a garden to water, water in late afternoon or evening so that evaporation will not waste water. The plants will have the whole night to benefit.

EROSION
ANIMAL WASTES
FERTILIZER
INSECTICIDES
FEEDLOT WASTES

DETERGENTS
SEWAGE
HOUSEHOLD TRASH
YARD WASTE

GARBAGE
SEWAGE
TRASH
MUNICIPAL WASTES

CHEMICALS
SLUDGE
INDUSTRIAL WASTES

CHEMICALS
SLUDGE
OIL SPILLS
MUNICIPAL WASTES

Litter-Free Land

We sing of America: "O beautiful for spacious skies, For amber waves of grain, For purple mountain majesties Above the fruited plain! ..." But as you hike along you find this beauty desecrated by millions of thoughtless litterbugs. They travel along, scattering their trash far and wide along our highways, across the countryside, throughout state and national parks, and in and on our waters.

It costs nearly a billion dollars a year to pick up the trash along America's highways and byways. Who pays that enormous bill? You and your family and every American taxpayer. Imagine how much good that money could do if we did not have to spend it to clean up after thoughtless and careless people!

The money waste is bad enough. But think also of the forests that go up in flames because some speeding litterbugs throw their cigarettes out their car windows. Think of streams being choked with discarded cans, bottles, cartons, metal trash, old tires. Think of bathing beaches made unsafe to bathers because of broken glass and boards with nails. Think of the beauty of the landscape made unsightly by tons of garbage, newspapers, cans, bottles, cardboard boxes, wrappers of all kinds, and the indestructible plastics.

But the litter plague is not just an open-country plague. It is a town and city plague as well. Take a look around your neighborhood. Are sidewalks, streets, or gutters littered with trash? Are empty lots and alleys filled with litter? Is the schoolyard clean? In towns and cities litter is not just an eyesore. It is a health and safety hazard as well. It can cause fires and accidents. It can cause boat accidents on the water.

WHAT YOU CAN DO ABOUT LITTER. Starting with yourself, get going on an antilitter spree.
- Become an antilitter fiend. Train yourself to refrain from littering. Put small trash—candy wrappers, ticket stubs—in your pocket for disposal in the nearest trash can.

- Make a tote-litter bag for the family car or a neighbor's car. Bring a litter bag to camp for toting out your trash.
- Don't be bashful about other people's litter. Pick it up— because it is there. If the litterers see you do it, so much the better. It may be the hint they need.
- Take part in a block cleanup campaign. Or organize one of your own, with your patrol helping.
- Select part of a beach or limited area in a park. Collect all rubbish in it. Exhibit it for a day or two, in a wire cage, at the entrance to the area for everyone to see. Put up a map to show where the trash was collected. Then get rid of it.
- In the inner city, adopt an empty lot. Find out who owns it. Get permission from owner or city department to clean it up. Then do it.
- Work with your patrol to clean up a rest area or a roadside near where you live. Many Scout patrols do this. Some of them consider cleaning up a roadside stretch of 150 m (500 ft.) a reasonable day's goal.
- For getting rid of large trash, report to your local sanitation department and get its help.

Take a 2-hour walk where you live. Make a list of things that please you, another of things that should be improved. Set out to improve them.

Clean Air

What do you get when you mix oxygen and nitrogen and sulfur dioxide and soot and smoke and exhaust fumes? Ordinary city air—that's what!

It wasn't always like that. There was a time when the air over America was sparkling clear. But many years ago when man began to gather in cities, the air began to lose its purity.

First came the smoke from thousands of home fires. Then the smoke from mills and manufacturing plants began filling the air with soot and poisonous fumes. The chemical industry added acid gases and other pollutants. The population increased. So did homes with coal- and oil-burning heating systems. Then the automobile—millions and millions of them—burning gasoline and spewing out hydrocarbons, carbon monoxide, nitrogen oxides, sulfur dioxide. As if this were not enough, the sun cooks the hydrocarbons and nitrogen into troublesome pollutants that sting the eyes and damage the lungs. They cause smog, injure plants, attack cloth and building materials.

The air around us seems limitless. It isn't. The layer of air around the earth is only about 15 km (10 miles) thick. Of this, only the first 5 to 6 km (3 to 4 miles) contain enough oxygen to be of use to human beings. Into this layer of air we dump our noxious wastes. This kind of waste does not disappear. What's there is there. The air is now so polluted that our lives are endangered.

The national and state governments have passed laws to cut down further pollution. A Clean Air Act was passed in 1970. And the Environmental Protection Agency was given power to set limits on the pollutants that are most dangerous to health. Industry is reducing smoke from its plants. Automobile manufacturers are building antipollution systems into their cars. Local governments are forbidding open burnings. Some improvements have been made. But we have a long way to go.

The big difficulty is that air pollution is the most insidious

MAIN CAUSES OF AIR POLLUTION

AIRCRAFT

HEAVY INDUSTRY

LIGHT INDUSTRY
OFFICE BUILDINGS
HOMES
   Trash burning
   Heating
   Leaf burning

TRUCKS
CARS
VANS
BUSES

DUST
FERTILIZERS
FUMES
HEATING

of all types of pollution. Litter pollution can be seen and the litter can be removed. Water pollution can be traced and the water can be treated. But when it comes to air pollution everyone is guilty. As a famous cartoon character, Pogo, once said, "We have met the enemy—and he is us!"

It is the task of every American to help clean up our air. But we can do it only if we change from being the problem to becoming the solution.

WHAT YOU CAN DO ABOUT AIR. Major air-pollution problems must be solved by the local and the Federal governments. But there are many things a citizen can do.

- If your family has a car, keep it correctly tuned. Have muffler, tail pipe, pollution device in good shape.
- Have family oil burner adjusted to give off as little pollution as possible. Use oil with a low sulfur content.
- In the fall, add fallen leaves to the compost heap.
- Never burn plastics. In burning they produce an acid gas—a dangerous pollution agent, damaging people's eyes.
- Smoking is not just harmful for your own health. It is also a serious air pollution problem affecting the health of others, particularly people with lung and heart diseases.
- Plant trees. Trees take in carbon dioxide and give up pure oxygen—the gas you breathe to keep alive. Trees will also filter or screen out pollutants in the air by collecting them on their leaves. Have you thanked a tree recently?
- Stop noise pollution—another form of air pollution. Loud playing of radios and record players can cause hearing defects to some and irritation to others.

Fertile Soil

Soil and water are inseparable. Without water, soil is unproductive. With sufficient water, soil is able to grow plants on which man and animals depend for their living.

Without soil and water all life would perish. And yet, we are careless with soil beyond belief. Experts have estimated that one-third of the topsoil of our country has been lost since America gained independence more than 200 years ago. This loss was caused by erosion. Rain swept over bare or poorly cultivated land and carried the soil downhill and away, polluting rivers and silting up lakes and reservoirs.

The loss of fertile soil through erosion is still the greatest danger to our land. More than 300 million of our 400-odd million acres of farm land are now eroding faster than soil is being formed. More than 4 billion tons of soil is carried off our fields every year by erosion.

"Charity begins at home." So does soil-and-water conservation. It begins with opening the eyes to features that show poor conservation: to the splash erosion on the bare ground below the spilling-over gutter, to the sheet erosion where the rainwater spreads over the sloping lawn, to the rill erosion as the water speeds downhill in tiny rivulets. By being aware of these erosions we can stop them before they become problems.

With the home conditions taken care of, the next steps could be the school grounds and the Scout camp. And then, eventually, the local watershed and other public lands.

Protect a low stream bank by willow planting, a steep bank by riprapping.

WHAT YOU CAN DO ABOUT SOIL. If you are a farm boy, your family has probably already adopted the soil conservation practices of contouring, strip cropping, crop rotation, stubble mulching, and many other methods. But whether farm boy or city boy you still have a chance to go in for soil conservation by fighting erosion in your backyard, in camp, and at your favorite hike destinations.

- Plant all bare areas to vegetation where possible.
- Repair an eroding downhill trail by installing water bars to direct the water off the trail. Cut a shallow channel across the trail at an angle to the slope. Then place a log or a row of stones in the channel.
- Stop the formation of a small gulley by diverting the water that may flow into it. Then plant grasses, vines, shrubs.
- Protect a low stream bank from erosion by planting willow cuttings. If planted in spring or early summer the cuttings will soon sprout roots to hold the soil.
- Protect a steep stream bank by riprapping. Place a row of stones against the foot of the bank. Build a wall against the bank to the height the rushing water might reach.
- If you have a family garden, establish a compost heap in some corner. Pile up grass cuttings, weeds, vegetable garbage. Keep it moist. Turn it over from time to time. It will decay into humus. Spade this into the soil to improve it.
- Earn the Soil and Water Conservation merit badge.

Repair an eroding downhill trail by putting in water bars to lead water off the trail.

A bucket can hold so much water. An area can hold so much wildlife.

Wildlife, Wild and Free

When naturalists speak of "wildlife," they generally mean the animals with backbones that inhabit our outdoors and waters: mammals, birds, reptiles, amphibians, and fish.

While our country was still a wilderness, the amount of wildlife depended on the ability of the animals to survive and reproduce. Today, when man has taken over the land, the amount of wildlife is determined by what food, water, cover protection, and living space for nesting and rearing young are available in man-managed areas.

But a certain area of a certain environment can carry only a certain amount of wildlife. Think of the area as a bucket. You

THE AMERICAN BISON—Mammal symbol of our country.

The bison—or buffalo—gave the Plains Indian his meat, skin for making his clothing and tepees, fur for his bedding. The white man, pushing westward, also depended on the bison for food. Bison were killed—some for food and hides, others for the "sport" of it. The result: If you want to see one today, you must go to a zoo, a park, or to the Philmont Scout Ranch near Cimarron, N. Mex.

335

You'll find designs for birdhouses in the *Bird Study* merit badge pamphlet. Wrens, chickadees, titmice, nuthatches, bluebirds, flycatchers, woodpeckers may take over a box-shaped birdhouse. Robins, phoebes, barn swallows prefer an open shelf.

can fill a bucket with just so much water. If you try to fill it beyond its capacity, it overflows and the water is wasted. If an area gets filled with wildlife beyond its "carrying capacity," the wildlife will die from lack of food or other wildlife need. That is why such areas must be managed. But within these areas we want whatever wildlife is there to be truly wild and free. We want wildlife to have a chance to survive.

In the last century the American bison roamed the prairies in vast numbers. Today you will find them fenced in herds or in zoos. In those early days the passenger pigeon was the most numerous of all American birds. They were hunted to extinction. The last of them died in a zoo on September 1, 1914. Other kinds of American wildlife are now near extinction.

You can help wildlife survive and flourish wherever it exists. And you can help in the efforts to protect and preserve some of the wildlife species that are now endangered. Among them are the eastern timber wolf, the Florida panther, the Sonora pronghorn, the brown pelican, the California condor, the southern bald eagle, the American peregrine falcon, the whooping crane, the ivory-billed woodpecker. There are many others—more than 200 endangered species in the U.S.A.

WHAT YOU CAN DO ABOUT WILDLIFE. The more wildlife you see on your hikes and in camp, the more you will want to conserve it. Get help from experts.

• Hunt and fish only in season. Respect bag limits and other hunting and fishing laws.

Some birds feed on fats. Make a suet stick: Drill holes in a short log. Push suet into the holes.

Make a food tray for seed-feeding birds. Build it so that it will swing with the wind to protect the seeds against rain and snow.

- Out driving, keep alert for animals, particularly at night. Warn the driver in time if you see an animal starting to cross the road.
- In late winter or early spring, build and put up birdhouses.
- In the fall, put up feeding stations for birds. Keep them stocked the entire winter.
- Put up brush piles as shelters for small animals where no cover exists.
- Protect a stream bank as suggested on page 334. You not only save the soil, you also improve the stream for the fish living in it.
- Get the approval and help of your local conservation department in building deflector dams, V-dams, or other devices for improving the flow in a local stream.
- Earn the Fish and Wildlife Management merit badge.

A pile of brush will help small animals survive the rigors of winter.

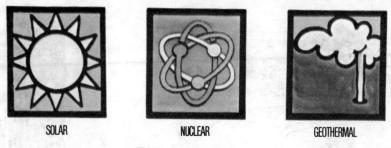

SOLAR   NUCLEAR   GEOTHERMAL

Energy to Spare

All energy is from the sun. The radioactive minerals in the ground that we use for nuclear energy were there when the earth wheeled away from the sun perhaps 4½ billion years ago—plus or minus 70 million years. The energy of hot water in the ground—geothermal energy—comes from water heated by the hot inner core that the earth brought with it from the sun. The oil and gas we burn come from ancient animal life that depended on the sun. The coal we use is from plantlife that grew with its help. So are the logs we throw into our fireplaces. We can also thank the sun for the waterfalls that drive our turbines and the wind that turns our windmills. And we can thank it for its heat, for solar energy, and for the food that sustains our lives and produces the energy of our bodies.

We can depend on the sun for countless years. And we can depend on water and wind power and the energy from growing things as long as the sun provides the climates.

We can depend on no other sources of energy. The known United States oil reserves may be gone in 15 years. Within 20 years the demand for gas may exceed our domestic supply. The coal we have may last 400 years. The sources of nuclear energy will eventually be exhausted. What then?

Right this moment, the people of the United States are squandering more energy than any other people in the world. And we are paying for it dearly. The high prices we pay for imported oil has weakened the American dollar. The reliance on imported oil has made us vulnerable to foreign nations who can control our future by higher prices or embargoes.

Anything—ANYTHING— that you and your family and your friends can do to cut down the use of energy will help.

OIL GAS COAL

WHAT YOU CAN DO ABOUT ENERGY. You can save energy directly by cutting down on the use of gas and oil and other fuels. You save double when you cut down on electricity: you save the energy used by the appliance and the energy used by the power company.

There are many energy-saving tricks you can do in your home. Most of them are pictured on the next two pages.

- Get there by walking and bicycling instead of driving.
- Encourage family members to drive within the national speed limit of 55 miles an hour. It is the most effective use of gas—and it's the law.
- Is your home weather-sealed for heat and cold? Check insulation. Check for drafts around doors and windows.
- Avoid overuse of air conditioners. A fan may be enough. An attic fan will help.
- Open your windows at night to let in the cool air. Close them during the day to keep out the hot air.
- Do you actually need an electric toothbrush, can opener, carving knife, and a gas-power mower? Won't muscle power do?
- Find out where your local recycling center is. Collect and bring in steel cans, aluminum cans, glass jars, and bottles.
- Tie up bundles of your family's newspaper for recycling. Use twine and tie with the packer's knot (pages 90-91). Use the same method on a newspaper drive with your troop.
- Earn the Energy merit badge.

WATER WIND PLANTS

Attic vents and fan reduce use of air conditioners

Use smaller bulbs

A sweater gives warmth without fuel

Storm windows add comfort, cut costs

Fluorescent lighting uses less current

Turn off heat in unused rooms

Turn off lights and T when leaving room

Turn tap tight—replace worn washers

Replace insulation if it is worn

Cook several things at once

Don't keep refrigerator open needlessly

Pres cook save ener

Save heat—keep out drafts

Cool leftovers before refrigerating

Use appliances during "non-peak" h

Run power equipment at peak efficiency

Run washer or dryer with full load

340

Family Tips for Saving Energy

Insulation warms in winter, cools in summer

Weatherstrip and caulk all openings

Draw shades and drapes

Set thermostat to lowest comfort level

Lower heat 5 to 6 degrees at bedtime

A 100-watt bulb is better than two 60's

Lower thermostat when family is away

Close damper

Close garage doors to prevent heat loss

NO!
GAS

A properly tuned car saves gas

Properly inflated tires save fuel

Recycle glass, aluminum, paper, steel cans

GLASS   METAL

Old newspapers make new newspapers through recycling

341

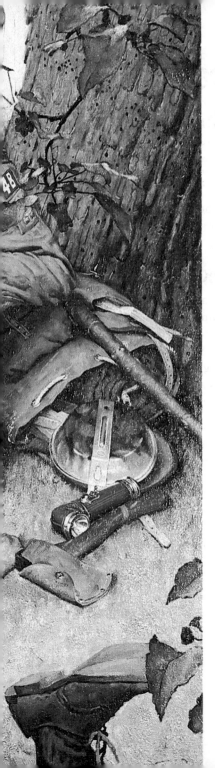

YOU AND OTHER PEOPLE

NOTE: At the time this picture
was painted the den chief cord
was worn on the right shoulder;
it is now worn on the left.

The Adventure Trail
by Norman Rockwell, 1952

Communication

Every day you are among people. Most of them you pass by. But often you stop for a greeting, or to tell a person something, or to ask someone a question. The better you can express yourself, the better will be the impression you make. The clearer will be the information you will get.

On those occasions you are practicing the skill of communication. It is the most important skill for getting along with people. It is also the most important for learning.

THE SPOKEN WORD

The most common form of communication is the two-way kind using the spoken word. It's the kind you have when you talk directly with someone. This can be face-to-face, over the phone, or by ham radio, or CB (citizens' band).

Radio and TV, newspapers, magazines, and books are all examples of one-way communication. You can listen or read. You are informed. But you can't talk back or ask questions.

DIRECT COMMUNICATION. Let's try a sample of each of the two kinds of communication, using the spoken word:

Making an Announcement. Your patrol has planned an event to which you want to invite the other patrols. You have a spot on the troop program for making the announcement. Keep it brief and to the point. Then ask for questions. Answer all of them. That makes it two-way communication.

Making Introductions. Names are the key part of any introduction. They must be right and said clearly.

Let's say you want your Scoutmaster to meet your parents. Here are three ways of making the introduction:

"Mr. Jones, I'd like you to meet my mother and father."

"Mom and dad, this is Mr. Jones, my Scoutmaster."

"Mr. Jones—my mother and father."

That's one-way communication. It will be followed by the two-way kind as your parents talk with your Scoutmaster.

TELEPHONE COMMUNICATION. Be prepared. Have a card close by the phone with the numbers of the persons you usually call. And also with the emergency phone numbers you may need someday (see page 362).

Making a Call. Dial, then let the phone ring up to 10 times—one minute—before you hang up. When someone answers, say right away who you are—"This is Bill Jones" (or whatever it is)—and to whom you wish to speak. If what you have to say will take a long time, ask if the person has time to talk now. If not, ask when you may call back.

Be careful in your timing when you call. Don't phone too early or too late in the day or at mealtime.

When you make a call, it's up to you to cut it off when you have done what you called for. Make the call short—others may want the phone.

Taking a Call. Pick up the phone as soon as it rings. Say who you are—"Bill Jones here." If the call is for you, go ahead. Let the one calling finish the conversation. If the call is for another, get that person to the phone quietly.

The ultimate in communication is to be able to tell a story or relate an incident so vividly that you hold your audience spellbound.

THE PRINTED PAGE

The kind of communication you can get from the printed page is some of the best you'll ever receive. A good author can tell you what you want to know. A good artist or photographer can show you what's involved. From newspapers, magazines, and books you can find out about your world. From the printed page you can learn to do things by yourself.

Learn by Yourself. The illustrations in this book and the text that accompanies them will give you all the information you need for doing what you'll want to do in Scouting. By applying what you read you will be able to master most of the skills of Scouting.

Let us say that you became interested in the special skill you saw on page 114: How to make fire by friction. No one in the troop knows how. You have to learn by yourself.

By reading the text you find out what equipment you need. By looking at the pictures you learn how to make it. By assuming the position in the illustration and following the instructions, you know how to use the fire-by-friction set.

You may not get fire the first time you try. But you will if you persevere.

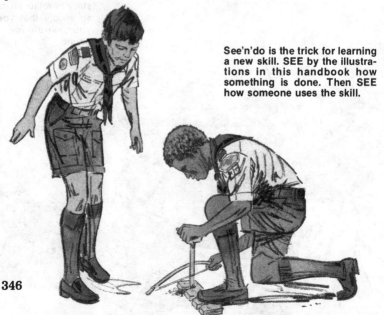

See'n'do is the trick for learning a new skill. SEE by the illustrations in this handbook how something is done. Then SEE how someone uses the skill.

SHOWING

A Scout in the troop may become so fascinated by your special skill that he'll want to learn it. He may say, "Please teach me how to do it." Your first reaction may be, "Sure." But hold it!

A successful educator once said, "You can't teach anybody anything. The best you can do is inspire him and help him learn for himself." That's the way it's done in Scouting.

So, instead of saying "Sure" you say "No." But add quickly, "But I'll help you learn for yourself."

Show Him. If your special skill is fire by friction, put the parts of the set together slowly so that he can follow what you are doing. Then go through the process of making fire. Ask him questions about what he sees you use. Have him describe what you are doing. Draw him out—that's education. Don't tell him what you are using and doing. Don't pour it in—that's just instruction.

Let Him Do It. Then give him the set and let him make fire himself. Go on drawing him out. "Why are you doing that? Why are you pressing down so hard? Why are you speeding up your bow strokes?" Soon there'll be smoke, fire—success!

You haven't taught him, yet he has learned. And, paradoxically, by definition this makes you the perfect teacher: "If the learner has learned, the teacher has taught."

After seeing, DO. If you want to learn to make fire by friction, for instance, make a set. Then DO what you have seen.

HAND SIGNS
Silent Scout Signals

For games and contests, and for moving the troop or the patrol, the Scouts have to get into formation quickly and smartly. In Scouting, this is not done with shouted commands. It is done with hand and arm movements.

TROOP SIGNALS. All formations start with the leader in charge first making the "Attention" signal (page 37).

- **Single Rank (Troop Line).** Leader extends both arms parallel to the line he wishes. The patrols fall in line, with the patrol leaders centered in front of their patrols.
- **Council or U (Horseshoe).** Leader raises both arms 45 degrees from the sides. The Scouts fall in, in a semicircle, with the patrol leaders to the right of their patrols.
- **Troop Circle.** Leader raises arms 45 degrees, then swings them from front to rear and back several times. The patrols form a complete circle around him.
- **Open Columns.** Leader extends arms forward, bent at elbows, with palms up. The Scouts fall in patrol lines, with the patrol leaders centered in front of their patrols.
- **Close Columns.** Leader extends arms as for open columns, but with hands fisted. The patrols line up, with the patrol leaders at their right.
- **Parallel File (Relay File).** Leader extends arms forward at shoulder height. The patrol leaders take position two paces apart. Their Scouts fall in behind them.
- **Dismissal.** Leader swings arms in a crossed-front position.

PATROL SIGNALS. On a hike or in a game in camp, your patrol leader can use silent signals to tell you what to do.

- "Move forward." Your patrol leader raises his right arm and swings it forward to horizontal position.
- "Hurry." The PL moves his right fist quickly up and down.
- "Halt." The PL raises his right fist up high.
- "Spread out." The PL swings his arms out to both sides.
- "Assemble." The PL swings his raised arm in a wide circle.

348   **SILENT SCOUT SIGNALS** ▶

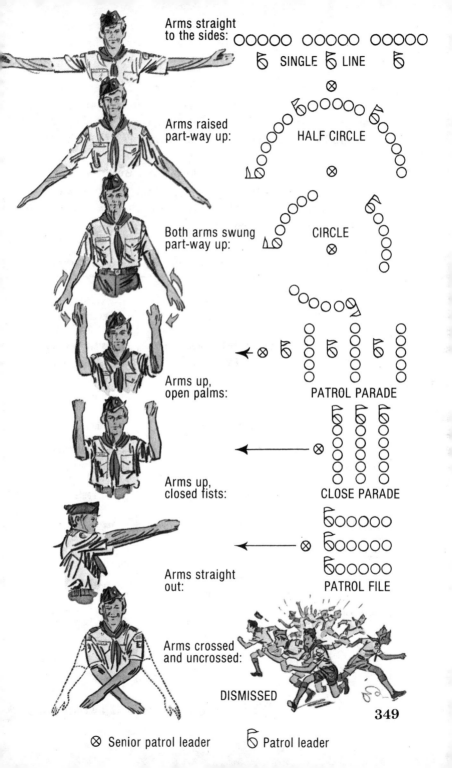

Arms straight to the sides: SINGLE LINE

Arms raised part-way up: HALF CIRCLE

Both arms swung part-way up: CIRCLE

Arms up, open palms: PATROL PARADE

Arms up, closed fists: CLOSE PARADE

Arms straight out: PATROL FILE

Arms crossed and uncrossed: DISMISSED

349

⊗ Senior patrol leader   🇫 Patrol leader

Indian Sign Language

Every Indian tribe had its own language. The languages were different. Therefore Indians from different tribes could not communicate with each other through the spoken word. But they could by making signs with their fingers and by hand motions.

Every tangible thing had a word sign. But to express abstract things the Indians had to put two or three signs together. The word signs used to express the 12 points of the Scout Law have deep meaning.

The points of the Scout Law	The Indian word sign	The meaning of the word signs
A SCOUT IS		
TRUSTWORTHY	TRUE	Like an arrow, straight from the heart and lips.
LOYAL	HEART + TRUE	Heart stays that way.
HELPFUL	HEART + BIG	Cares about others.
FRIENDLY	FRIEND	Growing up side by side.
COURTEOUS	TALK + GOOD	Good: a motion level with the heart.
KIND	GOOD + KILL + NO	These three word signs indicate no cruelty, no killing, but "good."
OBEDIENT	LISTEN	Listens—heeds what is being said.
CHEERFUL	HEART + SUNRISE	A remarkable picture: "sunrise in the heart."
THRIFTY	EXTERMINATE + NO	Leaves something for others.
BRAVE	BRAVE	Knuckle to knuckle unflinching.
CLEAN	HEART + MIND + TONGUE + GOOD	The meaning is evident. A beautiful statement.
REVERENT	KNOW + GREAT MYSTERY	The two fingers up is the sign for wisdom. God, the Great Mystery, above man, indicated by the waving motion.

SCOUT LAW IN INDIAN WORD SIGNS

Scout

True

Heart

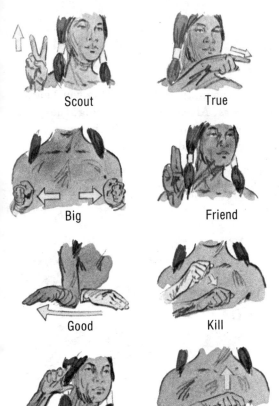

Big

Friend

Talk

Good

Kill

No

Listen

Sunrise

Exterminate

Brave

Mind

Tongue

Know

Great Mystery

A student of Indian languages, Wm. Tompkins, collected 761 word signs used by Plains Indians. Here, by permission, are 17.

Sign Language for the Hearing-Impaired

People who cannot hear can communicate with each other—and with others who know the method—by forming word signs with their hands and fingers. After special training, they can also use their lips to form the shape of words they can't say which can then be read by a lip reader.

MANUAL ALPHABET. Words for which there are no signs, the hard-of-hearing spell out in the signs of the manual alphabet. They use these signs also when they spell out the names of persons or places.

A

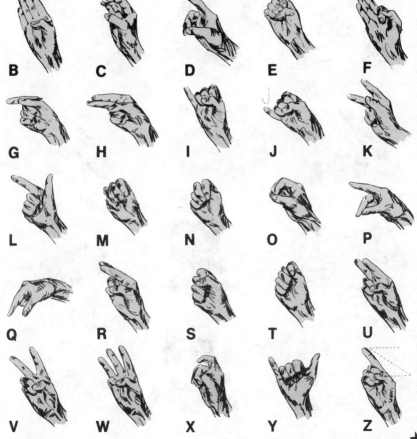

SCOUT LAW IN SIGN LANGUAGE

 THE

 SCOUT

 LAW

 A

 SCOUT

 IS

 TRUSTWORTHY

 LOYAL

 HELPFUL

 FRIENDLY

 COURTEOUS

 KIND

 OBEDIENT

 CHEERFUL

 THRIFTY

 BRAVE

 CLEAN

 REVERENT

353

Offside

Delay of game

Illegal procedure

Illegal motion

Clipping

Personal foul

Touchdown or
field goal

Illegal use of hands
and arms

Time-out

First down

Ball ready for play
FOOTBALL

Start the clock

Strike one

Out
BASEBALL

Safe

TOUCH

Blind people throughout the world can read and write by using the braille system. It was invented in 1824 by a blind Frenchman, Louis Braille.

Braille is a system of raised dots for touch reading and writing. The system is based on an arrangement of six dots. Each such arrangement is called a braille cell.

1 ● ● 4

2 ● ● 5   To aid in identifying the positions of the dots in each braille cell, Louis Braille numbered the dot positions 1-2-3 downward on the left, and 4-5-6 downward on the right.

3 ● ● 6

a	b	c	d	e	f	g	h	i	j
1	2	3	4	5	6	7	8	9	0

LINE 1, consisting of the first 10 letters of the alphabet is formed with dots 1,2,4,5 of the braille cell. These symbols also make the numbers.

| k | l | m | n | o | p | q | r | s | t |

LINE 2 adds dot 3 to each of the characters of line 1.

| u | v | x | y | z | and | for | of | the | with |

LINE 3 adds dots 3 and 6 to each of the characters of line 1.

| ch | gh | sh | th | wh | ed | er | ou | ow | w |

LINE 4 adds dot 6 to each of the characters of line 1.

| , | ; | : | . | en | ! | () | "/? | in | " |

LINE 5 uses dots 2,3,5,6. These are mostly punctuation characters.

Courtesy American Federation for the Blind

Flag signaling with Morse code uses one flag. Semaphore requires two.

SIGNAL CODES

From the start of Scouting in 1910, American Scouts have used codes for communicating over long distances—from lakeshore to lakeshore, from mountaintop to mountaintop.

- **Semaphore Code.** In this system, you use two flags. You send your message by swinging the flags into certain positions to indicate the letters of the alphabet.

- **Morse Code.** This code of dots and dashes was invented by Samuel Morse in 1835 for use in telegraphing by electricity. It can be sent with a single flag, by light (flashlight or mirror), sound (bugle or whistle), or ham radio. In flag signaling, the flag swung to the right is dot, to the left dash.

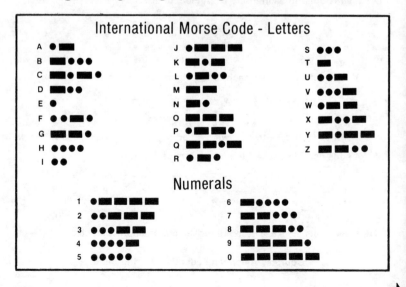

SEMAPHORE CODE ▶

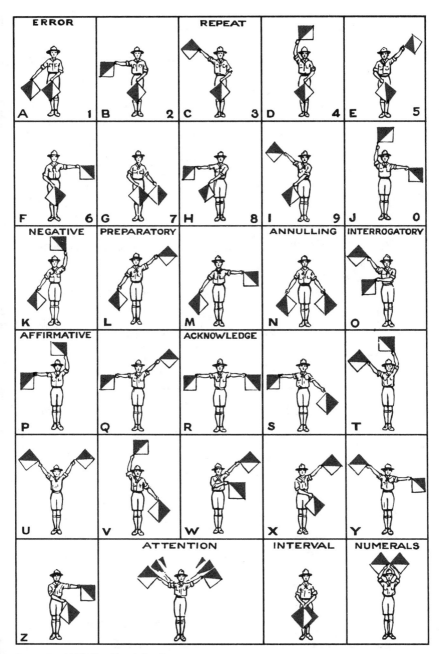

From the 1911 *Handbook for Boys.*

Procedure Signals for Sending Code Signals

Used by SENDER (Letters with line over them sent as one letter.)

Morse	Semaphore	Meaning	Explanation
A̅A̅A̅A̅	Attention (Flags swung overhead)	Attention	I have a message for you. Are you ready?
8 E's	8 E's	Error	I made a mistake. I will repeat beginning with last word that I sent correctly.
Front or Pause	Front (Flags down)	End of word	End of word. More coming. (Front with flags; pause in other methods.)
A̅A̅A̅	AAA	Period	End of sentence. More coming. (Punctuation is usually spelled out in long messages.)
A̅R̅	AR	End of message	That's all for now. Did you get it?

Used by RECEIVER (Letters with line over them sent as one letter.)

Morse	Semaphore	Meaning	Explanation
K	K	Go ahead	I am ready to receive. Start sending.
I̅M̅I̅	IMI	Repeat sign	Please send again; I missed it.
T	C	Word received	I understood word. TO BE SENT UPON RECEIPT OF EACH WORD (not used in telegraph and radio receiving).
R	R	Message received	I got it OK.

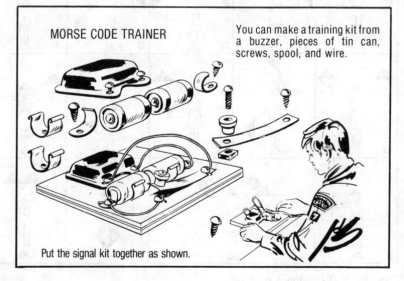

MORSE CODE TRAINER

You can make a training kit from a buzzer, pieces of tin can, screws, spool, and wire.

Put the signal kit together as shown.

V

Require
Assistance

X

Require
Medical
Assistance

N

No or
Negative

Y

Yes or
Affirmative

Proceeding in
This Direction

GROUND-TO-AIR SIGNALS. Make them in open area near camp. Tramp out in snow or sand as big as you can. Line with boughs or stones for shadow and contrast. Burn grass, turn over sod, or lay out any material that might be seen. Geometric designs will catch attention of aircraft overhead. Such signals work even if you are asleep or ill when plane comes. Destroy upon rescue.

DISTRESS SIGNALS

If you are ever completely lost, make your position known as soon as possible. The way to do this is by using some attention-getting device. This would be anything that would disturb the "natural" look or "natural" sound of the area.

- Fly a large flag of contrasting color—perhaps a blanket—from a tall tree.
- Set up the appropriate ground-to-air signal (top of page).
- Use the universal distress signal. This is some kind of signal repeated three times: Three shouts, three blasts of whistle or bugle, three gunshots, three columns of smoke. (For making fires, see pages 110-113.)
- Sweep the horizon with a mirror or a bright can lid at often-repeated periods during the day. On bright days the reflected light can be easily spotted by a plane. Even on hazy days it can be seen by aircraft.
- If in contact with someone, send the S O S Morse code distress call. Use a flag (shirt on a pole). Or send by interrupted light or sound: flashlight, lantern, mirror, bugle, whistle, spark coil, radio.

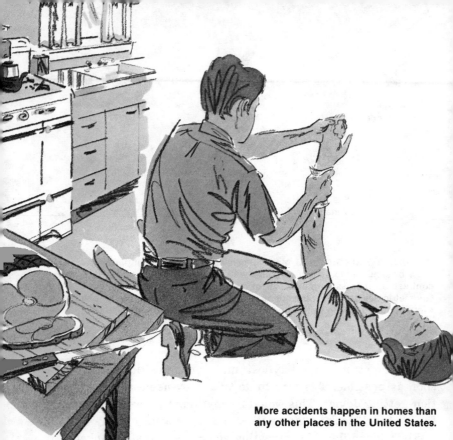

More accidents happen in homes than any other places in the United States.

Be Prepared for Accidents

"Accidents will happen." They shouldn't—but they do. There may be many times in your Scouting life when you will come face to face with an accident. Out alone or with friends, you may come upon an automobile smashup. Someday you may save a person from drowning. In camp, another Scout may cut himself with an ax. At home, some member of the family may have a fall. In each case, you may be the one to give first aid.

WHAT IS FIRST AID? First aid is definitely aid given at *first* in case of injury or sickness. That word "first" suggests that there is more to follow. The next aid should be given by someone who has special training for the job: a doctor. If a case is at all serious, get medical help immediately.

The way you act in an emergency has a great bearing on the patient's recovery. The *confidence* you show because you know what to do, the *common sense* you display in doing first things first, your *calmness* and *cheerfulness*—all these will make your patient feel at ease.

Close to 50,000 people die each year in auto accidents on the country's highways—many because help is not at hand. Be prepared to act in case of a crash.

DO FIRST THINGS FIRST. In a major accident, THINK! Then DO FIRST THINGS FIRST! In a car crash, for instance, proceed this way:

- **Protect yourself.** Be watchful as you go into action.
- **Secure car and passengers.** Turn off the ignition. Flag down other traffic. Keep anyone from smoking. If there's smoke or fire, get the passengers out quickly but carefully.
- **Phone for an ambulance.** Send somebody to phone. Give full information about your location and extent of injuries.
- **Decide priorities.** If several persons are injured, get at "hurry cases" first. Then other injuries.
- **DON'T MOVE THE INJURED** unless there is risk of a fire. Moving may turn a small injury into a big one.

GETTING HELP. The way to get help is not always the same. Your town may have an EMSS (Emergency Medical Services System). Or you may have a rescue squad, a hospital ambulance service, a police or sheriff's office, or a fire department emergency service. Or you can get help by dialing 0 (Operator). Find out the best way now and write it here:

Police _____

Fire _____

Ambulance _____

Doctor _____

Rescue or EMSS _____

Poison control center _____

Friendly neighbor _____

At home, write the emergency number on a card and place this near your phone.

Away from home, have a card with the emergency number written on it in your pocket. Carry a few "emergency coins" with you at all times—a couple of dimes, a couple of nickels. You'll need them to use a pay phone.

When you phone for help, say to the person answering, "I want to report an accident." Speak clearly. Use the three W's: WHO, WHERE, WHAT.

- WHO? Give your name and telephone number: "This is Scout Joe Brown calling from 555-2222."
- WHAT? Tell what is the matter: "I am reporting an automobile accident. Three people hurt, one unconscious."
- WHERE? "Where Route 130 and Route 1 cross."

362

Take for granted that shock comes with an injury. Act to prevent it.

SHOCK AND FAINTING

SHOCK occurs in every accident. It's a quick lowering of strength caused by pain, fear, and sometimes loss of blood. A shock victim is very weak. His face is pale. His skin is cold and clammy. He shivers from chills. He may vomit.

Don't Wait for the Symptoms to Show. Assume that injury and shock go together. Give shock care immediately. That may prevent it from setting in.

First Aid. Have the injured person lie down. Raise his feet slightly. In cool weather cover him to keep him warm. If it is hot, don't. If the patient is conscious, let him sip a little water. If he is unconscious, turn him to lie on his side, not on his back.

FAINTING is a mild form of shock. It is a "blacking out" caused by not enough blood going to the brain. It can be caused by fright, bad news, breathing bad air, standing too long. A victim gets pale. He may wobble or suddenly fall to the ground.

First Aid. Keep the victim lying down until he feels better. Loosen his collar. Raise his feet.

If he does not come to right away, treat for shock.

If you ever feel faint yourself, sit down and put your head between your knees. Even better, lie down and raise your legs.

"HURRY CASES"

Most of the accidents you will come upon will be minor. Here you can take your time to plan and to act. But someday you may be up against one of the "hurry cases." Life is at stake! You must move with utmost but carefully considered speed!

- Breathing has stopped. It must be started again.
- Blood is spurting or gushing from a wound. It must be stopped immediately.
- Poison has been swallowed. It must be made harmless.
- Heart attack. It must be acted upon quickly.

JUMP TO THE JOB! A second saved may be a life saved!

SEVERE BLEEDING. A car crash, a railroad accident, carelessness with a knife or an ax or with a power tool. You rush to the scene. There is a victim with blood spurting from a gash!

First Aid. Cover the wound with a bare hand and PRESS—HARD! Stop that blood! Then use your free hand to reach for your neckerchief or handkerchief. Or tear a piece off your shirt. If someone is near, call for a cloth folded into a pad or for a sterile gauze pad. Let go of the wound for the split second it takes to slap the pad on it, then press again. Finally, tie the pad firmly in place with some kind of bandage—cravat bandage, gauze bandage, or whatever you can manage. If pad gets blood-soaked, don't remove it. Just put another pad on top of the first, and another bandage, and continue pressure.

Then get the victim to a hospital.

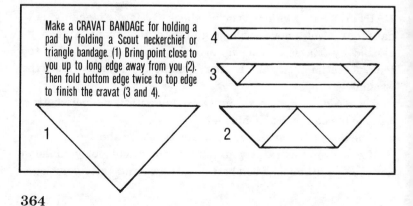

Make a CRAVAT BANDAGE for holding a pad by folding a Scout neckerchief or triangle bandage. (1) Bring point close to you up to long edge away from you (2). Then fold bottom edge twice to top edge to finish the cravat (3 and 4).

Spurting blood must be stopped quickly. Grab the wound with your bare hand and press down firmly. Raising the cut arm or leg above body level will help control bleeding.

Remember: MOST bleeding can be stopped by direct pressure.

Use your free hand to get a pad of cloth of some kind. Let go of the wound long enough to place the pad. Wrap something around pad to keep it in place. Get medical help.

Square knot

Spurting blood comes from an artery—one of the blood vessels that carry blood from the heart out into the body. Some bleeding from a cut artery can be controlled by pressure.

Pressure on four pressure points—two on each side of the body—can be used to control bleeding of arm and leg. Press the artery against the bone at the pressure point. It acts just like stepping on a water hose.

Arterial Bleeding from a Leg

Control it by pressing the artery with the heel of your hand against the pelvic bone at the pressure point.

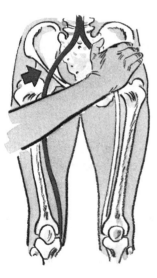

Arterial Bleeding from an Arm

Control it by squeezing the artery with the flat of your fingers against the upper-arm bone at pressure point.

365

RESCUE BREATHING. A drowning person is pulled out of the water ... a man is dragged out of a burning building ... an auto mechanic is dragged from under a car with its motor running ... a child is pulled away from an electric wire. In each of these cases, breathing may have stopped. Yet the victim's life may be saved. Someone must get to work right away. That someone could be YOU.

If you come upon an emergency, check if the victim is breathing. Look at his chest. Listen with an ear to his mouth. If he is not breathing, start giving him rescue breathing.

In rescue breathing you breathe your own breath into the victim's lungs. The air in your breath has enough oxygen in it to save a life. For an adult you breathe through the victim's mouth. For a child you breathe into both nose and mouth.

First Aid. Time is of the utmost importance. Act quickly.

Position the Victim. Place the victim face up. Tilt his head far back, chin pointing up. Lift with one hand under the neck. Press down with the other hand on the forehead. Pinch the nostrils shut with thumb and forefinger of this hand.

Then take a deep breath and give rescue breathing:

- *Step 1.* Open your mouth wide and seal it over the victim's mouth. Blow into his mouth to fill up his lungs. Look to see that his chest rises.
- *Step 2.* Remove your mouth. Take a deep breath. Look to see that the victim's chest falls as the air escapes.

Repeat steps 1 and 2 every 5 seconds for an adult, every 3 seconds for a child.

When the victim's breathing starts, time your efforts to fit his efforts to breathe for himself. Then care for shock.

Check the Effect. If no air is getting into the victim's lungs, move speedily to open up the airways:

- Give the victim four quick, sharp blows on the back.
- Place one of your hands on your other hand and press victim's abdomen with four quick upward thrusts.
- Probe victim's mouth with two fingers for obstructions.
  Then quickly resume rescue breathing.

Don't give up. Continue until a doctor tells you to stop.

To open airway, place victim face up. Tilt his head far back, chin pointing up. Lift neck with one hand, press forehead with other. Pinch nostrils.

Diagram shows importance of far-back position of head. With victim's head flat on the ground (top), his tongue closes the airway. With his head far back (bottom), airway is fully open.

STEP 1 IN RESCUE BREATHING
Seal your mouth over victim's mouth. Blow into his mouth to fill his lungs. Watch to see that his chest rises as air enters lungs.

STEP 2 IN RESCUE BREATHING
Remove your mouth. Take a deep breath. Watch to see that the victim's chest falls as the air escapes from lungs.

If airway is blocked, roll the victim toward you. Give him four sharp blows on the back.

Roll victim back on his back. Straddle him. Place heel of hand midway between rib cage and belly button. Push upward quickly four times.

Turn victim's head to side. Sweep a finger inside his mouth to remove any foreign objects.

Keep medicines and household chemicals where children cannot get hold of them.

POISONING BY MOUTH. One third of all deaths by accident among children is caused by poisons. It is hard to believe what kids will swallow: kerosine, turpentine, insecticides, rat poisons, peeling wall paint, lye, pills and tablets from medicine cabinet, weed killer from garden supplies.

First Aid. Your first thought in a case of swallowed poison is this: Dilute it! DILUTE IT! DILUTE IT!! Water! Water!! Have a child drink half a glass of water, an adult a full glass. Then more water. Or milk if you have it.

Find the container of the poison swallowed. Then call the poison control center or hospital emergency room listed in the phone book and noted by you on page 362. Give the name of the poison. If the instructions on the poison container tell what the antidote is, send someone for it. Use it quickly.

HEART ATTACK. Heart attack is the major cause of death in the United States. You may have to come to the help of someone who is having a heart attack. These are the signals:

- Uncomfortable pressure, squeezing, fullness or pain in the center of the chest behind the breastbone. The feeling may spread to shoulders, arms, and neck. It may last 2 minutes or longer and may come and go. It need not be severe. *Sharp, stabbing twinges of pain usually are NOT signals of a heart attack.*
- Sweating for no explainable reason, such as a hot room.
- Nausea: stomach distress with urge to vomit.
- Shortness of breath.
- Feeling of weakness.

First Aid. Get the patient under medical care as soon as possible. Follow steps for GETTING HELP on page 362.

368

Small wounds: Wash with soap and water. Let dry. Cover with sterile adhesive bandage.

OTHER FIRST AID CASES

CUTS AND SCRATCHES are wounds—openings in the skin. Even the slightest wound should be cleaned promptly. Otherwise germs may get to work and cause a dangerous infection.

First Aid for Small Wounds and Scratches. The best way to clean a wound is to wash it with soap and water. At home, use water right out of the faucet. On a hike or in camp, use water from your canteen or the clear running water of a stream. Wait until the skin around the wound dries, then put on an adhesive bandage. If you don't have such a bandage and the wound is small, simply wash it. Let it bleed. The bleeding will stop shortly when the blood has clotted.

First Aid for Larger Cuts. Wash a larger cut with soap and water. Cover it with a gauze compress that is sterile. That is, treated so that it is free of germs. Hold in place with adhesive tape or with a binder. If you don't have such a compress, fold a piece of clean cloth. The binder may be a gauze bandage from a first aid kit. Or use your Scout neckerchief, folded into a cravat bandage (page 364) or applied as shown on page 371.

If a wound is serious, see that the patient gets medical aid.

Large wounds: wash with soap and water. Cover with a sterile compress.

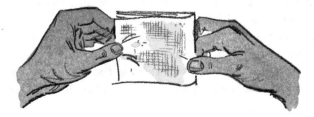

Arm sling
for hand fracture

Arm sling
for shoulder fracture

Placing arm sling with "pig's tail"

Overhand
knot
for
"pig's
tail"

Arm sling with "pig's tail"

SLINGS. A sling is used to support an injured hand or arm. You can use a Scout neckerchief, plain or with a "pig's tail"—an overhand knot tied in the large angle of the triangle.

Place the neckerchief over the chest, with the "pig's tail" at the elbow of the injured arm and one end over the shoulder. Bring the other end of the neckerchief up to the other shoulder. Tie the two ends together on the side of the neck so that the hand is held about 8 cm (3 in.) higher than the elbow.

SCOUT NECKERCHIEF AS A BANDAGE

Head bandage

Hand bandage

Knee bandage

Foot bandage

NOSEBLEED looks bad but is not very serious. It is usually from a small vein in the middle partition of the nose. It seldom lasts long.

First Aid. Be calm. Sit up and lean forward slightly. Press the bleeding nostril toward the center. Apply cold cloth to nose and face.

BURNS, SCALDS, AND SUNBURN. Someone touches a hot coal—result: an ordinary burn. Someone spills boiling water over his foot—result: a scald. Someone falls asleep on the beach after a swim—results: sunburn.

First Aid for Burns and Scalds. When a burn covers a large area, you can be certain that shock will set in. So give first aid for shock as well as for the burn.

First-Degree Burn. In minor burns and the usual sunburn, the skin gets red. Use cold water or ice cubes immediately. Keep the burn underwater until there is little or no pain. If cold water is not available, put on a clean, dry dressing.

Second-Degree Burn. If blisters form, the case is more serious. Blisters may break and become open wounds. Protect them by covering them with a dry, sterile gauze pad. Keep the pad in place with a bandage.

Third-Degree Burn. In the most severe burns, the skin may be burned away. Some of the flesh will be charred. There will be no pain. Do not try to remove any clothing. It may be sticking to the flesh. Wrap a clean sheet around the victim. Cover him with blankets if the weather is cool. Have him rushed to a hospital. His life is at stake.

CHEMICAL BURNS. Wash off with lots of water. Then treat the burn the way you would treat a burn of the same degree from any other cause. If the chemical gets in your eye, spray water into it or lie back and pour tap water into the eye. Put on a loose gauze bandage. Get medical help.

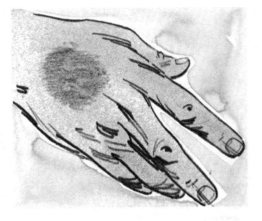

FIRST-DEGREE BURN

The skin is reddened. Patient may feel pain. Sunburn is usually a first-degree burn when sunning is stopped in time.

SECOND-DEGREE BURN

Blisters may have formed. Great care is necessary to keep the blisters from breaking. If they break, wound may become infected.

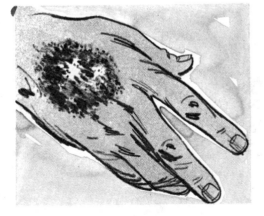

THIRD-DEGREE BURN

Some skin may be burned away and some flesh charred. Patient feels no pain. This burn is extremely dangerous because growth cells that form the new skin have been destroyed.

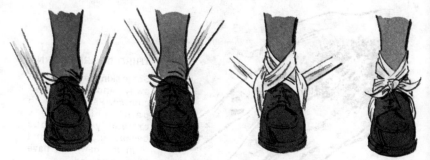

A blister can spoil a backpacking trip. Stop and give it proper care.

BLISTER ON HEEL. A shoe rubbing against a heel may cause a blister. If a blister starts forming, stop for first aid.

First Aid. Wash the foot with soap and water. When dry, cover with a sterile adhesive bandage or a sterile pad.

If you think that the blister may break, drain the fluid. Sterilize a pin in the flame of a match. Puncture the blister near its edge. Press out the liquid. Put on a sterile bandage.

SPRAINED ANKLE. A stumble may cause a sprained ankle. It swells up right away and is painful.

First Aid. Do not remove the shoe. Use it as a support. Tie an ankle bandage around foot and shoe. If foot is bare, have patient lie down. Then raise his leg and put a cold, wet towel around the ankle. Get patient under medical care.

Have a sprain checked by a doctor. A bone in the foot may be broken.

BITES AND STINGS of certain insects and spiders, chiggers, and ticks can be very painful. Some may cause infection.

First Aid. The pain of bites of mosquitoes, ants, and chiggers, and the stings of bees and hornets and yellow jackets can be relieved with a cold towel or ice water. If the stinger of a bee or wasp breaks off, flick it off with a finger. For further relief, you can apply a paste of household "meat tenderizer" and water. Use the same method for scorpion stings.

Ticks are small, hard-shelled relatives of the almost invisible chiggers. They may be infected with a disease. If a tick fastens itself to you, don't pull it off. The head may break off. Simply cover it with grease or oil. It will let go.

NOTE: Some people are allergic to insect and spider bites. They may have trouble breathing. They need special care:

- If the bite is on an arm or leg, tie a constricting band above the bite. It should be just tight enough to stop the blood in the skin. You should be able to put a finger under it.
- Put ice water or ice in a cloth on the bite.
- Keep the arm or leg lower than the body.
- Get the person under medical care. Be sure he keeps breathing. Give rescue breathing if needed.

SOME POISONOUS ARACHNIDS

Tick
(actual size)

Tick

Brown recluse spider

Black widow spider

Scorpion

JELLYFISH STINGS. The bell-shaped pink jellyfish of cool norther waters and the Portuguese man-of-war of warm southern waters have thousands of stinging cells on their tentacles. When touched, the poisons of these cells cause a sharp burning pain.

First Aid. Wash the affected area with diluted ammonia or rubbing alcohol. "Meat tenderizer" paste (page 375) may relieve the pain. Get the victim under medical care as quickly as possible. Some people are allergic to jellyfish stings. They may go into deep shock without any notice.

DOGBITES. A dogbite is not an ordinary wound. The dog may suffer from a disease called rabies. This can cause the death of the person bitten. The only way to find out if the dog is rabid is to have it caught and kept under observation. You have three jobs to do:

- Give first aid.
- Call for medical help.
- Call the police to come get the dog.

First Aid. Wash the bite in plenty of water to remove the saliva. Cover bite with a sterile dressing. Then to the doctor.

RATBITES. Infants and older persons are occasionally bitten while they sleep by rats nibbling at remains of food on face or clothing.

First Aid. Wash thoroughly with soap and water. Then cover the bite with a sterile dressing. Take the victim to a doctor for medical treatment.

Have a person bitten by a poisonous snake lie down quietly. Put a constriction band, such as a cravat made from a handkerchief, around his bitten limb. Get medical help.

376

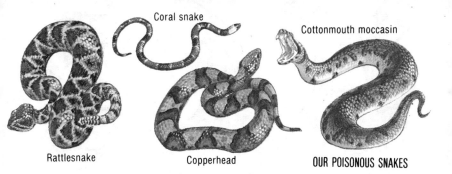

Coral snake

Cottonmouth moccasin

Rattlesnake

Copperhead

OUR POISONOUS SNAKES

SNAKE SAFETY. Although poisonous snakes may be common in certain areas, bites from them are not. When proper treatment is promptly given, few bites result in death.

But that doesn't mean that you should not be careful when you hike through snake-infested country. Our poisonous snakes are generally shy. They will try to get away. It is mainly if the snake finds itself cornered that it is likely to strike. So when you hike in rocky woods where rattlesnakes and copperheads are found, take along a stick that you can poke in among the rocks ahead of you. When climbing ledges watch where you place your hands. High-top boots will protect you in snake country since most snakebites are below the knee. When swimming or boating in the South, watch for cottonmouths sunning on banks or on tree branches overhanging the water.

SNAKEBITES. Both harmless and poisonous snakes are apt to strike when cornered. The bite by a nonpoisonous snake requires only ordinary first aid for small wounds (page 369). The bite of a poisonous snake involves more complicated first aid.

First Aid for Poisonous Snakes. Go to work quickly:

• Have the victim lie down, with the part bitten lower than the rest of the body. Calm him down. Keep him quiet.

• Put a constriction band 2 to 4 inches above the bite to slow the spread of the poison. Make it just tight enough so it's not easy to push your fingers between the band and his skin.

• Get medical help immediately. Tell the doctor the kind of snake, if known. This is especially important if antivenin is needed.

377

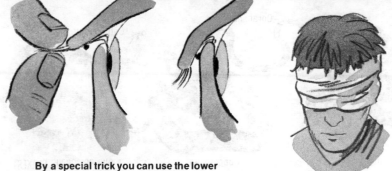

By a special trick you can use the lower lashes to brush out a speck in the eye.

SOMETHING IN THE EYE. Anything in the eye is not only painful but may endanger the eyesight.

First Aid. Get the person to blink his eyes—the tears may flush out the object. For something under the upper lid, pull the lid out and down. The lower lashes may brush the speck out. If the object is under the lower lid, place your thumb just below the lid. Move it down gently. Take out the speck with a corner of a clean handkerchief. If that fails, cover the eye with a sterile gauze pad. Take the patient to a doctor.

PUNCTURE WOUNDS may be caused by pins, splinters, nails, fishhooks, knife stabs, and gunshots. All are dangerous. Lockjaw (tetanus) germs may have gotten into the wound.

First Aid. After taking out any foreign matter, squeeze gently around the wound. Wash with soap and water. Apply a sterile bandage. Get to a doctor. He may decide on a tetanus antitoxin shot to prevent lockjaw.

If snagged by a fishhook so that the barb has gone through the skin, cut the line. Get to a doctor and let him remove the hook. In backcountry you may have to do the job: Push barb out through the skin and cut it off with wire cutters. The barbless hook can then be removed easily.

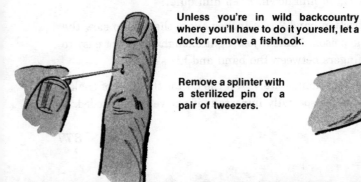

Unless you're in wild backcountry where you'll have to do it yourself, let a doctor remove a fishhook.

Remove a splinter with a sterilized pin or a pair of tweezers.

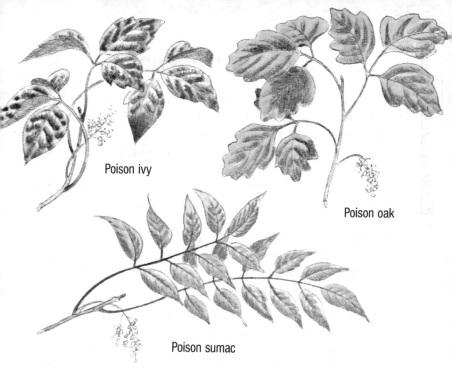

Poison ivy

Poison oak

Poison sumac

SKIN POISONING FROM POISON PLANTS. The poisoning from poison ivy, poison oak, and poison sumac is caused by an oily substance throughout the plant. Touching these plants may cause the skin to become red and itchy. Blisters may form.

First Aid. If you think you have touched a poison plant, wash immediately with soap and water, then with rubbing alcohol. Calamine lotion relieves the itching.

JEWELWEED FOR POISON IVY

Pale (yellow) and spotted (orange) jewelweed grow in damp places in eastern woodlands near spots where poison ivy is most rampant. It is also known as touch-me-not: the ripe seedpods pop when you touch them. The Indians used jewelweed for sting and poison-ivy medicine. They crushed a handful of the plant and applied the juicy mess to the itching areas for quick relief.

HEAT EMERGENCIES

HEAT EXHAUSTION. Heat exhaustion—as the name indicates—is caused by heat. It usually hits a person in an overheated room, but may also overtake him in the sun.

The patient's face is pale, with cold sweat on the forehead. Breathing is shallow. The whole body may be clammy from perspiration. Vomiting is common. NOTE: Do not confuse with heat stroke which requires a different kind of first aid.

First Aid. Heat exhaustion may be considered shock from heat. Regular care for shock therefore is in order. Move the patient to a shady, cool spot. Place him on his back. Raise his feet. Loosen his clothing. Fan him or apply cool, wet cloths. Give him sips of salt water: pinch of salt to a glass of water.

HEAT STROKE. Heat stroke is usually caused by exposure to sun. It's a life-and-death matter. Get a doctor at once.

The patient's face is like the sun: red, hot, dry. Breathing is slow and noisy. The pulse is rapid and strong. The body skin feels dry and hot. The patient may be unconscious.

First Aid. Get the patient quickly into a cool, shaded spot. Place him on his back with his head and shoulders raised. Undress him immediately down to his underwear. Then set out to cool him—especially his head—with water. Cover him with dripping wet towels, shirts, cloths. Keep him cool by dousing them with water or by wringing them out in cold water from time to time. When the patient's body has cooled, stop treatment for a while to see if it heats up again. If it does, resume cooling. When the patient regains consciousness, let him drink all the water he wants.

COLD EMERGENCIES

FROSTBITE. When you are out skating or skiing, someone in the party may complain of his ears, nose, fingers, or toes feeling numb. Or you may notice that a person's ears or nose or cheeks are looking grayish-white—a sure sign of frostbite.

First Aid. Get the frozen part thawed out. If part of the face is frozen, have the person remove a glove and cover the part with his hand. If a hand is frostbitten, bring it under the armpit next to the skin. Then get the patient into a warm room. Give him a warm drink. Warm the frozen part by holding it in warm—not hot—running water. Or wrap it in a warm blanket. When the frostbitten part is rewarmed tell the patient to exercise injured fingers or toes.

HYPOTHERMIA. When you hear of someone having "died from exposure" or "frozen to death," the killer may actually have been hypothermia—from *hypo*, low, and *thermia*, state of heat. It is caused by the body losing more heat than it generates. It occurs when a person is not clothed warmly enough for the air around him. Such a person is further endangered if he is exhausted, wet, and exposed to a strong wind as when caught in a rainstorm. Under such conditions the air doesn't have to be below freezing—a moderate air temperature of 40-50° may result in death.

Hypothermia starts with the patient feeling chilly, tired, irritable. If he is not helped at this stage, he will begin to shiver uncontrollably. Soon his shivering becomes violent. He may act irrationally. He may stumble and fall. If the shivering then stops, he is close to death.

First Aid. If you are on a hike or backpacking trip in severe weather and realize that someone in the party shows early symptoms of hypothermia, stop right then and there. Put up a shelter. Strip the patient gently and get him into a dry sleeping bag. A cold sleeping bag won't help much: a rescuer should also strip and get into the sleeping bag to use his warm body to warm the victim's cold body. If the victim is conscious and alert, offer hot liquids (sugary tea, chocolate, fruit juices). Careful, this may cause nausea. Get to medical care as soon as possible.

NOTE: The body temperature of a swimmer drops steadily in water cooler than himself. The shivering that results is the onset of hypothermia. Get out of the water. Cover up. Exercise to get warm.

BROKEN BONES

An automobile smashup, a fall, a violent blow, and you may be up against a fracture—a broken bone.

CLOSED AND OPEN FRACTURES. There's your patient. He is obviously suffering from shock. He complains of pain in a certain spot of leg or arm—or maybe side or back. A quick check shows that a bone is broken: The patient can't move the hurt part. It may look bent or shortened or have a bump. A swelling is setting in.

If that's the picture, your patient is lucky. His fracture is a *closed (or simple) fracture*—one with no open wound.

But if the sharp edges of a splintered bone have cut through flesh and skin, your patient is suffering from an *open (or compound) fracture*—a fracture plus an open wound.

The terrible danger in fractures is that incorrect handling by a well-meaning first-aider may turn a closed fracture into an open fracture. Such a fracture may cripple the patient or even endanger his life. So in fractures what you DO is important. What you DON'T DO may be even more important.

First Aid. There are three DO's and three DON'T's to the first aid for fractures:

- DO let the patient lie with as little motion as possible right where he is while you render first aid. Make him comfortable with something over and under him.
- DON'T let anybody bundle your patient into a car to rush him to a hospital. That's the easiest way of turning a simple closed fracture into an open compound one.
- DO call a doctor or an ambulance immediately.

Materials for splints: boards, sticks, umbrella, paper, cardboard tube

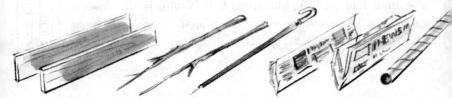

- DON'T try to set the bone—that's the doctor's job.
- DO treat for shock while waiting for the doctor.
- DON'T give stimulant if there is severe bleeding.

IMPORTANT: In an open fracture, cover the wound with a sterile dressing. If blood is spurting from an artery, stop it with hand pressure against pressure point (page 365).

Additional First Aid. In case of extreme emergency—when the accident happened on a heavily traveled highway or in the wilderness—you may have to move the patient before the doctor can get to him. In such a case heed this DO and DON'T:

- DO support the broken limb by making it immovable between well-padded splints. SPLINT HIM WHERE HE LIES!
- DON'T move the patient before the splinting is completed.

Splints. A splint is some stiff material that can be bound onto the fractured limb to prevent the broken bone from moving and tearing the flesh with its sharp edges. It should be longer than the bone on which it is to be used. It should be padded with soft material before being applied.

Look around where you happen to be. Use what is there: slabs of wood or lengths of saplings, pieces of bark, canes or umbrellas, broomsticks or shovel handles, rulers, heavy cardboard, cornstalks, wire netting, newspapers, magazines.

For padding, use cotton or wool batting, moss or grass, stockings, pieces of clothing, pillows, blankets, crumpled paper. Padding makes splints fit better and prevents hurting the patient.

For binding the splints use neckerchiefs, handkerchiefs, roller bandages, strips of cloth, belts.

Right now—this very moment—stop reading. Look around. What is within reach that you could use for splints, padding, and binding?

Materials for padding: clothing, crumpled paper, pillows, grass, moss

NOTE: In all fracture cases take for granted that the patient is suffering from shock as well. Start shock care immediately by having patient lie down while you give first aid for fracture. Follow up with other care for shock, as needed (see page 363).

COLLARBONE OR SHOULDER FRACTURE. No splint necessary. Place the forearm in a sling (page 370) with the hand raised about 8 cm (3 in.) higher than the elbow. Tie the upper arm against the side of the body with a wide cravat bandage. Make sure the bandage is not so tight that it stops the circulation in the arm.

LOWER-ARM OR WRIST FRACTURE. Use splint of magazine or thick newspaper. Or use two padded wooden splints, as long as the distance from elbow to knuckles. Place one on inside of arm, the other on outside, and bind together. Place arm in a wide sling with the thumb up and the hand slightly higher than the elbow.

UPPER-ARM FRACTURE. Use one padded splint only, slightly longer than the distance from shoulder to elbow. Bind it with two binders on outside of arm. Place forearm in narrow sling. Tie the splinted upper arm against the side of the body with a cravat bandage.

LOWER-LEG FRACTURE. Use two padded splints, as long as the distance from middle of thigh to just beyond the heel. Place one splint on each side of the injured limb and bind them together, using at least four binders.

THIGH FRACTURE. Use padded splints, one for outside the leg extending from heel to armpit, one for inside the leg from heel to crotch. Bind the splints together. Use four binders around the splints and leg, and three binders around the upper part of the outside splint and the body.

NOTE: Because of the strength of the muscles of the upper leg, they may pull the broken parts of the thigh bone out of line and into the flesh. For this reason the method given is early emergency care. The patient should not be moved any great distance without a traction splint. Ambulances carry such splints. A doctor will bring one if he is told of thigh fracture.

NOTE: All knots should be square knots.

BROKEN BONES

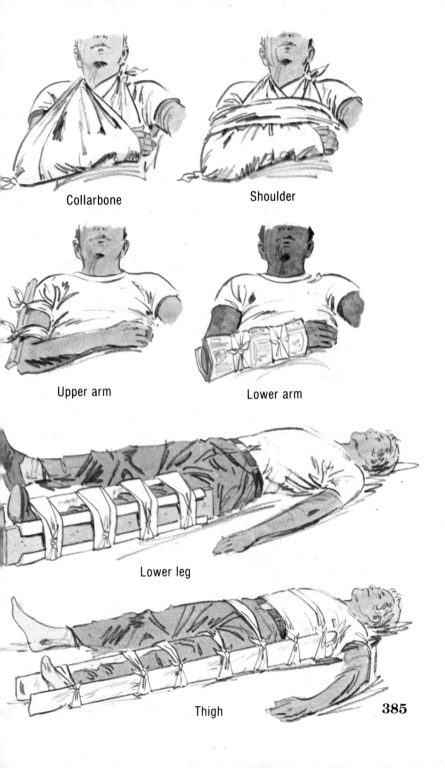

Collarbone

Shoulder

Upper arm

Lower arm

Lower leg

Thigh

385

TRANSPORTATION

The transportation of an injured person requires a lot of common sense and care. A SERIOUSLY INJURED PERSON SHOULD BE MOVED BY A FIRST-AIDER ONLY IN CASE OF EXTREME EMERGENCY. And then only after he has received first aid and has had possible fractures splinted.

ASSISTS AND HAND CARRIES. Walking Assist. A patient who has suffered a minor accident and feels weak may be assisted to walk. Bring one of his arms over your shoulder. Hold onto his wrist. Place your free arm around his waist.

One-Man Carry. This is best done piggyback. Bring your arms under the patient's knees. Grasp his hands over your chest.

Four-Hand Seat. This is a good method for two first-aiders to carry a conscious patient. Each bearer grasps his own right wrist with his left hand. The two bearers then lock hands with each other. The patient places his arms over the bearers' shoulders.

Two-Man Carry. Use this when the patient is unconscious. Bearers kneel on each side of the patient. Each bearer brings one arm under the patient's back, the other under his thighs. The bearers grasp each other's wrists and shoulders and rise from the ground with the patient.

STRETCHERS. When the patient has to be moved for some distance or his injuries are serious, he should be carried on a stretcher.

Emergency Stretchers. Use a not-too-heavy door, a short ladder, a gate, a sheet of heavy plywood.

Making a Stretcher. To make a stretcher, use two poles somewhat longer than the patient is tall. Use strong saplings, lengths of pipe, long tool handles, oars.

For the bed part turn two or three Scout shirts or coats inside out, button them up, and push the poles through the sleeves. Or use blankets. Or use burlap sacks with holes cut in the bottom corners. Or a sleeping bag with the bottom-corner seams opened. Or chicken wire.

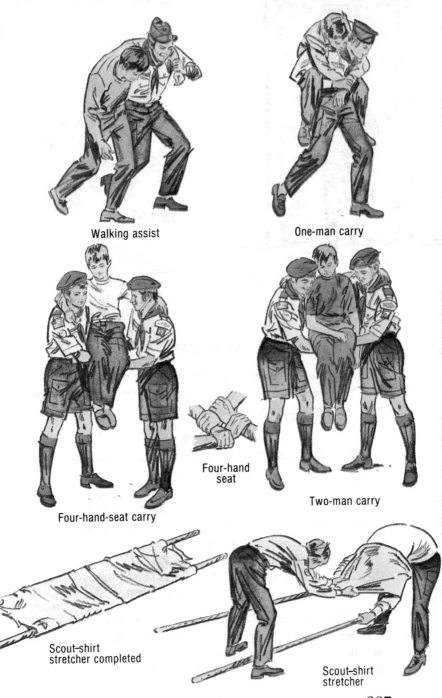

Walking assist

One-man carry

Four-hand-seat carry

Four-hand seat

Two-man carry

Scout-shirt stretcher completed

Scout-shirt stretcher

387

Building on Fire. **GET THE PEOPLE OUT!** Yell, hammer on the door, ring the doorbell. Have someone call the fire department. Or do it yourself.

RESCUES

First aid, in most cases, is something you do after an accident has happened. But there are cases where you may have to make a rescue before you give first aid.

Fires

A BUILDING ON FIRE. Every year, more than 6,000 Americans are burned to death! You may help hold down this ghastly number by going into action if you see a building on fire.

The first thing to do is: **GET THE PEOPLE OUT!** Yell, hammer on the door, ring the bell—**GET THEM OUT!** If the building has an alarm system, set it off.

Next: **CALL THE FIRE DEPARTMENT.** While waiting for the fire engines, figure out if there is something you can do—then do it with a cool head. Finally, **OFFER YOUR HELP.**

A PERSON ON FIRE. A person's clothes may catch fire from an open flame, or from burning oil, kerosine, or gasoline. The victim's first impulse is to run. It is the worst thing he can do. Running does not put out the fire—it fans the flame.

Rush up to the person, tackle him, if need be, to get him quickly to the ground. Then roll him over slowly as you beat out the flames with your hands. Be careful that your own clothes do not catch fire. If there is a blanket or a rug handy, wrap it around the victim to smother the flames. When the fire is out, give the victim the first aid he needs.

Live Wires

After a storm, someone may stumble over a live wire that has been knocked down. Or someone trying to fix an electrical outlet may get an electric shock. Or faulty house wiring may cause an electric accident.

ELECTRIC ACCIDENT FROM HOUSE CURRENT. If someone in a house is in contact with a live wire, shut off the current by pulling the main switch. Or grab the electric cord at a place where it is not bare or wet and pull it from the socket.

If you don't know where the main switch is and can't get the plug pulled out, you will have to try to remove the wire from the victim. To do this, take a DRY handkerchief, DRY towel, DRY sheet, or other cloth, encircle the wire with it, and pull the wire from the victim.

If you can't encircle the wire with the cloth, use it instead to pull the victim from the wire. Do not touch the victim until he and the wire are separated.

Be particularly careful in the case of a bathroom accident. Pull the main switch or call the electric company. It will probably be too difficult to get the victim away from the wire because of the many grounded objects, such as water pipes and a wet floor.

If the victim is not breathing after the rescue, start rescue breathing immediately. Call a doctor.

ELECTRIC ACCIDENT FROM OUTDOOR POWER LINE. Rescuing a person in contact with a live power line outdoors is extremely dangerous. Do not attempt a rescue yourself. Call the electric company, police, or fire department instead.

Drownings

WATER ACCIDENTS. This year, about 7,000 people—mostly boys and men—will drown while swimming or boating or playing in the water. You may have the chance, someday, to prevent one of these drownings.

If you have done lots of camping, you'll have learned to swim and will have had training in lifesaving. When a water accident occurs, it is simply a matter of making use of what you have learned. The methods are given on pages 156-57.

ICE RESCUE. During the winter, many people drown by falling through ice. If you witness such an accident, be quick—but think clearly! Do not rush headlong out on the ice—you may go in yourself. Decide on a safe way of saving the victim.

Try to reach the victim from shore with a pole or a coat or a rope. Tie a loop in the rope for the victim to put his arm through. It will be hard for him to hold on with numb fingers. At lakes where there is skating, you will often find an emergency ladder. Push the ladder out until the victim can reach it.

If you have to get to the victim over the ice, the main thing is to distribute your weight over as great a surface as possible. Lie down flat and snake out over the ice until you get close enough to throw the rope. When the victim has a firm grasp on it, then pull him out slowly.

If helpers are available, form a human chain (see illustration on page 43). Crawl out on the ice while someone holds on to your ankles, someone else to his. Grasp victim by the wrists and snake back. Even better, reach him with a pole (below and page 391).

After you have removed the victim from the ice, get him into shelter and give him first aid for hypothermia (page 381).

If the victim has stopped breathing, start rescue breathing.

Tornadoes and Floods

TORNADOES. Every year certain sections of our southern and central states are swept by tornadoes. Prepare for the tornado season by having on hand a battery-powered radio and a flashlight. Know where public shelters are located.

A tornado is a violent whirlstorm, sweeping along from southwest to northeast as a funnel-shaped cloud. In its awesome fury it can lift houses off the ground, tear up trees. Fortunately, its path is usually narrow, only a couple of hundred feet wide. So the chance of being caught is not very great.

When a tornado warning has sounded, immediately get out of any room that has windows and into shelter. The safest place to be during a tornado is underground in a storm cellar. In a home without a storm cellar, the corner of the basement nearest the approaching tornado is safest. If your house has no basement, crouch down low in an interior bathroom or closet.

If you are caught in the open with a tornado cloud directly southwest of you, and you can't get to safety, lie down flat in the nearest ditch, ravine, or other depression. If you are in a car, get out and get down.

FLOODS. In river valleys the thaws of early spring may bring ruin and destruction. When a sudden warm spell melts the snow in upstream mountains and sends the water foaming down, rivers often rise above their normal banks.

Most of the time there's plenty of warning before real danger comes. You can aid the authorities by helping people move out of their homes and directing them to high ground.

Someone falls through the ice! Form a human chain and attempt to rescue the victim.

YOU— AMERICAN CITIZEN

Our Heritage
by Norman Rockwell, 1950

393

Be a Knowing American

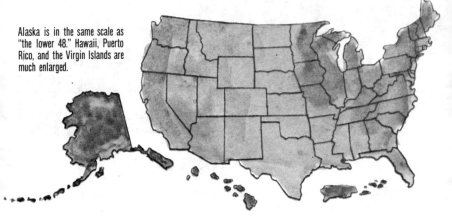

Alaska is in the same scale as "the lower 48." Hawaii, Puerto Rico, and the Virgin Islands are much enlarged.

The baby in its cradle, the boy or girl at school or at play, the man or woman at work or caring for a family or enjoying their leisure are all American citizens.

Citizenship is your privilege, your right. No one can take it away from you. You are a citizen now, this very minute.

But because America so generously bestows its citizenship upon you, you owe it to your country to be a good citizen. You owe it to your country to do your best to be a true American boy who will eventually grow into a true, upright American man and not to wait until you grow up to become a great man, but to be a **GREAT BOY, NOW!**

The way to become a good citizen is first to KNOW and then to DO.

America is a land, a people, and a way of life. By getting to know your country you will come to love it. By "helping other people at all times," by working with them, you will come to know the kind of people that Americans are. You will learn to get along well with all of them. By studying the past, by finding out about the American way of life, you will become an informed citizen. You will know what is needed to keep America great.

KNOW YOUR LAND

How well do you know America—your country? How much does it mean to you?

As a Scout you have hiked over its fields, camped in its woods. You have listened to the winds that speed across its plains, the brooks that gurgle through its meadows. But do you really know America? Have you realized its vastness, its beauty, its riches?

A HIKE OF AMERICA. Suppose you could take a hike of all America. Suppose you could sling your pack upon your back and could travel and travel, until you knew every corner of the country as well as you know your own backyard. Just suppose. . . . Such a hike may never become a reality. But let's try it in our imagination.

MAINE, NEW HAMPSHIRE, VERMONT, MASSACHUSETTS, RHODE ISLAND, CONNECTICUT . . . We'll set out from New England on a day in early spring. Sap is running strong in her maples. Snow still covers Boston Common. The waves are breaking over the "rockbound coast" of Maine and around Plymouth Rock. Clouds roll low over Mount Katahdin, over the White and Green Mountains. They hang even lower over the village green of Lexington where the first blood was shed for American independence April 19, 1775.

. . . **NEW YORK, NEW JERSEY, PENNSYLVANIA, DELA-WARE, MARYLAND** . . . We'll hike through New York State from the thunder of Niagara Falls to the hubbub of America's largest city. We'll wander through the farmlands of New Jersey. We'll walk the beaches of Delaware Bay. We'll stop at Valley Forge and at Gettysburg. There we will feel ourselves in tune with our past. And we'll stand before the Liberty Bell. It will never ring again. But, we'll hear it in our minds pealing out its message of liberty throughout the land.

. . . **VIRGINIA, WEST VIRGINIA, KENTUCKY, TENNES-SEE, NORTH CAROLINA, SOUTH CAROLINA, GEORGIA** . . . From the top of the Washington Monument in the heart of the Capital we'll look wide over the land of Dixie. We'll cross the calm Potomac and hike west through red clay fields. We'll climb the crest of the Alleghenies. We'll cross through the Cumberland Gap and explore the Great Smokies. Then go down onto the flatlands, among the pinewoods and the old plantations of Georgia.

. . . **FLORIDA, ALABAMA, MISSISSIPPI, LOUISIANA, ARKANSAS, MISSOURI** . . . We'll bask in the sun under Florida's swaying palms and explore the Everglades. We'll follow the old Spanish trail along the Gulf till we strike the "long-flowing" Mississippi. "Old Man River" himself will wel-

come us. We swing northward between cottonfields and sugarcane. We pass the hot springs of Arkansas and climb into the wild mysteries of the Ozark Mountains. Then, again, we reach the "great water" and go by riverboat up the Mississippi and the beautiful Ohio River.

...**OHIO, MICHIGAN, INDIANA, ILLINOIS, WISCONSIN, MINNESOTA, IOWA**... We enter states that are rich in industry and agriculture. Factories and warehouses crowd the busy cities. The hum from machines fills the air, night and day. But outside the cities the grass is green in the checkered fields. The corn is golden. The new-plowed soil is black and rich. And to the north are a thousand lakes for swimming, canoeing, fishing.

...**NORTH DAKOTA AND SOUTH DAKOTA, NEBRASKA, KANSAS**... The Great Plains spread before us as far as the eye can

reach. The wind ripples the wheat fields till they look like a yellow sea. A group of trees in the distance indicates a farm. A haze over the horizon shows the nearest town. Nowhere in our country will you get a feeling of its vastness as vividly as on the Great Plains. The only "islands" that rise above the flat distance are the Black Hills. Here, carved on the side of Mount Rushmore, the faces of Washington, Jefferson, Lincoln, and Teddy Roosevelt look to the future.

... MONTANA, IDAHO, WYOMING, COLORADO, UTAH ...

Beyond the hills the plains stretch out again. We follow them as they roll westward into still more states. But presently the plains become wavy hills that push higher and higher. We climb into the majestic beauty of the Rockies. As we follow the snaking road, snowcapped mountains rise high above us to one side, deep gorges drop a thousand feet or more to the

other. In Yellowstone Park we watch Old Faithful send up its steaming plume. We walk along the white shores of the Great Salt Lake and scale Pikes Peak.

... **OKLAHOMA, TEXAS, NEW MEXICO, ARIZONA** ... We roam through the oil lands of Oklahoma, Sooner State of the great land rush of 1893. We enter the immensity of Texas. We are in the land of the cowboy. Cattle by the thousands glare at us from behind strong wire fences. Then we lose ourselves in the underworld caves of New Mexico. Our hike continues through deserts that glare yellow and orange and red in the broiling sun.

... **CALIFORNIA, NEVADA, OREGON, WASHINGTON** ... California greets us with its sunshine as we wander through it from south to north. For a while we follow the Pacific coast line where stand majestic sequoias, our country's largest

trees. Then we look up. High above the orange groves of the valleys the snowy Sierras invite us to follow the trail of the eagle—up Mount Shasta and Mount Hood. We cross the mighty Columbia River and climb to the very top of Mount Rainier itself.

. . . ALASKA, HAWAII. After a jump over vast territories of Canada we reach Alaska—one fifth the size of all the rest of the United States. Mount McKinley invites us to scale our country's highest peak. The rivers invite us to pan for their gold. And finally, we leap across the Pacific to Hawaii. We hike to the rim of a smoldering volcano, surf in the breakers of Waikiki, and stand in silence by the Pearl Harbor memorial.

Our hike is done. We have seen America.
It is vast. It is beautiful. It is rich.
It is OURS—ours to know and to love.

THE AMERICAN'S CREED

I believe in
    the United States of America as a[1]
    Government of the people, by the people, for the people;[2]
    whose just powers are derived from the consent of the governed;[3]
    a democracy in a republic;[4]
    a sovereign Nation of many sovereign States;[5]
    a perfect Union, one and inseparable;[6]
    established upon those principals of freedom, equality, and justice,
    an humanity for which American patriots sacrificed their lives and
    fortunes.[7]

I therefore believe it is my duty to my country
    to love it;[8]
    to support its Constitution;[9]
    to obey its laws;[10]
    to respect its flag; and[11]
    to defend it against all enemies.[12]

The American's Creed was developed by William Tyler Page in 1917. It is a brief, clear statement of American traditions and ideals, as expressed by leading American statesmen and writers.

Key to The American's Creed: 1. Closing words of Preamble to the Constitution; 2. Lincoln's Gettysburg Address; 3. Declaration of Independence; 4. W. T. Page; 5. Speech by Daniel Webster; 6. Preamble to the Constitution; 7. Adapted from closing words of Declaration of Independence; 8. Speech by John Hancock; 9. United States Oath of Allegiance; 10. George Washington's Farewell Address; 11. War Department Circular, April 14, 1917; 12. Oath of Allegiance.

KNOW OUR DEMOCRACY

To you and me, America is the finest country in the world. But it is not just the land we love. It is also the kind of life for which America stands—our democracy.

It is your duty as a Scout and as an American to help keep that democracy alive. To do this, you must know the true meaning of Amerca. You must believe in her form of government. You must be willing to keep America great.

The American's Creed sums up, in the words of great Americans, the things for which America stands. It points out your rights and your duties as an American citizen.

I believe in the United States of America . . . The United States of America—that's the name of our country, given it by the men who founded int. United, the people of America have worked to give it its present high standards of living. United, we can go on to even greater prosperity and happiness.

. . . as a Government of the people, by the people for the people . . . Of, by, and for the people—not just for some of them, but all of them. Not just the rich or the poor, not just people of one color one creed, but all the people—the people of whom the Declaration of Independence speaks when it says: "All men are created equal . . ."—not equally gifted or equally rich, but equal under the law.

. . . whose just powers are derived from the consent of the governed . . . The word "democracy" itself tells of our form of government. It has come to use form the Greek: *demos*, the people, and *kratein*, to rule. But imagine more than 220 million people getting together some place at one time to rule a country! Such "absolute" democracy works in a small body such as a Scout patrol. But it wouldn't work in a whole country where the people are spread out over millions of square miles. Our democracy is therefore the "representative" kind. In this kind of democracy the governing is done by representatives elected by the people and responsible to them. A country ruled in this way is called a "republic."

SOME RIGHTS AS A CITIZEN

You and your family can:

- worship where you like
- say what you think
- own things and live where you like
- meet when you want to
- go to a good school
- vote
- have a trial by a jury
- keep people from searching your home—unless they have a special paper, called a warrant, issued by a judge.

Your rights as a citizen are found in the Bill of Rights and in your country's laws.

These rights are yours. Be proud they are yours. You keep them by using them.

... a Sovereign nation of many sovereign States ... The government of our nation is located in Washington, District of Columbia, the capital of our country. Here the Congress enacts federal laws, the Supreme Court interprets them, the executive branch of the government carries them out. But in addition, 50 separate state governments in 50 state capitals enact laws to suit the conditions of their "sovereign" states— each state with controlling power over its own affairs.

... a perfect Union, one and inseparable ... The Founding Fathers relied on divine providence in setting up what they hoped would be a "perfect union." Today, in the motto of our country, we express that same conviction that our union can be perfect only by God's help: "In God We Trust."

... established upon those principles of freedom, equality, justice, and humanity for which American patriots sacrificed their lives and fortunes ... Thousands of Americans gave their blood to create and protect our democracy. Their will-

SOME DUTIES AS A CITIZEN

You—and your family—should:

- obey laws
- respect the rights and things of others
- help police who keep the laws
- serve on a jury
- pay taxes
- vote
- keep up on what is going on around you
- help change things that are not good

It may be hard, but do what is right for you and others.

Your duties as a citizen are determined by laws, your living them by your conscience.

ingness to die for our country should make all of us even more determined to live for it.

I therefore believe it is my duty to my country to love it; . . . America is your country. Her soil feeds you. Her laws protect you and give you "the right to life, liberty, and the pursuit of happiness." America deserves your love. America has a right to expect you to express that love in your deeds.

. . . to support its Constitution; . . . The Constitution of the United States explains your rights as a citizen of our country. By supporting the Constitution you keep these rights. But remember that the rights that are yours are the rights of others as well. You have the right to worship God in your own way. See to it that others retain their right to worship God in their way. You have the right to speak your mind without fear of prison or punishment. Ensure that right for others, even when you do not agree with them.

. . . to obey its laws; . . . The laws of our country and the laws

405

of your state are written by the representatives of the American people for the good of all Americans. These laws govern much of what we do in our daily lives. They draw the line between what is right and what is wrong. They protect us against those who may want to do us ill. By obeying them you strengthen them and maintain the protection they afford.

. . . to respects its flag; . . . The flag is the symbol of our country. When we show it our respect, we show our respect and love for all that is America--our land, our people, our way of life.

. . . and to defend it against all enemies. It is the ferven prayer of all of us that never again shall American lives be lost on the battlefield. The way to ensure this is to keep America strong and prepared to stand up against any foreign power that might wish to destroy us. But it is just as important to defend America against the enemies within our own borders. These enemies are those who sow the seeds of distrust among our people, who try to stir up hatred, who attempt to ruin the lives of others by lies an smears, who break our laws.

The American's Creed is your creed as an American boy. By studying the creed you will know what is expected of you. By following it you will prove yourself a true American.

Spanish missionaries in California, Dutch settlers in New Amsterdam . . .

Four famous Americans
on a famous mountain monument

KNOW OUR COUNTRY'S GREATS

A great country is built by great people. Some of America's greats performed their greatness in small ways. They are the unsung greats—the men and women who opened the East and conquered the West. Other greats performed their deeds in ways that changed our country and the world. They did it in many different ways. Some by their statesmanship, others by their military skills. Some by their books, others by their inventions. Some by their oratory, others by sacrificing their lives. They are the famous ones. Their fame endures.

You should know these people. You will find some of them pictured on page 409. Read about them in an encyclopedia.

When you learn about their lives you will better understand the greatness of the United States of America.

. . . Pilgrims in New England, western explorers are parts of your heritage.

Susan Brownell Anthony (1820-1906): Advocate of women's rights, temperance, and abolition

Alexander Graham Bell (1847-1922): Scientist and inventor of the telephone

Daniel Boone (1734-1820): Pioneer frontiersman

Samuel Clemens (1835-1910): Better known as Mark Twain. Author of *Tom Sawyer* and *Huckleberry Finn*

Thomas Alva Edison (1847-1931): Inventor of phonograph, electric light, motion-picture projector

Albert Einstein (1879-1955): German-American physicist. Developed theory of relativity

Dwight David Eisenhower (1890-1969): Commander of Allied Forces in World War II. Thirty-fourth President of the United States

Henry Ford (1863-1947): Pioneer automobile manufacturer

Benjamin Franklin (1706-90): Signer of Declaration of Independence, statesman, author, inventor, ambassador, postmaster general

Samuel Gompers (1850-1924): Labor leader and president of American Federation of Labor

Matthew Henson (1867-1955): With Robert E. Peary at the North Pole, 1909

Martin Luther King, Jr. (1929-68): Civil rights leader. Awarded Nobel Peace Prize, 1964

Robert E. Lee (1807-70): Confederate general in chief

George Meany (1894-1980): Distinguished labor leader and president of the AFL-CIO 1955-79

Chief Plenty Coups (1849-1933): Last great Crow war chief

Walter Reed (1851-1902): U.S. Army medical officer, bacteriologist. Discoverer of yellow fever carried by mosquitoes

John Davison Rockefeller (1839-1937): Billionaire industrialist and philanthropist

Padre Junipero Serra (1713-84): Franciscan missionary; founder of first missions in California

Harriet Tubman (1820-1913): Abolitionist

Whitney Young, Jr. (1921-71): Civil rights leader. Executive director of National Urban League

Thomas Edison

Dwight D. Eisenhower

Robert E. Lee

Martin Luther King, Jr.

Benjamin Franklin

Henry Ford

Matthew Henson

Susan B. Anthony

John D. Rockefeller

George Meany

Samuel Gompers

Chief Plenty Coups

Padre Junipero Serra

Daniel Boone

Harriet Tubman

Alexander Graham Bell

Whitney Young, Jr.

Albert Einstein

Walter Reed

Samuel Clemens

FAMOUS SAYINGS. Many famous Americans are known mostly by their deeds. Others are remembered not only for what they did but for what they said. We have a wonderful heritage of their sayings. Here are a few. Find out the background of those who said them and where and why.

"Ask not what your country can do for you; ask what you can do for your country."   John F. Kennedy

"Dost thou love life? Then do not squander time, for that is the stuff life is made of."   Benjamin Franklin

"Liberty is the only thing you cannot have unless you are willing to give it to others."   William Allen White

"Labor to keep alive in your breast that little spark of celestial fire—conscience."   George Washington

"Injustice anywhere is a threat to justice everywhere." Martin Luther King, Jr.

"A candle loses nothing of its light by lighting another candle."   James Keller

"I never spoke to God, nor visited in heaven; yet certain am I of the spot as if the chart were given."   Emily Dickinson

"The only thing we have to fear is fear itself."   Franklin D. Roosevelt

"Always do right. This will gratify some people, and astonish the rest."   Samuel Clemens (Mark Twain)

"Speak softly and carry a big stick."   Theodore Roosevelt

"The only way to have a friend is to be one."   Ralph Waldo Emerson

"Give me liberty or give me death."   Patrick Henry

"Men, their rights and nothing more. Women, their rights and nothing less."   Susan B. Anthony

"As I would not be a slave, so I would not be a master. This expresses my idea of democracy. Whatever differs from this, to the extent of the difference, is no democracy." Abraham Lincoln

"If a man does not keep pace with his companions, perhaps it is because he hears a different drummer. Let him step to the music he hears, however measured or far away."   Henry David Thoreau

Spacecraft on the moon

KNOW AMERICA'S PAST

The history of our country is alive not only with men and women, their deeds and their words. It is full, also, of places and things, each of them with a story to tell.

On these pages and the next you will find a dozen pictures of places and things that have a meaning to every American. The pictures are meant to stimulate your thinking. How many places and things can you name? Do you know why they are famous? What is their importance to our history?

USS Arizona monument at Pearl Harbor

411

Wright airplane

Spirit of St. Louis

Minuteman Statue

The Alamo

412

Driving the "golden spike"

Wagon Train

Pony express

Liberty Bell

Statue of Liberty

Old Ironsides

413

KNOW THE PLEDGE OF ALLEGIANCE

The Pledge of Allegiance to the Flag
of the United States of America

I pledge allegiance to
the flag of the United States
of America
and to the Republic for which it stands,
one Nation under God,
indivisible, with liberty and
justice for all.

THE MEANING OF THE PLEDGE OF ALLEGIANCE. When you pledge allegiance to your flag you promise loyalty and devotion to your nation. Each word has a deep meaning:

I pledge allegiance . . . I promise to be true
. . . *to the flag* . . . to the sign of our country
. . . *of the United States of America* . . . a country made up of 50 states, each with certain rights of its own
. . . *and to the Republic* . . . a country where the people elect others to make laws for them
. . . *for which it stands,* . . . the flag means the country
. . . *one Nation under God,* . . . a country whose people believe in God
. . . *indivisible,* . . . the country cannot be split into parts
. . . *with liberty and justice* . . . with freedom and fairness
. . . *for all.* For each person in the country—you and me.

414

KNOW OUR COUNTRY'S FLAG

The flag ceremony is about to start. There is a signal. "Salute!" With your friends to the right and to the left, you pledge allegiance to your flag and to your country. And as you look at that flag and think of the pledge you are making, you feel again the thrill of being an American.

That flag is far more than the red, white, and blue cloth of which it is made. It is the living symbol of our America. It stands for the past and the present and the future of our country. It stands for our people, our land, and our way of life.

It stands for the men and women who built America. It stands for the Pilgrims setting out to find a place to worship their God in their own way...of pioneers hewing their homes out of the wilderness... of Washington fighting for a new nation...of Lincoln holding that nation together...of men and women who fought and died for their country.

Its stripes tell of the 13 states that gained our liberty. Its stars tell of the more than 200 million people of 50 states working and fighting to keep that liberty for themselves and for generations to come.

When next you pledge your allegiance to the flag, think of those things. Then promise yourself that you will show it your respect by always handling it, displaying it, folding it and saluting it in the right way.

The History of Our Flag—Old Glory

The flag of the United States of America today has 13 stripes—7 red and 6 white—and 50 white stars on a blue field—five rows of 6, four rows of 5. The stripes remind us of the 13 original colonies that gained us our liberty. The stars represent the states that are bound together into one country.

The flag you help hoist today grew out of many earlier flags raised in days gone by over American soil.

From the time America was discovered, different flags flew over different parts of the country: the flags of Spain, France, Holland, Sweden, and England. An English flag known as the Red Ensign waved over the American colonies from 1707 to the Revolution.

The flag that became known as the Grand Union flag was raised over George Washington's headquarters outside Boston on January 1, 1776. The Revolutionary War had started the year before, and the colonies needed a flag of their own.

The first official flag of the new nation—the United States of America—was created by a resolution of the Continental Congress meeting in Philadelphia. The resolution was passed on June 14, 1777. That is the date we celebrate every year as Flag Day.

The flag that waved over Fort McHenry when it was bombarded, September 13-14, 1814, was a 15-star and 15-stripe flag. Two stripes and two stars had been added to the original 13 on May 1, 1795. It became famous as the Star-Spangled Banner. That was the term that Francis Scott Key used for it in the poem he wrote about it.

When still more states joined the United States, it became evident that the flag would get to be an awkward shape if more and still more stripes were added. Therefore, on April 4, 1818, Congress passed a law that restored the design to the original 13 stripes. It also provided that a star be added to the blue field for each new state. The 50th star—for Hawaii—was added on July 4, 1960.

RED ENSIGN was the merchant flag of England. It was red with a union in the upper inner corner combining the cross of St. George (red on white), patron of England, with the diagonal cross (white on blue) of St. Andrew, patron of Scotland.

GRAND UNION FLAG raised over George Washington's headquarters retained the union of the English flag. But six white stripes broke the red field into seven red stripes—13 in all.

FIRST OFFICIAL FLAG of the United States of America was created by a resolution of the Continental Congress in 1777. It specified "that the flag...be 13 stripes alternate red and white; that the union be 13 stars, white in a blue field, representing a new constellation." Since the resolution did not tell how the stars were to be arranged, flag makers arranged them in different ways, among them: in rows, in a half circle, in a full circle.

STAR-SPANGLED BANNER of 1812 that inspired Francis Scott Key to write our national anthem had 15 stripes and 15 stars in the field. Two more of each had been added on May 1, 1795.

FLAG OF 1818 had the stripes reduced to 13. Five more stars had been added, for a total of 20. From then on, the number of stripes remained the same, but a star was added for each new state.

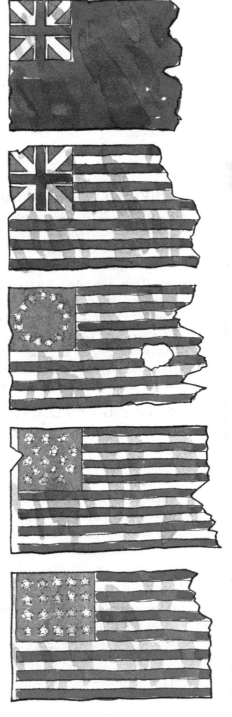

Respect to the Flag

The United States Flag Code adopted by Congress provides the rules for honoring and displaying the flag. The code states: "The flag represents a living country and is itself considered a living thing." For these reasons you give it your full respect.

What follows is an interpretation of the parts of the flag code that you should know as a Scout.

WHEN TO FLY THE FLAG. The flag of the United States should be flown every day when weather permits. If made of weather-resistant material it can be flown around the clock in any weather if properly illuminated.

It should be flown especially on New Year's Day, Inauguration Day, Lincoln's Birthday, Washington's Birthday, Easter Sunday, Mother's Day, Armed Forces Day, Memorial Day (half-staff until noon, full-staff to sunset), Flag Day, Independence Day, Labor Day, Constitution Day, Columbus Day, Navy Day, Veterans Day, Thanksgiving Day, Christmas Day, on other days proclaimed by the President, on the birthdays of states (dates of admission), and on state holidays.

HOISTING AND LOWERING THE FLAG. Joy is indicated by flying the flag at full-staff. You hoist it briskly in the morning, but not earlier than sunrise. You lower it slowly in the evening, but not later than sunset.

Mourning is indicated by flying the flag at half-staff. You hoist it to the peak first, hold it there for an instant, then lower it to half-staff, one-half the distance between the top and the bottom of the staff. When ready to take it down, you raise it to the peak, then lower it.

It takes two to hoist or lower the flag correctly.

Hoisting the Flag. No. 1 holds the folded flag to prevent it from touching the ground. No. 2—who is to do the hoisting—attaches the flag to the halyard, the flag line. He then raises the flag, briskly, keeping the line rather taut.

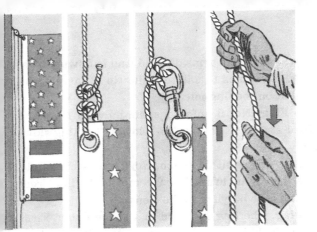

The flag can be attached to the halyard with two half hitches. A safer method makes use of two snap hooks.

It takes two to hoist and lower the flag correctly. No. 1 holds the flag. No. 2 attaches it to the halyard. No. 2 hoists the flag, keeping it close to the pole by holding the line rather taut (see hand positions in the illustration above). No. 1 steps back and salutes. No. 2 finally fastens halyard to the cleat on the pole.

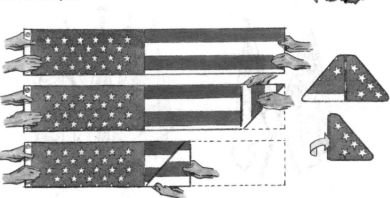

The flag is folded in a special way until only the blue field shows.

419

When the flag has left the arms of No. 1 and is flowing free, No. 1 steps back. He comes to salute while No. 2 fastens the halyard to the cleat on the flagpole.

Lowering the Flag. No. 2 unfastens the halyard from the cleat. While No. 1 stands at salute, No. 2 lowers the flag slowly, ceremoniously.

When the flag is down within reach, No. 1 drops his salute and gathers the flag in his arms. No. 2 removes the flag from the halyard and ties the halyard to the cleat.

Folding the Flag. The flag is folded in a special way. First fold it lengthwise in halves, then in quarters, with the blue field on the outside. Now, while you hold it by the blue field, another Scout makes a triangular fold in the opposite end. He continues folding the flag in triangles until it resembles a cocked hat, with only the blue field showing.

GREETING OUR FLAG. In Scout uniform, with or without a cap, you greet the flag with the Scout salute. You do this whenever you see it being hoisted or lowered, or when you pass it or are passed by it. You also make the Scout salute when you give it the Pledge of Allegiance.

When the flag passes you in a parade, come to attention and face it. Salute just before the flag reaches the point opposite you. Hold the salute until it has passed.

When displayed on staffs, the flag is at its own right or in the center.

When carried, the flag is at its own right or in front of other flags.

When you pass the flag, come to salute six steps before you reach it. Hold the salute until you are six steps past. In formation, salute at command of your leader.

In civilian clothes, use the civilian salute: greet the flag by placing your right hand over your heart. If you have a hat on, remove it and hold it at your left shoulder with the right hand over the heart.

CARRYING THE FLAG. The flag is always carried aloft and free, never flat or horizontally.

When the flag is carried alone, there should be an honor guard to the left of it or one on each side of it. When carried with other flags, the flag should be in front of the others or to the right if the flags are arranged in line.

The flag of the United States is never dipped in salute to any person or thing.

DISPLAYING THE FLAG. On certain occasions you may have a chance to help put the flag on display. There are special rules for doing this.

Displayed against a wall with another flag, with staffs crossed, the flag of the United States should be on its own right, with its staff in front of the other. In a group of flags on staffs, the flag of the United States goes in the center, at the highest point.

421

Displayed on a flagpole in line with other flags on poles of the same height, the flag of the United States goes to its own right. It is hoisted first and lowered last.

Hoisted on the same halyard with a troop, city, or state flag, the flag of the United States is at the peak of the pole.

In a church or auditorium, the flag on a staff may be placed to the clergyman's or speaker's right whether the platform or stage he stands on is raised or not, and whether or not the flag is placed on the same level as the clergyman or speaker.

When the flag is displayed flat against a wall, horizontally or vertically, the union should be at the top, at the flag's own right (to the left as you look at it).

When displayed from a staff that projects from a window or from the front of a building, the flag goes to the peak of the staff, except when displayed at half-staff.

Across a street, the flag is hung vertically with the union to the north in an east-and-west street, to the east in a north-and-south street.

When displayed on an automobile, the staff should be firmly clamped to the right front fender. It should not be draped on or over any part of the car.

The only time the flag is flown upside down is as a distress signal, to call for help.

NOTE: It may seem difficult to remember all the ways in which the flag should be displayed. But it really isn't. Not if you remember this simple rule:

"Consider yourself the flag. Consider your right shoulder the blue field. Face people with yourself to the right."

CARE OF THE FLAG. When handling the flag, never let it touch the ground, the floor, or water under it. Nothing is ever placed on the flag. And the flag is never used as drapery—use red, white, and blue bunting instead.

Clean the flag when it gets soiled. Mend it if it gets torn. When worn beyond repair, destroy it in a dignified way, by burning.

422

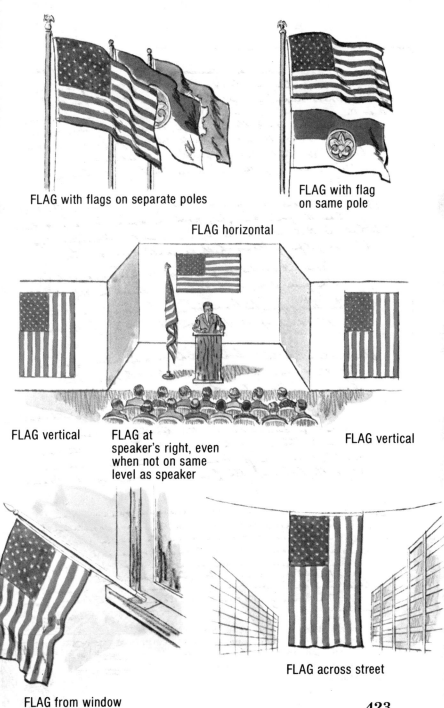

FLAG with flags on separate poles

FLAG with flag on same pole

FLAG horizontal

FLAG vertical

FLAG at speaker's right, even when not on same level as speaker

FLAG vertical

FLAG from window

FLAG across street

O say can you see by the dawn's early light
What so proudly we hail'd at the twilight's last gleaming,
Whose broad stripes & bright stars through the perilous fight
O'er the ramparts we watch'd, were so gallantly streaming?
And the rocket's red glare, the bomb bursting in air,
Gave proof through the night that our flag was still there,
O say does that star spangled banner yet wave
O'er the land of the free & the home of the brave?

On the shore dimly seen through the mists of the deep,
Where the foe's haughty host in dread silence reposes,
What is that which the breeze, o'er the towering steep,
As it fitfully blows, half conceals, half discloses?
Now it catches the gleam of the morning's first beam,
In full glory reflected now shines in the stream,
'Tis the star-spangled banner — O long may it wave
O'er the land of the free & the home of the brave!

And where is that band who so vauntingly swore,
That the havoc of war & the battle's confusion
A home & a Country should leave us no more?
Their blood has wash'd out their foul footstep's pollution
No refuge could save the hireling & slave
From the terror of flight or the gloom of the grave,
And the star-spangled banner in triumph doth wave
O'er the land of the free & the home of the brave.

O thus be it ever when freemen shall stand
Between their lov'd home & the war's desolation!
Blest with vict'ry & peace may the heav'n rescued land
Praise the power that hath made & preserv'd us a nation!
Then conquer we must when our cause it is just,
And this be our motto — "In God is our trust,"
And the star-spangled banner in triumph shall wave
O'er the land of the free & the home of the brave. —

The poem that Francis Scott Key wrote on September 14, 1814, became our national anthem in 1931. You can read the verses above in a reproduction of the poem in the author's own handwriting.

424

KNOW OUR NATIONAL ANTHEM

During the War of 1812, a British fleet attacked U.S. Fort McHenry near Baltimore. A young lawyer watched the bombing that lasted through the whole night. He worried whether our soldiers could withstand the attack. As morning came, he gazed toward the fort and wondered;

"O say can you see, by the dawn's early light,
What so proudly we hail'd at the twilight's last gleaming,
Whose broad stripes and bright stars through the
      perilous fight
O'er the ramparts we watched, were so gallantly streaming?"

The bombardment ended at 8 a.m., September 14, 1814. As the smoke cleared, the young lawyer saw that the flag was still flying over the fort. That day he wrote down the feelings he had had during the night and the trust he had in his country's future. A friend had his poem printed. And shortly afterward his words were sung throughout the country. What Francis Scott Key had written became our national anthem.

To get the full meaning of every line that Key wrote, read them in his own handwriting on the opposite page. Study them carefully. Then try to express them in your own words.

Whenever you hear our national anthem played or sung, stand up. Salute if you are in uniform. Place your right hand over your heart if you are in civilian clothes. And think of your own future under the Star-Spangled Banner.

425

KNOW YOUR LOCAL FLAG

Find the flag of your state, commonwealth, territory, or island possession.

Alabama

Alaska

American Samoa

Arizona

Arkansas

California

Colorado

Connecticut

Delaware

District of Columbia

Florida

Georgia

Guam

Hawaii

Idaho

Illinois

Indiana

Iowa

Kansas

Kentucky

Louisiana

Maine

Maryland

Massachusetts

Michigan

Minnesota

Mississippi

Missouri	Montana	Nebraska	Nevada
New Hampshire	New Jersey	New Mexico	New York
North Carolina	North Dakota	Ohio	Oklahoma
Oregon	Pennsylvania	Puerto Rico	Rhode Island
South Carolina	South Dakota	Tennessee	Texas
Utah	Vermont	Virginia	Virgin Islands
Washington	West Virginia	Wisconsin	Wyoming

When a boy becomes a Scout, his whole family joins the Scouting family.

Strive for a Happy Family

When you are a Scout your whole family is part of the Scouting family. Scouting takes you away from the family for hikes and camps, meetings and projects. But through these activities of yours, Scouting comes right into your home. Every family member gets involved in Scouting. Everyone wants to help you have all the fun that Scouting promises. They want to see you reach the goals you set for yourself in Scouting. And in helping you, each of them is influenced by Scouting.

WHAT IS A FAMILY? Your family is made up of the people you live with. Father, mother, brothers, and sisters are the family of most people. But relatives like grandparents, uncles and aunts, and cousins are also family, even though they may be scattered all over the country. Some people have no relatives. Their family is the group of people they grow up in— perhaps in foster homes, boarding schools, or orphan homes.

Two parents, one, or none—what makes up a family is not the number of people or whether they are related by blood. It is the way they care for each other, share with each other.

Your family provides love, shelter, food, clothing, and things to do together. It guides you to certain religious beliefs. It gives you your first values, your first understanding of what is right and wrong. As you grow, these family values become a part of yourself.

There's nothing much more important than being part of a warm, loving family. Show your love for the members of the family. And be grateful when they show their love for you. In such a family, each person is truly a member of the team, striving to do his share to make the family a happy one.

A family like this, like yours, multiplied millions of times makes up the great family of families—these United States.

THE FAMILY COUNCIL. In families where the children are old enough, they may share in making some of the family decisions. This may happen around the dinner table. Here you may discuss what jobs need to be done and who will do them. Here you may settle on what to do for the weekend—whether to take a trip or have your grandparents visit you.

Sometimes such a "family council" may be more serious.

It is in family council that you'll discuss what to do in case of fire. Everyone must know how to give the alarm if he smells smoke. Everyone must know the quickest route for getting out of the house. Everyone must know where to gather with the rest to be sure that everyone is safely outside. Then, when everyone knows what to do, you go through the steps to make sure the scheme will work.

Most of the time, a "family council" is a happy chat around the table.

Family jobs may be daily routines or special tasks to improve the home.

FAMILY JOBS

Making a family run smoothly takes a lot of effort. Some of the jobs that need to be done involve everybody. Some of them are your personal responsibilities.

What are some of the things your family has to do? Food must be bought or grown. Meals must be cooked. Floors, windows, walls, furniture, dishes, utensils, and kitchen and bathroom fixtures must be cleaned. Laundry must be done. Garbage and trash must be taken out. Some families have jobs that others don't: shoveling snow, mowing lawns. All of these are necessary family jobs. They really belong to everybody.

Your Special Jobs. There are some jobs that belong to you and only you. They include taking care of your things. Keeping your living space clean and neat. Hanging up your clothes. Putting away your things. Making up your bed. Cleaning up litter from a craft project. Washing dishes used for a snack. Your rule should be, "If it's mine or I did it, I'll clean it up." If you don't, someone else will have to. That's not playing fair.

You also have the duty to respect the feelings of others. Keep your noise level down—radio, TV, record player, even your voice. Don't take over the TV or telephone. Don't use someone else's things without asking. Get home when you said you would so your parents won't worry. Share your things with others. Respect the rights of your brothers and sisters to their own opinions and they will respect yours.

Caring for Younger Children

If you have younger brothers or sisters, one of the most important jobs you have is caring for them. This does not just mean looking after them when they are sick. It means showing them that you care, at all times.

What you do for them and with them will have a great effect on their growing up.

By being cheerful you can cheer them up when they are sad. By helping them whenever you see that they need help, they will learn to help others. By being their best friend, you help them to become friendly to others. By showing them that you love them, they will give love in return.

Playtime. Take time off often from your busy schedule to play with the younger members of your family.

If they are very small, make them a simple, safe toy once in a while. If somewhat older, put up a tent for them to play in. Even a tarp spread over a table to reach the floor will do. If they are getting close to Scout age, show them some of the things you have learned.

Baby-sitting is a responsible task. Be prepared for it by considering these points and living up to them:

- Know where the parents can be reached.
- Know a neighbor who could help if needed.
- Have emergency phone numbers handy to use in case of accident or fire (page 362).
- Keep the children out of danger areas.
- Lock the doors. Don't open for anyone unless you know the person.
- Know if the children are to eat anything.
- Know when the children are to go to bed.
- After the children are in bed, check them every half hour or so.
- Stay awake until the parents return.

One of the most important tasks that a boy will ever have is to look after and care for his younger brothers and sisters.

Family Finances

Your family has money coming in and money going out. It is part of our economic system. It is a business. Businesses have budgets. Families should have them, too. A budget is an estimate of how much money will come in and how much will go out.

The main source of income for most families is salaries for work done. Some get money from the sale of things the family grows or makes. Others have interest from invested money.

Out of what your parents earn, they provide you with the necessities of life such as housing, food, and clothing. They give you as many extras as they can afford. Show them that you appreciate what they do for you and what they give you.

You can help the family income by doing jobs that your parents would have to pay to have done: baby-sitting, mowing the lawn, painting the fence, polishing the car. Don't wait for them to ask you. Volunteer.

FAMILY PROBLEMS. "All happy families resemble one another. Every unhappy family is unhappy in its own fashion." That's a famous quotation from a famous author. But whether happy or unhappy, all families have problems, some small, some big.

If the problem that strikes your family is illness, you can help by giving active assistance. If the problem is lack of money, you can do your part by saving and by pitching in with what you can earn.

Your parents try to protect you from worry. You can help them by not being a problem yourself. You won't be if you live up to your Scout Oath and follow the Scout Law.

A large percentage of the money that a family spends is used to buy food. Go shopping with your family so that you can learn to pick the purchases wisely and to take advantage of bargains.

HOME EMERGENCIES

In most families life runs smoothly day by day. But occasionally some emergency arises. Most of the time, the adult members of the family will handle the emergency. But there may be times when the responsibility will be yours. You may be alone or home with younger brothers or sisters.

Some emergencies may be handled by summoning help by phone. That's why it is important always to have the emergency numbers close to the phone (see page 362). Others may involve immediate action on your part. Think clearly. Then act.

Medical Emergency. For a minor accident, use the first aid you have learned as a Scout (pages 360-91). For a major accident, get help as you also learned in your first aid. Use one of the emergency phone numbers you listed on page 362.

Police Emergency. Be wary of strangers around your home. If a stranger arouses your suspicions, call the police. Note how the stranger looks so that you can describe him or her. If a burglar breaks into your home, play it cool. Don't try to stop him. Flee and seek help.

Fire Emergency. Follow your family exit plan as developed in your family council (page 429). This should call for two ways of escaping and for a place to meet outside. After the escape get the fire department.

Utility Emergencies. Call the service department of the utility company involved and explain the emergency. Here are some typical problems:

Electrical Problems. Power off, a tree fallen on wires, a cat up a power pole, a burned-out streetlight.

Gas problems. No gas, gas smell in house, pilot light out and won't relight.

Water problems. No water, not enough water pressure, water leaks, broken water main, hydrant leak or break.

Telephone problems. Line is dead, line is blown down in a storm, nuisance calls. If your phone is out of order, call from a neighbor's phone or from the nearest public phone.

TRASH is a major safety hazard. It's a serious fire danger. It can cause bad falls and injury from broken glass. Clean it up—indoors and outdoors.

GARBAGE is a health menace. Rats, flies, roaches, and other disease-carrying vermin are attracted to it. Keep it sealed in plastic bags or garbage cans with tight lids, ready for pickup by the sanitation people.

HOME SAFETY

"Safe at home." Don't you believe it! More accidents happen at home than any other place. One reason, of course, is that people spend so much of their time at home. But another is that it is so easy to get careless around the house.

SAFETY-INSPECT YOUR HOME. While many home accidents are caused by carelessness, many more are caused by overlooking dangerous conditions. So inspect your home. Look for health and safety hazards. Correct any that you find.

FALLS. Falls rank tops among accidents in the home.
- Remove clutter and toys from stairways. Place toys not in use in the storage box where they belong.
- Remove weak or broken stair railings.
- Put nonslip backing on throw-rugs and mats.
- Use nonskid strips in bathtub or shower for safe footing.
- Remove tripping hazards from areas where people walk: electric cords, wires, ropes, and hoses.
- Put stronger light bulbs in poorly lighted places.
- Use a safe stepladder when you want to reach an object on a high shelf.

Falls and fires are the main causes of accidents in the home. Secure loose rugs by skidproof backings. Keep matches out of the reach of children.

FIRES. Fires, and burns caused by fires, are next in line.
- Place matches out of the reach of children.
- Remove trash from the vicinity of stoves and heaters.
- Replace frayed electric wires and broken plugs.
- Wet down contents of an ashtray before throwing them out.
- Wrap up oily rags in aluminum foil and get rid of them.
- Place a spark-catching screen in front of a fireplace that has a fire burning in it.

WOUNDS. Accidents that cause wounds occur most often in the kitchen and in the home workshop.
- Store knives and other sharp tools where children cannot get hold of them.
- Get rid of broken glass the safe way: Remove the bigger pieces with brush and dustpan, the tiny splinters with a wad of wet cotton or a wet, crumpled-up paper towel.

POISONS. Poisoning in the home happens mostly to unsupervised children.
- Place medicines, cleaning items, and pesticides where children cannot get at them.
- Scrape off and get rid of paint that may have lead in it. This danger is generally confined to old houses.

Family picnic

Father-and-son outing

Bowling game

Birthday party

FAMILY RECREATION

"All work and no play makes Jack a dull boy." It makes a dull family, too. The family needs recreation. In the freedom of fun, family members can talk more easily with each other. The adults can relax. The young ones can enjoy themselves. Family recreation helps build family spirit and unity.

There are a great many things that a family can do for recreation. Some of them cost no money, others cost a lot. All of them have to be thought up and suggested by somebody. Why not you? Think up an idea. Then say, "Why don't we . . . ."

Think Small. Figure out first some of the things that can be done right at home, with no extra cost.

County fair or
amusement park

Boat ride

Family swim

Think of a new game the whole family can play after supper. Make simple handicrafts together. Plan a special kind of birthday party and make decorations for it. Have a picnic. Visit a museum. Take part in a community activity—many of these are free.

Think Big. Recreation that involves money takes more planning. What's decided should be something that everyone will be happy doing. The best kind is something that's worth working for, saving for, everyone doing his or her share.

You might start with a bowling tournament for the whole family, or a swimming meet in a local pool. Then maybe a vacation trip by car into the country or a boat trip up the river. Possibly a visit to relatives. Perhaps even a family camping trip or backpacking expedition.

Know Your Community

People have always gathered together in communities. At first they did it for protection from animals and other people. Then they learned that by living close together they could help each other. As communities grew, needs arose for jobs to be done, for homes to be built. Markets had to be set up to supply food and goods. Institutions had to be established to educate the young and care for the old. Leaders had to be chosen to make and keep laws. Governments were formed.

But whether a community has remained small or has grown large, the basic reason for having it still remains: A community can do things that no one person or family can do alone.

WHAT IS YOUR COMMUNITY? Your community is the place where you live. It can be made up of a few blocks near your home or a few farms in a valley. It can be a town or a city. It can be a state or a country.

Who you are and who you will become are affected by the community in which you live. So for your own well-being, it is important for you and your family to do all you can to make your community a good place in which to live.

It should be a place in which people get along reasonably well in spite of differences in heritage and politics, education and religion. It should be a place where people care for each other.

To help make your community this kind of place, three things are required of you:

- Know your community.
- Take part in community life. Get involved.
- Feel pride in your community. Do things with and for it that will make it worthy of the pride of every citizen in it.

HOW YOUR COMMUNITY IS RUN. To manage the affairs of the community, the citizens vote into positions of leadership those fellow citizens who seem to have the needed abilities. Some of these leaders

438

Mayor or city manager
City councilmen
School board members
Municipal judge
City attorney
School superintendent
Church leaders
Head of Federal agency
Block-club leaders
Members of municipal committees
Municipal department heads
Service-club presidents
Ethnic-group leaders
Volunteer agency directors like
   Red Cross or Scout council
United Way of America officials

To better understand your community, visit one of the men or women who are the leaders in it. If you have an idea for improving the community, tell it.

take up positions in town government. Others are leaders in organizations that influence community life. These leaders make plans for the good of the whole community and act on them. This may happen in town or city councils, or in community action groups, tribal councils, farm co-ops, businessmen's associations.

GET TO KNOW THE LEADERS OF YOUR COMMUNITY. To find out how your community is run, sit in on some of the meetings of the council, or in the planning session of an action group or an organization.

For even more information, visit one of the men or women who are the leaders in your community. You will find a list of some of them on the top of this page. Such a visit will give you a better understanding of your community.

Community leaders are busy people. So arrange for the meeting beforehand. Explain why you want it. Then keep the appointment. Be on time. Find out quickly the things you want to know. Make notes so you can tell your patrol and your family of your visit. Thank the person as you leave.

The world became a different place when families moved together in cities.

MEETING COMMUNITY NEEDS

PUBLIC UTILITIES AND SERVICES. In the past, when families lived far apart, each family had to take care of its own needs. For water they would dig a well. For light they would make their own candles. For heat they would chop up trees into firewood. For communication they would walk or ride to the houses of their nearest neighbors.

Today, in the community in which you live, all these needs are taken care of by public utilities. One of them, your water department, makes safe water available to all households. A gas company makes gas from coal or brings in natural gas for cooking and heating. An electric company produces electricity for lighting and heating and hundreds of other uses. Your local telephone company, working with telephone companies everywhere, makes it possible for you to speak to anyone who has a telephone, in this country and around the world.

Other needs of the community are provided by public services. They include such things as fire fighting, police protection, garbage pickup, public schools, hospitals. There are many others: special homes and schools for handicapped, family counseling, probation services, orphanages, jails, and

TERMS YOU SHOULD KNOW REGARDING THE COMMUNITY

PUBLIC UTILITIES. People need water, gas, telephones, and electricity. Public utilities supply these things. Some utilities are run by private companies, and some are run by government.

PUBLIC SERVICES. Other needs of people are things like fire and police protection, schools, and trash pickup. These needs are often taken care of by public services. We pay for these services with taxes.

RESOURCES. Resources are things which help meet community needs. Libraries, museums, zoos, and parks are resources. People may be resources. Farms and stores and camps are resources, too. Resources are for you to take care of. *You* can also be a resource.

ETHNIC GROUP. A group of people with like backgrounds and language, or of the same race. Blacks, native Americans, Poles, and Hispanic Americans are ethnic groups. Each ethnic group usually has its own customs and ideas.

GOVERNMENT. The way people agree to run their communities. Governments make and keep laws. They give services. The people vote for some government leaders. Other leaders are appointed.

PRIVATE AGENCY. This kind of agency runs on money which people give, not money from taxes. The Red Cross is one type of private agency that aids people during times of trouble like floods or tornadoes.

GOVERNMENTAL AGENCY. Some agencies are run by the government. They run on the taxes we pay. The welfare department and the county agent's office are two.

TRADITION. A belief or way of doing things that has been handed down from generation to generation. Holiday celebrations, food, dress, and language are traditions.

COMMUNITY PROBLEM. A community problem is anything that hurts people and families. Poor schools, lack of jobs, and drugs are problems.

COMMUNITY ORGANIZATION. Any group of people which comes together to meet needs. Parents might get together to put crossing guards at a bad street corner. A block club might be formed to keep a block looking good.

VOLUNTEER. A person who gives his time freely to help the community. That volunteer might be *you.*

many more. We pay for these services through our taxes. The idea is that each family pays a portion so that all can benefit.

The churches and synagogues of your community can be considered "service." They give you spiritual guidance and active help when needed. They are supported by your family's contributions.

There are still other public services available to you and your family. Among them are newspapers, radio, and TV. They are usually owned by private companies.

AGENCIES AND ORGANIZATIONS. Other community needs are met by agencies and organizations. Some of these are government-run. Others are private.

The county agent's office, the department of welfare, and the motor vehicle department are samples of government-run agencies.

The private agencies and organizations are mostly volunteer. That means that they depend on the help of people who work without pay. Most communities depend on the services that volunteer organizations provide. Among such services are these: running blood banks, giving training in first aid and

From time to time, the troop leaders may arrange for the troop to visit one of the services of your community. After a trip to the fire department, you may decide to earn the Firemanship merit badge.

442

If you live in a city or large town, your local Scout council is sure to have a service center where you can buy books and many other Scout items.

lifesaving, running children's day-care centers, and helping in time of trouble like floods and tornadoes. Without volunteers, you wouldn't be a Scout. Your Scoutmaster is a volunteer, and he is helped by many other volunteers. Some of them are directly related to your troop: your assistant Scoutmasters, your troop committee members. Others help with the work that needs to be done in your Scouting district or council.

The money it takes to run these organizations comes from individuals, businesses, and groups who believe in the things they do. Many of the organizations are members of their community's fundraising agency, the United Way.

Sometimes people get together to set up a community organization for a special purpose. A group of parents might organize to get crossing guards at a dangerous street corner. When they get the guards, the group might disband; its job is done. But some community organizations keep going. For instance, a block club may help keep a block clean and in good repair. Or a neighborhood group may give transportation to the elderly.

When people work together as volunteers they learn to get along better with each other. It creates good feelings. It builds pride in each person. It helps improve the whole community. Some of these organizations or groups need the kind of help you could give.

If your town has a museum, a visit to it will prove an interesting troop or patrol activity.

COMMUNITY RESOURCES. People also need to relax and enjoy life in other ways. Many communities have special resources to meet these needs.

Your community may have a library, a museum or a zoo, and one or more playgrounds. It probably also has a park. Maybe even a lake or ocean beach. These tax-supported things are for all people to use. They are generally free.

There are sure to be other community resources available: theaters, movie houses, concert halls, baseball and football parks. These are usually privately owned and privately run. In these you have to pay for admission.

It is the job of all the people of the community to keep these resources going. It means taking care of libraries, parks, playgrounds, and all the other things owned and run by the community. When some of these things are permitted to run down or are vandalized, the money for restoring them comes out of the pockets of your family and your neighbors. The money must be raised through higher fees or higher taxes. Otherwise the services may be closed down. You have a part to play in preserving these resources and in making other people care about their community.

444

Libraries and playgrounds are created for your benefit. Make use of them.

Using Community Resources. The best way to have all these resources prospering and kept in good shape is to make use of them.

In your local library you can find all you want to know about the world in which you live. You can read the finest books ever written. The more you and your friends and other people visit your library and make use of its services, the better its chance to get the financial support it needs to keep growing. The more you use the parks and beaches and playgrounds, the more evident the need becomes to keep them clean.

The same idea works for special events that take place in your community. As more people come out for them, more will be planned for the future.

To find out what is happening in your community, check your local newspaper. It will have a list of coming events. Look at the bulletin boards in your school, the community centers, and supermarkets. Walk down the street and watch for posters in store windows that tell of things about to happen.

Then make your choice. Take part in those activities and events in your community that will enrich your life and give you the greatest satisfaction.

COMMUNITY GROUPS

In every community, groups of people get together for a great variety of activities.

Some of these groups may be social clubs meeting for fun and fellowship. Some of them may be service groups discussing plans to improve the community. There will be sports clubs with members playing different sports and helping others learn. There will be religious groups celebrating special holidays or working to make life a little better for the sick and the elderly. Among these groups, the ethnic groups have a special significance.

ETHNIC GROUPS. Every person has an ethnic background— a background of race or people with common traits and customs, languages, and traditions.

Unless you are a full-blooded Indian, you have in your veins and arteries the blood of immigrants—people who came to America from the country in which they were born. Your forebears may have arrived in this country before the American Revolution. More probably they didn't. They may have come, many years later, from Europe, Africa, or Asia. Your grandparents may have brought your father and mother to the United States. Or your parents may have brought you from "the old country." It doesn't matter. What matters is what your ancestors have given to America and what you can give our country because of your rich heritage.

The Importance of Ethnic Groups. If it were not for ethnic groups, America would not have so many different kinds of music, inventions, and ideas. And we would not have a literature as rich as we have. From our native Americans, the Indians, to the newest citizen from South Vietnam, we benefit from the knowledge and skills, the traditions and customs of these many groups of people.

What we need to do is respect each other, enjoy the differences we find in each other, learn from each other, and build understanding among all groups.

446

Many ethnic celebrations, such as Chinese New Year, are very colorful.

Take Part in Activities. You may belong in a family that is keeping alive traditions that you inherited from your forebears—a belief or a custom that has been handed down from generation to generation. It may be a song, a kind of dance, a way of dressing, or a holiday. Whatever it is, the tradition is a part of your life.

Other ethnic groups have their own traditions and activities. Find out the background of members of your patrol. Find out about the ethnic groups in your community. Learn something about their history and some of their customs. Try to get to know some of the people. They will probably be proud to tell you about the background of their group and the contribution it has made to America. Then arrange to take part in some of their activities. These may be small, local celebrations of events in the past, or religious occasions. But there are large ethnic events also in which everybody gets involved—as when the Irish celebrate St. Patrick's Day; the Chinese, Chinese New Year's Day; the Indians, American Indian Day; the Scandinavians, Leif Ericson Day; the Polish, Pulaski Day. And some of us take the day off on Columbus Day to celebrate, with the Italians, the anniversary of the discovery of America.

COMMUNITY PROBLEMS

A perfect community would run smoothly. Difficulties that arose would be quickly recognized and managed before they turned into problems. But communities are not perfect. All have problems. Yours has right now.

Most community problems involve money. It takes money to provide for all the services a community needs. The money comes from taxes paid by your family and all other families. When there is not enough money coming in, services must be cut or taxes raised. If raised too little, the problem persists. If raised too high, people may move out and businesses close down, creating other problems. It takes wisdom to do the right thing.

There may be other big problems. More schools are needed. Rundown neighborhoods must be rebuilt. Ways must be found to provide more water. Garbage collection must be improved. New buses or snow-removal equipment must be purchased. There is no end to things that must be done. And then there are the problems of vandalism, crime, drugs, and many other things.

WHAT YOU CAN DO. You can't do the big things that are needed to solve big problems—they must be handled by the leaders of your community. But you can do small things toward their solution.

Let's take an example. Let's say your town has a problem with its water supply.

Here are steps you can take to help:

- **Get to Know the Facts.** In this case, visit the waterworks. Find out where the water comes from, how it is treated, how it is distributed.
- **Recognize the Problem.** On one of your patrol hikes you may have passed the town's water reservoir. You will have noticed that the level of the water was far below normal. It may have been caused by drought, or by people using too much.

- **Think Up Ideas.** You realize that saving water will help toward solving the problem. So you and your family and your patrol discuss possible ways of saving. The suggestions on page 326 should get you started.
- **Settle on Something Practical.** Some of your ideas may be farfetched and impractical. Some will make sense and should work. Persuade your family to accept the workable ideas and get your patrol members' families to do the same.
- **Carry Out the Ideas.** Do what you've decided on—and continue doing it.

CRIME PREVENTION. Visit your police department and find out how it works. Get to know the problems your town has in regard to crime prevention. Learn what you and your family can do to reduce the likelihood of crime in your home and neighborhood. There may be a number of things:
- Burglar-proof your home with good locks and windows that cannot be jimmied open.
- Protect the family car by always removing the key and locking the doors.
- Safeguard your bicycle by chaining it in the daytime, bringing it indoors at night.
- Report to the police any suspicious persons hanging around the neighborhood.

A hike to your town's water reservoir may show you the need for water conservation.

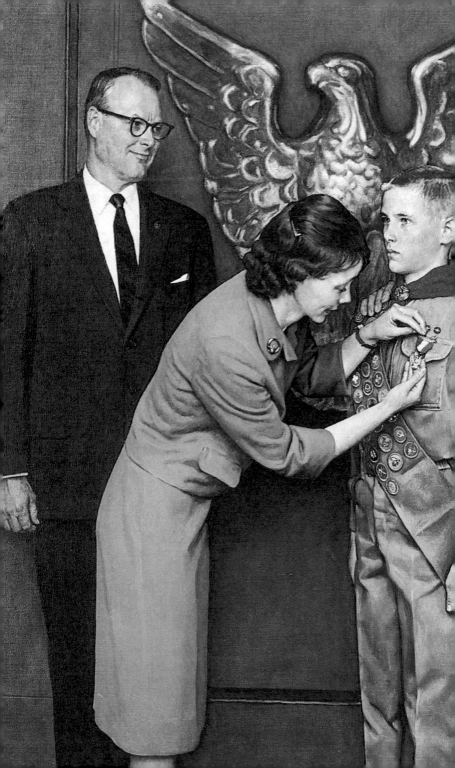

UPWARD TO EAGLE

A Great Moment
by Norman Rockwell, 1965

451

Scout Advancement

When Baden-Powell founded the Scouting movement, he felt that any boy who took the time and trouble to master certain Scoutcraft skills should be rewarded for his effort. And so he came up with this idea: He gave each Scout who passed certain tests a badge to wear on his uniform. It showed other people what the Scout had done. That is how the badge system got into Scouting. It is a system of learning that is different from all other learning systems.

In most other kinds of learning you are taught in a class. You do a certain amount of required work in a certain required subject in a certain length of time.

Not in Scouting. Here you decide for yourself what you want to learn and move ahead in your own way at your own speed. Your rate of advancement depends on your own interest and effort and ability. Remember, skill awards, merit badges, and Eagle palms must be earned before your 18th birthday.

Also, in other kids of learning and in games and sports you are often urged to "lick" the other fellow.

Not in Scouting. Here you compete with yourself against your own standard. You can get as far as your own ambition will carry you.

ADVANCEMENT IN SCOUTING. The advancement program of Scouting provides a forward-moving series of tests. It sets standards for passing them. It offers awards to the Scout who meets the tests, in the form of special badges.

As you study the tests for each major step forward, for each rank in Scouting, you will see that there is a certain pattern to them. For all ranks, you are required to show active Scout participation in your troop and your patrol. You are required to master certain Scout skills. You must show Scout spirit: you must show that you know the ideals of Scouting and are trying to live up to them.

Good luck to you as you move onward and upward on the Scouting trail!

For each rank you reach, you will receive
an award for your progress in the form of a
colorful badge, such as those for Tenderfoot, Second, and First Class.

ONWARD TO FIRST CLASS

Do you know how to eat an elephant? No? The answer to that very "weighty" question is simply: "One bite at a time."

Becoming a Tenderfoot Scout is but the first bite of Scouting. There are many other bites you need to take and chew before you can consider yourself a real Scout.

Set off as quickly as possible on the biggest meal of your life: Second Class, then onward to First Class. For each bite you digest, you receive an award for your progress.

How to Advance

Active Scout participation and advancement go together. So, if you want to advance, first and foremost, take part in all the activities of your patrol and troop.

When you do, you will pick up most of the Scoutcraft skills you need for your advancement. Work with the other Scouts of your troop on service projects. When you do, your Scout spirit will grow stronger. Help other Scouts. As you do, your leadership abilities will develop.

Then when you have completed the tests for the award you are aiming for, tell your Scoutmaster. He will sit down with you for a Scoutmaster conference. After this, he will arrange for a board of review. When this review is over, your Scoutmaster will order the badge you have earned. It will be presented to you at a ceremony.

SCOUT PARTICIPATION. For each of the ranks you are required "to be active in troop and patrol" for a certain length of time.

Three *A*'s count high for showing how you live up to this test of Scout participation: your *A*ttendance, your *A*ppearance, your *A*ttitude.

Attendance. Your attendance at troop and patrol events is good. You are there on the dot for all meetings, hikes, and camps. When sickness or some other reason prevents you from coming, you tell your patrol leader in advance. Then he can announce, "All present or accounted for."

Appearance. Your appearance—well, how about it? Do you always show up for Scout events in uniform? Is it neat and complete? Do you wear your badges correctly? You can hardly expect to be taken for a real Scout unless you look like one.

Attitude. Your attitude shows in everything you do when you take part in troop and patrol events. It shows in the way you come to attention the moment the signal is given. It shows in the way you get ready for a game or a contest, the way you take part in the program.

Your Scoutmaster gives his time and his effort and his best thoughts to make the troop as good as possible. He should be able at all times to count on each of "his" boys. Back him up in what he is trying to do for the good of all of you.

Most of your advancement will be the natural outcome of the activities of your patrol and troop. To advance, take part in all of them.

SCOUT SPIRIT. Your standing as a Scout does not depend just on the skills of your hands or the badges on your uniform. It depends even more on the spirit in your heart, on the way you try to live the Scout Oath and Law.

Your Scout leaders will know how you live the Oath and Law in your patrol and troop. But that is not enough. Before they are sure that you are worthy of the higher Scout awards, they will ask other people. These people will tell what they think of you as a Scout. Your attitude in your home shows your parents what being a Scout means to you. Your teachers judge you by the way you act in school. Your religious leader will know the effect Scouting has had on you. By weighing all the evidence, your leaders will know what kind of Scout you are.

The way you help at home, in school, church or synagogue, and in your community should be more and more effective the higher you climb in Scouting. Your Good Turn habit should be growing stronger. Going out of your way to help and comfort other people should have become natural for you.

You get better and better as you move upward in Scouting. You expect more and more of yourself as you follow the trail to Star, Life, and all the way up to Eagle. The kinds of service projects you take on and the leadership you give are clues. They will tell your Scout leaders what kind of boy you are. From these clues they will judge what kind of man you will become.

Doing a daily Good Turn is one of the best ways in which you can show your Scout spirit.

The award for learning a Scout skill is a metal loop you put on your belt.

SCOUT SKILLS. The skills of a Scout cover the whole wide outdoors. They also deal with your everyday life and with your striving to become a true American citizen.

These skills fall into 12 groups:

Five of these groups deal with outdoor skills: *Camping, Cooking, Hiking, Environment,* and *Conservation.* Two of them will help you have a healthy body: *Physical Fitness* and *Swimming.* Two others have to do with people: *Communications* and *First Aid.* The last three deal with your family, your community, and your country: *Family Living, Community Living,* and *Citizenship.* When you meet all the tests in any one of these skills you receive an award for having passed them: a skill award. And skill awards count toward your advancement in rank.

To become a Tenderfoot, you must pass the Citizenship tests. Second Class aims to make you a good hiker and a good helper. For this you must earn the Hiking and First Aid skill awards. First Class aims to make you a good camper. Here you must earn the Camping and Cooking skill awards.

How to Earn Skill Awards. First turn to pages 538 to 548. Here, in alphabetical order, you will find the tests for all the 12 skill awards. Decide on the ones you want to earn. You can work on more than one at a time.

Study the tests and set out to learn the skills. Some of them will be easy for you. You will pass the tests quickly.

Some skill awards are required for ranks: Citizenship for Tenderfoot, Hiking and First Aid for Second Class, Camping and Cooking for reaching First Class.

457

Some can be earned very naturally during the regular activities of your patrol and troop. For others you may need help from the other Scouts in your patrol.

When you are ready to be tested, tell your patrol leader. He will test you himself or send you to another Scout leader who will do it. When you have done everything necessary for an award, have your patrol leader sign your record. Take it to your Scoutmaster. He will give you the belt loop you have earned.

Patrol Work on Skill Awards. The earning of skill awards becomes even more fun if you work on them together in the patrol.

The outdoor skill awards would then be your first choices. The skills are those you use when you go hiking or camping with the patrol and the troop. Physical Fitness and Swimming, Communication and First Aid also fit into the life of the patrol. The rest require mostly your own effort.

After some hard work, your patrol could be a Hiking or a First Aid skill award patrol. At least three boys must then have the award if yours is a five-boy patrol. At least four boys must earn it in a six-boy patrol, and five in a seven- or eight-boy patrol. To show off what you have done, get an extra skill award belt loop. Flatten it and snip off top and bottom. Make holes in the four corners. Round the metal somewhat and tack the award onto your patrol flagpole. Hurray for your patrol!

A Scoutmaster conference is a friendly chat between a boy and a man.

Scoutmaster Conference

One of the aims of Scouting is to help you grow. You will have no difficulty seeing yourself growing taller and heavier. But you are also growing in ways you can't see. Your actions and thoughts are growing and changing, too. These are the things that make up your personality and character. They help determine the kind of man you will be.

Your Scoutmaster is interested in you. He wants to know about you. Only then can he help you have fun in Scouting. Only then can he know what you have to bring to the troop and to your patrol.

YOUR FIRST CONFERENCE. Soon after joining you will have your first Scoutmaster conference. You and he will sit down for a quiet talk.

Tell him about yourself and about your family. Tell him about your father and mother and what they do. Describe your brothers and sisters and tell the things you like to do with them. If you have a pet, tell him about that, too.

Your Scoutmaster will probably ask what things you like to do. Sports? Which ones? Music? Do you play an instrument? Do you like to read? What kinds of books do you like? Were you a Cub Scout? What things did you like to do? Did you like to make things, to play

459

games, to earn activity badges? Were you a Webelos Scout? Did you earn the Arrow of Light Award? How about school? What do you like best in school?

Your Scoutmaster will also want to know what things you do especially well. These are the things you will build on as you grow.

SETTING A GOAL FOR YOURSELF. Your Scoutmaster will ask you to set a goal for yourself in which you will use much of your strength. This goal could be something you will do with your family. It could be something you will do in your patrol or troop, school, religious group, community. It could even be something you will do alone. Whatever your goal, it is important that you set it yourself. Because it will be up to you to meet it. The right kind of goal is something you have to work at to reach. When you reach it, you will be proud of yourself.

Your Scoutmaster might ask you first about what goal you may have set for yourself in Scouting. You may have a leadership goal. Or it could be a goal in advancement. Your Scoutmaster might have ideas that will help you choose what skill awards or merit badges you will want to earn next.

But you will have goals outside Scouting as well. Suppose you are good at sports—baseball, for instance. Your goal might then be to organize some ball games for the troop. You might even plan to be the umpire since you know all the rules.

Maybe you like to do handicraft such as woodworking. Your goal could be to build a candle stand for use at a troop ceremony or to repair chairs for your neighborhood day-care center.

Perhaps music is your strength. You might then set a goal of entertaining the troop with your guitar at a number of troop campfires. Maybe you play the trumpet. How about becoming the troop bugler?

These are just a few examples. Get the idea? You don't just let things happen. You set it as a goal, then do it.

At each conference your Scoutmaster will want to find out from you how close you came to reaching your previous goal. He will help you set the next. As you become older and more experienced you will, of course, set even bigger goals. But each time the goal will be your own.

460

Your progress is reviewed by your troop leaders before you get your badge.

Your Progress as a Scout

Each time you move ahead in Scouting, from one rank to another, you will have a Scoutmaster conference. Each conference will be along the line just described. At the end of this conference, your Scoutmaster will tell you when the board of review will take place.

BOARD OF REVIEW. The board of review is done by your troop leaders. They will talk to you about your progress. They want to make sure that you have done all the things you were supposed to do. They will also want to learn what kind of Scout you are. They want to help you become an even better one.

The patrol leaders' council will review you for Tenderfoot, Second Class, and First Class. The troop committee will review you for Star and Life. Your council has a procedure that's followed for the Eagle Scout review.

The board of review members certify that you've completed the requirements by signing your handbook and the advancement report. This report is sent to your council service center. In addition, for the Eagle Award, an application is required; your council will send this application to the BSA national office for approval.

Soon after, the badge will be given to you at a ceremony. This may be at a troop meeting or perhaps at a parents' night.

You get a beautiful, embroidered badge when you reach Star, Life, and Eagle ranks. For Eagle, you also get the Eagle badge, a silver eagle suspended from a red-white-blue ribbon (see page 19).

UPWARD TO EAGLE

Before you set out on the upward trail to Eagle, through Star and Life, study carefully the requirements for these three ranks on pages 534-37. You will then find that each of the ranks calls for three added tests beyond those that carried you to First Class. One is a certain number of merit badges, with some of them specifically required. Another calls for giving leadership in the troop. The third deals with service.

MERIT BADGES. You probably started to earn merit badges soon after you became a Scout. Now you need to concentrate on the merit badges that are required for Eagle. You will find the requirements for them on pages 549-61.

LEADERSHIP IN THE TROOP. Some of the leadership positions or opportunities in Scouting you can seek—others may seek you.

If you have interests along certain lines, you may offer your services to the troop as scribe or quartermaster or librarian or chaplain aide, whatever troop jobs are open.

If there's a Cub Scout pack connected with or near your troop, you may become a den chief.

If you prove yourself the right kind of Scout, the fellows in your patrol may someday elect you for patrol leader. Or you may be elected senior patrol leader. Still another possibility may be a leadership project given you by your Scoutmaster.

SERVICE. Star and Life Service. The service project for Star and Life calls for you to give 6 hours of service for each award. You can do this service on your own. Or you can do it with your patrol and troop. The service project must be approved by your Scoutmaster before you start.

Eagle Service Project. There is a major difference between the service project for Star and Life, and that for Eagle. In the first two you can be a follower. For Eagle you must be a leader. You must plan, develop, and give leadership to a project of help to any religious group, school, or community. The project must be of real value when finished.

The project idea must be approved by your Scoutmaster and your troop committee and reviewed by your council or district before you start.

You may ask, "Does the project for Eagle have to be original? Must it be something I dreamed up that has never been done before?" The answer is "No, but it could be!"

Another point: How big does it have to be?" It should take many more hours in planning and carrying out than your Star and Life service. Here are a few projects that other Scouts have done for Eagle:

- Organized a bicycle safety campaign. Trained fellow Scouts as inspectors and judges. Ran a bike rodeo that included a bike safety check and a safe-bike-riding contest.

- Trained fellow students as audiovisual aides for the school. Arranged for more than 200 hours of audiovisual work.

- Set up a used-toy collection and repair service within the troop. Gave the toys to a school for handicapped children.

- Designed a footbridge across a brook to make a safe short-cut for children between their homes and school. Got permission to put it up. Supervised the Scouts building it.

- Surveyed the ruins of an old Spanish mission. Mapped it out. Then got the help of other Scouts to restore the ruin.

All of these projects required the help of other Scouts. The Eagle candidate planned the project. He lined up the manpower. He directed the work.

MERIT BADGES

Why do we have merit badges in Scouting? For two reasons. First, to encourage you to increase your skill in things you like to do. And second, to challenge you to try out new activities that may result in new interests or hobbies. These may even start you on your lifework.

PICKING A MERIT BADGE. Check the complete list of merit badges on pages 465-72. Pick one that interests you. If it is one that is required for Eagle, you will find the requirements on pages 549-61. If not, you need to get a copy of the *Boy Scout Requirements* booklet. This will tell you what you have to do. You may be able to borrow this booklet from your patrol or troop library. Or you may want to buy one for yourself. Then study the requirements.

Now, find out from your Scoutmaster who the counselor is for that badge. Merit badge counselors are people who want to help Scouts advance. They know their subjects.

EARNING A MERIT BADGE. These are the steps:
- Get signed merit badge form from your Scoutmaster.
- Phone the merit badge counselor and tell that person you want to earn the badge. Go to see the counselor to find out what is expected of you.
- Get the merit badge pamphlet on your subject. Your patrol or troop may have one you can borrow. So may your library. Or you may buy one in your Scouting service center.
- Learn and do the things that the pamphlet describes as being required for the badge.
- When you are ready, call the counselor again to make an appointment. Bring along the things you have made to meet the requirements or proof of what you have done. The counselor will spend time with you to make sure that you know your stuff. When the counselor is satisfied that you have done what is required, he signs your merit badge form.
- Give the signed form to your Scoutmaster. He will get the badge for you and will present it to you in front of the troop.

Agribusiness provides our food and fiber.

Art can reflect the real world or the world of your imagination.

American Business helps you understand the free-enterprise system.

Astronomy is the study of the universe.

American Cultures is about customs and traditions of others.

Athletics tests your skill in track and field.

American Heritage helps you enjoy our country's history.

Atomic Energy is power for many uses.

American Labor represents the work force of our nation.

Aviation makes the world a neighborhood for business and pleasure.

Animal Science leads you to explore farm and animal production.

Backpacking is being ready for outdoor adventures.

Archery helps you develop skills for safe and accurate shooting.

Basketry is an ancient art and skill in a world of machines.

Architecture is the art and science of planning homes and buildings.

Beekeeping produces honey, beeswax, and crop pollination.

465

Bird Study can be fun for as long as you live wherever you live.

Citizenship in the World helps you know that you are a world citizen, too.

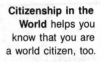

Botany will give you an introduction to the plants that grow nearby.

Coin Collecting is a special interest that can last a lifetime.

Bugling can make you the man of the hour as you sound the calls.

Communications is how to get your message to others.

Camping experience makes outdoor living a ot more fun.

Computers make it possible to condense and control facts and figures.

Canoeing can take you to faraway places.

Consumer Buying helps you be a thrifty Scout.

Chemistry is a part of the nature of things; how they work and what they do.

Cooking can be fun for the Scout who learns how to make tasty meals.

Citizenship in the Community is where you work with your neighbors.

Cycling for fun and transportation puts you in the driver's seat for safety.

Citizenship in the Nation is a birth-right that is yours to use wisely.

466

Dentistry shows you how to care for your teeth.

Dog Care shows that a dog deserves a master who knows dogs.

Drafting is the way we transfer ideas about making things.

Electricity is an invisible force that powers our lights and appliances.

Electronics applies magic to electricity in doing specialized work.

Emergency Preparedness helps you to know how to help in times of trouble.

Energy needs to be conserved to keep the world going.

Engineering is designing and building the world's largest structures.

Environmental Science helps you know the world around you.

Farm Mechanics helps you to know how to care for equipment.

Fingerprinting is a natural means of identification. Prints are unique.

Firemanship teaches fire prevention and rescue.

First Aid helps a Scout meet serious emergencies.

Fish and Wildlife Management helps conserve our outdoor friends.

Fishing is always fun because excitement may hit at any time.

Forestry helps us make the best use of our trees for many uses.

Hiking the trails of adventure and fun.

Gardening your own vegetables can be done almost anywhere.

Home Repairs will always require a handyman around the house.

Genealogy helps you trace your ancestry.

Horsemanship involves learning how to ride and care for horses.

General Science leads you into experiments that are fun.

Indian Lore is the story of our native Americans.

Geology is for anyone who wants to find out about the earth's features.

Insect Study is about the familiar and strange insects that live near us.

Golf is the only game where you are your own "official."

Journalism searches for stories that the public should know about.

Graphic Arts is the way to spread ideas and images.

Landscape Architecture visualizes and plans for pleasing scenes.

Handicap Awareness helps you know about and work with disabled persons.

468

Law helps you to know your rights and responsibilities as a citizen.

Leatherwork skill helps you make many useful things.

Lifesaving skills help you make water rescues.

Machinery speeds our manufacturing ability, but machines need service.

Mammal Study helps you get to know more outdoor friends.

Masonry is building with bricks, stones, or blocks and mortar.

Metals Engineering studies metals and the alloys made from them.

Metalwork is using metals to make useful articles and tools.

Model Design and Building includes land, air, space, and water vehicles.

Motorboating can place you at controls of excitement.

Music may be your thing if you play an instrument and can read music.

Nature helps you understand the world around you.

Oceanography takes you deep into ocean life and movement.

Orienteering is a fast-moving sport with compass in hand.

Painting preserves and beautifies the surface of things.

469

Personal Fitness is a debt you owe to yourself, your mind and body.

Personal Management helps you use your time and money wisely.

Pets, other than dogs, require their own special care from their owners.

Photography is a skill in handling equipment, and an art in stopping time.

Pioneering makes use of primitive building materials.

Plant Science helps you know how plants produce food.

Plumbing brings water in and takes waste out of our buildings.

Pottery provides the bowls, dishes, and jars that we use every day.

Public Health is guarded by government and informed citizens.

Public Speaking helps you tell your story to others.

Pulp and Paper provides us with many things we use every day.

Rabbit Raising is a source of meat and fur for market.

Radio is a worldwide hobby of operators, young and old.

Railroading hauls the freight and captures the interest of model builders.

Reading for fun and information can give you a lifetime of adventure.

Reptile Study is fascinating for some and frightening for others.

Rifle Shooting trains your eye and mind

Shotgun Shooting is the big bang in marksmanship.

Rowing a boat, so that it does what you want it to do, is fun.

Signaling is an old skill that can be fun.

Safety first is the smart way of doing things anytime.

Skating is fun and helps keep you in shape.

Salesmanship says opportunity hides in every selling situation.

SALE

Skiing makes us think snow even when it's summertime.

Scholarship makes the best of time and talent; you have both.

Small-Boat Sailing can thrill you as you try to catch up with the wind.

Soil and Water Conservation must be followed, or our future will be sad.

Sculpture is art in the round or in relief, and it is your creation.

Space Exploration is exploring the last frontier.

Sports can last a lifetime and help keep you in good condition.

471

Stamp Collecting helps you become a better citizen.

Veterinary Science can lead you into a career of animal care.

Surveying marks the boundaries of land sections.

Water Skiing is as exciting as it looks; learn the fundamentals.

Swimming is one of the sports to enjoy throughout your lifetime.

Weather forecasting isn't perfect, but it's getting better every day.

Textile includes natural and synthetic fibers for many uses.

Whitewater is excitement with safety.

Theater can be a way to understand another person by playing a role.

Wilderness Survival skills are important to every outdoor activity.

Traffic Safety is important in your everyday life.

Wood Carving is creative expression in design and form.

Truck Transportation moves the country's goods.

Woodwork is for carpenters, cabinetmakers, and home handymen.

HOW TO WEAR MERIT BADGES, Up to six merit badges may be worn on the right sleeve of the long-sleeve shirt starting 3 inches from the bottom edge of the cuff in rows of two. No merit badges may be worn on the short-sleeve shirt. For the merit badge sash, see the illustration on page 517. Only merit badges may be worn on the sash.

On a foggy day in 1909, a British Boy Scout guided an American businessman, William D. Boyce, to his destination and refused a tip for his Good Turn. Boyce, impressed with the boy's spirit, brought Scouting to the U.S.A.

Years later, the unknown Scout was honored for his deed with the Silver Buffalo Award.

THE STORY OF A GOOD TURN

How good must a Good Turn be to be GOOD? The answer is best given by telling you the story of how Scouting came to America. It shows that it isn't the size of the Good Turn that counts. It's the doing of it, whether large or small.

A GOOD TURN TO AN AMERICAN. One day in the year 1909 the great city of London was in the grip of a dense fog. An American businessman, William D. Boyce, stopped under a street lamp to locate himself. Out of the gloom a boy approached him and asked if he could be of help.

"You certainly can," said Boyce. He told the boy that he wanted to find a certain business office in the center of the city.

"I'll take you there," said the boy.

When they got to the destination, the American reached into his pocket for a tip. But the boy stopped him.

"No thank you, sir. I am a Scout. I can't take anything for helping."

"A Scout? And what might that be?" asked Boyce.

And so the boy told the American about himself and his brother Scouts. Boyce became very interested. After finishing his errand, he had the boy take him to the British Scout office. There the boy disappeared.

At the office Boyce met Baden-Powell, the famous British general who had founded the Scouting movement. Boyce was so impressed with what he learned that he decided to bring Scouting home with him.

And so, on February 8, 1910, in Washington, D.C., Boyce and a group of outstanding men founded the Boy Scouts of America. Ever since then this day has been known as the birthday of Scouting in the United States.

What happened to the boy? No one knows. He was never heard of again, but he will never be forgotten. In the British

Scout Training Center at Gilwell Park, England, a statue of a buffalo was put up in honor of this "Unknown Scout." His Good Turn had brought the Scouting movement to our country.

One Good Turn to *one* man became a Good Turn to millions of American boys. Such is the power of a Good Turn. You never can tell. . . .

THE FOUNDER OF SCOUTING. The man who founded the Scouting movement, Robert Baden-Powell, had had a great military career. He got his early training in India. He then saw service in Africa. At the turn of the century he was an officer in the war between Britain and the descendants of Dutch settlers, the Boers, in South Africa. Here he gained world fame by holding a key town, Mafeking, for 217 days against a big enemy force. He stood fast until another army group broke through the Boer lines and relieved him and his men.

Baden-Powell came home to England as the greatest hero of the Boer War. He decided to make use of his fame to help British boys become better men.

He slowly developed his ideas. He based them on his own experiences as a boy in England and a soldier in India and Africa. He then tested them with a group of boys. He held the world's first Boy Scout camp on the English island of Brownsea, in 1907. Out of this testing came a book he called *Scouting for Boys*. It was an instant best-seller. Boys by the thousands bought it and decided to become Scouts. Within a few weeks Scouting spread like wildfire throughout England and soon afterward around the world.

Baden-Powell learned the skills of outdoors camping with his older brothers in England and on military service in India and Africa. He became world-famous in 1900. He decided to use his fame to promote a program to help boys become better men. He tested it out in 1907 and published a book about it in 1908. It quickly spread around the world, arriving in U.S.A. in 1910.

Daniel Carter Beard
National Scout
Commissioner

Ernest Thompson
Seton, first
Chief Scout

James E. West, first
Chief Scout Executive

EARLY DAYS IN AMERICA. Among the founders of the Boy Scouts of America, two men had started programs that boys liked. They were Ernest Thompson Seton and Daniel Carter Beard. They were both well-known authors. Seton became the first Chief Scout of the Boy Scouts of America. Beard was made the National Commissioner.

Soon after Scouting started, James E. West, a young Washington lawyer, became the first Chief Scout Executive. He had had a tragic boyhood. His father died before he was born. His mother died when he was 7. He was sent to an orphan asylum. Here it was discovered that he had an incurable disease in one leg that made him a cripple for life. In spite of his handicap, he put all his ambition, ability, and energy into becoming a lawyer. He succeeded and dedicated himself to help all children, healthy, sick, or handicapped, to have a better life. He led the Boy Scouts of America for 32 years. He was a strong, wise leader. He helped build Scouting into the largest boy movement in the country and in the free world.

THE FIRST HANDBOOK. The first *Official Handbook* of the Boy Scouts of America was published hurriedly in 1910. It was an Americanized version of Baden-Powell's *Scouting for Boys.*

In it, the boys of America could read about joining a Scout patrol, about fun in the outdoors, about hiking and camping. There were games to play, badges to earn.

Immediately, boys by the thousands became Scouts.

Altogether, nine editions have been published. With the edition you are now reading, 32,560,000 copies of *Boy Scout Handbooks* have been printed from the start of the Scouting movement.

BOYS' LIFE. From the very beginning, James E. West, as Chief Scout Executive, felt that the Boy Scouts of America needed a magazine that would tell every Scout what to do and would provide him with good reading.

In Providence, Rhode Island, an 18-year-old youth, Joseph Lane, had started a boys' magazine. He had given it the ideal title for a magazine for boys: *Boys' Life.* The Boy Scouts of America decided to buy it for a sum equivalent to one dollar for each subscription. The number was determined at 6,100 – and the purchase price consequently at $6,100.

NORMAN ROCKWELL
The best-known and most-beloved American artist.
In 1912, at 18, Rockwell joined *Boys' Life* magazine as illustrator and art director. During his career, he did more than 500 paintings for the BSA. Twelve of them are reproduced in this book. His success was based on his skill and his high standards. Once he wrote on the top of his easel "100%" in gold paint. A friend asked him, "What does that mean?" He answered, "That's what Norman expects of Norman."

From 6,100 in 1912, *Boys' Life* grew to be a national magazine with more than 2,000,000 subscribers. It is still going strong as a magazine for you and for every other Scout.

BOY SCOUT SERVICE. When the United States joined the Allied Forces in the war against Germany in 1917, the Boy Scouts were firmly established and ready for service. Their work in the war effort made people realize the importance of Scout training for boys. The Congress of the United States granted a charter to the Boy Scouts of America.

With this great acceptance of the program and ideals of Scouting, boys became Scouts by the hundreds of thousands and, eventually, by the millions.

THE FIRST WORLD JAMBOREE. By 1920, Scouting had spread around the world. To strengthen this world brotherhood, Baden-Powell called Scouts from all nations where the movement had taken hold to a world jamboree in London in 1920. During this first world gathering of Scouts, Baden-Powell was acclaimed "Chief Scout of the World."

When you became a Boy Scout, you joined the largest youth movement in the free world, with more than 14 million members in more than 100 countries. You can help Scouting around the world by contributing, through your troop, to the World Friendship Fund.

The jamboree was a great success. It showed the people of the whole world what Scouting was and what Scouts could do.

The Scout leaders of the world decided that the jamboree idea should be kept alive. Since 1920, world jamborees have been held every 4 years, with the exception of the World War II years.

The Boy Scouts of America took up the idea on a national basis. National jamborees have been held between world jamborees since 1937, with as many as 50,000 Scouts taking part.

THE GROWTH OF SCOUTING. The Boy Scouts of America continued to grow. More and more Boy Scouts joined. And other groups increased the membership.

Sea Scouting had been established in 1912 to hold the older boys. Then it became Senior Scouting and showed a spurt in membership. Later, it was turned into Exploring which is now the program for young men and women in the Boy Scouts of America.

The Lone Scouts of America, organized by William D. Boyce who brought Scouting to the United States, merged with the Boy Scouts of America in 1924.

And in 1930, a younger-boy program, first called Cubbing, but now known as Cub Scouting, began drawing boys from 8 years up into the movement. Tiger Cubs, BSA, was added in 1982.

"Shake my hand and call me friend." All Scouts use the left hand.

Scouting Opportunities

LEADERSHIP OPPORTUNITIES. Most boys who have had a happy Boy Scouting experience want to help the younger boys who are following in their footsteps have just as much Scouting fun as they had. You can be a great influence in the lives of this next generation of Scouts by offering your services to your troop for leadership in troop activities or in one of the capacities illustrated by the badges above and below.

If you have shown that you are a real leader, the Scouts in your patrol may choose you for a patrol leader. Or you may be elected the senior patrol leader.

Den Chief

Webelos Den Chief

Special Opportunities

Below are some of the awards you can earn. Requirements are outlined in *Boy Scout Requirements* or on the application forms.

SNORKELING, BSA, AWARD. You can earn this award by completing the requirements on the application form.

MILE SWIM, BSA. You can earn this award by completing the requirements outlined in the *Swimming* merit badge pamphlet, including swimming 1 mile.

BSA LIFEGUARD. If you hold the Swimming, Lifesaving, and Rowing merit badges you can earn this badge. You do it by meeting the further tests outlined on the application form.

481

HORNADAY AWARD AND BADGE. These awards go to Scouts who have done exceptional and distinguished service in conservation. If you desire to make an extra effort toward saving our natural resources, aim for this award. Get an application for it at your council service center. Then get to work.

WORLD CONSERVATION AWARD. You can get this by earning certain skill awards and merit badges. The skill awards are Environment and Conservation. The merit badges are Environmental Science, Citizenship in the World, and either Soil and Water Conservation or Fish and Wildlife Management.

YOUTH LEADERSHIP IN AMERICA AWARD FOR SENIOR PATROL LEADERS. This award may be earned by any senior patrol leader who meets the six requirements and is approved by his Scoutmaster.

INTERPRETER. If you are good at languages, a special interpreter badge is available to you. To earn this, you must be able to carry on a conversation in a foreign language or in sign language. You must write a letter in the foreign language (not required for signing). And you must translate orally and in writing from the language.

BENGALI

If you can speak a foreign language, you can earn the Interpreter strip.

50-MILER AWARD. You earn this award by taking part in a troop event involving a wilderness trip. You go on foot, by canoe or boat. The trip must cover 50 consecutive miles over at least 5 consecutive days. On the trail you must do service projects to improve the environment.

HISTORIC TRAILS AWARD. For this award you must work with other members of your troop to locate a historic trail or site. You must also find out about its significance. You must then hike to camp 2 days and 1 night along the trail or near the site. You finish the tests by working with a group of adults. You help them mark and restore the trail or site.

PAUL BUNYAN WOODSMAN. If you like axmanship this award is for you. You must have earned the Totin' Chip and helped a Scout to earn his. You must show your skill with a three-quarter ax or a saw and do a forestry job. You must also teach other Scouts how to use woods tools.

DEN CHIEF SERVICE AWARD. A special recognition given to den chiefs who complete certain service and training requirements.

WORLD CREST. A recognition for Scouts who participate at least 5 days in an official international Scouting event or provide home hospitality to foreign Scouts or Scouters for at least 5 days.

RELIGIOUS EMBLEMS

"A Scout is reverent." All Scouts show this by being faithful in their duty to God. Some go further and give special service. This may qualify them for a religious emblem. Such an emblem is not a Scouting award. It is conferred on a Scout by his religious leader. Each faith has its own requirements for earning its emblem. Listed below are the emblems and where to find out about them. Before writing, check with your religious leader.

Ad Altare Dei. Roman Catholic—pastor or Scoutmaster.

Alpha Omega. Orthodox—Orthodox Scouting Commission, 1345 Fairfield Woods Road, Fairfield, CT 06430-3214.

Ararat. Armenian—Armenian Church, Diocese of America, 630 Second Avenue, New York, NY 10016-4885.

Bog I Ojczyzna. Polish National Catholic—Thaddeus R. Rudnicki, 11491 Tonawanda Creek Road, Akron, NY 14001.

God and Country. Baptist—Association of Baptists for Scouting, Boy Scouts of America, 1325 Walnut Hill Lane, Irving, TX 75038-3096; Episcopal—for information contact your diocesan office; Protestant—minister or Scoutmaster.

God and the Salvation Army. The Salvation Army, 120 West 14th Street, New York, NY 10011-7301.

"In the Name of God." Islamic—Islamic Committee on Scouting, 7016 Heather Heath, West Bloomfield, MI 48033-5412.

Liahona. Reorganized Church of Jesus Christ of Latter Day Saints, Box 1059, Independence, MO 64051-0559.

Light Is Life. Eastern Rite Catholic—Religious Relationships, Boy Scouts of America, 1325 Walnut Hill Lane, Irving, TX 75038-3096.

Living Faith. Lutheran—Lutheran Council in the U.S.A., 360 Park Avenue South, New York, NY 10010-1761.

Ner Tamid. Jewish—Religious Relationships, Boy Scouts of America, 1325 Walnut Hill Lane, Irving, TX 75038-3096.

"On My Honor." Church of Jesus Christ of Latter-day Saints, Church Distribution Center, 1999 West 1700 South, Salt Lake City, UT 84104-4233.

Pope Pius XII. Roman Catholic—pastor or Scoutmaster.

Religion in Life. Unitarian Universalists or members of other liberal groups—Unitarian Universalist Association, 25 Beacon Street, Boston, MA 02150-4398.

Sangha. Buddhist—Buddhist Churches of America, 1710 Octavia Street, San Francisco, CA 94109-4398.

Altare Dei

Alpha Omega

Ararat

Bog I Ojczyzna
Polish National Catholic

God and Country
Baptist

God and Country
Episcopal

God and Country
God and Church
Protestant

God and the
Salvation Army

"In the Name of God"

Liahona

Light Is Life

Living Faith
Lutheran

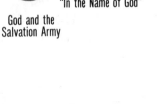

Ner Tamid

"On My Honor"

Pope Pius XII

Religion in Life

Sangha

MORE OPPORTUNITIES

ORDER OF THE ARROW. This is a national brotherhood of Scout campers. The honor of becoming a member of the Order of the Arrow is one that you cannot set out to earn on your own. This honor is bestowed on a Scout by the members of his troop. This is done when he has proved himself worthy of receiving it. He must be an outstanding Scout and an unselfish camper.

ALPHA PHI OMEGA. A national college service fraternity active on many campuses. It is based on the ideals of the Scout Oath and Law.

NATIONAL EAGLE SCOUT ASSOCIATION. Any Eagle Scout may join this national association. Many local councils have active chapters on both a formal and informal basis. If you are an Eagle Scout and want to join—and you should—request an application from the national office, Boy Scouts of America. (For address, see page 10.)

EXPLORING. When you have completed the eighth grade and are at least 14 years of age, or are 15 years of age or older, you may join an Explorer post. As an Explorer, you are still a member of the Boy Scouts of America. You may also be in a Scout troop. Explorer posts often do some form of career exploration. Young women as well as young men may become Explorers.

LIFESAVING AWARDS

AWARDS BY THE NATIONAL COURT OF HONOR. The National Court of Honor makes awards for rare Scoutlike action and for saving life.

Honor Medal. The highest special award in Scouting is the gold Honor Medal for saving life. This is awarded by the National Court of Honor. It is given to Scouts and Scouters who show heroism, resourcefulness, and skill by saving or trying to save life at the great risk of their own. In rare cases it is awarded with crossed palms.

Heroism Award. Awarded for heroic action where there is minimum or no risk to self.

Medal of Merit. The Medal of Merit is awarded by the National Court of Honor. It is given to Scouts who put into practice the skills and ideals of Scouting, by doing some great act of service. This act need not necessarily be a rescue or involve risk to self.

Honor Medal   Heroism Award   Medal of Merit

YOU— FROM BOY TO MAN

Growth of a Leader
by Norman Rockwell, 1966

489

The leadership you give shows that you are willing to help.

The way you live up to the Scout Oath will show what kind of man you are aiming to become.

Living the Scout Oath

What kind of person do you want to be? There is a simple way to find the answer. You do it by first answering another question: "What kind of person do I most admire?"

Sit down quietly and alone with a piece of paper. Then ask yourself, "Which Americans—past and present—do I look up to?" Put their names down. "Why do I admire them? What do I like about them?" Write down the whys and the whats.

High on your list may be your mother and father. And perhaps the names of relatives, your Scoutmaster, your religious leader, your best friends.

Your list may include Washington because of his loyalty to his country . . . Lincoln for his simplicity and steadfastness . . . Theodore Roosevelt for his enthusiasm and fighting spirit . . .

Edison for his energy and perseverance . . . heroes from our wars for their daring and self-sacrifice . . . athletes for their endurance and sportsmanship . . . men of science and arts for their accomplishments.

You have made your list. There before you in black and white are the qualities you admire most in others.

Study those qualities closely. Then notice how they add up until they cover each part of the Scout Oath.

The Scout Oath Your Guide. They are bound to come out that way, because in the Scout Oath you have the qualities that make men fine and great.

On My Honor . . . Heroes have died rather than betray their honor. As a Scout, you count your honor one of your most valuable possessions.

. . . *I Will Do My Best* . . . No person who has accomplished anything worthwhile did this by doing his second best—or his third or fourth best. He gave the very best that was in him—his best thoughts, his best work.

. . . *To Do My Duty to God and My Country* . . . The kind of man you will be depends on your ability to know your duty and to do your utmost to live up to your obligations.

. . . *And To Obey the Scout Law;* . . . That law fits you as a boy. It will fit you just as well when you become a man—for a real man is everything the Scout Law stands for.

. . . *To Help Other People at All Times;* . . . It is not enough to have the willingness to help other people—you need to have the ability as well. You develop this ability as you advance in Scouting and learn how to act in an emergency.

. . . *To Keep Myself Physically Strong, Mentally Awake, and Morally Straight.* You owe it to yourself, your country, and your God to develop your body, to train your mind, to strive to be a boy and man of high character.

In all these things Scouting helps you. By taking part enthusiastically in all activities of patrol and troop, by learning the skills that Scouting has to offer, by living up to the ideals of Scouting, you will become the man you want to be.

DUTY TO GOD

The men and women who founded our nation held the strong conviction that all persons "are endowed by their Creator with certain unalienable rights." When they signed their names to the Declaration of Independence they did this "with a firm reliance on the protection of Divine Providence."

But these courageous people recognized also that for these "unalienable rights" and that "protection," they owed certain obligations and duties to God.

You learn what these religious duties are from your family and religious leader. They teach you about God. By following these teachings in your daily life, by taking part in the practices of your faith, by using your leadership ability in your religious activities, you perform your duty to God.

As a Scout, living in close contact with nature, you learn to know God's handiwork more deeply. As you see the wonders around you, your reverence toward God is strengthened. Sometimes when you look up from your campsite into the starlit sky on a quiet night, thank God for all things.

Show your gratefulness to God by using your gifts and talents in your daily activities.

You have a wonderful body and a thinking brain. Artists use the gift of painting so that they can inspire their fellowman. Writers use the power of words so that they can form word pictures of beauty and can lead others to beauty. Composers can stir other people with their music; statesmen can work for their country. Teachers help us to grow in wisdom.

The way to thank God for your abilities is to develop these abilities to the fullest and make the best possible use of them. Learn as much as you can in your youth and use your knowledge for the rest of your life.

All human beings are important in the sight of God. One way to express your thankfulness to God is to help others. This, too, is a part of your Scout Oath.

We Thank Thee, O Lord
by Norman Rockwell, 1974

PHILMONT GRACE
For food, for raiment,
For life, for opportunity,
For friendship and fellowship,
We thank Thee, O Lord.
—Amen

493

DUTY TO COUNTRY

Our country was built upon a trust in God. As you look into the past, you learn about men and women who toiled to make our America, who raised it to where it is today.

The duty you have as a Scout to carry this work forward is contained in *The American's Creed* (pages 402-06).

OBEYING THE SCOUT LAW

WHAT OTHERS SEE. Several points of the Scout Law have to do with your behavior toward people with whom you come in contact. These people have a chance to judge whether you are trustworthy, loyal, helpful, friendly, courteous, kind, obedient, and cheerful. You prove all these things in your actions.

The most important of these people are the members of your own family. They must be able to trust you and depend on you. The way you act in your own home shows better than anything else what kind of boy you are.

Other people you deal with soon discover that you can be trusted by the way you keep your promises. They see your loyalty in the way you act at home and in school. They notice your willingness to be of help. They feel your friendliness and courtesy. They observe your kindness. They notice the obedience you show your parents, your teachers, your leaders. They respond to your cheerfulness.

WHAT YOU KNOW WITHIN YOURSELF. The way you live up to the remaining points of the Scout Law—thrifty, brave, clean, and reverent—is hidden to other people. Some of these traits have certain outward signs. But it is what happens within your heart that makes you know to what extent you have obeyed them.

Thrift, for instance, is more than going to the bank teller's window and passing over money. It is the way you make use of your earnings, your time, your ability. Bravery is not often shown in heroic deeds. It is often a matter of overcoming your fear, a decision within yourself to do what is right regardless of the consequences. Cleanliness is more than having a clean face and clean hands. Only you know whether your thoughts are clean. Reverence is more than going to your church or synagogue. It is the way your faith makes you act when only God is your witness.

HELPING OTHER PEOPLE

When you dedicated yourself to the Scout Oath, you promised to "help other people"—not once or twice, but all the time.

As you have moved onward and upward in Scouting, your eyes have been opened to the needs of other people. You have learned skills for serving these needs. And the daily Good Turn has become a habit.

To people who know about Scouting, the daily Good Turn is one of the finest features of our movement. The record of Good Turns, small and large, that have been done by Scouts since the day Scouting was founded is truly impressive.

Think of the small everyday things done by individual Scouts, by patrols and by troops: assistance to the weak and the old, service to the sick, first aid to injured people, help in directing traffic, and numerous other things.

Then think of the work that Scouts have done in big national Good Turns involving conservation and safety, in get-out-the-vote campaigns. And also of the Scout services in two World Wars—service upon service, day in and day out.

And think of the part Scouts have played over the years in floods, tornadoes, and hurricanes: messenger service, caring for the wounded, aiding the police, helping relief workers.

What Scouts have done, Scouts can do! What has been done by others YOU can do! But remember: those others were trained, prepared, willing to help other people.

So get yourself trained to meet any accident, any emergency. Then, when the chance comes, you will be ready to do your part, ready to keep alive the tradition of Scout service.

To Keep Myself Physically Strong
by Norman Rockwell, 1964

Do you know Latin? Probably not. But you should know an old Roman proverb: *Mens sana in corpore sano*—A sound mind in a sound body. There's a goal to strive for.

A plane is checked before its journey. You should be checked as well.

PHYSICALLY STRONG

Imagine yourself at one of our country's great airports. Tremendous jet planes are lined up for trips to Europe or South America or around the world. The passengers stream on board. The crew members are at their posts.

The pilots know exactly where they are going and the steps for getting there. But how do they make sure that they'll reach their goal and return?

Do they have their planes thoroughly checked before take-off? You bet your life they do.

Do they have their instruments tested? Of course they do.

Do they have all possible defects corrected before they speed down the runway? Well, what is your guess?

They don't even trust themselves, alone, to make the final check. They call in master mechanics to inspect the engines, experts to test the instruments, specialists to look over wings and fuselage and landing gear.

CHECKING YOUR MACHINE. Your body is much like a plane in which you set out on your trip through life. But it is a far more wonderful and far more complicated machine than any built by human hands.

You are the pilot. You should know if it is in order for the journey.

Part of the checking you can do yourself.

If you are in good health, you should hardly feel your body at all. There should be no pains or discomfort. Your appetite should be good. You should awake in the morning cheerful and refreshed, full of pep for the day's play and work. You should go to bed at night tired, perhaps, but quickly dropping off to sleep.

But there may be a "knock" in the "engine" somewhere, or a weak part of which you are not aware. Someday it may cause you trouble. That's why the proper thing to do is to have an expert give your body a thorough check at regular intervals. Do it once a year. The expert, of course, is a doctor, and the check is known as a medical examination. This check should be made by your family physician. Or it could be some other doctor in whom you have confidence.

If the doctor finds your body in fine working order, he or she will give you a clean bill of health. If weak points are discovered, the doctor will tell you how to strengthen them.

GROWING INTO MANHOOD. In building health and strength, you should realize that you may feel like an adult and act like one. But your body is not yet that of an adult. You must remember that you are not yet fully grown. Be patient and use your willpower and common sense.

By following simple and sensible rules of health, you can build a body ready for action, with plenty of reserve energy to carry you through life.

BODILY MEASUREMENTS

HOW TO MEASURE. Height: Barefoot. Weight: Stripped. Neck: Thinnest part. Chest: Across nipples, chest expanded. Waist: Thinnest part, stomach relaxed, NOT pulled in. Hips: Widest part. Biceps: Around tensed biceps, arm bent. Forearm: Thickest part, arm straight, fist clenched. Wrist: Thinnest part. Thigh: Thickest part at top of leg. Calf: Thickest part. Ankle: Thinnest part.

KEEP TRACK OF YOUR GROWTH

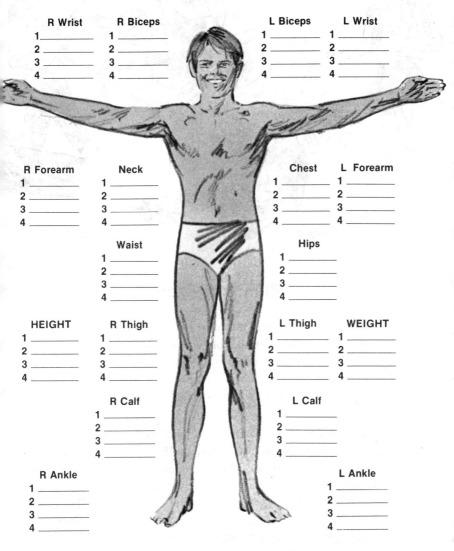

R Wrist
1 _____
2 _____
3 _____
4 _____

R Biceps
1 _____
2 _____
3 _____
4 _____

L Biceps
1 _____
2 _____
3 _____
4 _____

L Wrist
1 _____
2 _____
3 _____
4 _____

R Forearm
1 _____
2 _____
3 _____
4 _____

Neck
1 _____
2 _____
3 _____
4 _____

Chest
1 _____
2 _____
3 _____
4 _____

L Forearm
1 _____
2 _____
3 _____
4 _____

Waist
1 _____
2 _____
3 _____
4 _____

Hips
1 _____
2 _____
3 _____
4 _____

HEIGHT
1 _____
2 _____
3 _____
4 _____

R Thigh
1 _____
2 _____
3 _____
4 _____

L Thigh
1 _____
2 _____
3 _____
4 _____

WEIGHT
1 _____
2 _____
3 _____
4 _____

R Calf
1 _____
2 _____
3 _____
4 _____

L Calf
1 _____
2 _____
3 _____
4 _____

R Ankle
1 _____
2 _____
3 _____
4 _____

L Ankle
1 _____
2 _____
3 _____
4 _____

Measure yourself at 3-month intervals and fill in the spaces above.
The numbers refer to the following dates that you fill in:

1 ___/ ___19___   2 ___/ ___19___   3 ___/ ___19___   4 ___/ ___19___

499

Hiking

Canoeing

Swimming

Camping

Axmanship

Plenty of Exercise

If you want strong arms, you must use them. You must pull, push, and swing them in work and play. You must lift with them, throw with them. If you want to strengthen your legs you must walk and hike, run and jump. If you want to have an agile, supple body covered with flat, firm muscles, you must bend it, twist it.

DAILY EXERCISE. When you are out Scouting with your patrol or your troop you get plenty of exercise. Hiking, games and contests, swimming, rowing, axmanship, and many other activities give your body a workout. Even indoors, at patrol and troop meetings, you get exercise through games or in strength tests with your fellow Scouts.

Play team games. Baseball, football, soccer, and basketball are good. But also get going, while still a boy, on a game that has a strong "carry-over value." That is, a sport you will want to pursue after you grow up. Swimming and skiing and skating, and golf and tennis have strong "carry-over value." Wrestling and football and other body-contact sports have none.

Indian arm wrestling

Chest push

Stick fight

Pull apart

YOUR POSTURE. Good posture itself is good exercise: Your are using your muscles to keep yourself upright against the pull of gravity. Get into the habit of standing tall, sitting tall. Here is a simple trick for doing this: Try to touch, with the top of your head, an imaginary ceiling just an inch above your head.

Good posture means keeping your head high, your shoulders easily back, your chest up, and your stomach in.

STRENGTHEN YOUR BODY. There are three steps for making certain that you are actually strengthening your body:

• Test yourself in the five tests on page 502. Write the results in the top line of your personal chart on page 503.

• Decide now the standards you want to reach in 30 days. Write them next to the word AIM.

• Set out with determination to improve your record. Write down every few days what you accomplish.

After you have exercised for a full month, retest yourself in the five tests and record the results on the chart. How did you make out? Continue to improve yourself until you reach the EXCELLENT standard for your age in each of the five tests.

Sit-up

Pull-up

Your Age	SIT-UPS		PULL-UPS		LONG JUMP		50-METER DASH* 50-YARD DASH		600-METER RUN/WALK* 600-YARD RUN/WALK	
	Number of times		Number of times		Meters (feet/inches)		Seconds		Minutes:Seconds	
	Good	Excellent	Good	Excellent	Good	Excellent	Good	Excellent	Good	Excellent
11	41	45	5	6	1.75 (5' 9")	1.83 (6')	8.2 *7.5*	7.8 *7.2*	2:24 *2:12*	2:18 *2:06*
12	43	48	5	7	1.83 (6')	1.90 (6' 3")	8.0 *7.3*	7.6 *7.0*	2:16 *2:04*	2:08 *1:57*
13	47	50	6	9	1.96 (6' 5")	2.08 (6' 10")	7.6 *7.0*	7.3 *6.7*	2:08 *1:57*	2:00 *1:50*
14	48	52	8	10	2.08 (6' 10")	2.18 (7' 2")	7.2 *6.6*	7.0 *6.4*	2:00 *1:50*	1:54 *1:44*
15	49	52	10	12	2.21 (7' 3")	2.32 (7' 7")	7.0 *6.4*	6.8 *6.2*	1:55 *1:45*	1:49 *1:40*
16	49	52	10	12	2.29 (7' 6")	2.41 (7' 11")	7.0 *6.4*	6.8 *6.2*	1:52 *1:42*	1:47 *1:38*

* 50 m (54½ yd.) 600 m (656 yd.). Times for 50-yard dash and 600-yard run/walk are set in italics.

PRESIDENTIAL PHYSICAL FITNESS AWARD. These five tests are a part of the nationwide fitness program for schools, clubs, and Scout troops. If you wish to earn the award certificate and emblem, write to the President's Council on Physical Fitness and Sports, 400 Sixth Street, SW., Room 3030, Washington, D.C. 20201. Share this information with your Scoutmaster.

SIT-UPS. Lie on your back with legs bent. Have someone hold your ankles or put your feet under a heavy object. Clasp your hands behind your neck. Sit up. Touch the right elbow to the left knee. Lie down. The next time, sit up, touch the left elbow to the right knee, and lie down. Count one sit-up each time you lie down.

PULL-UPS. With the palms facing forward, grasp an overhead bar. Hang with arms and legs fully extended and feet off the ground. Pull yourself up with the arms, without kicking the legs and without swinging, until you can place your

502

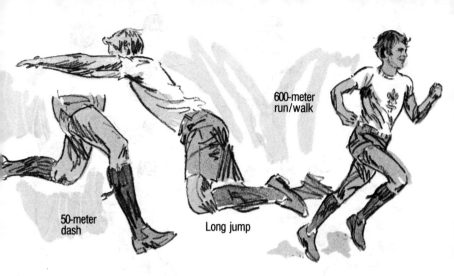

600-meter
run/walk

50-meter
dash

Long jump

Date	SIT-UPS Aim: _____	PULL-UPS Aim: _____	LONG JUMP Aim: _____	50-METER DASH Aim: _____	600-METER RUN/WALK Aim: _____

chin over the bar. Now lower yourself. Count one pull-up each time your chin is over the bar.

STANDING LONG JUMP. Stand on a level surface with the feet comfortably apart. Flex the knees. Swing the arms back and forth. Then jump, swinging the arms forcefully forward and up. Measure the distance from the takeoff line to the spot where the heel or any part of the body touched the ground.

50-METER DASH. Measure out a 50-m course. Have someone with a stopwatch stand at the finish line to act as the starter. He raises one hand, then brings it down smartly. As he hits his thigh, you start to run. As you cross the finish line, the starter notes the time in seconds to the nearest 10th.

600-METER RUN/WALK. Measure out a 600-m course. On the starter's signal, run the distance. You are permitted to walk if necessary, but the idea is to cover the distance as quickly as possible. Record the time in minutes and seconds.

503

As a boy, get into as many body-contact sports as you can manage without interfering with your family life, your school work, and your Scouting. But get started also on sports with a "carry-over value" into adult life.

Baseball, football, soccer, basketball, hockey, and wrestling are sports for the young and for professionals. Golf, tennis, swimming, skiing, bicycling, hiking, and backpacking are sports you'll enjoy as an adult.

RELATIVE PHYSICAL-FITNESS VALUES OF SPORTS

SPORT	Legs, hips	Abdomen	Lateral muscles	Arms, shoulders	Back	Endurance	Flexibility	Carry-over value
Archery	L	M	M	H	M	L	L	M
Backpacking	H	M	M	H	H	H	M	H
Badminton	M	M	L	M	M	M	M	M
Baseball	M	M	M	M	M	M	M	L
Basketball	H	M	M	H	M	H	M	L
Bicycling	H	L	L	L	L	M	L	H
Bowling	M	L	L	M	L	L	L	H
Camping	M	L	L	M	L	M	L	H
Canoeing	L	M	M	H	M	H	M	H
Climbing, Rock	H	M	M	H	M	H	M	M
Dancing, Folk	H	M	M	L	M	H	M	M
Dancing, Social	H	M	M	L	M	M	M	H
Fencing	M	M	M	H	M	H	M	M
Field Hockey	H	M	M	H	M	H	H	L
Football	H	H	M	H	H	H	M	L
Golf	M	L	M	M	L	L	L	H
Handball	H	M	M	M	M	M	M	M
Hiking	H	M	L	L	M	H	M	H
Horseback Riding	M	L	L	L	M	L	L	H
Orienteering	H	M	L	L	M	H	M	H
Rowing	M	M	M	H	M	H	M	M
Running	H	M	L	L	M	H	M	M
Skating	H	L	L	L	L	H	H	H
Skiing	H	M	M	M	H	H	H	H
Soccer	H	M	M	L	M	H	H	L
Softball	M	M	M	M	M	M	L	L
Swimming	H	M	M	H	M	H	H	H
Tennis	H	M	M	H	M	H	H	H
Volleyball	M	L	M	M	L	L	M	M
Water Polo	H	M	M	H	M	H	H	L
Weight Lifting	H	H	M	H	H	H	M	M
Wrestling	H	H	H	H	H	H	H	L

H—High   M—Medium   L—Low

Proper Nourishment

YOUR FOOD. Almost anything you eat and drink gives you some nourishment. Even a hot dog and a bottle of soda pop. But if you should try to get along on a steady diet of junk food you would soon run into trouble. Why? Because they lack a lot of things you need.

The food you eat should do three things:

- It should build your body and keep it in repair. Protein and minerals in meat, fish, eggs, and milk products will do this.
- It should give your inside organs—liver, spleen, intestines, and others—what they need to run smoothly. Vitamins and minerals in citrus fruits and vegetables, and protein and bulk in other foods work together to do this.
- It should provide fuel for the energy you need for what you do. And it must give you warmth on cool days. Bread and cereals, fats and oils take care of this. There is some fuel in everything you eat.

The four basic food groups on the next page form the basis for a balanced diet. They have all the foodstuffs, vitamins, and minerals that are needed for good health. They can be put together in millions of variations.

DRINK WATER. Besides solid nourishment and milk, you need plenty of water during the day. Water is needed to digest food. It carries away waste through the kidneys. Water regulates the heat of the body when you sweat.

GETTING RID OF WASTE. If you eat the right foods, exercise, and drink plenty of water, you'll develop a time for elimination.

Don't worry about how often your bowels move. Worrying often causes constipation. And don't take a laxative. It could throw your body out of order.

The idea that your bowels should move once a day or every other day is out of date. The only right schedule is your own schedule.

FOUR BASIC FOOD GROUPS

MILK GROUP
MILK, CHEESE, ICE CREAM, YOGURT
Every day

MEAT GROUP
MEAT, FISH, POULTRY, DRIED PEAS, BEANS, LENTILS
Two or more servings a day

EGGS
At least four or five a week

VEGETABLE-FRUIT GROUP
CITRUS FRUITS AND TOMATOES
At least one serving a day

LEAFY GREEN AND YELLOW VEGETABLES
At least one serving a day

OTHER VEGETABLES AND FRUITS
Two or more servings a day

BREAD-CEREAL GROUP
BREAD AND CEREALS
At every meal

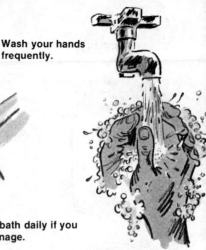

Wash your hands frequently.

Take a bath daily if you can manage.

Thorough Cleanliness

A clean body is a good defense against disease.

The skin is far more than just a covering of the body. Unbroken, it is an armor that keeps out germs and helps control your body temperature. Besides, the skin is the largest organ of the body and an important one. So keep it clean.

BATHING. Bathe regularly—daily is recommended. If you can't get a full bath or shower, you can wash your whole body every day with a wet cloth or towel. Follow this by a brisk rub down until your skin tingles.

In addition to this quick daily bath, take a more leisurely bath, with plenty of soap and warm water, twice a week or more often. Do this always after a hike or a camp or a strenuous game when you come home grimy and perspiring.

YOUR HANDS. Look at your hands. Other people do and often judge you by the kind of hands you have. If they are clean, with well-kept nails, they give a good impression of you. If they aren't—well. . . .

Get into the habit of washing your hands with soap and nailbrush morning and night, before each meal, following each trip to the bathroom. Wash them at such other times as they need it. Dry them thoroughly. Also clean under your nails.

Trim your nails regularly to match the tips of your fingers. Use clippers or a small pair of curved nail scissors. After cutting your nails, use the thumbnail to push back the skin around the lower part.

Here is a hint: If you do a lot of work that causes dirt to collect under the nails, scrape them over a piece of soap before you start working. The soap under the nails keeps dirt out and makes washing so much easier for you.

YOUR FEET. To have good posture you need sound feet. There is a very good reason why one-fourth of all the bones of your body are in your feet. They have to support you and move you around throughout your lifetime.

Wash your feet every night. Start each day with clean socks. Cut the nails straight across to prevent ingrown toenails.

The correct way to walk is to bring the feet down flat, not heel first or toe first. Keep your feet parallel, with the toes pointed straight ahead.

YOUR HAIR. Wash your hair as often as necessary to keep it and your scalp clean. Exercise your scalp by daily brushing and massaging with your fingertips.

YOUR TEETH. Your teeth are important to your appearance and digestion. Keep them in good working order.

Brush and floss your teeth at least twice a day—in the

Keep your hair well groomed.

Brush teeth after each meal.

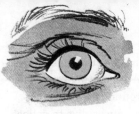

If your eyes bother you, have them examined.

As the old doctor said, "Never put anything but your elbows into your ears."

morning and at bedtime. Brush them also after each meal if possible. This will remove the sticky, colorless plaque that causes tooth decay and gum disease. Use fluoride toothpaste to help protect your teeth against decay.

Cleaning the teeth is only one part of tooth care. Eat well-balanced meals and cut down on sweet snacks. Have your teeth checked by a dentist twice a year.

YOUR EYES. One of the worst calamities that can happen to you is to lose your sight. You have only two eyes. Take good care of them!

Look in the mirror to see whether the pupils of your eyes are black, the colors of the iris bright, and the white a clear white. They should be. If your eyes are bloodshot, or if they hurt or get watery often, it is a sign of eyestrain. This may be caused by wind or smoke, lack of sleep, reading too much in poor light, an eye defect, or disease.

If your eyes bother you in any way, have them examined by an eye specialist and follow his advice.

YOUR EARS. As far as your ears are concerned, keep the outside part of them—the "trumpet"—as clean as the rest of your head by using a damp cloth over the end of a finger. Let nature take care of the inside. Never dig in your ear with any hard object. You may infect it or even break the eardrum.

Eardrums can be broken by jumping feetfirst into deep water without holding the nose. This may force water through the nostrils up into the inner ear and cause trouble. In swimming, if the water fills your ear canal, use rubber earplugs.

If you have any trouble with your ears, such as constant ringing in them, "running ear," or earache, see your doctor.

Fresh Air

To live and grow, each cell of your body must have a steady supply of oxygen from the air, day and night. If your air supply were cut off, you would die within minutes.

BREATHING PROPERLY. If it were just a matter of getting air to the lungs, it wouldn't make much difference whether you breathe through your nose or your mouth. But it isn't. The nose prepares the air for the lungs, the mouth doesn't. The damp lining of the nose moistens the air. The warmth of the nasal chambers warms it. The numerous tiny hairs that cover the inside of the nose help stop the germ-filled dust from entering the lungs. Thus, by breathing through the nose the lungs receive moist, warm, filtered air. By breathing through the mouth, colder, drier, dirtier air fills them.

So keep your mouth closed and the passage through your nose clear. Always blow your nose gently and one nostril at a time, never both together. If you have trouble breathing through your nose, let a doctor take a look at it.

Rest and Sleep

By the time you are 60 years old, you'll have spent 20 years in bed. A terrific waste? Not at all! Sleep is nature's way of recharging the human battery, of storing up new energy in the body. It also gives the body the chance to replace old tissues and to build new—in other words, to grow.

HOW MUCH SLEEP? How much is enough? A boy from 11 to 14 needs 9 to 10 hours of sleep each night. The reason for so much sleep is that you are at the age when the greatest growth occurs and when most sleep is required. And it's also the time when you go in for all kinds of strenuous activities.

It isn't how little you can get by on—it's how much you should have to be at your best. It will take planning to see to it that you get enough rest and sleep and yet get everything done you want to do and have to do, including school work.

511

Sleeping under the stars in camp is a treat you will always remember.

HOW TO SLEEP. To sleep well, your bed should be firm. If it sags, get a sheet of plywood to place under the mattress. Your covering should be light and just warm enough.

Sleep in fresh air. At home, have a window open so some fresh air will come in during the night, but not so much that you'll get cold. Sleep outdoors as often as you can—under open sky or in a tent. If you use a tent, leave the flaps open to let fresh air enter.

Staying Healthy

PROTECT YOURSELF AGAINST ACCIDENTS. More young people die from accidents than from any other single cause. In addition to those who die, thousands are injured—many of them permanently. Don't let that happen to you.

Here's what you can do about it:

Learn Skills to Make You Safe. There is a safe way of doing everything: swimming, bicycling, skateboarding, paddling a canoe, using an ax, playing baseball, soccer, or football, driving a car when you are qualified to do so. Practice the proper use of tools. Learn thoroughly the rules of sports you like. "Safety through skill" is a Scout slogan. Follow it.

Use Sense to Keep You Safe. It doesn't take skill to cross a railroad track. But it takes common sense not to do it when a train is coming. It is common sense to use a stepladder instead of a chair when you have to reach high. To keep away from strange dogs. To pick up broken glass before you or someone else gets hurt.

PROTECT YOURSELF AGAINST DISEASE. Your best weapon against disease is a healthy body. But that is not enough unless you use ordinary care.

Get yourself protected against catching certain diseases by immunization, that is, by getting shots that will keep you from getting the diseases. That goes for such diseases as tetanus (lockjaw), diphtheria, poliomyelitis (infantile paralysis), measles, and mumps.

Keep away from anyone who suffers from a communicable disease—that is, a disease that spreads from one person to another. Avoid persons who are coughing or sneezing.

Never use a drinking cup or eating utensils that have been used by others, until they have been properly washed and dried.

Use your own bath towel, washcloth, and handkerchief.

Keep flies away from yourself and your food.

Avoid persons who are coughing or sneezing.

PROTECT YOURSELF AGAINST YOURSELF. Many young people are bored because they have little interest in anything. Many others get themselves into all kinds of troubles. And so, they take what they consider the easy way out: they turn to drugs to get a "high" for excitement, or a "low" for forgetting their problems. They often wind up being no good to themselves and no good to anybody else.

What is a drug? A drug is a substance other than food that has an effect on the body or the mind, or on both. Drugs are of great value to doctors. Physicians can prescribe drugs to ease pain, to fight infections, to relax muscles, to quiet nerves, to cause changes in the body.

But some drugs are abused for "kicks" without being prescribed by a doctor. All of them affect the health, one way or another, of all persons using them.

Mild Drugs. *Coffee, tea*, and *cola drinks* (unless marked otherwise) contain a mild drug called caffeine. It stirs up the nervous system and speeds up the heart. Milk or water is far better. Milk is nourishment. Coffee and tea are not except for the milk added.

Tobacco. After many years of careful research, doctors agree that smoking endangers health. It causes lung cancer and weakens the heart. Tobacco has nicotine. But even worse is the tar from tobacco smoke. Imagine having the inside of your lungs tarred up!

Dangerous Drugs. Some drugs are dangerous to have. The possession of one of them—alcohol—by a person not of legal age is against the law. The possession of most of the others, without a doctor's prescription, is illegal in all states.

Alcohol. One look at a drunk staggering down the street is enough to tell you that alcohol slows down the body and the brain. Alcohol can turn a strong man into a weeping child. It can change a person into a raving maniac. It destroys families. It kills people outright and by drunken drivers.

Marijuana smoking may distort hearing, vision, and sense of time. Heavy use may produce boredom, disinterest in things and friends, and dropping away from normal activities.

Hallucinogens cause a change in the way a person sees, hears, tastes, smells, feels, and thinks. These sensations are often called "trips." They may turn into "bad trips." A gentle dream can switch to a violent nightmare. Many drugs of this type are known by the initials of the chemicals. LSD is one of these drugs. When using it, a person may lose knowledge of himself. He does not know what is real and what is not. His emotions may swing abruptly from bliss to horror.

Stimulants. A drug that excites or overworks the brain is a stimulant. Some are known as "speed" or "pep pills." They are used by persons who want to push themselves beyond their normal limits. Abuse of stimulants may cause liver and kidney damage and higher blood pressure. The users of stimulants may get upset and act strangely.

Sedatives and Tranquilizers. Sedatives are used to bring about sleep. Some of them—barbiturates—make their users "goof off" and go to sleep. They are therefore called "goof balls" or "sleepers." An overdose of sedatives can kill.

Narcotics. When correctly prescribed by a doctor, they will relieve pain and bring sleep. The dangers of narcotics use are extreme. A user comes to depend on them. When he is hooked, he can't help himself. He must have more and still more. To get money he needs to buy drugs from some "junkie," he may stage a holdup. He may even commit murder.

WHAT TO DO ABOUT DRUGS

Baden-Powell, the founder of Scouting, sometimes thought of adding one more point to the Scout Law: "A Scout is not a fool." But he decided against it. He figured that a boy smart enough to base his life on the Scout Oath would be smart enough to stay away from anything that was unhealthful or illegal or both.

As a Scout, you will agree with him. If you have been foolish, there is no law that says you have to stay that way.

Other Substances. Substances such as model-airplane glue, paint thinner, and other solvents contain chemicals that give off fumes. These fumes were never meant to be inhaled. Many of the containers warn against doing this. Sniffing the fumes produces a clouded mental state and may cause the sniffer to black out. Death can occur when the fumes are inhaled without enough oxygen.

FROM BOY TO MAN. At the age of 13, 14, or 15 (sometimes earlier, sometimes later) you not only grow, but many changes take place in your body. Your voice deepens. Your sex organs mature. These changes are caused mainly by the function of the sex glands, or testicles. They produce fluids that have a great effect on your development.

While all of this is going on, you may be wondering what is happening to you. You may have strange feelings that you have never had before. There are so many questions you would like to have answered.

Set out to get the answer to any question you may have about your development from boy to man. But be sure to seek your information from a good source. Information about sex you get from your friends often may be in error.

Start by asking your parent or family head. Your religious leader or your family doctor can help. So can a trained health adviser. These people may suggest books for you to read. Follow their advice.

A Healthy Attitude

You will find that living the Scout Law is a great help.

Being friendly, cheerful, brave, and clean makes you feel better. It helps reduce your worries and irritations. It also sets a fine example for your friends. A healthy attitude reduces fatigue, increases appetite, and helps you sleep soundly. You gain a feeling of success, ambition, and confidence.

"As a man thinketh in his heart, so is he!"

Think yourself fit and strong. Do something about it—and you will be fit and strong!

The badges on your uniform show that you are taking advantage of all the opportunities that Scouting is ready to offer you.

MENTALLY AWAKE

"Mentally awake..." in everything you do or think—that's part of our Scout Oath. What you make of yourself depends to a large extent on your mental alertness.

The boy who is mentally awake gets more out of life. And he gives more to other people. But also, he has a far better chance of creating a successful career for himself.

Learn to Think

In today's world, the most important thing you can learn to do is to THINK.

The ability to think—and especially to think fast—usually goes with a mind that is alert and interested and always inquiring. Thinking fast in an emergency also depends on the habit of figuring out in advance what you would have to do if an accident should happen.

THE ART OF CONCENTRATION. Does your mind jump from one thing to another like a flea? Or does it stick to the job at hand? You have to keep your mind constantly alert if you expect to keep it from drifting. Are you able to do it?

Alphonse Bertillon, a French criminologist, studied people to find a system for recognizing criminals. This eventually led to the worldwide use of fingerprints.

Some fellows seem to accomplish as much in one hour as others do in two. They can finish their studies more quickly.

They have ample time for all sorts of other interests—hobbies, athletics, reading. Often this is not so much because of superior ability. It's because they have learned to keep their minds on what they are doing. They know how to concentrate.

Concentration is made up of willpower and self-control.

During an exciting baseball game you often become so absorbed in the play that you are unaware of anything around you except the ball and the players. No difficulty about concentration here. Bring that same intense quality to your work and see how much more you can get done.

Give yourself a definite length of time to accomplish a certain amount of work—say, tomorrow's algebra or the next day's English composition. Force yourself to keep your attention on the job you are doing. Then finish on time.

Don't put off a job that has to be done until you feel like doing it. Do it and get it over with!

Do things often enough in this determined way for it to become a habit. After that you'll be sitting pretty while someone who hasn't learned to concentrate struggles along, never quite making the grade.

518

Alexander Fleming, working with germs, noticed that some of them died in his glass dishes. He asked himself, "Why?" Trying to learn, he discovered penicillin.

THINK WITH YOUR EYES, TOO. There's a way of thinking with your eyes in addition to your brain. How? By observing instead of just looking. The observation games you play in Scouting help you develop this power of thinking with your eyes. Things you see impress themselves on your mind. From what you see you are often able to make valuable deductions.

James Watt noticed that the lid of a kettle of boiling water popped up and down. Thousands of others had seen the same thing, but Watt observed. And from what he observed he deduced that it was the steam that had the power to lift the lid. The steam engine was the result.

Thomas Edison, while developing the light bulb, noticed a peculiar glow at the base of the bulb. He thought it important enough to patent what he had observed. The "Edison effect" later laid the foundation for modern radio and television.

Alexander Fleming, working in his laboratory with cultures of various germs, noticed that in some of his glass dishes the germs were not thriving. He decided to find out why and discovered that a mold was killing the germs. The result of his investigation was penicillin.

There is a saying among scientists that "luck favors the trained observer." The same holds true in life in general.

Gather Knowledge

Thinking, alone, is not enough to keep you "mentally awake." It must be coupled with accurate knowledge.

Much of this knowledge you absorb from other people. You get your early knowledge from your father and mother and from older brothers and sisters. Your Scout leaders have much to give you. So have your schoolteachers.

A foreign visitor once asked three American schoolboys: "Why do you go to school?"

The first schoolboy said, "Because I have to—it's the law."

The second said, "Because I want to—all my friends are there."

The third said, "Because I need to—if I am going to amount to anything."

Until a few years ago many Americans could truthfully say, "I never had a chance to get an education." Today America says to every boy and girl, "Here's your chance for an education—take it!" You have the chance. What you make of it depends on YOU!

LEARNING NEW SKILLS. You have a great help for gathering knowledge and learning new skills in the Scout advancement program. But in addition to Scouting, you need other interests, other hobbies.

The ability to read well and understand what you read will be one of your greatest assets as you strive to get on in life and make a career for yourself.

Don't choose all your hobbies along the same line. If you're interested in stamp collecting, try to learn something also about computers. If you like wood carving, take a fling at chemistry too. If you go in for collecting rocks and minerals, make a hobby of some outdoor sport as well. In most of these hobbies, there are merit badges awaiting you.

LOOKING AND LISTENING. Television and radio give you a chance to look at and listen to history at the very moment it is being made. You can see and hear the men and women who are making it. Through these two media you can also become acquainted with the finest music in the world.

Looking at crime and horror movies on TV and listening for hours to the latest fad in pop music on the radio won't do much to improve your mind. Try a varied diet for a few days. You are certain to decide on a better fare.

READING FOR A FULL LIFE. Reading worthwhile things sharpens your mind. Reading trash all the time makes it impossible for anyone to be anything but a second-rate person.

Keep up with what is happening in the world by reading

Reading is a magic carpet that will take you all over the world, into the history of the past and the promises of the future.

some of the more important items in the daily newspaper and in the weekly news magazines, if you have access to them.

Read a good magazine from time to time. Look into *Boys' Life*, the official magazine of the Boy Scouts of America. You will find it full of interesting stories and articles, Scouting and hobby features. If you aren't already a subscriber, talk to your Scoutmaster about becoming one.

Start a library of your own, even if you can afford only a few books. Get acquainted with your local librarian and ask for suggestions. Take out a library card. Talk to your school-teacher and others who can advise you about books.

Have Initiative

Thinking is good, knowledge is good. But no one will get very far with either unless he also has initiative.

Initiative is the ability to act without being told what to do. The boy with initiative often advances more rapidly than a more brilliant boy who doesn't have it. The boy who sits around and waits for somebody to give him directions, who does only what he is told and nothing more, is not going to advance very rapidly or very far.

Begin to exercise initiative right now in your own home. Do things around the house that need to be done, even though no one has told you to do them.

In your schoolwork, don't confine yourself merely to what the teacher tells you to study. Try to learn more about the subject than you find in the textbook.

Show initiative in your patrol and troop by bringing in suggestions for activities and things to display in your meeting room. Accept responsibility by offering to help a Cub Scout den, to get the troop's camp equipment in shape, to investigate new campsites, to run games and contests, to line up new activities. The boy who shows initiative is usually the one who is chosen to be a leader by his fellow Scouts.

The world will not advance without initiative. Someone has to show it. It might as well be you! You may make mistakes at first. Don't let that worry you—everyone does. Learn from

BOYS' LIFE

CONTENTS   Cover photograph by Mark Sosin.

your mistakes so that you don't make the same mistake twice. Be sure in your mind that you are right—then go ahead!

Control Yourself

"Know thyself" was good advice 2,000 years ago. It's just as good today. The trouble with it is that it is the hardest thing in the world to do.

Know yourself—know what makes you tick. If you know that, you have the answer to what makes the other fellow tick.

There is a constant battle going on inside all of us. It is a battle between the desire to do certain things or not to do them; to give our best efforts to accomplish something great or to try to get away with things the easy way. Sometimes a fellow feels like kicking up in an outburst of temper—the next moment he is too lazy to do anything. He may be irritated for a good reason or for none at all and show it in a sour spirit. He may hurt someone he loves with thoughtless words or with a silly act. Everybody does things like that at one time or another.

The main thing is to be strong enough to suppress these moods. If you keep yourself "mentally awake" they'll never have a chance to take over. Sometimes it helps to place yourself, figuratively speaking, outside yourself and try to see yourself as others see you. Then your behavior may strike you as being silly, and you can quickly do something about it.

At times you may have to disagree with other people. Learn to disagree without being disagreeable. If you present your view in a pleasant manner, people will listen. But if you get up on your high horse they'll feel like knocking you off—and you will have lost your point.

Learn to take with good spirit anything that comes. Do your best to shut out the things that might annoy you. Forget yourself. Get into the habit of thinking of other people. And keep busy doing interesting things.

Then you'll have no trouble keeping "mentally awake." Your life will be so full of things to be explored and lived that there won't be enough hours in the day to crowd them in.

MORALLY STRAIGHT

Deep within each human being is laid a precious thing, possessed by no other living creature. It is the thing we call a conscience. No one can tell you where it is located or what it looks like. But it is there just the same. Occasionally, in some people, it seems fast asleep. But in most people it is like an inner voice that is very much awake. Sometimes it whispers to you, at other times it seems to yell out loud. It is your conscience that makes it possible for you to distinguish between right and wrong, that helps you follow the right trail through life.

YOUR CONSCIENCE SPEAKS TO YOU OF YOURSELF. It tells you the moral obligation you have to make your life count.

This very moment, while you are still a boy, you must make decisions that will shape the rest of your life. The way you work in school will set the pattern for your future. Failing a subject may close the door forever to the lifework for which you are best suited, where you might possibly be of the greatest benefit to all mankind.

YOUR CONSCIENCE SPEAKS TO YOU ABOUT YOUR RELATIONSHIP TO OTHER PEOPLE. Respect their rights. Treat them justly. Give them a fair chance.

As you go about your own "pursuit of happiness," think of other people. Baden-Powell once said, "Happiness comes of happifying." He meant that real happiness is to be able to make others happy. Pleasure is a temporary, personal matter. Lasting happiness is something you share with others.

The knights of old were pledged to protect women. It was their duty to keep them from harm. The Scout of today treats women with the same high regard.

While you are a boy you have the chance to prepare yourself for life through Scouting. But eventually you leave boyhood behind. You become a man. You must "Be Prepared" to act like one.

As a young man you are capable of becoming a father. God has given you this very high trust.

Some young people destroy their lives by failing in that great trust. They let their health be undermined by venereal disease (VD). They may even cause others to lose their health through these diseases spread by sexual contact.

When you live up to the trust of fatherhood your sex life will fit into God's wonderful plan of creation. Fuller understanding of wholesome sex behavior can bring you lifelong happiness. A moment of so-called sexual freedom can turn into a lifetime of regrets. "The good life that could have been" is wrecked for many unwed teenagers burdened by babies for whom they are unable or unready to shoulder full responsibility of parenthood.

You owe it to yourself to enter adult life without regrets. You owe it to yourself to learn what is right. Proper sex education will give you the knowledge you need. It will enrich your life.

Turn to the persons who helped you during your sexual growth. They are the best people to advise you as you reach sexual maturity. First among them is your parent or family head. Next comes your religious leader or your physician.

YOUR CONSCIENCE TELLS YOU TO OBEY THE LAWS OF OUR COUNTRY. Those laws were created to benefit all our people. They were established to keep all people safe in their persons and in their property, to protect them in their homes and on the streets and highways. Obey those laws. If you disagree with some of them, work to have them changed through the ballot box. In the meantime, obey them.

"Let your conscience be your guide." Know what is right. Do what is right.

One of the finest tasks a man can take on is helping boys starting in Scouting follow the trail he traveled himself. He can do this as a Scouter— a Scoutmaster or an assistant Scoutmaster.

ONCE A SCOUT, ALWAYS A SCOUT

Eventually, your days as a Boy Scout or Explorer will be over. You are an adult. But as an adult you may want to keep a close association with Scouting. There are several ways to do this:

You can do it by becoming a Scouter—a leader of a Cub Scout pack, a Boy Scout troop, or an Explorer unit. This task— the task of making Scouting come alive in the lives of boys—is one of the most gratifying that a man can have.

Or you may offer your services as a member of the troop committee that backs the active Scouters in that "good old troop" of yours. Or you may become a member of a committee working for Scouting in your local district or council.

Or you may decide, as many others have, to make Scouting your lifework as a professional member of the Boy Scouts of America.

If your work does not permit you to take active part in Scouting, you can still maintain identification with the Scout movement by registering as a Scout alumni member. As an alumnus you commit yourself to perpetuate the aims, purposes, and ideals of the movement—as you did as a boy.

527

BECOME A VOTING CITIZEN. But whether you stay on actively in Scouting or not, what you have learned as a Scout will be with you always.

When you reach the age of voting citizenship you will know the true meaning of democracy and of liberty. You will be able to carry out your duties to your country—obeying its laws, taking your place in the community.

Be a thinking citizen—not a thoughtless one.

Keep yourself informed on the happenings of the day in your own community, your country, and throughout the world.

Learn how your country, your own state, your city, town, or village is governed. Find out how you fit into that government. Discover where that government is strong and where it is weak. Do your part as a citizen in the big task of upholding its strength and overcoming its weaknesses.

But be prepared as well to do your part in the smaller tasks—in such everyday things as obeying traffic regulations, obeying game laws when you go hunting or fishing, serving on jury duty when called, and many other things.

Find out about our political parties and what they stand for—all of them, not just one. Study all sides of a question that concerns the welfare of your community, your state, your country. Then take your stand and vote as your conscience bids you. Vote to place those people into public office who you feel are best fitted to do what you think is right.

That's the way to make democracy work.

But don't stop here.

Remember that America is not a gift that is freely given us. Each of us must deserve it. We must work for America, live for it and, if the call should come, die for it!

"A chain is as strong as its weakest link." A nation is as strong as each of its citizens. America is as strong as YOU are!

On hikes and in camp, through climbing and swimming and pioneering, you have developed your body into that of a healthy American—straight-backed, strong.

As you move from boyhood into manhood, keep the faith you gained in Scouting and the trust people have in you.

Your mind has been sharpened as you practiced observation and reasoning, as you mastered new skills, as you learned to go through nature with your eyes wide open.

By following the Scout Oath and the Scout Law you have set a high standard for yourself. You have built yourself into the kind of citizen our country needs.

As a man you are able to step forward unflinchingly, take your place with our country's finest, and say with them:

"AMERICA! Here I stand!
My body strong to fight your battles!
My mind trained to keep your democracy strong!
My spirit true to uphold your ideals!
To God and to you I pledge my service:

ON MY HONOR, I WILL DO MY BEST . . . !"

My Trail to EAGLE

Skill Awards, merit badges, ranks, and Eagle palms must be earned before your 18th birthday.

BOY SCOUT
(Joining Requirements)

	Handbook Pages	Date/Leader's Initials
1. Complete fifth grade and be at least 10½ years old or 11 years of age or older, but not yet 18.	10	
2. Understand and intend to live by the Scout Oath or Promise.	27-29	
Scout Law	30-41	
Scout motto	42-43	
Scout slogan	44-45	
and Outdoor Code	54-57	
3. Know the Scout sign, Scout salute, and handclasp and when to use them.	46-47	
4. Understand the significance of the Scout badge.	48-49	
5. Take part in a Scoutmaster conference.	459-60	

Became a Boy Scout on _____ 19____

TENDERFOOT RANK

	Handbook Pages	Date/Leader's Initials
1. Be active in your troop and patrol for at least 2 months.*	12-23, 455	_____ _____
2. Scout spirit: Repeat from memory the Scout Oath or Promise and Law.	27, 31	_____ _____
Explain the meaning of each point of the Law in your own words.	30-41	_____ _____
Demonstrate that you have practiced these ideals in everyday life.	456	_____ _____
3. Earn Citizenship and one other skill award.	538-48	

Citizenship skill award   539   _____ _____

_____ skill award   _____ _____

4. Take part in a Scoutmaster conference.   459-60   _____ _____

Became a Tenderfoot Scout on _____/_____/19____   _____

Board of review initials

*The Scoutmaster may waive the 2-month service requirement for the Tenderfoot rank for a new Scout who has earned the Arrow of Light Award as a Webelos Scout.

SECOND CLASS
RANK

	Handbook Pages	Date/Leader's Initials
1. Be active in your troop and patrol for at least 2 months as a Tenderfoot Scout.	12-23, 455	____ ____
2. Show Scout spirit.	456	____ ____
3. Earn Hiking, First Aid, and one other skill award (so that you have five in all).	538-48	

	Hiking skill award	546	____ ____

	First Aid skill award	545	____ ____

_____ skill award		____ ____

4. Take part in a Scoutmaster conference.	459-60	____ ____

Became a Second Class Scout on ____/____/19____ _____

Board of review initials

532

FIRST CLASS RANK

	Handbook Pages	Date/Leader's Initials
1. Be active in your troop and patrol for at least 2 months as a Second Class Scout.	12-23, 455	_____ _____ _____ _____
2. Show Scout spirit.	456	_____ _____
3. Earn Camping, Cooking, and one other skill award (so that you have eight in all).	538-48	

	Camping skill award	538	_____ _____
	Cooking skill award	542	_____ _____
_____ skill award			_____ _____

4. Earn First Aid merit badge.   556   _____ _____

5. Swimming. Tell what precautions must be taken for a safe swim. Jump feetfirst into water over your head in depth. Swim 50 m (or 50 yd.). During the swim, stop, make a sharp turn, level off, and resume swimming.*   152-53   _____ _____

6. Take part in a Scoutmaster conference.   459-60   _____ _____

Became a First Class Scout on _____/_____/19___ _____

Board of review initials

_____

*This requirement may be waived by the troop committee for medical or safety reasons.

533

STAR
RANK

	Handbook Pages	Date/Leader's Initials
1. Be active in your troop and patrol for at least 4 months as a First Class Scout.	12-23, 455	_____ _____
2. Show Scout spirit.	490-526	_____ _____
3. Earn five more merit badges (so that you have six in all), including any three more from the required list for Eagle.*	464-72 549-61	
_____ merit badge		_____ _____
_____ merit badge		_____ _____
_____ merit badge		_____ _____
_____ merit badge		_____ _____
_____ merit badge		_____ _____
4. While a First Class Scout, take part in service projects totaling at least 6 hours of work. These projects must be approved by your Scoutmaster.	463	_____ _____
5. While a First Class Scout, serve actively for 4 months in one or more of the following positions (or carry out a Scoutmaster-assigned leadership project to help the troop): patrol leader, senior patrol leader, assistant senior patrol leader; den chief; scribe, librarian, historian, quartermaster, bugler, chaplain aide, member of the leadership corps, instructor; junior assistant Scoutmaster.		
_____	462, 480	_____ _____
_____		_____ _____
6. Take part in a Scoutmaster conference.	459-60	_____ _____

Became a Star Scout on _____/_____/19____ _____

Board of review initials

*The required list for Eagle has 14 merit badges in 11 categories. First Aid was earned for First Class. Any of the remaining 13 may be used for this requirement.

LIFE
RANK

	Handbook Pages	Date/Leader's Initials
1. Be active in your troop and patrol for at least 6 months as a Star Scout.	12-23, 455	____ ____
2. Show Scout spirit.	490-526	____ ____
3. Earn five more merit badges (so that you have 11 in all), including any three more from the required list for Eagle.*	464-72 549-61	

_____ merit badge   ____ ____

_____ merit badge   ____ ____

_____ merit badge   ____ ____

_____ merit badge   ____ ____

_____ merit badge   ____ ____

4. While a Star Scout, take part in service projects totaling at least 6 hours of work. These projects must be approved by your Scoutmaster.   463   ____ ____

5. While a Star Scout, serve actively for 6 months in one or more of the leadership positions listed in requirement 5 for Star Scout (or carry out a Scoutmaster-assigned leadership project to help the troop).

_____   462, 480 ____ ____

_____   ____ ____

6. Take part in a Scoutmaster conference.   459-60   ____ ____

Became a Life Scout on ____/____/19___ _____

                                              Board of review initials

*The required list for Eagle has 14 merit badges in 11 categories. First Aid was earned for First Class. Any of the remaining 13 may be used for this requirement.

EAGLE

NOTE: If you have a permanent physical or mental disability you may become an Eagle Scout by qualifying for as many required merit badges as you can and qualifying for alternate merit badges for the rest. If you seek to become an Eagle under this procedure, you must submit a special application to your council service center. Your application must be approved by your council committee for advancement BEFORE YOU CAN WORK ON ALTERNATIVE MERIT BADGES.

	Handbook Pages	Date/Leader's Initials
1. Be active in your troop and patrol for at least 6 months as a Life Scout.	12-23, 455	____ ____
2. Show Scout spirit..	490-526	____ ____

3. Earn a total of 21 merit badges (10 more than you already have), including the following: (a) First Aid, (b) Citizenship in the Community, (c) Citizenship in the Nation, (d) Citizenship in the World, (e) Communications, (f) Safety, (g) Emergency Preparedness OR Lifesaving, (h) Environmental Science, (i) Personal Management, (j) Personal Fitness OR Swimming OR Sports, and (k) Camping. *   464-72   549-61

_____ merit badge		____ ____
_____ merit badge		____ ____
_____ merit badge		____ ____
_____ merit badge		____ ____
_____ merit badge		____ ____
_____ merit badge		____ ____
_____ merit badge		____ ____
_____ merit badge		____ ____
_____ merit badge		____ ____
_____ merit badge	464-72	____ ____

4. While a Life Scout, serve actively for a period of 6 months in one or more of the following positions: patrol leader, senior patrol leader, assistant senior patrol leader; den chief; scribe, librarian, quartermaster, member of the leadership corps, junior assistant Scoutmaster; chaplain aide; instructor.   462, 480 ____ ____

5. While a Life Scout, plan, develop, and give leadership to others in a service project helpful to your religious institution, school, or com-

*You must choose only one merit badge listed in items *g* and *j*. If you have earned **536** more than one of the badges listed in items *g* and *j*, choose one and list the remaining badges to make your total of 21.

munity. The project idea must be approved by your Scoutmaster and troop committee and reviewed by the council or district before you start. — 463 ___ ___

6. Take part in a Scoutmaster conference. — 459-60 ___ ___

Became an Eagle Scout on ___/___/19___ _____

Board of review initials

 # EAGLE PALMS

	Handbook Pages	Date/Leader's Initials

After becoming an Eagle Scout, you may earn palms by completing the following requirements:

1. Be active in your troop and patrol for at least 3 months after becoming an Eagle Scout or after award of last palm. — 12-23, 455 ___ ___

2. Show Scout spirit. — 490-526 ___ ___

3. Make a satisfactory effort to develop and demonstrate leadership ability. — 462-80 ___ ___

4. Earn five additional merit badges beyond those required for Eagle or last palm. (Merit badges earned any time since becoming a Boy Scout may be used for this requirement.) — 464-72 ___ ___

5. Take part in a Scoutmaster conference. — 459-60 ___ ___

Bronze palm

_____ merit badge ___ ___

_____ merit badge ___ ___

_____ merit badge ___ ___

_____ merit badge ___ ___

_____ merit badge ___ ___

Bronze palm earned on ___/___/19___ _____
Board of review initials

Gold palm earned on ___/___/19___ _____
Board of review initials

Silver palm earned on ___/___/19___ _____
Board of review initials

You may wear only the proper combination of palms for the number of merit badges you earn beyond Eagle. The Bronze Palm represents 5 merit badges; Gold, 10; and Silver, 15. For example, if you earn 10 merit badges (two palms), you would wear **only** the Gold Palm. If you earn 20 merit badges (four palms), you would wear a Silver and a Bronze Palm.

SKILL AWARD
REQUIREMENTS

Camping Skill Award

	Handbook Pages	Date/Leader's Initials
1. Present yourself to your leader, properly dressed, before going on an overnight camping trip.	63	____ ____
Show the camping gear you will use, including shelter and food. Explain how you will use the gear.	64-65	____ ____
Show the right way to pack and carry it.	66-67	____ ____
2. Go on two overnight camping trips with your troop, patrol, or other Scouts, using the gear.	12, 23	

On each overnight camp, do the following:

	Handbook Pages	Date/Leader's Initials
a. Carry the gear on your back for at least 2 km (1¼ mi.) to your camp. After camping, carry it 2 km (1¼ mi.) back.	189	
b. Pick a good place for a tent.	74	
Pitch a tent correctly in the place you picked and sleep in it overnight.	72	
Store the tent correctly after use.	72	
c. Make a bed on the ground. Sleep on it overnight.	73	
d. Follow good health, sanitation, and safety practices. Leave a clean camp.	76-77, 133	
e. After each trip, tell your leader what you achieved and learned. Tell how good camping practices proved useful.	60	
Overnight camp No. 1		____ ____
Overnight camp No. 2		____ ____
3. a. Whip the ends of a rope.	89	____ ____
b. Tie the following knots: square knot, sheet bend, two half hitches, clove hitch, taut-line hitch, bowline. Show their correct use.	92-95	____ ____
4. a. Lash poles together with the following lashings: square, shear, and diagonal lashings. Show their correct use.	96-99	____ ____
b. Use lashing for making a simple useful camp gadget.	97	____ ____

NOTE: If you use a wheelchair, crutches, or if it is difficult for you to get around, you may substitute "transport the gear" for "carry the gear on your back" in requirement 2a. You must travel under your own power.

538

Citizenship Skill Award

	Handbook Pages	Date/Leader's Initials
1. a. Describe the flag of the United States.	416	____ ____
Give a short history of it.	416-17	____ ____
b. Explain why you should respect your country's flag.	418	____ ____
Tell which special days you should fly it in your state.	418	____ ____
c. Using a flag and with another Scout helping you, show how to hoist and lower the flag, how to hang it horizontally and vertically on a wall, and how to fold it.	418-19 422-23 419	____ ____
d. Tell when to salute the flag and show how to do it.	420-21	____ ____
2. a. Repeat from memory the Pledge of Allegiance. Explain its meaning in your own words.	414	____ ____
Lead your patrol and troop in the proper ceremony of reciting the pledge.	415	____ ____
b. Tell about the meaning of our National Anthem and how it was written.	424-25	____ ____
3. a. Explain the rights and duties of a citizen of the United States.	404-06	____ ____
b. Tell about two things you have done that will help law-enforcement agencies.	449	____ ____
c. Explain what a citizen should do to save our resources.	324	____ ____
4. Do one of the following:		
a. Visit a community leader. Learn about the duties of the job or office. Tell your patrol or troop what you have learned.	439	____ ____
b. Learn something about a famous U.S. person of your own choosing. Tell your reasons for picking that person and give a short report of what that person did to gain this recognition.	407-09	____ ____
c. Make a list of 10 things, places, or sayings that have some relationship to the history of the United States. Explain their meaning.	410-13	____ ____
d. Know the history and tradition of your state, commonwealth, or territorial flag.	426-27	____ ____

Communications Skill Award

	Handbook Pages	Date/Leader's Initials
1. Do the following:		
a. Make a phone call correctly and answer properly.	344	_____ _____
b. Show how to make an emergency phone call.	362	_____ _____
Put these emergency phone numbers near your home phone.	362	_____ _____
c. Do two of these:		
(1) Introduce a guest.	344	_____ _____
(2) Make an announcement.	344	_____ _____
(3) Tell of some special past event.	345	_____ _____
2. Teach a Scout skill to two (2) or more Scouts.	347	_____ _____
3. Get a message to others without speaking or writing using two of these:		
a. Silent Scout signals	348-49	_____ _____
b. Manual alphabet	352	_____ _____
c. Sign language for the deaf	352-53	_____ _____
d. Indian sign language	350-51	_____ _____
e. Sports signals	354	_____ _____
f. Morse code	356-58	_____ _____
g. Semaphore code	356-58	_____ _____
h. Scout trail signs	248-49	_____ _____
4. Tell how to get to a place selected by your leader. (It must be 1 km [0.6 mi.] away and not in a straight line.) Use speaking, writing, and sketches.		_____ _____
5. Take part in or plan an emergency mobilization for your patrol or troop.	205	_____ _____
6. Know five emergency distress signals.	359	_____ _____

540

Community Living Skill Award

	Handbook Pages	Date/Leader's Initials
1. Explain what is meant by the terms: public utility; public service; government; community problems; community organization; volunteer or private agency; government agency; ethnic group; tradition; resources; crime resistance	441	_____ _____
2. Do three:		
a. Make a list of five organizations working in your community. Visit one. Tell what it does.	442-43	_____ _____
b. List five activities that take place in your community during a month. Explain the reason for each. Take part in one. Tell what you did.	447	_____ _____
c. Make a list of five community problems. Explain how each affects you, your family, and the community.	448-49	_____ _____
d. Tell some of the history, traditions, contributions, and ways of living of two ethnic groups in your community.	446-47	_____ _____
e. Visit your police department. Find out what you can do to help reduce the likelihood of crime in your home and neighborhood. Tell about your visit.	440, 449	_____ _____
f. Take part in a service project that will help a volunteer or private agency in your community. Tell what you did.	442-43	_____ _____
3. Describe two public services. Visit a place that provides one of these services. Tell about your visit.	440-42	_____ _____
4. Show that you know how to get around using a map or transportation schedule.	203	_____ _____

NOTE: "Community" is the place where you live.

Conservation Skill Award

	Handbook Pages	Date/Leader's Initials
1. Show by what you do that you follow the Outdoor Code when you are in the outdoors.	54-57	_____ _____
2. a. Explain the main causes and effects of water pollution. Tell how we can have clean water.	325-27	_____ _____
b. Explain the main causes and effects of air pollution. Tell how we can have clean air.	330-32	_____ _____
3. a. Make a list of present major sources of energy and the major alternate sources.	338-39	_____ _____
b. Make a list of 10 ways in which you and your family can save energy.	339	_____ _____
4. a. Take a walk around where you live for 2 hours and make two lists related to conservation:	328-29	
List things that please you.		_____ _____
List things you feel should be improved.		_____ _____
b. Plan and carry out your own conservation project. Get it approved by your patrol leader before you start.	324-39	_____ _____
5. Take part in one of these projects with your patrol or another Scout:		
a. Clean up a roadside, picnic ground, vacant lot, stream, lake shore, or ocean beach.	328-29	_____ _____
b. Work on erosion control of stream bank, gully, or trail.	333-34	_____ _____
c. Plant trees, do forest improvement, or insect control.	292-301 296	_____ _____
d. Improve backyard or other wildlife habitat.	328-29	_____ _____
e. Help with energy conservation.	339	_____ _____

Cooking Skill Award

	Handbook Pages	Date/Leader's Initials
1. Show you know how to buy food by doing the following:		
a. Plan a balanced menu for three meals— breakfast, lunch, and supper.	506-07 118-25	_____ _____

		Handbook Pages	Date/Leader's Initials

b. Make a food list based on your plan for a patrol of eight Scouts.   104-05   _____ _____

c. Visit a grocery store and price your food list.   104   _____ _____

d. Figure out what the cost for each Scout would be.   104   _____ _____

2. Sharpen a knife and an ax properly and give rules for their safe use.   79-85   _____ _____

3. Use a knife, ax, and saw correctly to prepare tinder, kindling, and firewood.   79-87 108-09   _____ _____

4. a. Locate and prepare a suitable fire site.   107   _____ _____

b. Build and light a cooking fire using not more than two matches.   111-12   _____ _____

5. a. In the outdoors, cook, without utensils, a simple meal. Use raw meat (or fish or poultry) and at least one raw vegetable, and bread (twist or ashbread).   128-29   _____ _____

b. In the outdoors, prepare, from raw, dried, or dehydrated food, for yourself and two others:

(1) A complete breakfast of fruit, hot cooked cereal, hot beverage, and meat and eggs (or pancakes), and   118-20   _____ _____

(2) A complete dinner or supper of meat (or fish or poultry), at least one vegetable, dessert, and bread (biscuit or bannock).   122-25   _____ _____

6. After each cooking, properly dispose of garbage, clean utensils, and leave a clean cooking area.   _____ _____

NOTE: When laws do not let you do some of these tests, they may be changed by your Scoutmaster to meet the laws.

Environment Skill Award

	Handbook Pages	Date/Leader's Initials

1. a. Tell what is meant by environment.   214-15   _____ _____

b. Describe how plant life, animal life, and environment relate to each other.   215   _____ _____

c. Explain the oxygen cycle.   216-17   _____ _____

d. Explain the water cycle.   218-19   _____ _____

2. Tell how sun, air, water, soil, minerals, plants, and animals produce food used by man.   216-17   _____ _____

3. a. Make a 3-hour exploration of a forest, field, park, wetland, lake shore, ocean shore, or desert. Make a list of plants and animal life you recognize.   222-38 ____ ____

   b. In the outdoors, spot and name 10 wild animals by sight or sign (mammals, birds, fish, reptiles, mollusks).   258-85 232-33 ____ ____

   c. In the outdoors, spot and name 10 wild plants.   296-308 ____ ____

   d. Know how to identify poison ivy, poison oak, and poison sumac.   379 ____ ____

4. Do one:

   a. Study a plot of ground, 1 m² (10 sq. ft.). Report on the plants and animals you find.   240 ____ ____

   b. Make a closed terrarium that includes animals. OR make an aquarium that includes both plants and animals.   240-41 241 ____ ____

   c. Keep a daily weather record for at least 2 weeks. Tell how weather affects the environment.   314-15 ____ ____

5. Display at least six newspaper or magazine clippings on environment problems.   322-41 ____ ____

Family Living Skill Award

	Handbook Pages	Date/Leader's Initials

1. Tell what is meant by: family, duty to family, family council.   428-29 ____ ____

2. a. Make a chart listing the jobs you and other family members have at home.   430 ____ ____

   b. Talk with your family about other jobs you may take on for the next 2 months.   430 ____ ____

3. Show that you can look after yourself, your family, and home. Do four of these:

   a. Inspect your home and grounds. List any dangers or lack of security seen. Tell how you corrected one.   434-45 ____ ____

   b. Explain why garbage and trash must be disposed of properly.   434 ____ ____

   c. Look after younger children for 3 hours. Use good health and safety practices.   431 ____ ____

   d. List some things for which your family spends money. Tell how you can help your family in money matters.   432 ____ ____

e. Tell about what your family does for fun. Make a list of fun things your family might do at little cost. Do one of these with a member of your family.   436-37 ____ ____

f. Carry out a family energy-saving plan.   340-41 ____ ____

4. Explain how you can get help quickly for these problems: 438

    medical.   ____ ____

    police; fire; utility.   ____ ____

    housing; serious family problem.   ____ ____

Post a list of these directions in your home.   362   ____ ____

First Aid Skill Award

	Handbook Pages	Date/Leader's Initials
1. a. Explain what first aid is. Tell how to act in case of an accident.	360-61	____ ____
b. The dangers of moving a badly injured person.	382	____ ____
c. Tell the best way to get medical help quickly. Show that you keep the names, addresses, and phone numbers for medical help where you can find them quickly.	362 362	____ ____ ____ ____
2. a. Show how to treat shock.	363	____ ____
b. Show what to do for "hurry" cases of:		
serious bleeding.	364-65	____ ____
stopped breathing.	366-67	____ ____
internal poisoning.	368	____ ____
heart attack.	368	____ ____
3. Show first aid for the following cases:		
cuts and scratches.	369	____ ____
burns and scalds.	372-73	____ ____
blisters on feet.	374	____ ____
bites or stings of insects, chiggers, ticks.	375	____ ____
bites of snakes and mammals.	376-77	____ ____
skin poisoning.	379	____ ____
sprained ankle.	374	____ ____
object in eye.	378	____ ____
nosebleed.	372	____ ____
4. Explain first aid for puncture wound from splinter, nail, or fishhook.	378	____ ____

5. Use a bandage to hold a dressing in place on the head, hand, knee, and foot. 371 ____ ____
6. Make an arm sling. 370 ____ ____
7. Tell the five most common signs of heart attack. 368 ____ ____
   Tell what action you should take. 368 ____ ____

Hiking Skill Award

	Handbook Pages	Date/Leader's Initials
1. Tell how to take a safe hike:		
a. Cross-country, day and night.	180	____ ____
b. Along a highway, day and night.	180-81	____ ____
2. a. Tell how to keep from getting lost.	210	____ ____
b. Tell what to do if you are lost.	210-11	____ ____
3. a. On a map, point out 10 different symbols, including contour lines. Tell what they represent.	186-87	____ ____
b. Orient a map.	188	____ ____
c. Point out on a map where you are.	188	____ ____
4. a. Show how a compass works.	189	____ ____
b. Give its eight principal points.	189	____ ____
5. a. Show how to use a compass and map together.	193	____ ____
b. Using a compass and map together, follow a route you marked on the map far enough to show you know how.	192	____ ____
6. Take a hike in the field:		
a. Before leaving, have your plan approved by your leader, including purpose, route, and clothing.	176	____ ____
b. Take an 8 km (5-mi.) hike in the field with your troop, patrol, or two or more other Scouts. Wear the right clothing. Take the right equipment. Follow good hike rules.	177-83	____ ____
7. Take a hike in your town.*		
a. Before leaving, have your plan approved by your leader including purpose, route, and clothing.	202	____ ____

*The hikes for requirements 6 and 7 must be taken on separate days.

b. Take an 8 km (5-mi.) hike in a place of interest outside your neighborhood with your troop, patrol, an adult, or two or more other Scouts. Wear the right clothing. Take the right equipment. Follow good hike rules. 202-03 ___ ___

c. After you get back, tell what you did and learned. ___ ___

NOTE: If you use a wheelchair, crutches, or if it is difficult for you to get around, you may substitute "trip" for "hike" in requirements 1 and 7, and "trip to a specific objective" for "hike in the field" in requirement 6. You must travel under your own power.

Physical Fitness Skill Award

	Handbook Pages	Date/Leader's Initials
1. a. Show that within the past year you have had a health examination by a doctor licensed to practice medicine.	497-98	___ ___
If the doctor told you some things to do, tell what you are doing about one of them.	498	___ ___
b. Show that you have had a dental examination within the past year.	510	___ ___
2. a. Record your best in the following tests: ___ pushups; ___ pullups; ___ sit ups; standing long jump ___m ___cm; run walk ___mins. ___secs.	502-03	___ ___
b. Set goals to do better.	501	___ ___
c. Keep a record of how you are doing for 30 days.	503	___ ___
3. a. List the four groups of basic foods needed in the daily diet of a boy your age.	506-07	___ ___
b. Tell how this diet helps your body.	506	___ ___
4. a. Satisfy your adult leader that you have good daily health habits.	500-13	___ ___
b. Tell how the use of tobacco, alcohol, and drugs can hurt your health.	514-16	___ ___

Swimming Skill Award

	Handbook Pages	Date/Leader's Initials
1. a. Tell what must be done for a safe swim with your patrol, troop, family, or other group.	150-51	_____ _____
b. Tell the reasons for the buddy system.	144-51	_____ _____
2. Jump feetfirst into water over your head. Swim 100 m (or 100 yd.), with at least one change of direction. For the first 75 m (or 75 yd.) use any stroke. For the last 25 m (or 25 yd.), use the elementary backstroke. Right after the swim, stay in the water and float for a minute with as little motion as possible.	154-55, 158	_____ _____
3. Water rescues:		
a. Show reaching.	156-57	_____ _____
b. Show throwing.	156-57	_____ _____
c. Describe going with support.	157	_____ _____
4. Show rescue breathing.	366-67	_____ _____

Advancement for Lone Scouts

Lone Scouts are not generally registered with a Boy Scout troop and must rely on their lone friend and counselor for leadership and guidance. They cannot be expected to meet the specific advancement requirements in the same way a member of a troop does.

The Boy Scouts of America allows the Lone Scout's friend and counselor to suggest alternative requirements. This is important, since a boy cannot meet all the advancement requirements by reason of not being in a troop or patrol.

All such alternative requirements should be equal to the replaced requirement and be approved by the local council advancement committee. Any unequal or dissimilar requirement should be allowed only in extreme circumstances or when such like requirements could not be met without extreme hazard or hardship.

MERIT BADGE REQUIREMENTS
for Badges Required for Eagle

Camping

1. Make a layout of a typical patrol campsite. Show cooking spots, dining fly, latrine, and at least three two-man tents. Explain how and why weather, season, and water supply are considered when choosing a site. Explain what care to take with regard to safe water, sanitary facilities, and emergencies.
2. Make a written plan for getting to and from a camping spot on foot or by vehicle.
3. Make a chart showing how a typical patrol is organized for an overnight camp. List assignments for each member.
4. Prepare a list of clothing you would need for an overnight camp in:
   (a) Summer
   (b) Winter
   Discuss the kinds of footwear for different kinds of weather. Explain care of the feet.
5. Describe four kinds of tents. Give their good and bad points.
6. Prepare for an overnight camp with your patrol by doing the following:*
   (a) Make a checklist of personal and patrol gear that will be needed.
   (b) Prepare a lightweight camp menu that is right for the time of the year. Give recipes. Make a food list for your patrol. List foods

---

*May be part of a troop trip.

you can get from your grocery store. Plan two breakfasts, three lunches, and two suppers. (Some canned foods may be used.)
   (c) Pack your own gear and your share of the patrol gear and food for proper carrying. Protect it against bad weather. Show that your pack is right for getting what's needed first: comfort. weight, balance, size, and neatness. Explain how the rest of the patrol gear and food is divided among members.
   (d) Show the right way to pack your full gear on a pack frame. Use a diamond hitch or other good hitch.
7. Complete the following while on an overnight camp:
   (a) Present yourself with your pack for inspection. Be correctly clothed and equipped for an overnight camping trip.
   (b) Working with another Scout, pitch a two-man tent. Consider weather and terrain. On this campsite, where allowed, make a latrine for your patrol. (Where not allowed as in state parks, etc., describe how to build it.)
   (c) Make a comfortable ground bed. Use it for 2 nights. Use ground cloth and padding of clothing, pack, grass, leaves, or straw.
   (d) Where it's allowed, build up a fireplace area of nonburnable soil. Show proper use of woods tools in getting and preparing fuel for a cooking fire. Show how, on a rainy day, you would get, prepare, and protect your wood. Show how you would properly prepare a meal when it's raining.
   (e) Build three kinds of top-of-the-ground fires. Use charcoal for one. Show how to put out a fire properly. (Where open fires cannot be used, show how to build

the fires, but don't light them.)

(f) Show the right way to protect your camp, including food and gear, against animals, insects, and wet or bad weather. Discuss how you would protect yourself against kinds of weather if caught out on the trail with only a pocketknife.

(g) Strike camp. Fold or roll your tent for packing. Pack all gear. Leave a clean camp. Show the right way to get rid of garbage and rubbish.

8. Show experience in camping by the following:

(a) Camp out a total of at least 20 days and 20 nights. Sleep each night under the sky or under a tent you have pitched. (You may use a week of summer camp as a part of the 20 days and 20 nights.)

(b) On one of these camping trips, hike 2 km (1¼ mi.) or more each way to and from your campsite. Pack your own gear plus your share of the patrol gear and food. (This is in addition to the two trips required for the Camping skill award.)

(c) Serve as one of the cooks for your patrol for at least five meals prepared in camp.

9. Discuss how the things you did to earn this badge have taught you personal health and safety, survival, public health, conservation, and good citizenship.

Citizenship in the Community

1. Describe your community to your counselor giving:
(a) Short history
(b) Cultures and ethnic groups
(c) Major places of employment
What is the future of your community?

2. Mark or point out on a map of your community the following:
(a) Chief government buildings
(b) Fire station, police station, and hospital nearest your home
(c) Schools, churches, and synagogues near your home
(d) Main highways to neighboring cities and towns
(e) Nearest railroads and bus stations and airport, if any
(f) Chief industries or other major places of employment
(g) Historical and other interesting points

3. Do the following:
(a) Chart the organization of your local or state government. Show the top offices and tell which are elected or appointed.
(b) Name the political parties in your community government and list four persons active in the politics of your community and what positions they hold.

4. Attend one:
(a) County or parish board meeting
(b) City council meeting
(c) School board meeting
(d) Municipal, county, or state court session

5. After visiting the governmental meeting, obtain a copy of that body's published budget. Review

the major sources of income and expenses for its operation with your counselor.

6. List the services your community provides to the citizens in return for the taxes paid by you and your parents.

7. Select a city, county, or school problem or issue under consideration from the local newspaper or news broadcast and write a letter expressing your views to the mayor, administrator, or school board president. Show this letter and any response to your counselor.

8. List and describe the work of five volunteer organizations through which people in your community work together for the good of your community.

9. Tell how to report an accident or an emergency in your community.

10. List five ways you can demonstrate good citizenship in your community, religious institution, school, or Scouting unit.

2. Name the three branches of government and explain their functions. Explain the checks and balances on each branch of government.

3. Outline the relationships between state and federal governments.

4. Do ONE of the following:
   (a) Visit the National Capitol.
   (b) Visit your state capitol.
   (c) Tour a federal installation.
   Explain your experiences to your counselor.

5. Name your two senators and the congressman from your congressional district. Write a letter to one of these elected officials on a national issue sharing your view with him or her. Show your letter and any response to your counselor.

6. What are five important functions of your national government? Explain how these functions affect your family and local community.

7. Discuss the main ways by which our federal government is financed.

Citizenship in the Nation

1. After reading, discuss with your counselor the following documents:
   (a) Declaration of Independence
   (b) Preamble to the Constitution
   (c) Constitution
   (d) Bill of Rights
   (e) Amendments to the Constitution

Citizenship in the World

1. Explain how communications and transportation have changed relationships between countries.

2. Discuss the importance of international organizations with your counselor. Tell how the following organizations provide a

551

means for countries to work together.

(a) United Nations
(b) World Court
(c) World Scout Association
(d) International Red Cross

3. Show on a world map countries that have different forms of government and ideologies from that of the United States.

4. Tell how the geography, natural resources, and climate of a country affect its economy. Tell how they may affect relations with other countries.

5. Explain to your counselor what is meant by:
(a) International trade agreement
(b) Foreign exchange
(c) Balance of payments
(d) Tariffs
(e) Free trade
How does world trade affect your community and state?

6. Show your counselor how the American dollar fluctuates in relationship to three or more major foreign currencies. Why are these currencies important to the United States?

7. How does the U.S. State Department help us in foreign countries? What is meant by the following:
(a) International treaty
(b) Diplomatic exchange
(c) Ambassador
(d) Consul
(e) Cultural and educational exchange

8. Obtain the form to secure a passport. Fill it out and show it to your counselor.

9. Do ONE of the following:
(a) Attend a world jamboree
(b) Take part in an international event in your area.
(c) Visit with a foreign exchange student and discuss his or her country and customs.
(d) Take a year of foreign language in school.

(e) Write an embassy or consulate and secure material from it about its country and discuss the material with your counselor.

Communications

1. Develop a plan to teach a skill. Have it approved by your counselor. Then, create and make teaching aids. Carry out your plan. With the counselor, check to see if the learner has learned.

2. Pick an item or product. It may be real or imagined. Build a sales plan based on its good points. Try to "sell" the counselor on buying it from you. Talk with him about how well you did in telling him about the item and the wisdom of buying it.

3. Show how you would make a telephone call inviting someone who is an expert fisherman to give a demonstration on fishing to your unit.

4. Do the following:
(a) Write a 5-minute speech. Give it at a meeting of a group.
(b) Show how to introduce a guest speaker.

5. Attend a town meeting where two or three points of view are being given. Record what you hear. Make a report from your notes. Tell your troop or patrol what you think you heard.

6. Plan a troop court of honor or campfire program. Give it to the patrol leaders' council for approval. Write the script.

Prepare the program for reproduction. Act as master of ceremonies.
7. Prepare an autobiographical resume that you would use in applying for a job.
8. Check careers in the field of communications. Prepare a statement on the one you like. Talk it over with your counselor.

Emergency Preparedness

1. Earn First Aid merit badge.
2. Do the following:
(a) Tell what you would do to prevent injury and possible loss of life to yourself and others in each of the following emergencies: fire or explosion at home and in a public building, car stalled in blizzard or desert, motor vehicle accident, mountain accident, food poisoning, boating accident, search for lost person, lost or marooned group, gas leak, earthquake, flood, tornado or hurricane, atomic emergency, and avalanche (snow or rock).
(b) Show that you know what to do in at least TWO of the above.
3. Show how you could safely save a person from the following:
(a) Touching a live electric wire
(b) A room with carbon monoxide or other fumes or smoke
(c) Clothes on fire
(d) Drowning using nonswimming rescues (including ice accidents).

4. Tell the things a group of Scouts should be prepared to do, the training needed, and the safety precautions to be taken for the following emergency service:
(a) Crowd and traffic control
(b) Messenger service and communication
(c) Collection and distribution services
(d) Group feeding, shelter, and sanitation.
5. Take part in an emergency service project, either real or a practice drill.
6. Show three ways of attracting and communicating with rescue planes.
7. With another person, show a good way to move an injured person out of a remote and rugged area, conserving the energy of the rescuers.
8. Do the following:
(a) Prepare a written plan for mobilizing your troop when needed to do emergency service. If there is a plan, explain it. Tell your part in making it work.
(b) Take part in at least one troop mobilization. Describe your part.
(c) Show the personal "emergency pack" which you have prepared to be ready for a mobilization call. Show a family kit (suitcase or box) for use by your family in case an emergency evacuation is needed. Explain the need.
9. Show proper use of ropes and lines for rescue work by doing the following:
(a) Tie knots for joining lines. Tie knots for shortening or adjusting lines. Tie knots for lashings.
(b) Lower a person from a height sufficient to show how.
(c) Coil and accurately throw light and heavy 50-foot heaving lines.

Environmental Science

1. Explain the meaning of the following: ecology, environment, biosphere, ecosystem, plant succession, limiting factor. Give an example of the last two.
2. With the help of your counselor, pick an area of 10 acres* for study.
3. Visit the area four times—2 hours each time. Do this at different times, one day a week for a month; or if at camp, on four different days of the week at different times of the day.
   (a) Record the temperature, precipitation, and wind.
   (b) List the animals you saw and tell what they were doing.
   (c) List the plants you saw.
   (d) Name the kinds of rocks and describe the soil.
4. Write about your study in 500 words or more showing:
   (a) How the climate, topography, and geology have influenced the number and kinds of plants and animals.
   (b) How the living and nonliving elements of the environment are interrelated.
   (c) Why it is important that people understand this.
5. With your counselor, plan and carry out a project in one of the following:
   (a) The effect of water-holding capacity of soil on plant life. The relation of plant cover to runoff. How both are related to the water and oxygen cycles.
   (b) The influence of land plants on temperature, light intensity, wind velocity, and humidity. The influence of water plants on the water environment. How both land and water plants affect animal life.
6. Make a report, in the form of a short talk to a Scout group, on what you did in requirement 5.
7. Show you understand the following:
   (a) The causes of water pollution. Tell what it does to rivers and lakes.
   (b) The causes of land pollution. Tell what it does to the environment.
   (c) The causes of air pollution. Tell what it does to the environment.
   (d) How some chemicals get into the tissues of animals miles from where they were used.
8. Describe what you and others can do to help solve a local problem of air pollution, water pollution, or land pollution.
9. Describe the duties of three positions in environmental science.

*City Scouts may pick an area in a large park, if a better place is not available.

First Aid

1. Earn the First Aid skill award. Show you know the skills by doing any of them asked by your counselor.
2. Do the following:
   (a) Describe the signs of a broken bone. Tell first aid rules for handling fractures, including compound (open) fractures.
   (b) On a person lying down, and using improvised materials, show the first aid for any two of the following fractures as asked for: forearm, upper arm, wrist, collarbone, upper leg, lower leg, crushed foot, spine.
3. Do the following:
   (a) Explain what should be done for severe bleeding.
   (b) Tell when the use of a tourniquet may be justified.
   (c) Show how to stop bleeding from a severe cut of the lower leg and wrist.
4. Do the following:
   (a) Tell the dangers of moving a seriously injured person.
   (b) If a sick or injured person must be moved, tell how you would decide what way to do it.
   (c) Show alone, and again with help, two carries for moving an injured person as selected by your counselor.
   (d) Improvise a stretcher. With helpers under your direction, move a presumably unconscious person.
5. Show the proper way to put on an adhesive bandage. Show how to put on a large gauze compress held in place with tape. Show how to put a dressing on the eye with a cravat.
6. Show the proper way to put a roller bandage on the ankle and foot, the wrist and hand, the forearm, and a finger.
7. Do the following:
   (a) Tell the causes and proper first aid for unconsciousness.
   (b) Tell what first aid you would give a person with an epileptic convulsion.
   (c) Tell what to do for the following: heatstroke, heat exhaustion, frostbite, boils and pimples, bruises, stomachache, choking on food, hypothermia, and arm and leg cramps.
8. Make a list of things you should have in a home first aid kit, first aid equipment for an automobile, or a patrol first aid kit.
9. Help in teaching the skills in the First Aid skill award to two or more persons.

Lifesaving

1. Before doing the following requirements:
   (a) Earn Swimming merit badge.
   (b) Swim 400 meters (400 yards).
2. Explain:
   (a) The Safe Swim Defense.
   (b) The order of methods in water rescue.
3. Show reaching rescues using such things as arms, legs, branches, sticks, towels, shirts, paddles, and poles.

4. Show rescues using items that can be thrown, such as lines, ring buoys, and free-floating supports.

5. Show or explain the use of rowboats, canoes, and other small craft in making rescues.

6. With a helper and a subject, show a line rescue both as tender and as rescuer. Use a 15-meter (50-foot) length of line. If available, demonstrate the use of a torpedo buoy and rescue tube.

7. Show twice that you can remove street clothes* on shore (except underwear or swim trunks) in 20 seconds or less. Explain the importance of disrobing before a swimming rescue.

8. Explain the importance of avoiding contact with a subject; explain "lead" and "wait" tactics; and explain why equipment should be used in a swimming rescue.

9. Swim 9 meters (9 yds) and make the correct approach to a tired swimmer. Move him 9 meters (9 yds) to safety using: (a) under-arm swim-along, (b) two-man assist, (c) tired swimmer carry.

10. Keeping the practice victim in sight at all times, make a leaping entry, swim 9 meters (9 yds) with a strong approach stroke, and tow the subject back to pier or poolside using:
(a) a shirt or other equipment
(b) the rear approach and cross-chest tow
(c) the front approach and wrist tow.
Remove the practice victim from the water and place in position for resuscitation.

11. Show in deep water your defense against grasps by blocking, and escaping. Free yourself from both front and rear holds.

12. Make four surface dives in 2.4 meters (8 feet) of water. Retrieve an object three times. Bring up a 10-pound weight once.

13. Show search techniques:
(a) As a part of a lost swimmer drill,
(b) As a diver using mask, fins, and a snorkel (not scuba).

14. Explain cardiopulmonary resuscitation (CPR) and show evidence of having a minimum of 3 hours of instruction† (not certification) in CPR skills.

---

*"Street clothes" means low shoes, socks, underwear (or trunks), pants, belt, and long-sleeve shirt. A jacket or sweater or sweat shirt also may be worn.

†Resources for CPR instruction include local chapters of the American Red Cross, the American Heart Association, rescue squads, fire departments, hospitals, medical societies, BSA aquatics instructors, YMCA aquatics instructors, or any person having completed the CPR basic life support course.

Personal Fitness

If meeting Nos. 1 and 5 are against the Scout's religious convictions, they will not have to be done if the boy's parents and proper church officials state in writing that:
(a) To do so would be against religious convictions.
(b) The parents accept full responsi-

bility for anything that might happen because of such exemption. They release the Boy Scouts of America from any responsibility.

1. Before you try to meet any other tests, have your physician give you a thorough health examination. He is to use the Scout medical examination form. Describe the examination. Tell what questions you asked about your health. Tell what recommendations your doctor made. Report what you have done about them.

2. Explain what physical and mental health means to you, including:
   (a) Reasons for being fit.
   (b) Normal differences in rate of growth and development.
   (c) What it means to be mentally healthy. Discuss three healthy personality traits.

3. Show you know health facts by answering questions asked on the following:
   (a) Basic foods needed in the daily diet of a person of your age.
   (b) Cleanliness of the hands, food, and dishes and the control of illness.
   (c) Bad effects of tobacco and alcohol, and the use and abuse of drugs.
   (d) The illnesses against which you may be immunized or otherwise protected.

4. Present a list of your health habits including:
   (a) Number of hours of sleep.
   (b) Care of your skin, hands, fingernails, toenails.
   (c) Care of your eyes.
   (d) Care of your ears.

5. Have an examination made by your dentist. Get a statement saying that your teeth have been checked and cared for. Tell how you care for your teeth.

6. Carry out daily for 4 weeks six exercises for all-around physical development. Use those that strengthen your arms, shoulders, chest, abdomen, back, legs, and one for endurance. Pick three activities from No. 7. Test yourself at the beginning and weekly during the 4 weeks. Show the record of your test. This is to be completed before starting No. 7.

7. Fitness Tests: Earn a minimum of 200 points. These 200 points must come from not more than 5 events. Only one alternate, A or B, is allowed in each event.
   EVENT 1 Swimming (50 point maximum)
   A. 20-yard speed swim—5 points for each second faster than 25 seconds
   B. Distance swim—50 points for swimming 1 mile, 25 points for swimming ½ mile.
   EVENT 2 Arm Strength (50 point maximum)
   A. Pull-ups—10 points for each pull-up
   B. Push-ups—2 points for each push-up
   EVENT 3 Abdominal Power (50 point maximum)
   A. Bent-knee sit-ups—1 point for each sit-up
   EVENT 4 Speed Running (50 point maximum)
   A. 50-yard dash—2 points for each 1/10 of a second faster than 9 seconds
   B. 40-yard shuttle run—2 points for each 1/10 of a second faster than 12 seconds
   EVENT 5 Endurance Running or Walking (50 point maximum)
   A. 600-yard run-walk—1 point for each second faster than 2 minutes 50 seconds
   B. Mile walk—10 points for each minute faster than 18 minutes
   EVENT 6 Jumping (50 point maximum)
   A. Standing long jump—5 points for each inch over 5 feet
   B. Vertical jump and reach—5 points for each inch over 9 inches
   EVENT 7 Body Coordination (50 point maximum)
   A. Basketball throw—2 points for each foot over 50 feet
   B. Softball throw—1 point for each foot over 100 feet

8. Show that you are reasonably good in one team or one individual sport.

Personal Management

1. Talk over with parents or guardian how family funds are spent to meet day-to-day and long-term needs. Tell how you can help with the family budget.
2. Make a budget for yourself for 90 days. Keep a record of income and expenses for that period. Review it and report.
3. Help to choose and buy family groceries for 1 month. Make a report of what you learned.
4. Explain the possible use, advantages, and risks in using $100 in each of the following ways. Tell how it might help you and others.
   (a) Hide it in a mattress.
   (b) Put it into a savings account at a bank or savings and loan association. (Explain the difference.)
   (c) Buy a bicycle.
   (d) Open a checking account.
   (e) Buy a U.S. Savings Bond.
   (f) Buy a power mower or paint sprayer.
   (g) Invest in a mutual fund.
   (h) Start a life insurance policy.
   (i) Buy fishing gear.
   (j) Buy common stock.
5. Talk about things you would like to do within the next 90 days. Tell how you plan to get these done. After 90 days, tell what you did. Tell how you did them.
6. Tell how important credit and installment buying are to our economy and the individual and the family. Visit an officer of a bank or credit department of a store. Find out and tell what you must do to establish a good "credit

rating." Tell what it means to you now and in the future.
7. Check out jobs or career opportunities through interviews or reading. Tell what the "next step" would be to prepare yourself for one of these careers.

Safety

1. Prepare a safety notebook. Include: (a) newspaper and other stories showing main kinds of accidents, (b) similar materials showing five causes of accidents, (c) the approximate yearly loss for main kinds of accidents in terms of deaths, injuries, and cost in dollars, (d) how a serious fire or accident involving you or your parents can change your life, (e) how safe practices and safety devices make your life easier and more pleasurable.
2. At three appropriate and safe locations spend a total of 3 hours observing and listing safe and unsafe practices by (a) motor vehicle drivers, (b) pedestrians, (c) bicycle riders, (d) passengers (car, bus, train, or plane). Show this list to your counselor.
3. Do the following:
   (a) Using a safety checklist approved by your counselor, make an inspection of your home. Explain the hazards found, why they are hazards, and how they can be corrected.
   (b) Review your family's plan of escape in case of fire in your home.
4. Sketch your troop meeting place (or another public building where people gather) and show exits. Are

558

they adequate? Show which exit you would use in an emergency. Explain what should be done in a panic.

5. Make two safety checklists, one each for school and recreation. Include 10 points on each.

6. Make a plan for an accident prevention program for the following outdoor situations: (a) camping and hiking, (b) storm and wind, (c) water activities. Each plan should include an analysis of possible hazards, proposed action to correct the hazards, and reasons for the correction you propose.

7. Do ONE of the following:
(a) Report on a safety project that you helped to plan or took part in.
(b) Go with a company representative on a safety inspection tour of his company's premises (plant or other place where people work). Make a report.
(c) Join a building or fire inspector on an inspection tour of a public building. Make a report.
(d) Plan a farm safety project to correct unsafe conditions and equipment hazards.

8. Tell how you contribute to the safety of yourself, your family, and your community.

Sports

1. Explain sportsmanship. Tell why it is important. Give several examples of good sportsmanship in sports. Relate at least one of these to everyday citizenship off the sports field.

2. Take part for one full season as a member of an organized team in ONE of the following sports: baseball, basketball, bowling, cross country, diving, fencing, field hockey, football, golf, gymnastics, ice hockey, lacrosse, rugby, skating (ice or roller), soccer, softball, swimming, team handball, tennis, track and field, volleyball, water polo, and wrestling. (Or any other recognized team sport approved in advance by your counselor, except boxing and karate.)

3. *Take part in ONE of the following sports on a competitive basis in two organized meets or tournaments: archery, badminton, bait or fly casting, bowling, canoeing, cycling, diving, fencing, fishing, golf, gymnastics, handball, horsemanship, horseshoes, judo, orienteering, paddleball, rifle or shotgun shooting, sailing, skating (ice or roller), skiing, swimming, table tennis, tennis, track and field, waterskiing, and wrestling. (Or any other recognized sport approved in advance by your counselor, except boxing and karate.)

4. Make a set of training rules for the sports you picked. Tell why these rules are important. Follow these rules. Design exercises for these sports. Keep a record of how you do in these sports for one season. Show how you have improved.

5. Show proper techniques in your two picked sports.

6. Explain the attributes of a good team leader and a good team player.

7. Draw diagrams of the playing areas for your two sports.

8. Explain the rules and etiquette for your two sports. List the equipment needed. Describe the protective equipment. Tell why it is needed. Tell what it does.

*This cannot be the same sport used to meet No. 2.

559

Swimming

1. Fulfill all requirements of the Swimming skill award. Explain how swimming should be run safely for a group.
2. Swim continuously for 150 meters (150 yards) using the following strokes in good form: Sidestroke for 50 meters (50 yards), elementary backstroke for 50 meters (50 yards), and any of the following strokes for the last 50 meters (50 yards): trudgen, crawl, back crawl, or breast.
3. Surface dive headfirst into water over your head but not to exceed 2½ meters and bring up an object from the bottom. Repeat using the feetfirst method of water entry.
4. Show a plain front dive from a low board, if available. Show a headfirst dive from a dock. Show a racing start.
5. Enter water over your head wearing clothes. (Clothes means shoes, socks, underwear or trunks, long pants, belt, and long-sleeve shirt.) Remove shoes and socks. Inflate shirt and show that you can float using the shirt for support. Remove the pants and use them for support while floating. Swim 50 meters (50 yards) using inflated clothing for support.
6. Do the following:
   (a) Float faceup in a resting position, as nearly motionless as possible, for 1 minute.
   (b) Float facedown in a related position using minimum movement of arms and legs to raise head for breathing and keep body afloat for 10 minutes or longer.
7. Do the following:
   (a) Demonstrate rescuing a person from water by reaching with arm or leg, by reaching with a suitable object, and by throwing lines and floating objects.
   (b) Explain why swimming rescues should not be attempted when a reaching or throwing assist or boat rescue can be done. Explain why and how a person making a swimming rescue should avoid contact with the victim.

BOOKS YOU'LL ENJOY READING

CAMPING AND HIKING
Walking Softly in the Wilderness: The Sierra Club Guide to Backpacking. John Hart.
The New Way of the Wilderness. Calvin Rutstrum.
Backpacking, One Step at a Time. Harvey Manning.
Complete Book of Camping. Leonard Miracle with Maurice Decker.
Wildwood Wisdom. Ellsworth Jaeger.
Woodcraft and Camping. Bernard S. Mason.
Roughing It Easy. Dian Thomas.
Survival. Department of the Air Force.
Outdoor Survival Skills. Larry Dean Olsen.
Camp Cookery for Small groups. Arthur Walrath.
Be Expert With Map and Compass—The Orienteering Handbook. Bjorn Kjellstrom.
Merit Badge Pamphlets: *Backpacking, Camping, Cooking, Cycling, Hiking, Orienteering, Skiing, Surveying, Wilderness Survival.* Boy Scouts of America.

CAMP ACTIVITIES
Indian Crafts and Lore. Ben Hunt.
The Book of Indian Crafts and Indian Lore. Julian H. Salomon.
Dances and Stories of the American Indian. Bernard S. Mason.
Boy Scout Songbook. Boy Scouts of America.
Knots and How to Tie Them. Boy Scouts of America.
Progressive Pioneering. John Thurman.
The Gilwell Camp Fire Book. John Thurman and Rex Hazlewood.
Merit Badge Pamphlets: *Archery, Athletics, Indian Lore, Pioneering, Signaling, Sports, Surveying.* Boy Scouts of America.

AQUATICS
Swimming and Diving. David A. Armbruster et al.
Canoeing. The American National Red Cross.
Canoeing. Carle W. Handel.
Lifesaving, Rescue, and Water Safety. The American National Red Cross.
Pole, Paddle, and Portage. Bill Riviere.
The Complete Wilderness Paddler. James West Davidson and John Rugge.
Basic River Canoeing. Robert E. McNair.
Piloting Seamanship and Small Boat Handling. Charles F. Chapman and E.S. Maloney.
Merit badge pamphlets: *Canoeing, Lifesaving, Motorboating, Rowing, Small-Boat Sailing, Swimming, Water Skiing.* Boy Scouts of America.

NATURE—GENERAL
Joy of Nature. Reader's Digest.
Fieldbook. Boy Scouts of America.
New Field Book of Nature Activities and Hobbies. William Hillcourt.
Outdoor Things To Do. William Hillcourt.
Amateur Naturalist's Handbook. Vinson Brown.
Animal Tracks and Hunter Signs. Ernest Thompson Seton.

Wild Animals I have known. Ernest Thompson Seton.
Field Guide to Edible Wild Plants. Lee Peterson.
Wild Mushrooms Worth Knowing. Ansel Stubbs.
Merit badge pamphlets: *Astronomy, Bird Study, Botany, Environmental Science, Fish and Wildlife Management, Fishing, Forestry, Geology, Insect Life, Mammals, Nature, Oceanography, Reptile Study, Soil and Water Conservation, Weather.* Boy Scouts of America.

NATURE GUIDEBOOKS

Golden Nature Guides. Edited by Herbert Zim. Separate volumes on *Mammals, Birds, Gamebirds, Reptiles and Amphibians, Fishes, Seashores, Seashells, Pond Life, Insects, Butterflies and Moths, Spiders, Flowers, Nonflowering Plants, Trees, Rocks and Minerals, Fossils, Weather, Stars*

Peterson's Field Guides. Edited by Roger Tory Peterson. Separate volumes on *Mammals, Animal Tracks, Eastern Birds, Western Birds, Birds' Nests, Reptiles and Amphibians, Shells of Atlantic and Gulf Coasts, Shells of Pacific Coast, Butterflies, Rocks and Minerals, Wild Flowers, Trees and Shrubs, Ferns, Stars and Planets.*

Putnam's Field Book. Separate volumes on *Mammals, Eastern Birds, Birds of the Pacific Coast, Snakes, Reptiles and Amphibians, Ponds and Streams, Seashore Life, Insects, Flowers, Western Flowers, Trees and Shrubs, Mushrooms, Rocks and Minerals, Stars.*

PHYSICAL FITNESS

The Boy's Book of Physical Fitness. Hal G. Vermes.
The Complete Book of Running. James F. Fixx.
The New Aerobics. Kenneth H. Cooper.
How To Be Fit. Robert Kiphuth.
The West Point Fitness and Diet Book. James L. Anderson and Martin A. Cohen.
Merit badge pamphlets: *Athletics, Hiking, Personal Fitness, Sports, Swimming.* Boy Scouts of America.

SERVICE TO OTHERS

Standard First Aid and Personal Safety. The American National Red Cross.
Advanced First Aid and Emergency Care. The American National Red Cross.
Merit badge pamphlets: *Emergency Preparedness, Firemanship, First Aid, Public Health, Safety.* Boy Scouts of America.

CITIZENSHIP

Your Rugged Constitution. Bruce A. Findlay and Esther B. Findlay.
The United Nations and How It Works. David C. Coyle.
Merit badge pamphlets: *American Heritage, Citizenship in the Community, Citizenship in the Nation, Citizenship in the World.* Boy Scouts of America.

SCOUTING HISTORY

Baden-Powell—The Two Lives of a Hero. William Hillcourt with Olave, Lady Baden-Powell.
Boy Scouts—An American Adventure, The. Robert W. Peterson.
250 Million Scouts. Laszlo Nagy.

INDEX

Bill of Rights

Congress of the United States, begun and held at the City of New York, on Wednesday, the fourth of March, one thousand seven hundred and eighty nine.

The Conventions of a number of the States, having, at the time of their adopting the Constitution, expressed a desire, in order to prevent misconstruction or abuse of its powers, that further declaratory and restrictive clauses should be added: And as extending the ground of public confidence in the Government, will best insure the beneficent ends of its institution:

Resolved, by the SENATE and HOUSE OF REPRESENTATIVES of the UNITED STATES of AMERICA in Congress assembled, two thirds of both Houses concurring. That the following Articles be proposed to the Legislatures of the several States, as Amendments to the Constitution of the United States; all, or any of which articles, when ratified by three fourths of the said Legislatures, to be valid to all intents and purposes, as part of the said Constitution, viz.

Articles in addition to, and Amendment of the Constitution of the United States of America, proposed by Congress, and ratified by the Legislatures of the several States, pursuant to the fifth Article of the Original Constitution.

ARTICLE THE FIRST . . . After the first enumeration required by the first Article of the Constitution, there shall be one Representative for every thirty thousand, until the number shall amount to one hundred, after which, the proportion shall be so regulated by Congress, that there shall be not less than one hundred Representatives, nor less than one Representative for every forty thousand persons, until the number of Representatives shall amount to two hundred, after which, the proportion shall be so regulated by Congress, that there shall not be less than two hundred Representatives, nor more than one Representative for every fifty thousand persons. [Not Ratified]

ARTICLE THE SECOND . . . No law, varying the compensation for the services of the Senators and Representatives, shall take effect, until an election of Representatives shall have intervened. [Not Ratified]

ARTICLE THE THIRD . . . Congress shall make no law respecting an establishment of religion, or prohibiting the free exercise thereof; or abridging the freedom of speech, or of the press; or the right of the people peaceably to assemble, and to petition the Government for a redress of grievances.

ARTICLE THE FOURTH . . . A well regulated Militia, being necessary to the security of a free State, the right of the people to keep and bear Arms, shall not be infringed.

ARTICLE THE FIFTH . . . No Soldier shall, in time of peace, be quartered in any house, without the consent of the owner, nor in time of war, but in a manner to be prescribed by law.

ARTICLE THE SIXTH . . . The right of the people to be secure in their persons, houses, papers, and effects, against unreasonable searches and seizures, shall not be violated, and no Warrants shall issue but upon probable cause, supported by oath or affirmation, and particularly describing the place to be searched, and the persons or things to be seized.

ARTICLE THE SEVENTH . . . No person shall be held to answer for a capital, or otherwise infamous crime, unless on a presentment or indictment of a grand jury, except in cases arising in the land or Naval forces, or in the Militia, when in actual service in time of War or public danger; nor shall any person be subject for the same offense to be twice put in jeopardy of life or limb; nor shall be compelled in any criminal case, to be a witness against himself, nor be deprived of life, liberty, or property, without due process of law; nor shall private property be taken for public use without just compensation.

ARTICLE THE EIGHTH . . . In all criminal prosecutions, the accused shall enjoy the right to a speedy and public trial by an impartial jury of the State and district wherein the crime shall have been committed, which district shall have been previously ascertained by law, and to be informed of the nature and cause of the accusation; to be confronted with the witnesses against him; to have compulsory process for obtaining witnesses in his favor, and to have the assistance of counsel for his defense.

ARTICLE THE NINTH . . . In suits at common law, where the value in controversy shall exceed twenty dollars, the right of trial by jury shall be preserved, and no fact, tried by a jury, shall be otherwise re-examined in any Court of the United States, than according to the rules of the common law.

ARTICLE THE TENTH . . . Excessive bail shall not be required, nor excessive fines imposed, nor cruel and unusual punishments inflicted.

ARTICLE THE ELEVENTH . . . The enumeration in the Constitution of certain rights, shall not be construed to deny or disparage others retained by the people.

ARTICLE THE TWELFTH . . . The powers not delegated to the United States by the Constitution, nor prohibited by it to the States, are reserved to the States respectively, or to the people.

Bill of Responsibilities

Preamble. Freedom and responsibility are mutual and inseparable; we can ensure enjoyment of the one only by exercising the other. Freedom for all of us depends on responsibility by each of us. To secure and expand our liberties, therefore, we accept these responsibilities as individual members of a free society:

To be fully responsible for our own actions and for the consequences of those actions. Freedom to choose carries with it the responsibility for our choices.

To respect the rights and beliefs of others. In a free society, diversity flourishes. Courtesy and consideration toward others are measures of a civilized society.

To give sympathy, understanding and help to others. As we hope others will help us when we are in need, we should help others when they are in need.

To do our best to meet our own and our families' needs. There is no personal freedom without economic freedom. By helping ourselves and those closest to us to become productive members of society, we contribute to the strength of the nation.

To respect and obey the laws. Laws are mutually accepted rules by which, together, we maintain a free society. Liberty itself is built on a foundation of law. That foundation provides an orderly process for changing laws. It also depends on our obeying laws once they have been freely adopted.

To respect the property of others, both private and public. No one has a right to what is not his or hers. The right to enjoy what is ours depends on our respecting the right of others to enjoy what is theirs.

To share with others our appreciation of the benefits and obligations of freedom. Freedom shared is freedom strengthened.

To participate constructively in the nation's political life. Democracy depends on an active citizenry. It depends equally on an informed citizenry.

To help freedom survive by assuming personal responsibility for its defense. Our nation cannot survive unless we defend it. Its security rests on the individual determination of each of us to help preserve it.

To respect the rights and to meet the responsibilities on which our liberty rests and our democracy depends. This is the essence of freedom. Maintaining it requires our common effort, all together and each individually.